DDC

Visual Reference Basics

Microsoft® Excel® 2000

Karl Schwartz

DDC Publishing

Acknowledgements

English Editor
Emily Hay

Technical Editor
Howard Peterson

Layout and Design
Karl Schwartz

Copyright 1999 by DDC Publishing, Inc.

Published by DDC Publishing, Inc.

ISBN 1-56243-743-7

Catalog No. G46

All rights reserved, including the right to reproduce this book in any form whatsoever. For information, address DDC Publishing, Inc., 275 Madison Avenue, New York, New York, 10016.

Internet address: http://www.ddcpub.com

First DDC Publishing, Inc. Printing

10   9   8   7   6   5   4

Printed in the United States of America.

Microsoft®, Microsoft Excel®, AutoSum®, PivotTables®, and Windows® are registered trademarks of Microsoft Corporation.

IBM® is a registered trademark of International Business Machines.

Screen shots reprinted with permission of Microsoft Corporation.

The DDC Banner is a registered trademark of DDC Publishing, Inc.

All registered trademarks, trademarks, and service marks mentioned in this book are the property of their respective companies.

Introduction

DDC's *Visual Reference Basics* series is designed to help you make the most of your Microsoft software. Newly updated to reflect changes and enhancements in Microsoft 2000 applications, the *Visual Reference Basics* are equally useful as instruction manuals or as desktop reference guides for the experienced user. With illustrations and clear explanations of every step involved, they make even complex processes easy to understand and follow.

The most distinctive feature of this series is its extensive use of visuals. Buttons, toolbars, screens, and commands are all illustrated so that there is never any doubt that you are performing the right actions. Most information can be understood at a glance, without a lot of reading through dense and complicated instructions. With *Visual Reference Basics*, you learn what you need to know quickly and easily.

This book contains one hundred functions essential for optimal use of Microsoft Excel 2000. These functions are arranged for ease of use. Cross-references in chapters help you to find related topics. Notes on each page give additional information or tips to supplement the directions given. The only thing *you* need to get the most out of the *Visual Reference Basics* series is a basic understanding of Windows and the desire to become more familiar with Excel.

The *Visual Reference Basics* series is an informative and convenient way to acquaint yourself with the capabilities of your Microsoft application. It is a valuable resource for anyone who wants to become a power user of Microsoft 2000 software.

Visual Index

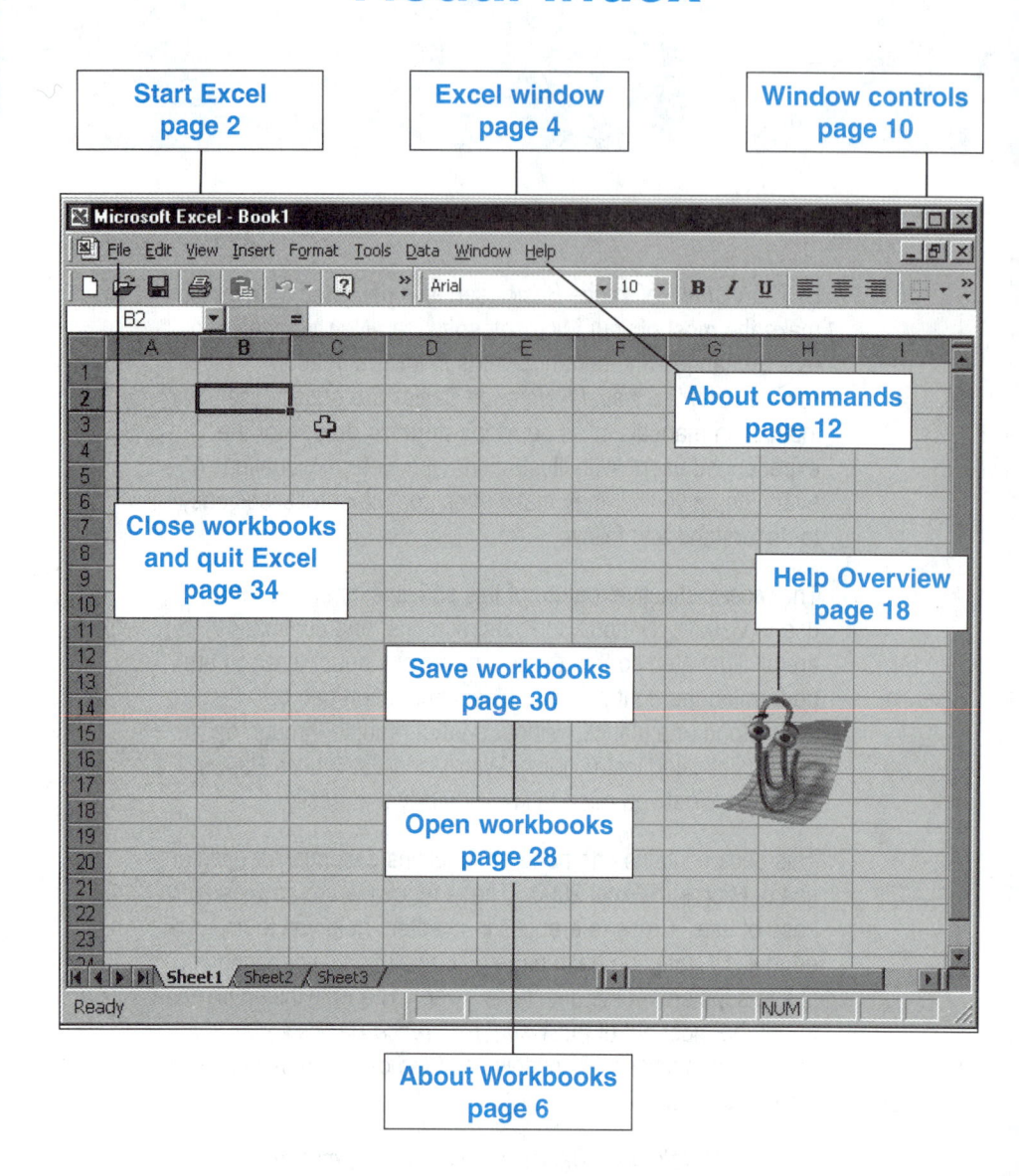

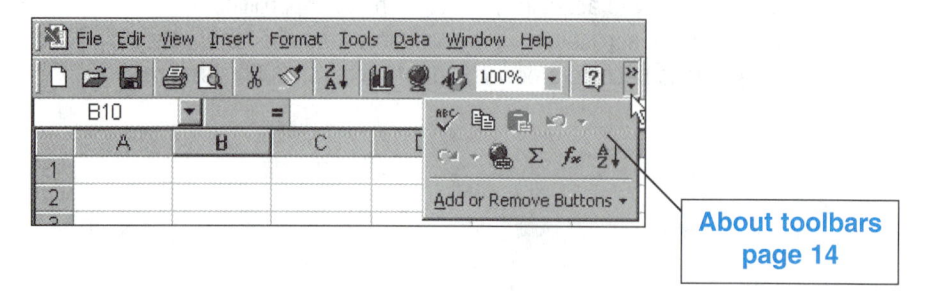

- Start Excel — page 2
- Excel window — page 4
- Window controls — page 10
- About commands — page 12
- Close workbooks and quit Excel — page 34
- Help Overview — page 18
- Save workbooks — page 30
- Open workbooks — page 28
- About Workbooks — page 6
- About toolbars — page 14

iv

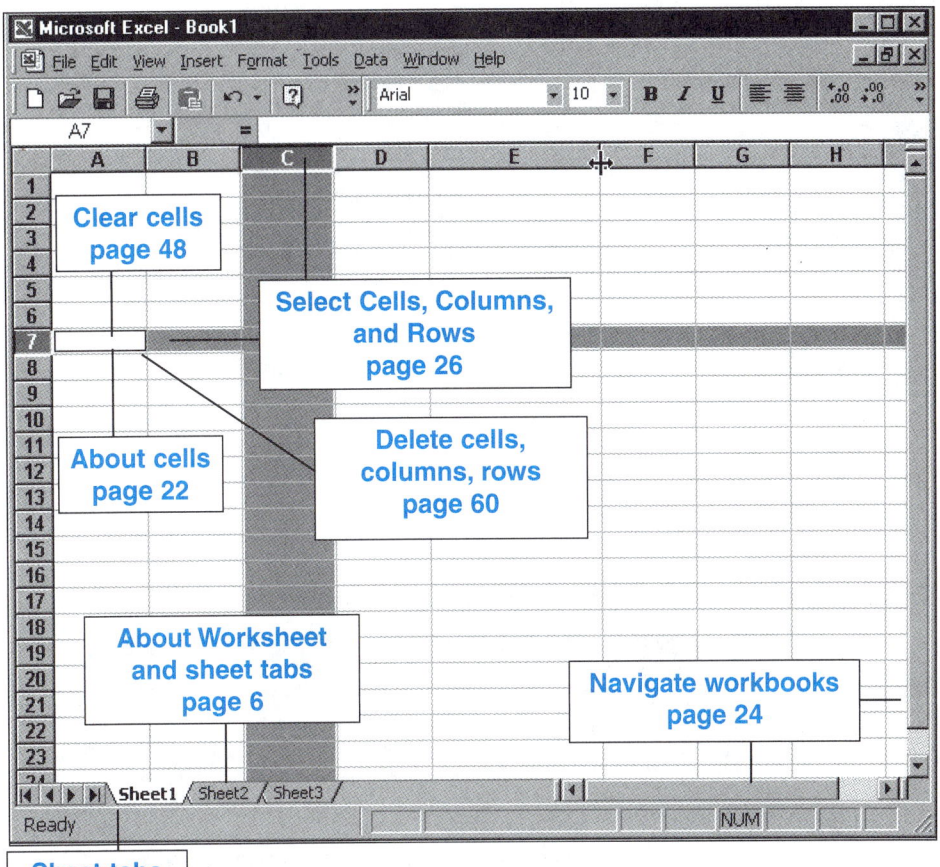

Visual Index (continued)

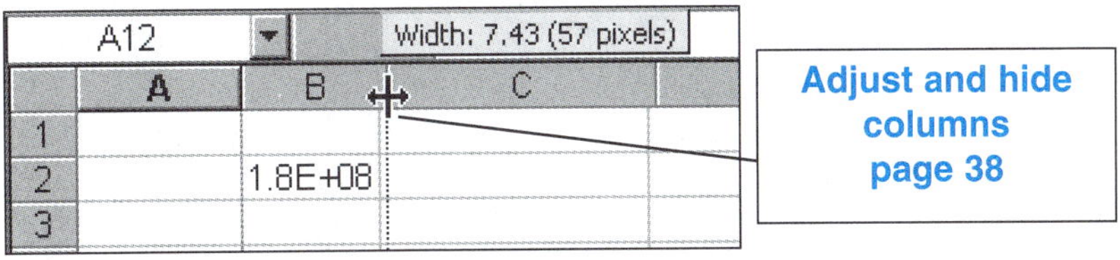

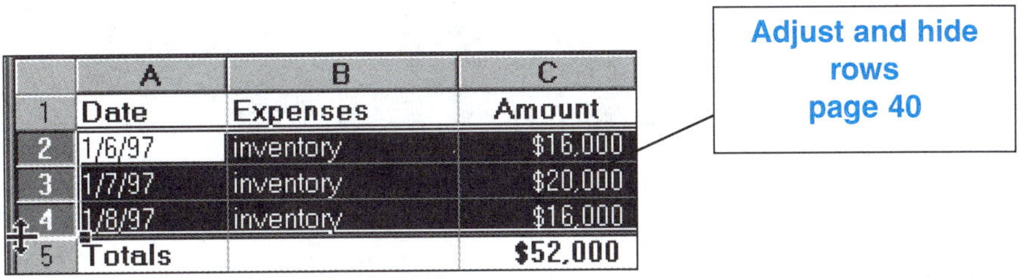

Callouts on Excel worksheet screenshot:
- Clear cells — page 48
- Select Cells, Columns, and Rows — page 26
- About cells — page 22
- Delete cells, columns, rows — page 60
- About Worksheet and sheet tabs — page 6
- Navigate workbooks — page 24
- Sheet tabs — page 110
- Adjust and hide columns — page 38
- Adjust and hide rows — page 40

Sample data table:

	A	B	C
1	Date	Expenses	Amount
2	1/6/97	inventory	$16,000
3	1/7/97	inventory	$20,000
4	1/8/97	inventory	$16,000
5	Totals		$52,000

v

Visual Index (continued)

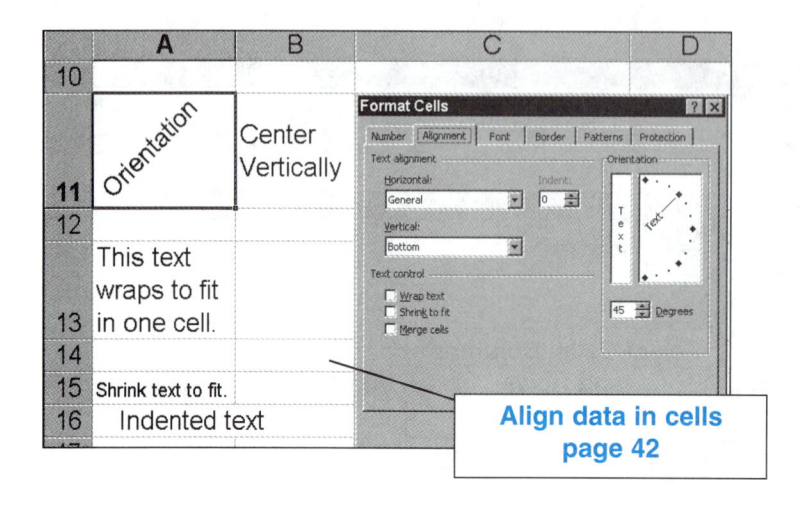

Align data in cells
page 42

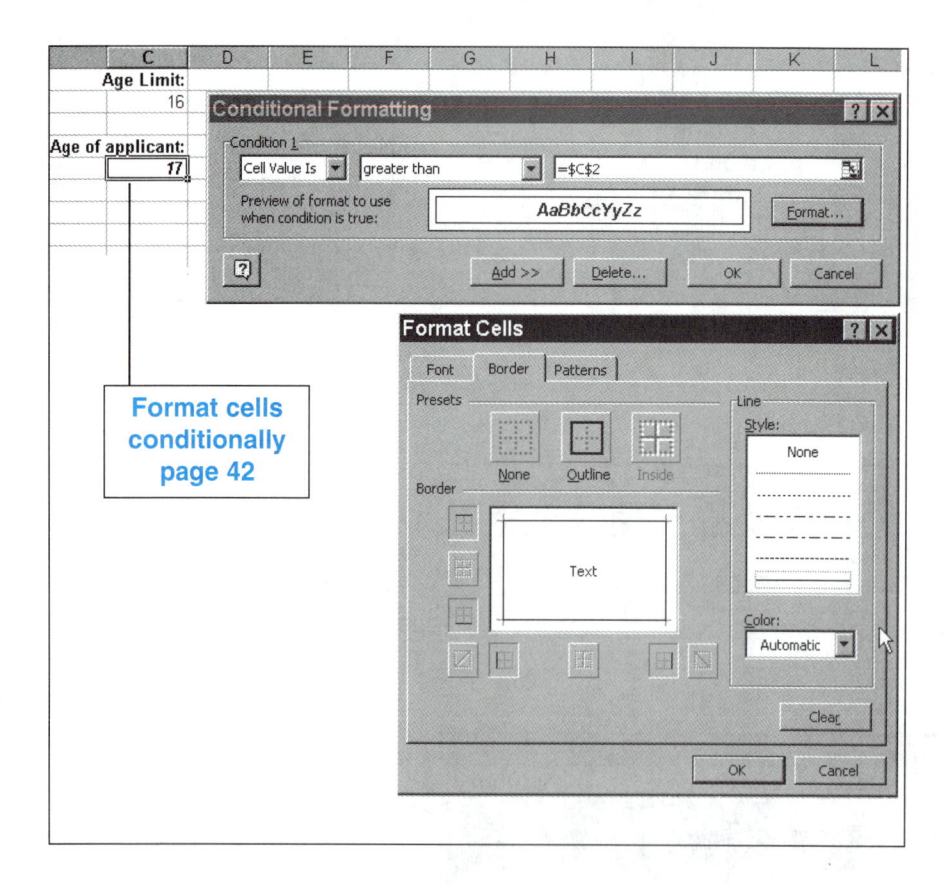

Format cells conditionally
page 42

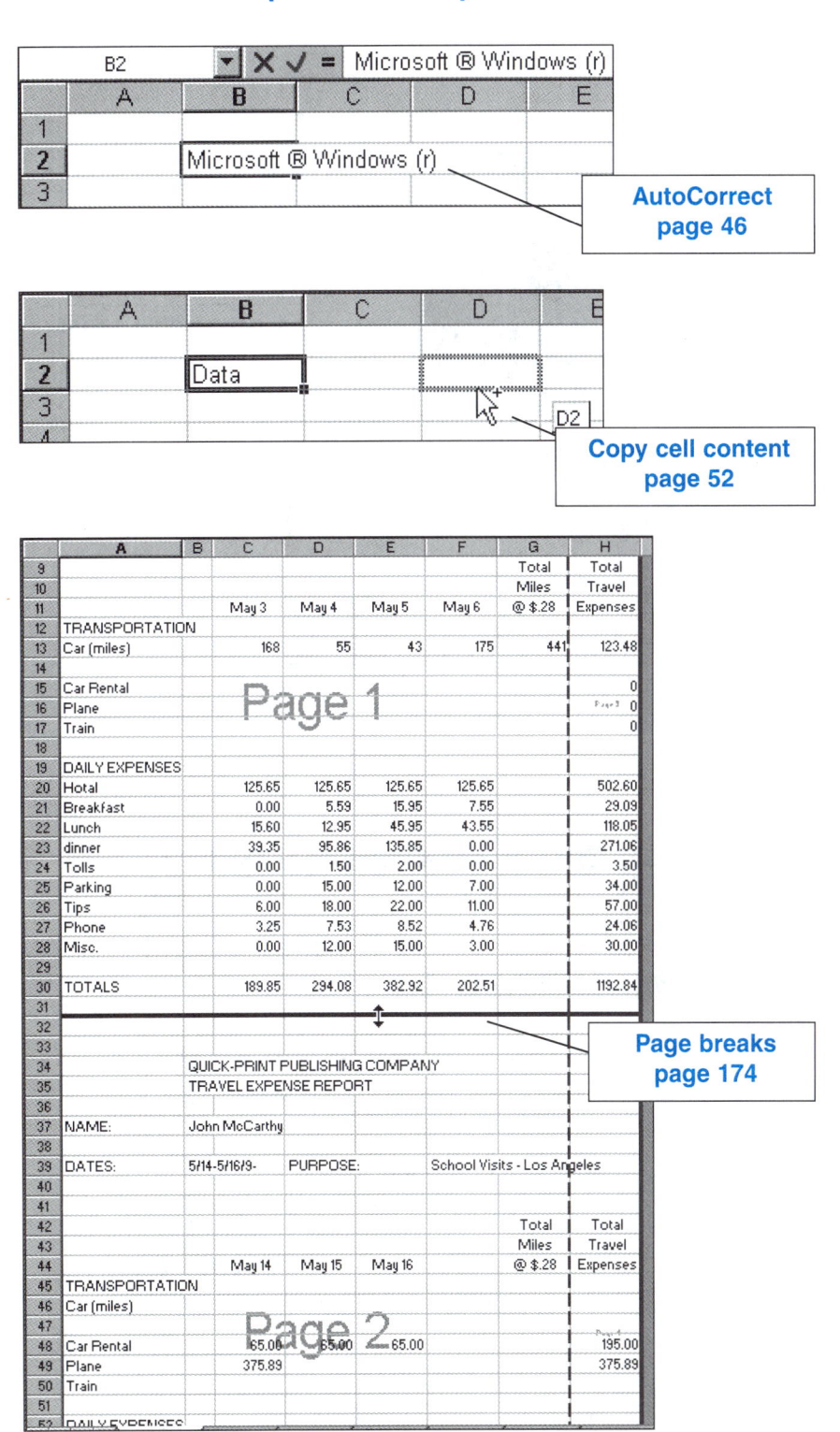

Visual Index (continued)

AutoCorrect page 46

Copy cell content page 52

Page breaks page 174

vii

Visual Index (continued)

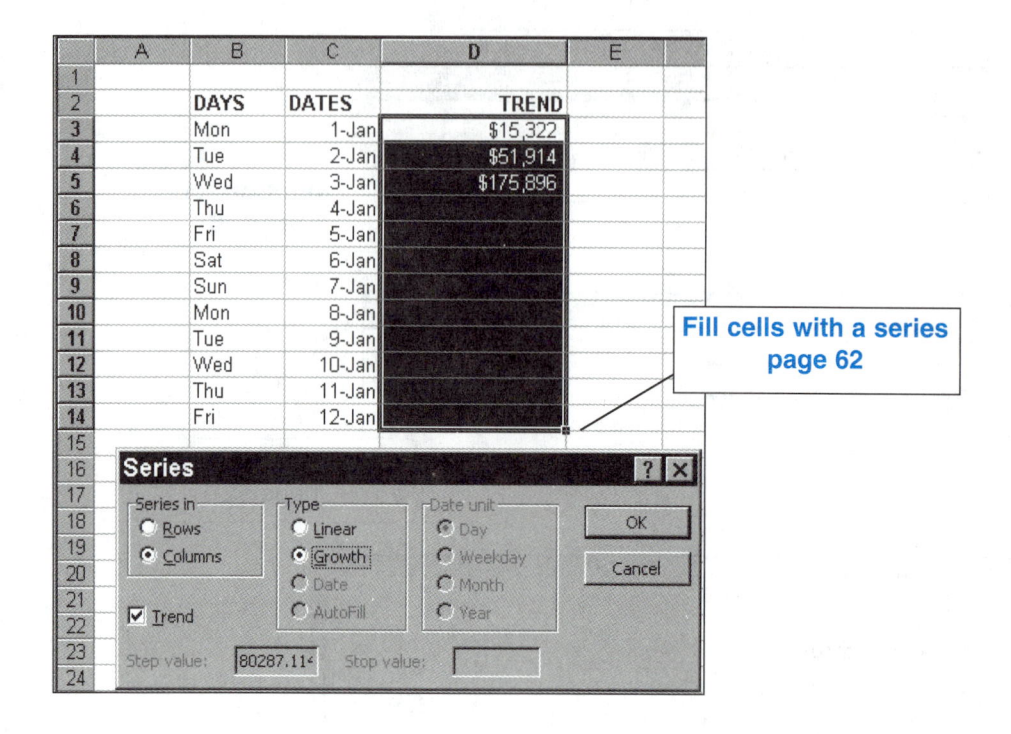

Fill cells with a series
page 62

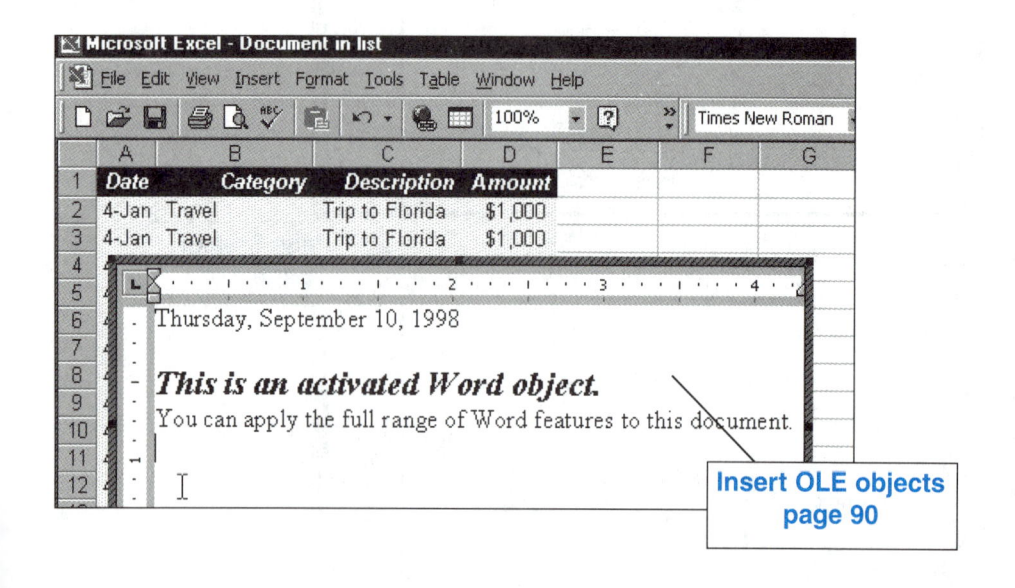

Insert OLE objects
page 90

Visual Index (continued)

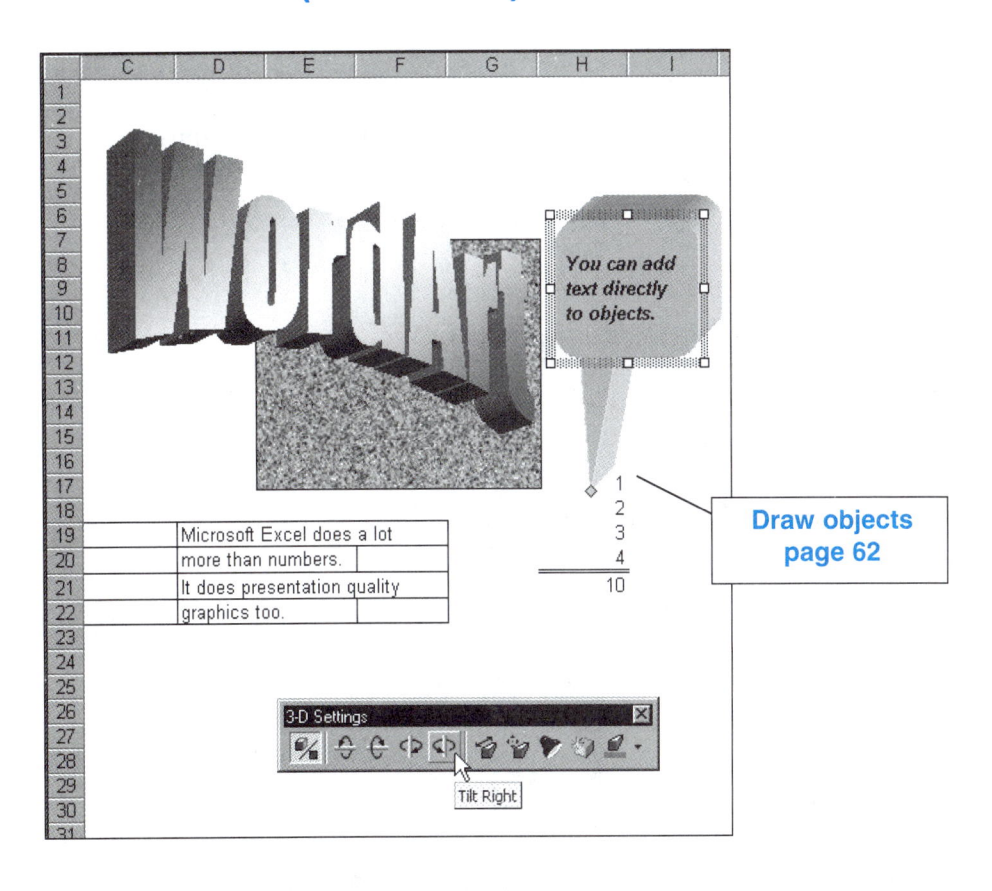

Draw objects page 62

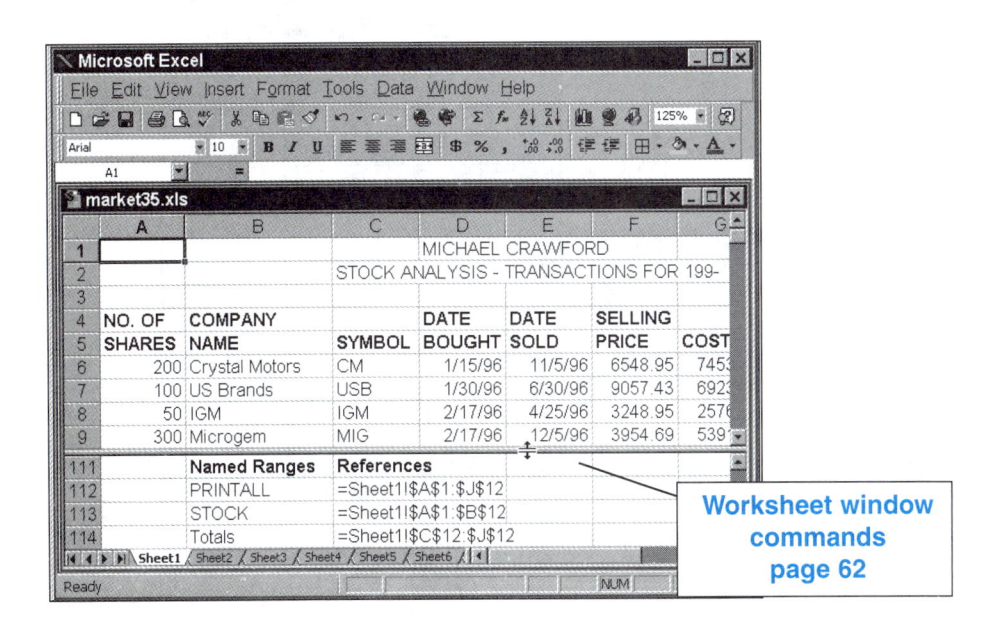

Worksheet window commands page 62

ix

Visual Index (continued)

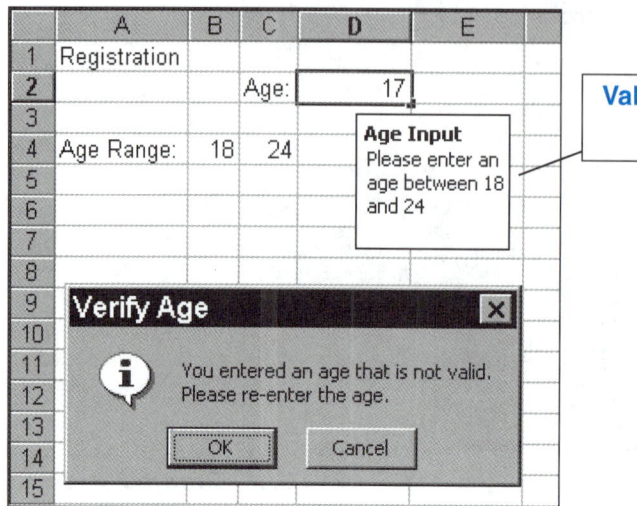

Validate cell entries — page 124

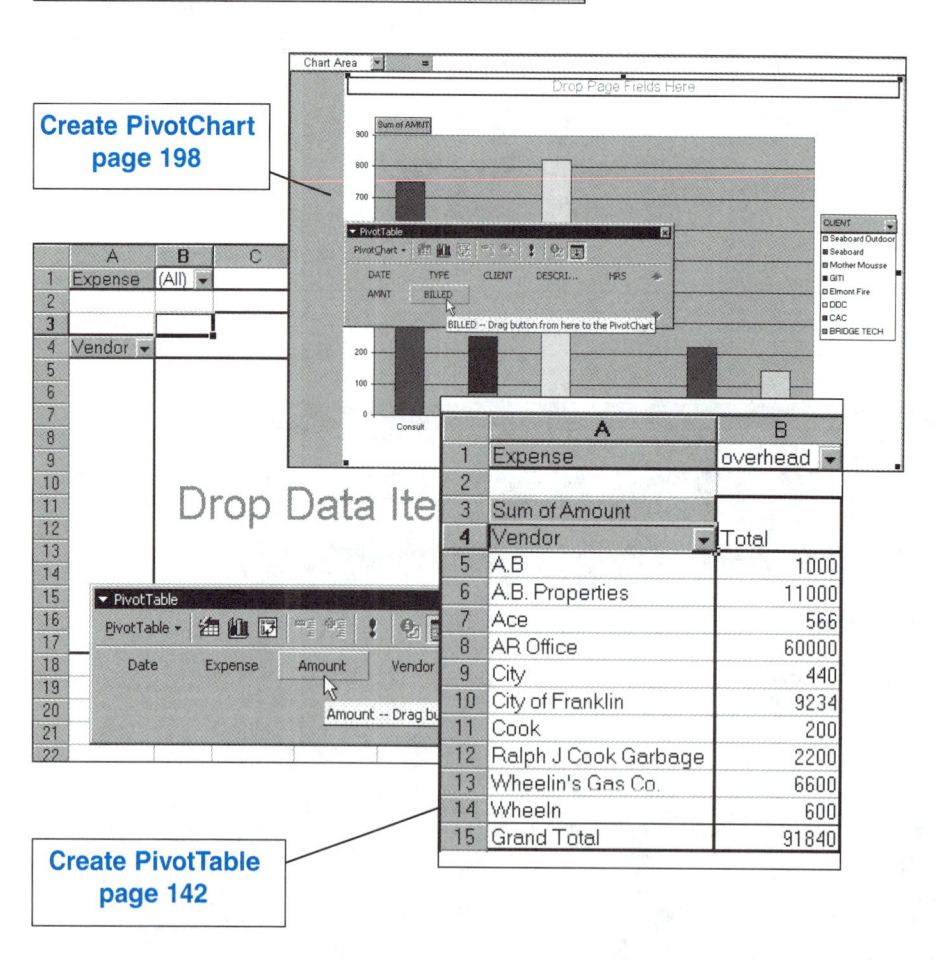

Create PivotChart — page 198

Create PivotTable — page 142

Visual Index (continued)

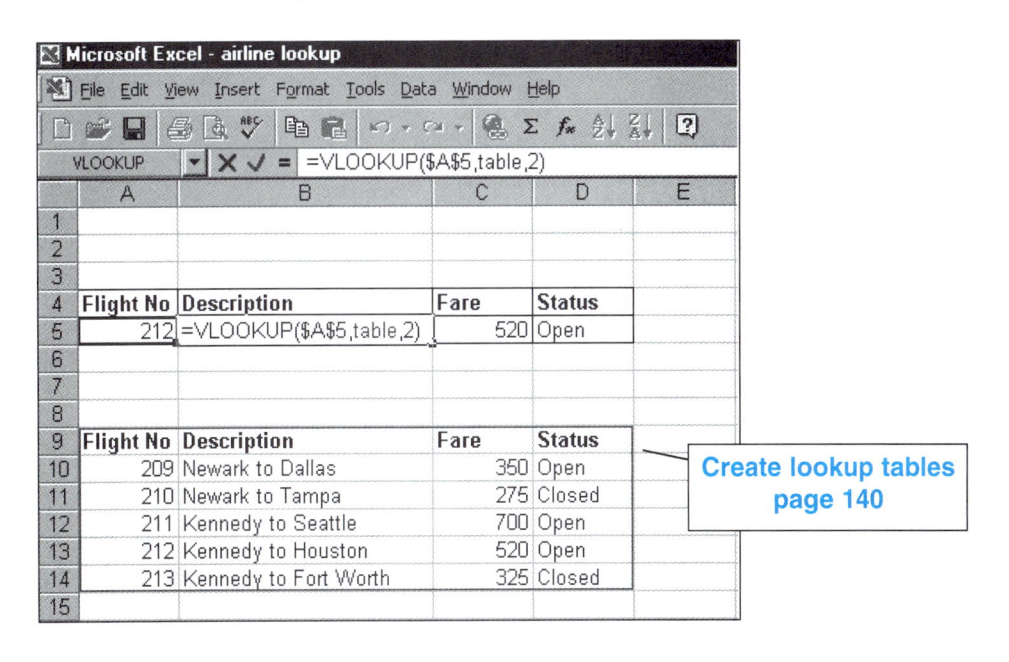

**Create lookup tables
page 140**

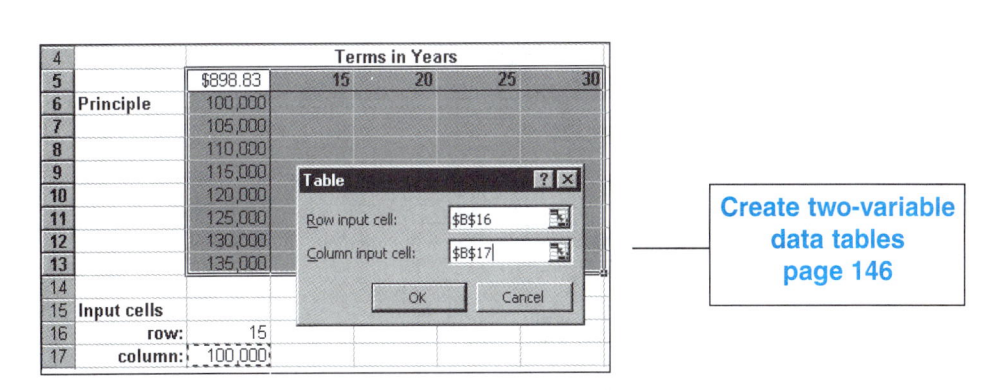

**Create two-variable
data tables
page 146**

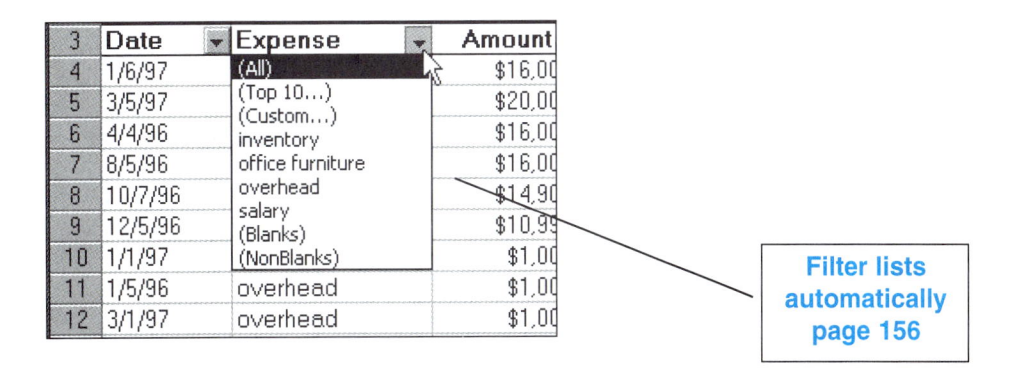

**Filter lists
automatically
page 156**

xi

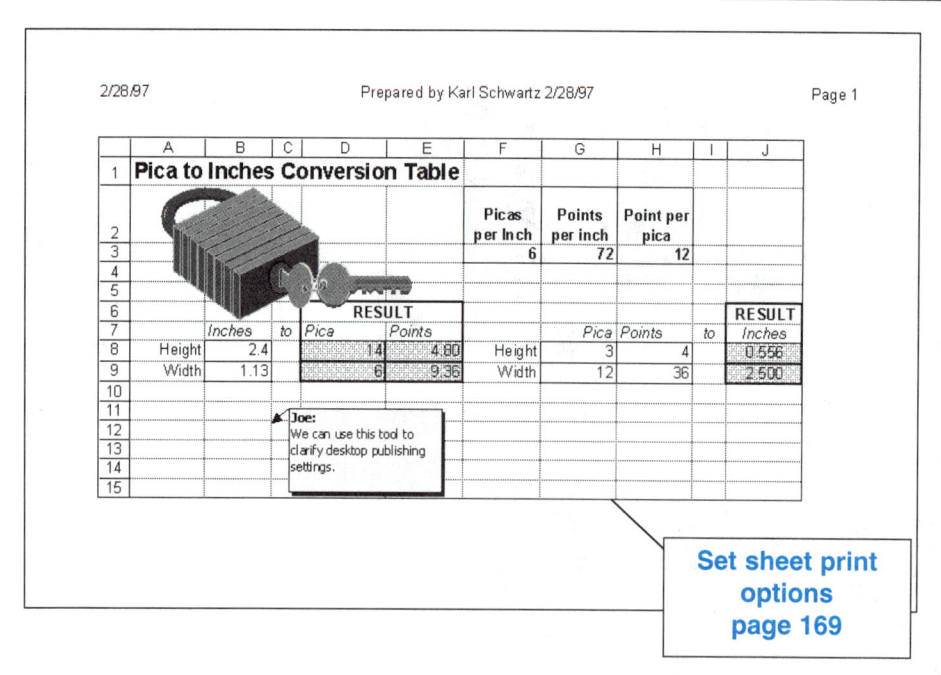

Visual Index (continued)

	A	B	C	D
10	Date	Expense	Amount	Vendor
11	1/6/98	inventory	$16,000	SW Wholesale
12	3/5/98	inventory	$20,000	SW Wholesale
13	10/7/98	inventory	$14,900	SW Wholesale
14	12/5/98	inventory	$10,997	SW Wholesale
15			$61,897	
16	3/31/98	overhead	$1,000	A.B. Properties
17	4/30/98	overhead	$1,000	A.B. Properties
18	6/14/98	overhead	$5,000	AR Office
19	11/14/97	overhead	$5,000	AR Office
20	12/14/97	overhead	$5,000	AR Office
21	2/5/98	overhead	$440	City of Franklin
22	2/5/98	overhead	$500	City of Franklin
23	11/4/97	overhead	$200	Ralph J Cook Garbage
24	12/4/98	overhead	$200	Ralph J Cook Garbage
25		overhead Total	$18,340	
26	2/5/98	salary	$1,890	Jim Parsons
27	3/5/98	salary	$1,890	Jim Parsons
28	3/14/98	salary	$945	Jim Parsons
29		salary Total	$4,725	
30		Grand Total	$84,962	

Outlines page 164

Subtotal lists automatically page 169

2/28/97   Prepared by Karl Schwartz 2/28/97   Page 1

Pica to Inches Conversion Table

	Picas per Inch	Points per inch	Point per pica
	6	72	12

RESULT

Inches	to	Pica	Points
Height	2.4	14	4.80
Width	1.13	6	9.36

	Pica	Points	to	Inches
Height	3	4		0.556
Width	12	36		2.500

Joe:
We can use this tool to clarify desktop publishing settings.

Set sheet print options page 169

xii

Visual Index (continued)

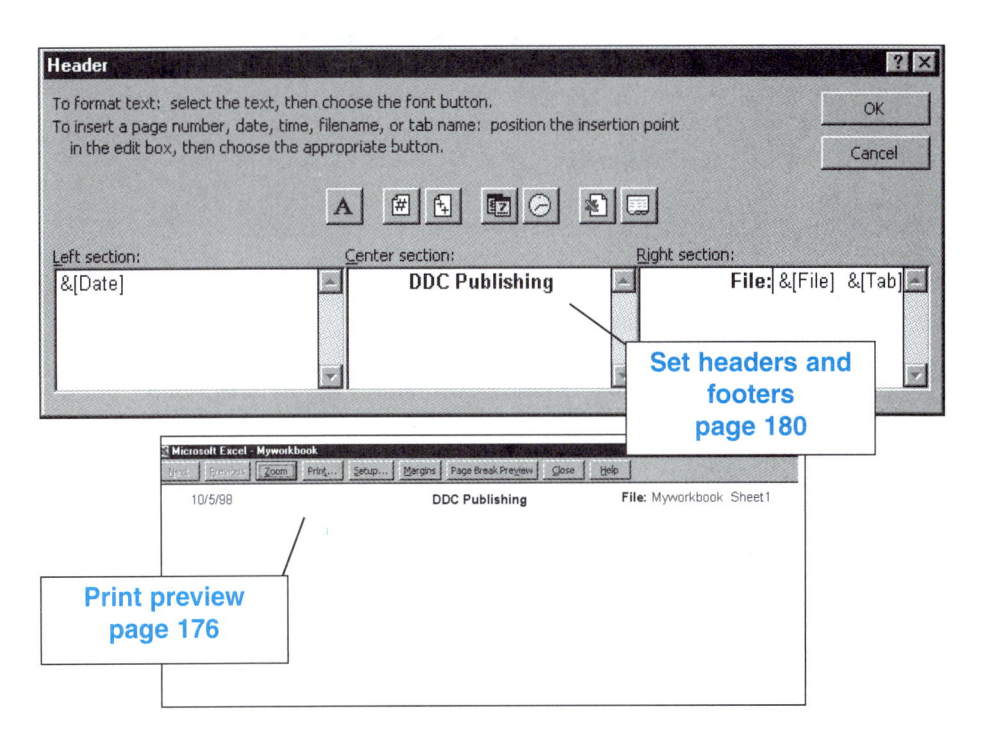

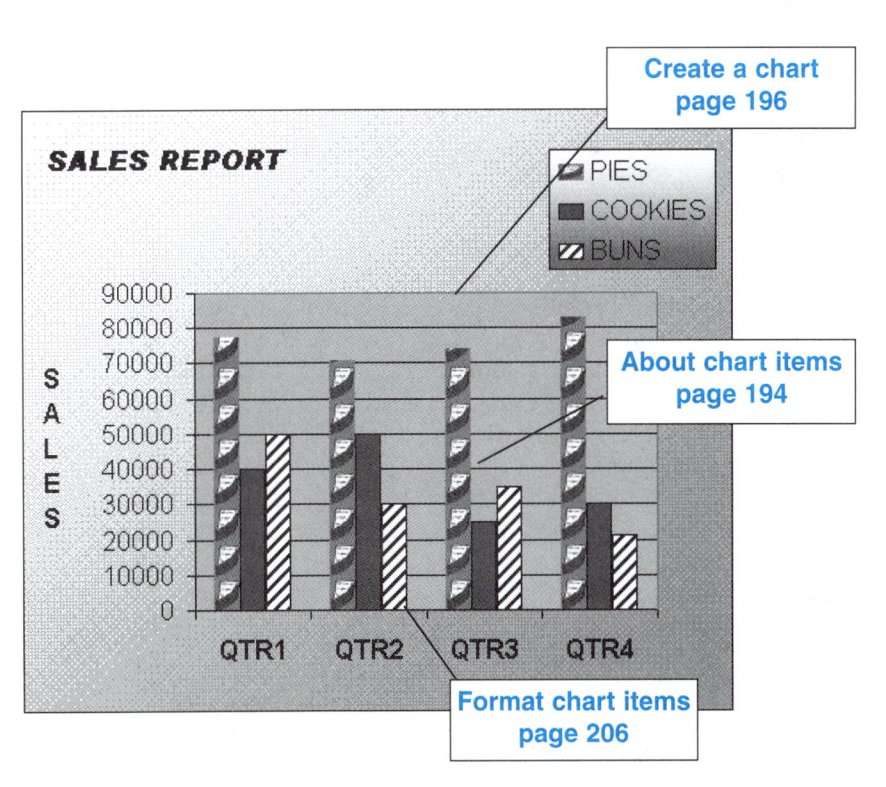

Set headers and footers page 180

Print preview page 176

Create a chart page 196

About chart items page 194

Format chart items page 206

xiii

Table of Contents

Getting Started

Start Excel. 2
About the Excel Window 4
About Workbooks 6
About Worksheets and Sheet Tabs. 8
Use Window Controls. 10
About Commands 12
About Toolbars. 14
Use Dialog Box Controls 16
Help Overview 18
About Cells 22
Navigate Workbooks 24
Select Cells, Columns, and Rows. 26
Open Workbooks 28
Save Workbooks 30
Close Workbooks and Quit Excel. 34

Basic Skills

Adjust and Hide Columns 38
Adjust and Hide Rows 40
Align Data in Cells. 42
AutoCalculate 44
AutoCorrect. 46
Clear Cells 48
Copy and Paste Special 50
Copy Cell Contents 52
Collect and Paste Multiple Items 54
Customize Excel 56
Delete Cells, Columns, and Rows 60
Draw Objects. 62
Edit Cells. 64
Enter Cell Data 66
Fill Cells With Series 68
Find and Replace 70
Find Workbooks 72
Format Cell Borders and Fill 74
Format Cells Conditionally. 76
Format Cells Using Format Painter 78
Format Data Tables Automatically 80

xiv

Format Font. 82
Format Number 84
Insert and Remove Comments 86
Insert Cells, Columns, and Rows 88
Insert OLE Objects 90
Macros 92
Move Cell Contents 94
Name Cells 96
Protect Workbooks 98
Protect Worksheet Data. 100
Set Calculation Options 102
Set Edit Options 104
Set General Options 106
Set View Options 108
Sheet Tabs 110
Spell Check 112
Templates 114
Workbook Properties 116
Workbook Window Commands 118
Worksheet Window Commands 120
Undo and Repeat Actions 122
Validate Cell Entries 124

Formulas, Lists and Data Tables

About Formulas 128
About References in Formulas 130
Audit Formulas 132
Create Formulas (Simple) 134
Create Formulas (Complex) 136
Create Functions 138
Create Lookup Tables 140
Create PivotTable 142
Create One-variable Data Tables 144
Create Two-variable Data Tables 146
Edit Formulas 148
Edit PivotTable 150
Filter Lists Automatically 156
Filter Lists (Advanced) 158
Goal Seek 160
Lists 162
Outlines 164
Sort Lists 166
Subtotal Lists Automatically 168
Use Data Forms with Lists 170

XV

Printing and Page Setup

Page Breaks 174
Print Preview 176
Print Workbook Data 178
Set Headers and Footers 180
Set Margins 182
Set Print Area 184
Set Repeating Print Titles 186
Set Scale and Orientation 188
Set Sheet Print Options 190

Charts

About Chart Items 194
Create a Chart 196
Create PivotChart 198
Edit PivotChart 200
Insert Objects in Charts 204
Format Chart Items 206
Move and Size Chart Items 208
Print Charts 210
Select Chart Type 212
Set Chart Options 214
Set Location of Chart 216
Set Source of Chart Data 218
Special 3-D Chart Effects 220

Getting Started

This section contains essential information for new users of Microsoft Excel 97. Topics, in this section only, are listed in a logical order beginning with **Start Excel**.

Start Excel

When you start Excel, Windows copies the program into memory, and Excel opens with a blank workbook named Book1. You can start Excel in a variety of ways.

Notes:

- You can always start Excel from the **Start** menu, which is visible on the bottom of the Windows desktop.

- For information about the Excel window, see *About the Excel Window* in this section.

- Excel always opens a blank workbook named Book1 when it starts. *(See About Workbooks.)* You can use this workbook to create new spreadsheets, or you can open a workbook that you have previously saved to a disk *(see Open Workbooks).*

  If a blank workbook is not to your liking, click the **File** menu, then **New** to access templates on the **Spreadsheet Solutions** tab.

- You can also start Excel by opening a recently used Excel document. Click the **Start** menu, point to **Documents**, and click the desired Excel document from the menu.

Start Excel Using Start Menu

1 Click the **Start** button on Windows toolbar.
2 Point to **Programs** on **Start** menu.

   A submenu appears.

3 Click **Microsoft Excel** icon.

   The Excel application starts and opens a blank workbook named Book1.

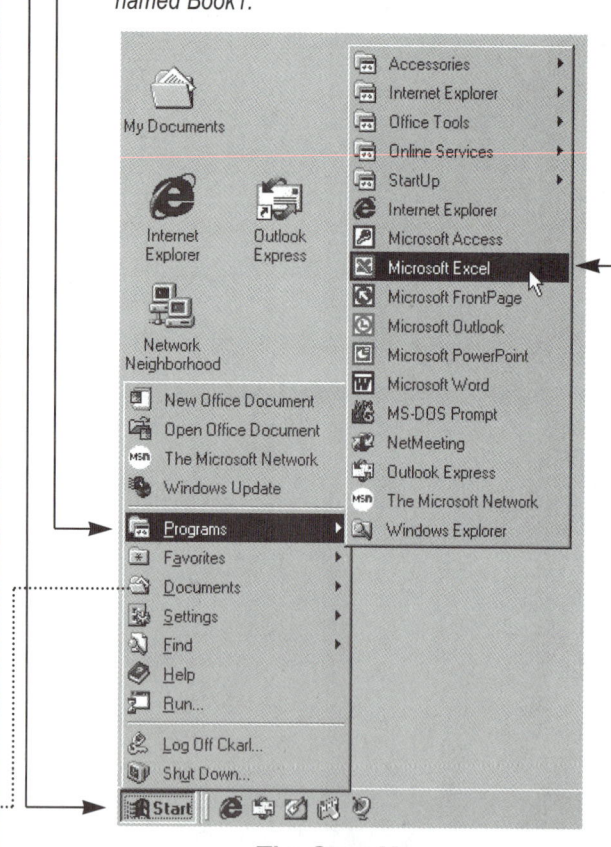

The Start Menu

Notes:

- Depending on how you set up Office, the **Office Shortcut Bar** may appear on your desktop. If it is not installed, you can add it by running Office setup: Open Control Panel, click **Add/Remove Programs**, select **Microsoft Office** from the list, then click the **Add/Remove** button.

- In the **New Office Document** dialog box, you can click the **Spreadsheet Solutions** tab to open an Excel template, instead of starting a new document from scratch.

Start Excel from Microsoft Office

This method requires that you install Excel as part of Microsoft Office 2000.

1 Click the **Start** button on the Windows toolbar, then click **New Office Document**.

OR

If the **Office Shortcut Bar** is installed and running, click the **New Office Document** button on the Shortcut bar.

2 From the **General** tab, double-click the **Blank Workbook** icon.

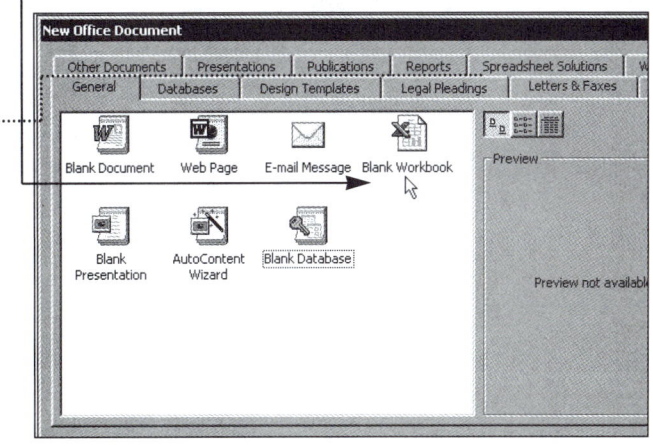

New Office Document Dialog Box

TIP: You can double-click any Excel document stored in a folder to start Excel and open that file. If Excel is already running, just the file opens.

3

About the Excel Window

Excel provides an interface (graphical tools and controls) for working with worksheet data. This topic will help you identify the purpose of the tools and indicators that appear in the Excel window.

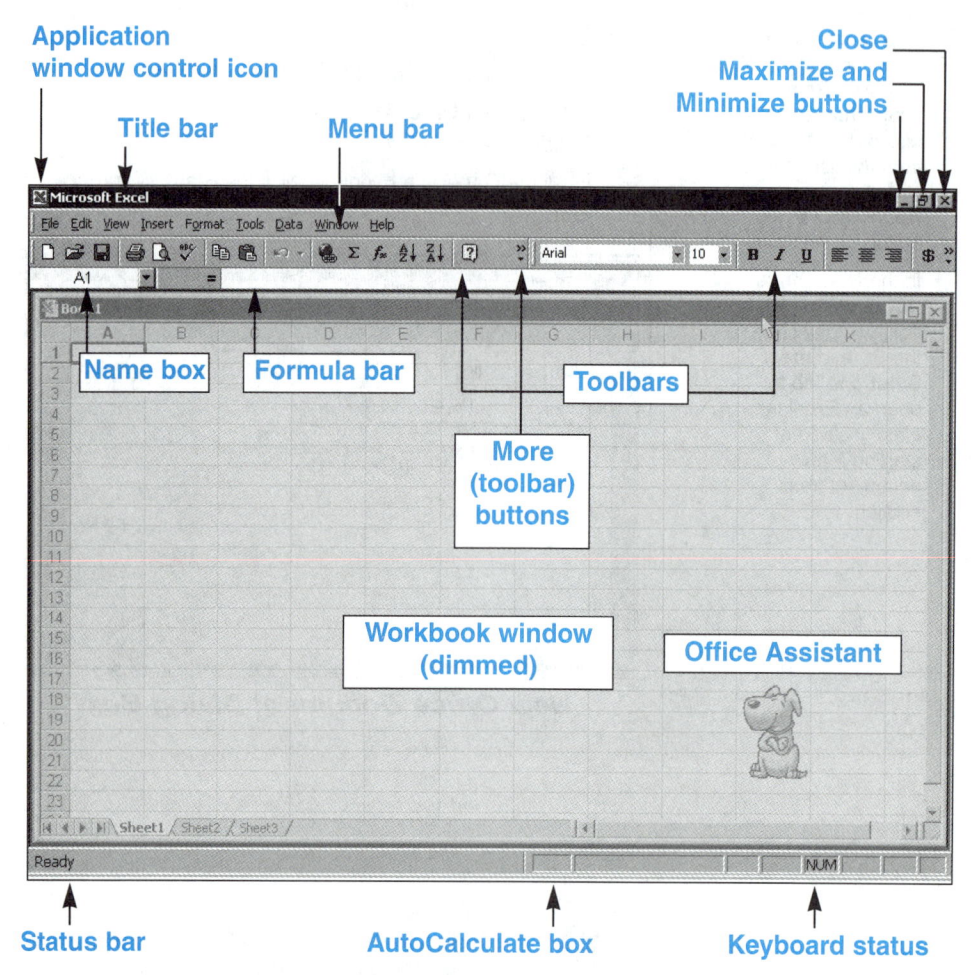

The Excel Application as it Appears When You First Open It

Labels on the illustration:
- Application window control icon
- Title bar
- Menu bar
- Close
- Maximize and Minimize buttons
- Name box
- Formula bar
- Toolbars
- More (toolbar) buttons
- Workbook window (dimmed)
- Office Assistant
- Status bar
- AutoCalculate box
- Keyboard status

> **TIP:** You can set Windows to show more screen area, thereby showing more Excel workspace and toolbar buttons: Right-click the desktop, click Properties, click the Settings tab, then adjust the slider to select a resolution appropriate to your vision and monitor size. The screen area in the illustration above is set to 800 by 600 pixels.

Notes:

- In the illustration, there are two sets of **Close**, **Maximize** and **Minimize** buttons: One for the Excel application window, and one for the workbook window. The **Maximize** button will appear as a **Restore** button if the window has already been maximized.

The Microsoft Excel Window

Application window control icon: Click to access a drop-down menu of commands that control the position and size of the application window.

Close, Maximize, and Minimize buttons: Click buttons to close, maximize, or minimize the Excel window. *(See Use Window Controls.)*

Formula bar: Provides a space for typing or editing cell data. *(See Edit Cell Data.)*

Microsoft Excel title bar: Displays the program name (Microsoft Excel), and may also display the file name of an open workbook window, if the workbook is maximized. You can drag the title bar to move the window, or double-click it to maximize the window.

Menu bar: Displays menu names which, when clicked, display drop-down menus. *(See About Commands.)*

More buttons: Click to open a submenu of additional toolbar buttons. By default, Excel will add buttons that you use often to your toolbars, and remove buttons from the toolbar that you do not use.

Name box: Displays the cell reference of the active cell. *(See About Cells.)*

Office Assistant: Appears when you open Excel, and can answer your questions about how to perform a task. *(See Help Overview.)*

Toolbars: Click toolbar buttons to select commands without opening a menu or dialog box. *(See About Toolbars.)*

Status bar: Displays information about the current mode, selected command, or option. The right side of the status bar shows the **keyboard status**. For example, NUM indicates that the numeric keyboard is toggled on (number lock). The middle of the status bar contains the **AutoCalculate box**, which displays the result of a selected AutoCalculate function (such as SUM or AVERAGE) when applied to a selected range of cells. *(See AutoCalculate.)*

Workbook window: Appears in, and is restricted to, the Excel window. Workbook windows contain the data that you enter in worksheets (purposely muted in this illustration). You can open multiple workbook windows within Excel. *(See About Workbooks.)*

About Workbooks

A workbook is a file in which you store and analyze information. Each workbook may contain multiple worksheets (sheets). This lets you organize related information in one workbook file. You can save workbooks with descriptive names and store and retrieve them from folders on a disk.

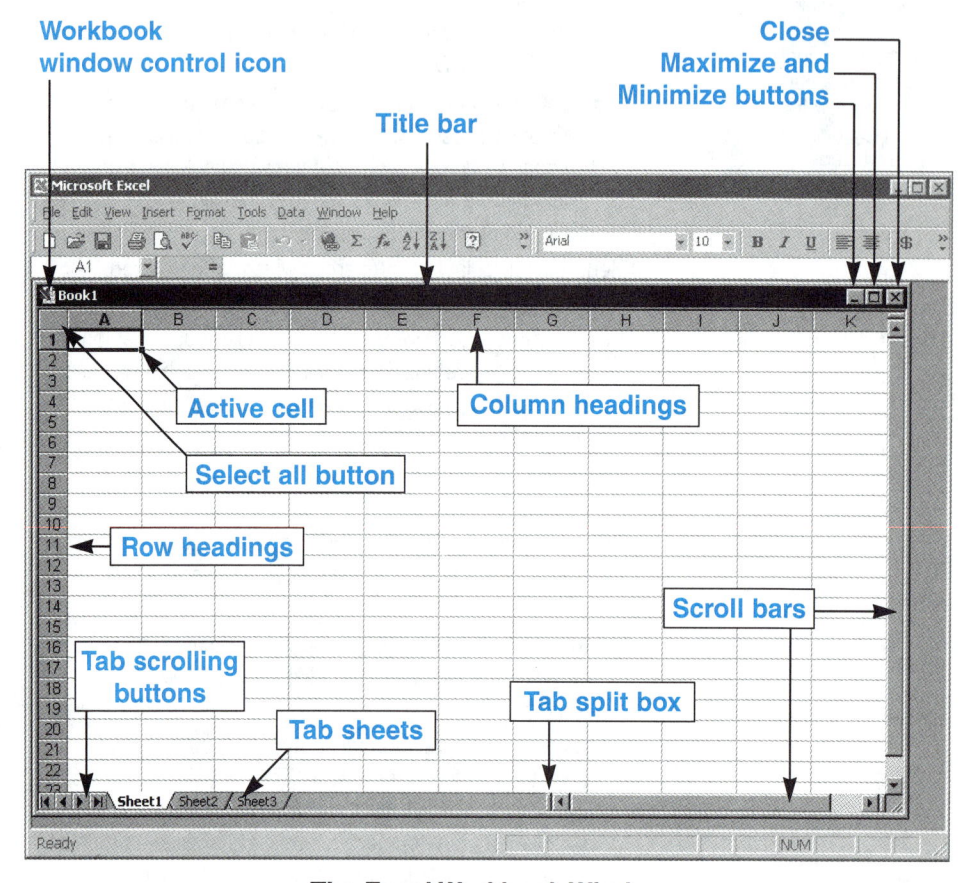

The Excel Workbook Window

Notes:

- If the workbook in the illustration were maximized, its name (Book1) would appear in the Excel application title bar, and the workbook title bar would not be available. *(See Use Window Controls for information about maximizing and restoring windows.)*

The Workbook Window

Active cell: The cell into which you can type data. The active cell has a dark outline (see cell A1 in the illustration on the previous page). *(See About Cells.)*

Row and column headings: Define a cell's location and let you adjust row and column dimensions with the mouse. Rows are numbered and columns are lettered. *(See Adjust and Hide Columns/Rows.)*

Scroll bars: Use to display areas of the worksheet that are not in view. *(See Use Window Controls.)*

Select all button: Click to select all the cells in the worksheet. *(See Select Cells, Columns, and Rows.)*

Sheet tabs: Indicate the names of worksheets and charts in the workbook. Click a sheet tab to display that sheet in the workbook window. The active sheet tab is shown in bold (see Sheet1 in the illustration on the previous page). *(See Sheet Tabs.)*

Tab scrolling buttons: Click buttons to scroll to sheet tabs that are not in view. *(See Sheet Tabs.)*

Tab split box: Drag to the right to display more sheet tabs or to the left to show more of the horizontal scroll bar. *(See Sheet Tabs.)*

Title bar: Displays the name of the workbook window. If the Workbook is maximized, however, its name appears on the Excel window title bar. You can drag the title bar to move the workbook within the Excel window.

Workbook (Book1): Displays the active worksheet (Sheet1), which is the document window that opens when you start Excel. By default, workbooks contain three worksheets (Sheet1– Sheet3) but can hold up to 255 sheets, which you can use to store data and formulas, charts, or macros.

Workbook control menu icon: Click the workbook window control menu box to access commands that control the workbook window. If the workbook window is maximized, its control menu icon is located on the left side of the Excel window menu bar. The workbook window **Close**, **Maximize**, and **Minimize** buttons let you control the size, minimize, or close the Excel window. *(See Use Window Controls.)*

Workbook window title bar: Displays the workbook file name. You can drag the title bar to move the window or double-click it to maximize the window size. A maximized workbook window does not have a title bar. Its file name appears on Excel's application window title bar.

About Worksheets and Sheet Tabs

By default, each new workbook contains three worksheets labeled Sheet1 through Sheet3, as illustrated below. Excel provides controls for working with sheet tabs as shown below. Also see *Sheet Tabs* for information about inserting, grouping, renaming, deleting, moving, and copying sheet tabs.

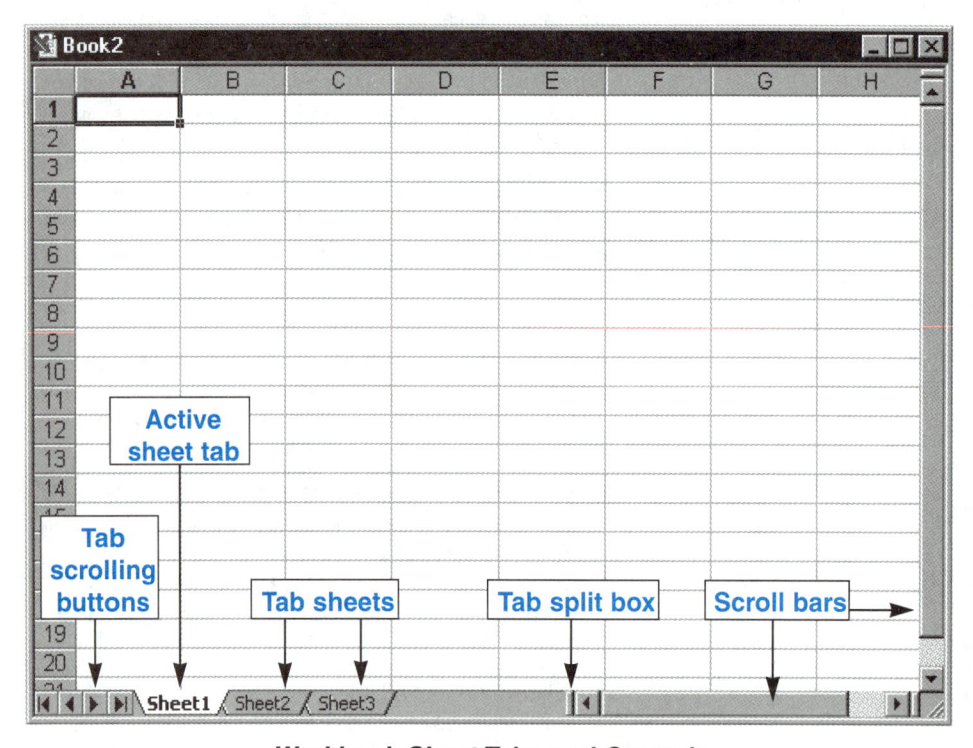

Workbook Sheet Tabs and Controls

8

Notes:

- A workbook can hold up to 255 sheets to display your data and formulas, charts, dialog boxes or macros. Excel 4.0 macros are stored on module sheets. Programmers can use dialog sheets to create dialog boxes containing application-like controls that interact with worksheet data.

- To change the number of sheets in a new workbook, click the **Tools** menu, then **Options**, select the **General** tab, and set the number in the **Sheets in new workbook** spin box.

- You can select (group) multiple sheets by pressing **Ctrl** and clicking the desired sheets. This lets you format or enter identical data in multiple worksheets in one step. *(See Sheet Tabs.)*

- Each sheet maintains its own settings, such as zoom, active cell, page margins, and gridlines.

- You can hide sheets, for example, to keep sensitive data hidden from a user: Click the **Format** menu, point to **Sheet**, then click **Hide**.

Worksheet Tab Controls

Scroll bars: Use to display areas of the active worksheet that are not in view. *(See Use Window Controls.)*

Sheet tabs: Indicate the names of worksheets, charts, and modules in the workbook. Click a sheet tab to display the sheet in the workbook window. The **active sheet tab** is shown in bold (see Sheet1 in the illustration on the previous page). You can insert, delete, move, and rename sheet tabs. *(See Sheet Tabs.)*

Tab scrolling buttons: Click to scroll to sheet tabs that are not in view.

Scroll to first/last sheet tab

Scroll sheet tabs left and right

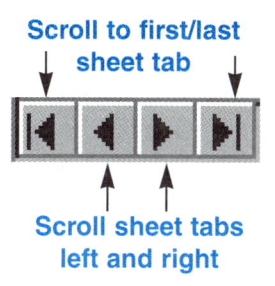

Tab split box: Drag to the right to display more sheet tabs or to the left to show more of the horizontal scroll bar. To drag the tab split box, rest your mouse pointer on the tab split box control. (Note that the mouse pointer changes to a left- and right-facing arrow as shown below.) Then drag the split box left or right.

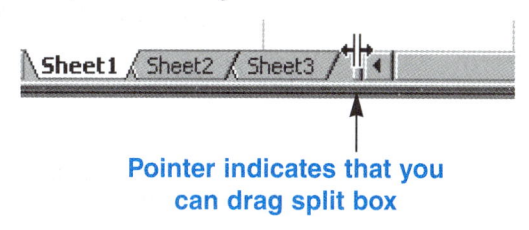

Pointer indicates that you can drag split box

9

Use Window Controls

Window controls are graphical elements such as window borders, title bars, and close buttons that you can use to control the size or position of the Excel and workbook windows.

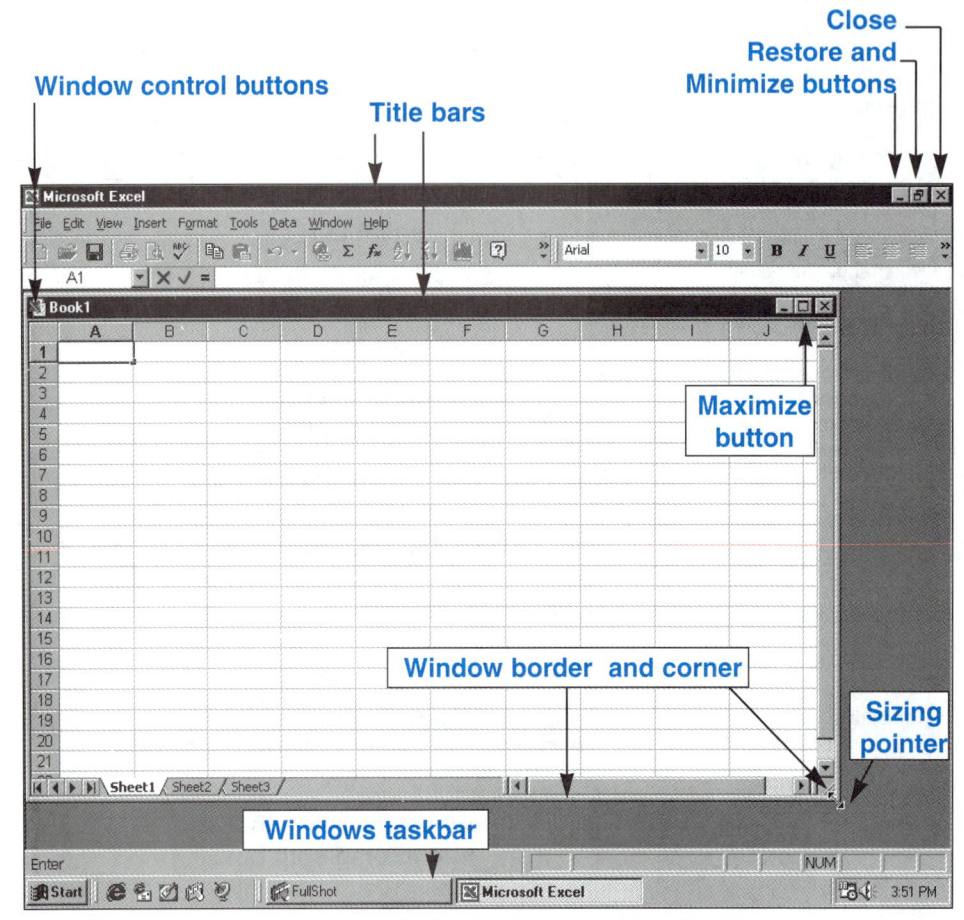

Excel Window Maximized, Workbook Not Maximized

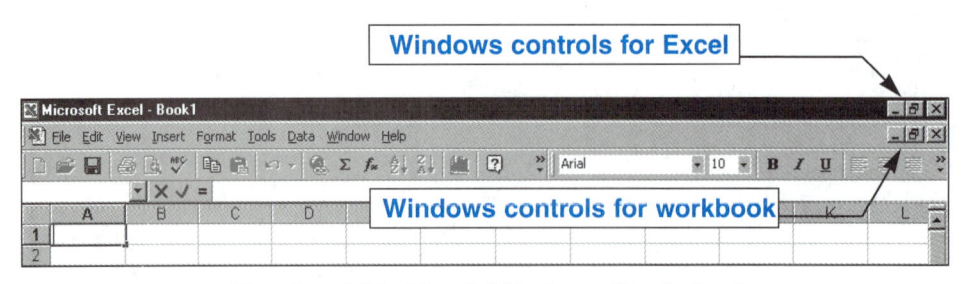

Excel and Workbook Windows Maximized

10

Notes:

- In the top illustration, the Excel window contains Close, *Restore*, and Minimize buttons, while the workbook window contains Close, *Maximize*, and Minimize buttons. You can size and move the workbook window when it is not maximized.

- In the bottom illustration, both windows have been maximized. The workbook's Minimize, Restore, and Close buttons appear on the Excel menu bar. You cannot size or move either window. Notice the workbook window does not have a title bar, and its name (Book1) appears in the Excel title bar.

Window Controls

Close button: Click to close the Excel or workbook window. You will be prompted to save changes to the workbook if you have not already done so.

Maximize button: Click to enlarge the window to fill the screen, or, for a workbook, to fill the Excel window.

Minimize button: In the Excel window, click it to reduce the window to a button on the taskbar. In workbook windows, click it to reduce the window to a button within the Excel application window.

Restore button: Click to restore a maximized window to its previous size.

Sizing pointer: The mouse pointer becomes a sizing pointer when you rest it on a window border or corner. This indicates that you can change the border by dragging it.

Taskbar: Click buttons on it to select a window that is not in view (hidden behind other windows), or to open a window you have minimized.

Title bar: Drag it to move a window, or double-click it to maximize/restore the window. Maximized windows cannot be moved or sized.

Window border or corner: Drag it to change the size of the window. The pointer becomes a sizing pointer when positioned on a window border or corner.

Window control buttons: Click to open a menu of commands that control the window, e.g., Restore, Minimize, and Close. You can open this menu with the keyboard:

Excel window   press **Alt+Space**
Workbook window   press **Alt+-** (hyphen)

11

About Commands

Commands allow you to tell Excel what actions to perform. For example, when you want to save the current workbook, you execute the Save command from the File menu. This topic will show you how to use the menu bar, shortcut menus, and keystrokes to execute commands.

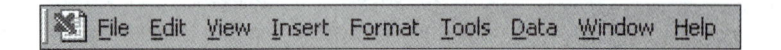

Notes:

- The item (cell, chart, text, etc.) you select in **step 1** will determine the available commands on the menu. If a command is not available for your selection, Excel will dim the command name.

- In **step 2**, the menu bar may change to reflect your selection. For example, if you have selected a chart, Excel will display **Chart** instead of **Data** on the menu bar.

- In **step 3**, if the menu name contains a submenu, ▶ appears to the right of the name. Excel will open the submenu when you click or point to this kind of menu.

- Excel will track commands you use most often and provide those menu items on the toolbars.

- To undo a command, click the **Edit** menu, then **Undo**.

Choose Menu Commands

1. If required, select item to which the command will apply.
2. Click desired menu name on menu bar.
   Excel opens a drop-down menu.
3. Open expanded menu options or submenu, then click desired command name.

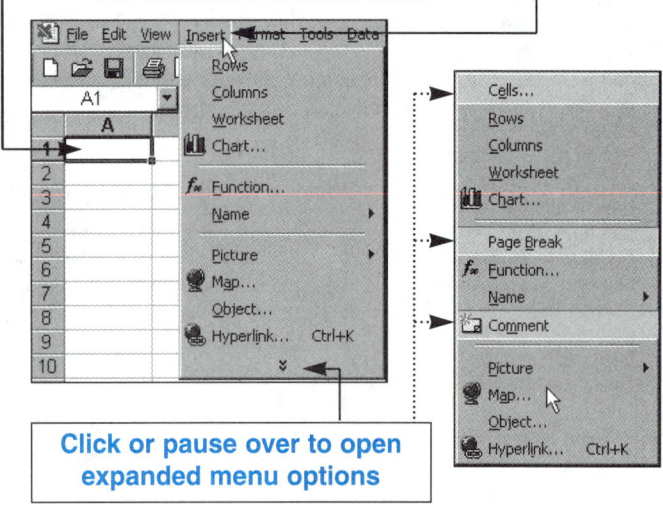

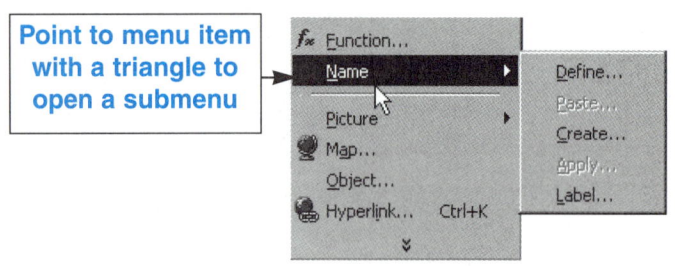

Click or pause over to open expanded menu options

Point to menu item with a triangle to open a submenu

Basics of Choosing Menu Commands

12

Notes:

- In **step 1**, as you move the mouse pointer, it will change its shape to indicate what action it can perform. When pointing to an object, the pointer must be shaped like a cross when you right-click.

- In **step 2**, right-clicking means to press and release the right mouse button.

- In **step 3**, available commands will vary depending upon your previous action. In the example, **Paste** and **Paste Special** are not available (dimmed) because no data has been copied to the Clipboard.

Shortcut Menu Commands

1 Select desired cell or object.
2 Right-click cell or object.
   Excel opens a context-sensitive menu.
3 Click the desired menu command.

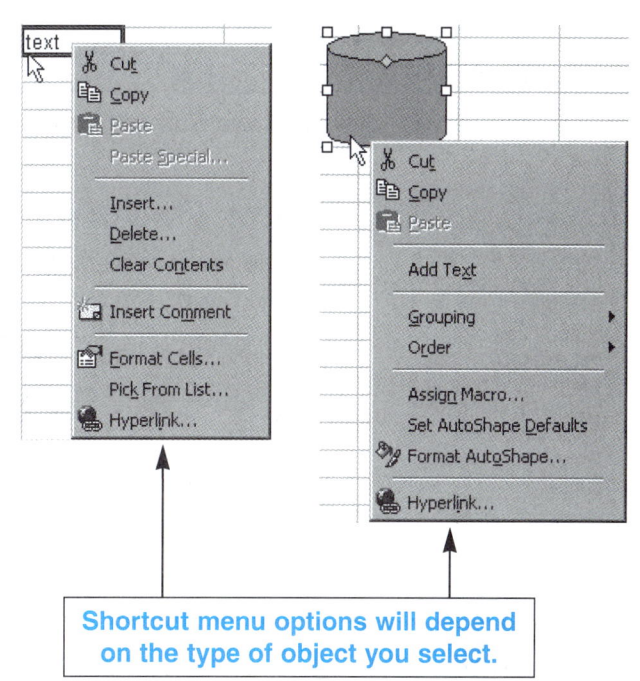

Shortcut menu options will depend on the type of object you select.

Notes:

- In **step 2**, press and hold **Ctrl** (the modifier key), while you press **1**. Then release both keys.

- For information about other kinds of commands, see *About Toolbars* and *Use Window Controls* in this section.

Keyboard Commands

1 Select cell or object to which the command will apply.
2 Press desired command key, such as **Ctrl+1** (Format Cells).
   Excel performs the action.

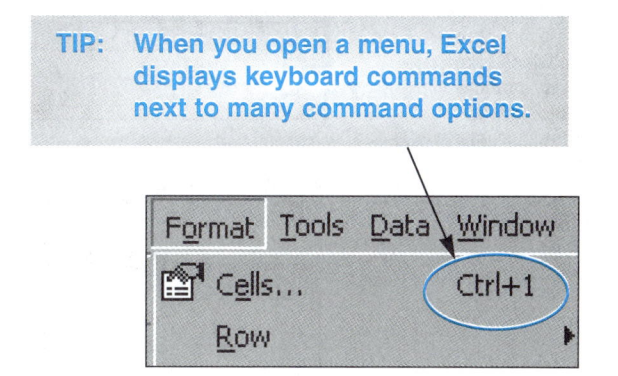

TIP: When you open a menu, Excel displays keyboard commands next to many command options.

13

About Toolbars

Excel displays the Standard and Formatting toolbars on a single row. These toolbars contain buttons that let you execute commands without opening menus and dialog boxes. As you work, Excel will display other toolbars for special tasks, such as editing a chart. *(Also see Customize Excel.)*

Standard and Formatting Toolbars

Notes:

- Excel may display additional information along with the button name. For example, when you rest the pointer on the **Print** button, it will show the name of the current printer.

Show Purpose of Toolbar Button

- Rest pointer on desired toolbar button.
  Excel displays the tool name.

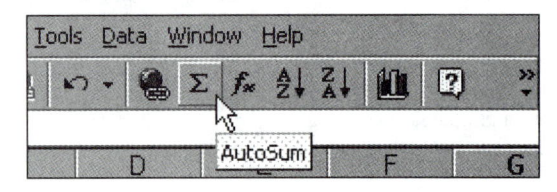

Notes:

- If you select a cell that has been bolded, the **Bold** button on the toolbar will invert to indicate the setting is in effect.

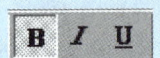

  Most buttons work this way, except the **Borders**, **Fill Color**, and **Font Color** buttons, which show the last attribute applied to any cell, not the current setting.

Use a Toolbar Button

1 Select cells or object to which the command will apply.

To show additional buttons on a toolbar:

- Click More Buttons on the right side of the toolbar.

2 Click desired button on toolbar.

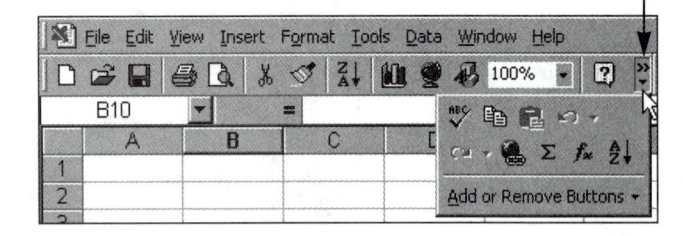

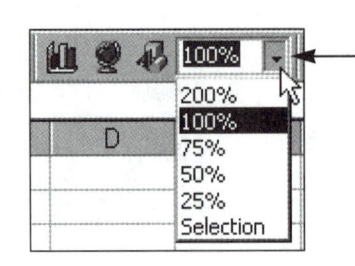

For toolbar buttons with drop-down arrows, click the arrow to open a list of options, then select the desired option.

14

Notes:

- In **step 1**, to right-click an item, point to the item, then press and release the right mouse button.

- In **step 2**, a check mark appears to the left of a currently displayed toolbar name.

- The **Customize** option lets you add and remove buttons on existing toolbars or create new toolbars. You can also change the size of toolbar buttons and enable or disable ScreenTips on toolbars using the the **Options** tab of the **Customize** dialog box. *(See Customize Excel.)*

Show or Hide a Toolbar

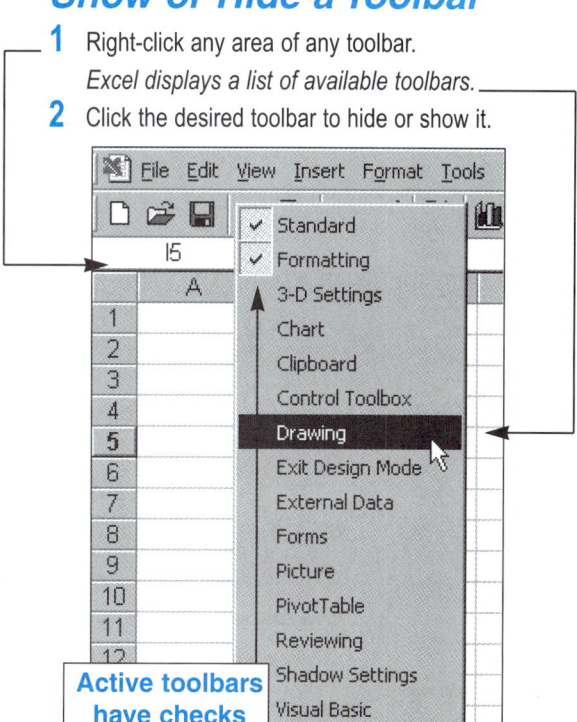

1 Right-click any area of any toolbar.

Excel displays a list of available toolbars.

2 Click the desired toolbar to hide or show it.

Active toolbars have checks

Notes:

- A **docked toolbar** is locked into a position on the Excel window border. Toolbars that have been moved into the workbook area are called **floating toolbars**.

- In **step 2**, when you drag a toolbar from its docked position to make it a floating toolbar, a title bar appears on it.

- To move a floating toolbar, drag its title bar.

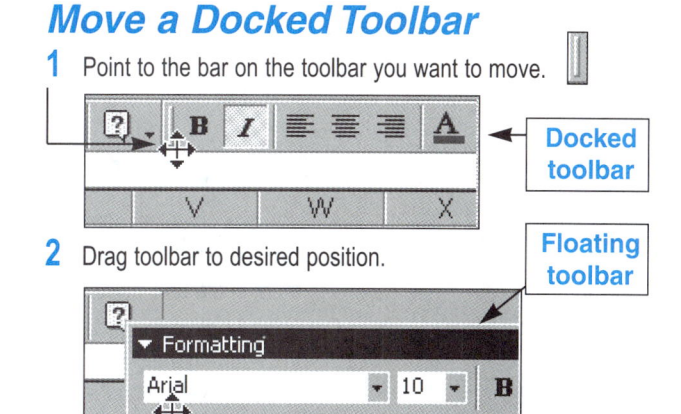

Move a Docked Toolbar

1 Point to the bar on the toolbar you want to move.

Docked toolbar

2 Drag toolbar to desired position.

Floating toolbar

Drag toolbar into a workbook area to create a **floating toolbar.** Drag it to any border of the Excel window to **dock it**. Drag a docked toolbar left or right to **size it** when two toolbars occupy the same row.

15

Use Dialog Box Controls

When you select certain commands, Excel opens a dialog box displaying related options. Some dialog boxes, such as Page Setup, contain tabs that you can click to display additional options. This topic describes the controls in a dialog box, such as option buttons and check boxes, so you can work efficiently with Excel.

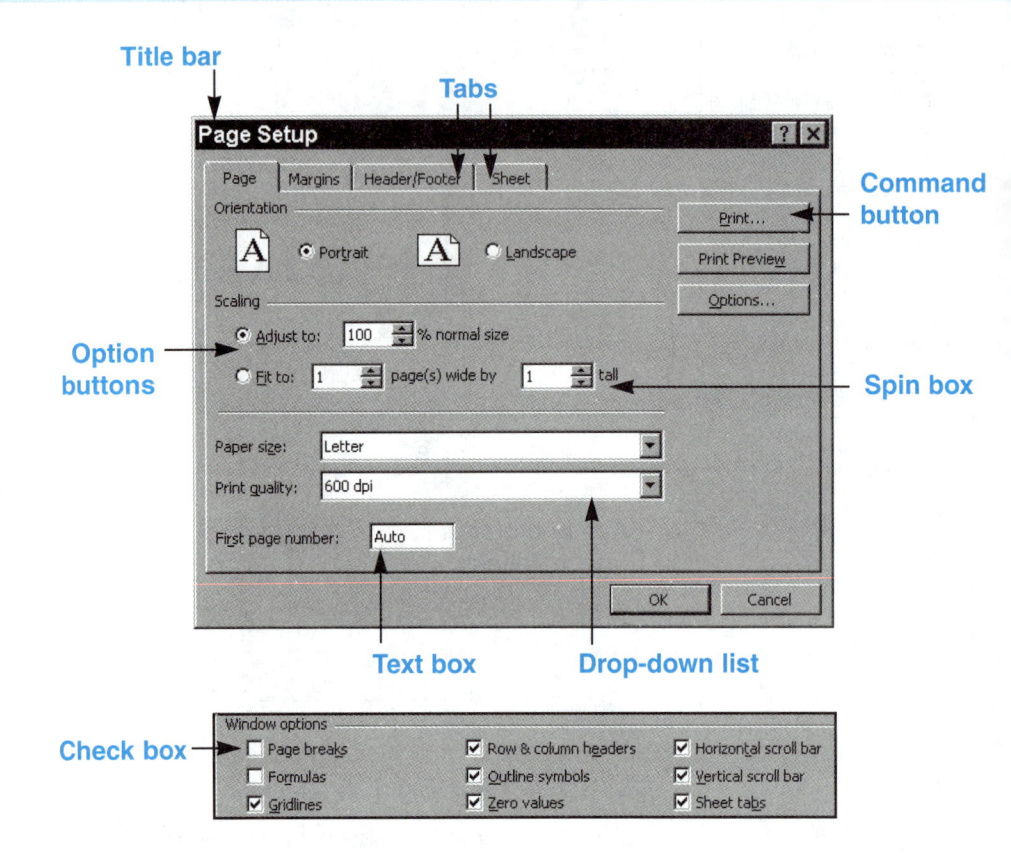

(Diagram of the Page Setup dialog box with labeled callouts: Title bar, Tabs, Command button, Option buttons, Spin box, Text box, Drop-down list, Check box.)

Notes:

- You can drag the title bar to move the dialog box. You might move it to view data behind it on a worksheet.
- You can click any area on a **drop-down list box** to open it.

Dialog Box Controls

A dialog box contains many ways to record settings:

Check box: Click to select or deselect an option. A check mark in the box indicates the option is selected.

Command buttons: Click to carry out actions described by the button name. When command names are followed by ellipses, clicking on them will access another dialog box.

Drop-down list: Click the drop-down list arrow to open a list of options. Choose from the options provided.

16

- If several **check boxes** are offered, you may select more than one option.
- You may choose only one option at a time from a set of **option buttons**.
- If a **text box** contains data you want to replace, double-click or drag through the data to select it, then type over the selection.

Option buttons: Click to select one option from a set. A selected option button contains a dark circle.

Spin box (or increment box): Type a value in the box, or click the up or down arrow (usually to the right of the box) to select a value.

Tabs: Display related options in the same dialog box. Click a tab to access its options.

Text box: Click in the box, then type information. Text boxes for cell references have collapse buttons (see below) that reduce the dialog box to allow a better view of the worksheet.

Title bar: Identifies the title of the dialog box (Page Setup in the illustration).

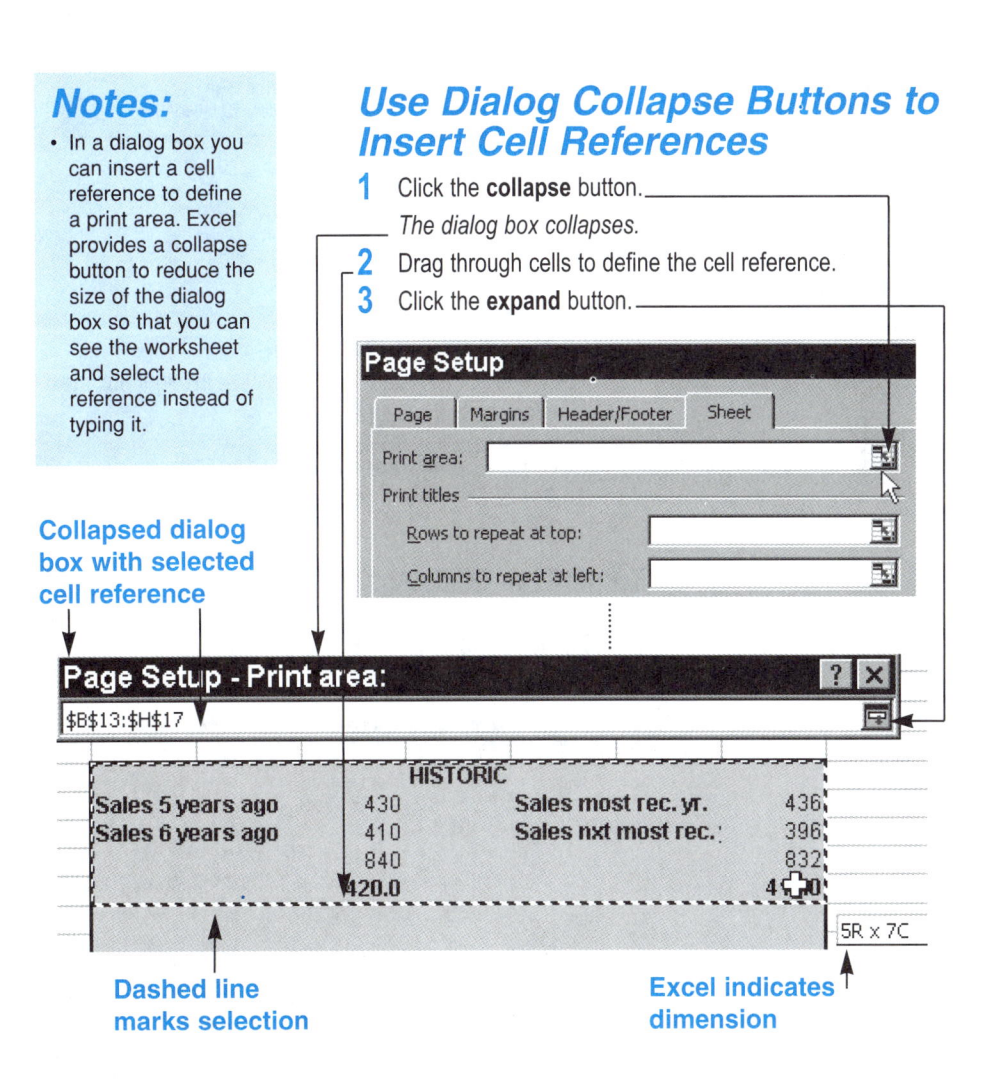

Notes:

- In a dialog box you can insert a cell reference to define a print area. Excel provides a collapse button to reduce the size of the dialog box so that you can see the worksheet and select the reference instead of typing it.

Use Dialog Collapse Buttons to Insert Cell References

1. Click the **collapse** button.
   The dialog box collapses.
2. Drag through cells to define the cell reference.
3. Click the **expand** button.

Collapsed dialog box with selected cell reference

Dashed line marks selection

Excel indicates dimension

Help Overview

When you need to learn how to perform a task, Excel's online Help system is always a few clicks away. Additionally, the Office Assistant will automatically suggest better ways to do your work.

Notes:

- If the Office Assistant is not available, click the **Help** menu, then click **Show the Office Assistant**.
- Click the Office Assistant animated icon to show or hide its prompt box.
- The Office Assistant will often display feature tips (time-saving hints) to help with procedures you use often.
- The Office Assistant dialog box contains options you can select to customize its behavior.

Help Overview

Microsoft Excel provides several ways for you to get help while you work.

Ask the Office Assistant:

- Click the Office Assistant icon, type a question and click **Search**, then follow any prompts that appear.

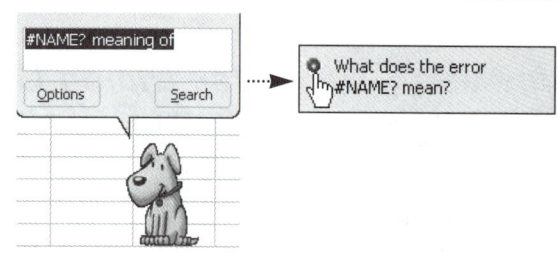

Use Office Assistant feature tips:

- Click the Office Assistant icon, then click the light bulb next to the feature in the bubble menu.

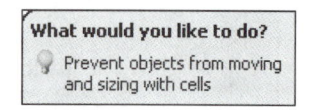

Turn off the Office Assistant to use classic Help:

- Click the Office Assistant icon, then click **Options**.
- From the **Options** tab deselect **Use the Office Assistant**, and click **OK**.

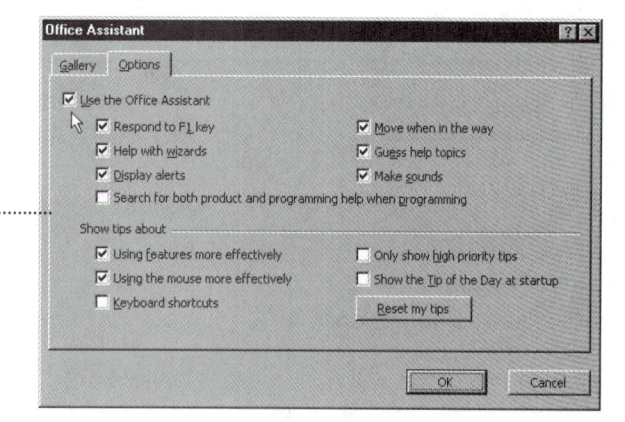

18

Use classic Help from the Help menu:

- If necessary, turn off the Office Assistant (see previous page).
- Click **Microsoft Excel Help**, then click the desired Help window tab.

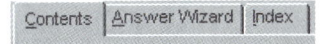

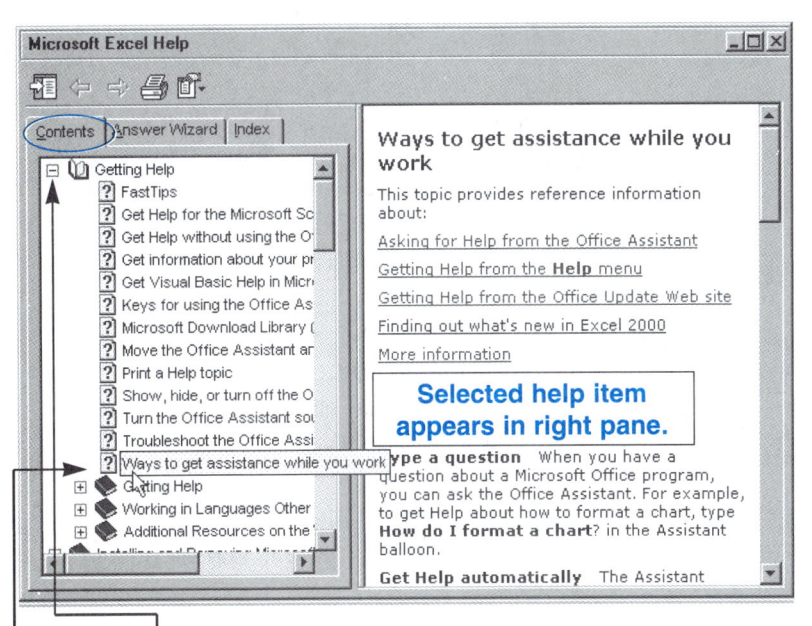

Contents: Click desired topic name to expand it, then click desired help item.

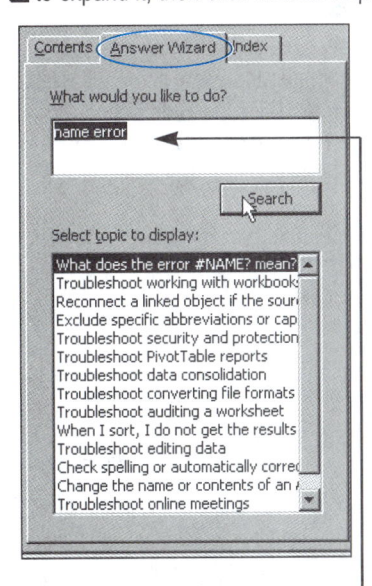

Selected help item appears in right pane.

Answer Wizard: Type description of help item, click **Search**, then click desired topic in the list that appears.

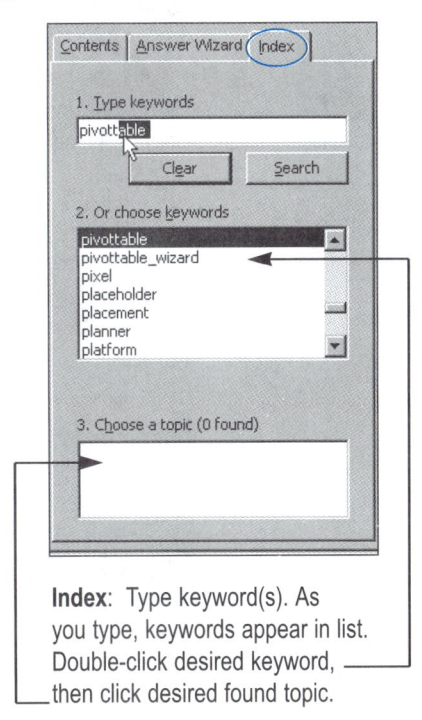

Index: Type keyword(s). As you type, keywords appear in list. Double-click desired keyword, then click desired found topic.

19

Help Overview (continued)

Notes:

- With the **What's This** command, you can identify the following:

    toolbar buttons.

    menus items.

    screen elements such as row headings or sheet tabs.

- You can also use **keyboard shortcuts** to get help:

    F1 — get classic or Office Assistant help

    Shift+F1 — use What's This help

- Rest the mouse pointer on any Help window toolbar button to identify it.

- When you need to view the left pane, click the **Show** button.

Identify screen items:

- Click the **Help** menu, then click the **What's This** command. A question mark prompt appears.

- Click the screen item, including menu commands, you wish to identify.

Get help in a dialog box:

- Click the **question mark** button, then click the desired option to view a description.

Get additional help on the Web:

- Click the **Help** menu, click the **Office on the Web** command.

Automatic and intelligent positioning of Help and Excel windows:

- When the Help window opens, its content pane takes up nearly one half of the screen, and the Excel screen is sized to fill the remaining area. Click the **Hide** button to hide the left pane of the Help window. This will increase your work space while you read the help information in the right pane.

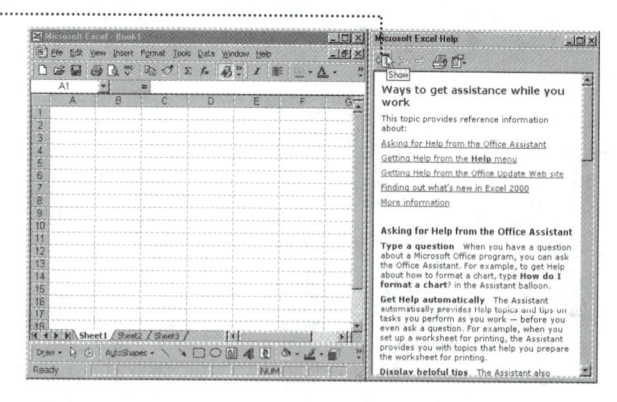

Common Causes of Error Messages Displayed in Cells

Below is a list of error values that may appear in a cell when Excel cannot calculate a formula value.

#DIV/0! — Indicates that the formula is trying to divide by zero.

Possible causes in formula: • Divisor is a zero. • Divisor is referencing a blank cell or a cell that contains a zero value.

#N/A — Indicates that no value is available.

Possible causes in formula: • An invalid argument may have been used with a LOOKUP function. • A reference in an array formula does not match range in which results are displayed. • A required argument has been omitted from a function.

#NAME? — Indicates that Excel does not recognize the name used in a formula.

Possible causes in formula: • A named reference has been deleted or has not been defined. • A function or named reference has been misspelled. • Text has been entered without required quotation marks. • A colon has been omitted in a range reference.

#NULL! — Indicates that the intersection of two range references does not exist.

Possible cause in formula: • Two range references (separated with a space operator) have been used to represent a nonexistent intersection of the two ranges.

#NUM! — Indicates a number error.

Possible causes in formula: • An incorrect value has been used in a function. • Arguments result in a number too small or large to represent.

#REF! — Indicates reference to an invalid cell.

Possible cause in formula: • Arguments refer to cells that have been deleted or overwritten with nonnumeric data. The argument is replaced with #REF!.

#VALUE! — Indicates the invalid use of an operator or argument.

Possible cause in formula: • An invalid value, or a referenced value, has been used with a formula or function, for example, SUM("John").

Circular — A message on status bar that indicates formula is referring to itself.

Possible cause in formula: • A cell reference refers to the cell containing the formula result. The Circular Reference toolbar may appear when a circular reference is detected. You can use the toolbar to locate the circular reference and to trace the references in the formula.

> NOTE: If a circular reference is intended, you can select **Options** from the **Tools** menu, then select **Iteration** from the **Calculation** tab. Iteration repeats a calculation until a specific result value is met.

About Cells

Cells are areas in a worksheet in which you store data. In formulas, you refer to cells by specifying their column and row locations in the worksheet. This is called a cell reference. You can enter text, values, and formulas in cells.

Notes:

- Each cell is defined by the intersection of a row and a column (e.g., A3 denotes column A, row 3). The cell's location is called a **cell reference** (or cell address).

- When you open a new workbook, it usually contains multiple worksheets. Each worksheet has 256 columns and 65,536 rows. Therefore, each worksheet contains 16,777,216 cells!

- **Columns** are labeled A through IV. **Rows** are numbered 1 through 65,536.

- Each cell can store up to 32,000 characters.

- To select a cell, click it, or press an arrow key in the direction of the cell you want to select. For more information about moving around in a worksheet, see *Navigate Workbooks*.

About Cell Locations

In the illustration below, cell B2 is the selected cell in Sheet1. You know this because:

- The reference B2 appears in the **name box**.
- Excel has outlined the column heading B and the row heading 2.
- Sheet1 is the active tab in the workbook window.

The contents of the selected cell also appear in the formula bar.

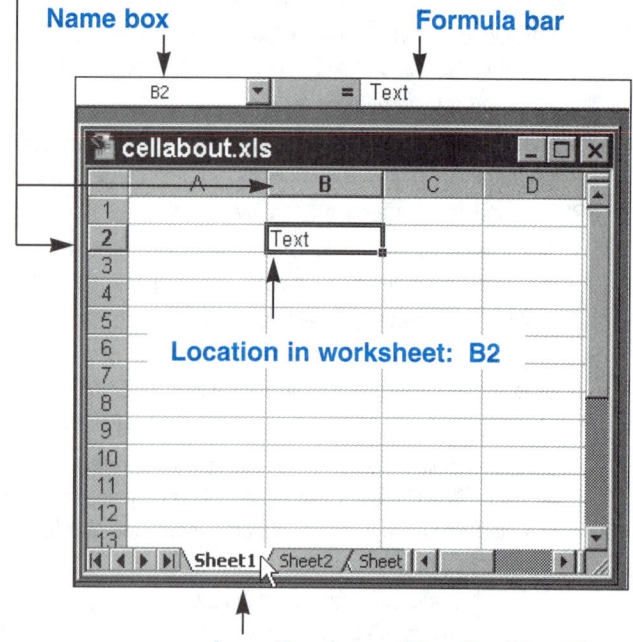

Name box   **Formula bar**

Location in worksheet: B2

Location in workbook: Sheet1

Cell Location in a Workbook

22

Notes:

- A **control** is any graphical element that allows you to perform an action or specify a setting.

- Excel changes the shape of the mouse pointer when you rest it on a cell control, such as a cell border or fill handle.

- A **cell reference** indicates a cell's location. Cell references are often used in formulas to calculate values stored in the worksheet. *(See About Formulas and About References in Formulas.)*

About Cell Properties and Controls

Cells are defined by the intersection of a column and a row. Therefore, the dimensions of a cell are defined by the column width and the row height. All cells have borders and fill properties. Selected cells have darkened borders and a fill handle (controls). These controls let you use a mouse to perform actions on the cell.

Border control: You can drag the border of a selected cell to move its contents. *(See Move Cell Contents.)*

Border style: You can apply line styles to one or more of the borders of a cell. *(See Format Cell Borders and Fill.)*

Fill: You can color or shade a cell to distinguish it from other cells. *(See Format Cell Borders and Fill.)*

Fill handle: You can drag the fill handle of selected cells to extend their content as a series, or, for a single cell, to copy its content to adjacent cells. *(See Fill Cells with Series.)*

Height/width: You can change the column width and row height to adjust the size of a cell. *(See Adjust and Hide Columns and Adjust and Hide Rows.)*

Location: You can identify the location of the selected cell by reading its cell reference in the **name box** (see illustration on previous page).

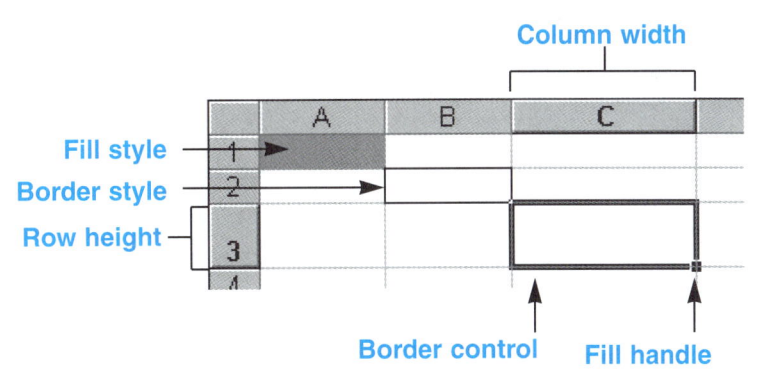

Cell Properties and Controls

Navigate Workbooks

You can use the mouse or the keyboard to move (navigate) between cells in a worksheet. When moving between worksheets, use the mouse. The new Microsoft mouse provides extra navigation features.

Notes:

- **Scrolling** moves an area into view without changing the active cell.
- The **size of the scroll boxes** is proportional to the dimensions of the data in the current worksheet.
- Excel displays the destination row or column in **ScrollTips** while you drag a scroll box.
- You can also use the Go To command to select a cell or cell range. Click the **Edit** menu, click **Go To**, then type a reference in the **Reference** box, or select a named reference from the list and click **OK**.

OR

Type a reference name in the Name Box and press **Enter** (see Name Cells).

Scroll to an Area in a Worksheet

TO MOVE:	CLICK:
one column left or right	left or right **scroll arrow**
one row up or down	up or down **scroll arrow**
one screen up or down	vertical **scroll bar** above or below scroll box
one screen right or left	horizontal **scroll bar** to right or left of scroll box

TO MOVE:	DRAG:
to any column with data	horizontal **scroll box**
to any row containing data	vertical **scroll box**

ScrollTip Appears when You Drag the Scroll Box

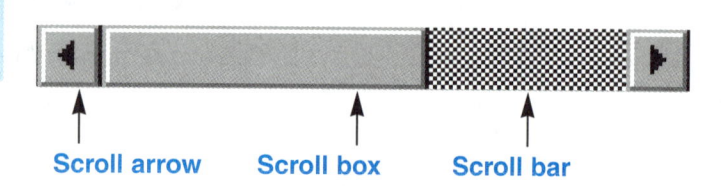

↑ Scroll arrow   ↑ Scroll box   ↑ Scroll bar

Horizontal Scroll Bar

Notes:
- To use a combination key like **Ctrl+Home**, press and hold the **Ctrl** key while you tap and release the **Home** key, then release **Ctrl**.
- To change the direction after pressing Enter: Click the **Tools** menu, then **Options**, select the **Edit** tab, then select **Direction** option.

Use Keyboard to Move to a Cell

TO MOVE:	PRESS:
one cell right	**Tab**
one cell down	**Enter**
one cell left or right	**left** or **right** arrow key
one cell up or down	**up** or **down** arrow key
first cell in worksheet	**Ctrl+Home**
last cell with data in worksheet	**Ctrl+End**
first column in worksheet	**Home**
one screen up or down	**PgUp** or **PgDn**

Notes:
- The **sheet tabs** indicate the names of worksheets, charts, and modules in the workbook. Clicking a sheet tab displays that sheet in the workbook window. The active sheet tab is shown in bold (Feet to Inches in the illustration). You can insert, delete, move and rename sheet tabs. *(See Sheet Tabs.)*

Select a Worksheet

1. If necessary, click tab scroll arrows to bring desired sheet tab into view.
2. Click desired sheet tab.

Tab scrolling button

Sheet tab

Notes:
- Use the outlined column and row heading to determine the location of the active cell. *(See About Cells.)*

Use Mouse to Move to Any Cell in Workbook

1. If necessary, click tab scroll arrows to bring desired sheet tab into view.
2. Scroll to desired area in worksheet *(see previous page)*.
3. Click desired cell.

Select Cells, Columns, and Rows

When working with worksheets, you will need to select a cell or range of cells to complete a variety of tasks. A range may consist of adjacent or nonadjacent cells. You can also name and select named cell ranges. Keyboard shortcuts for selecting cells are listed in Help, on the Contents tab, under the "Keyboard Reference" topic.

Notes:

- Excel will scroll the worksheet when you drag the selection beyond the visible area of the worksheet.
- The first cell you select is the active cell (cell A10 in the illustration).

Select Adjacent Cell Range

1 Click first cell you want to select.
2 Drag mouse through cells to include in selection.

	A	B	C	D
9				
10	Date	Expense	Amount	Vendor
11	1/6/91	inventory	$16,000	SW Wholesale
12	3/5/91	inventory	$20,000	SW Wholesale
13	6/4/91	inventory	$16,000	SW Wholesale
14	8/5/91	inventory	$16,000	SW Wholesale
15	10/7/91	inventory	$14,900	SW Wholesale
16	12/5/91	inventory	$10,997	SW Wholesale

Notes:

- The first cell in the last range you select is the active cell (cell C10 in the illustration).
- Selecting nonadjacent cells or cell ranges (multiple selections) is often used to select data to chart.

Select Nonadjacent Cell Range

1 Click first cell and drag through cells to select.
2 Press and hold **Ctrl**. Then drag through additional ranges to include in your selection.

	A	B	C	D
9				
10	Date	Expense	Amount	Vendor
11	1/6/91	inventory	$16,000	SW Wholesale
12	3/5/91	inventory	$20,000	SW Wholesale
13	6/4/91	inventory	$16,000	SW Wholesale
14	8/5/91	inventory	$16,000	SW Wholesale
15	10/7/91	inventory	$14,900	SW Wholesale
16	12/5/91	inventory	$10,997	SW Wholesale
17	1/1/91	overhead	$1,000	A,B

Notes:

- To select multiple columns and rows, drag through row or column headings, or press **Ctrl** and click nonadjacent headings.

Select Entire Column or Row

- Click row or column heading to select.

Row heading

Column heading

TIP: You can click this Select All button to select the entire worksheet.

Notes:

- You can also name nonadjacent ranges, as shown on the previous page.
- You might want to name ranges that you frequently chart or print.
- You can also use the <u>Go</u> To command (Ctrl + G) to select named ranges.
- For more information about naming cells see *Name Cells* in the Basic Skills section.

Name a Range

1 Select the range to name.

2 Click in the **name box** and type descriptive name.

  NOTE: Range names may contain uppercase and lowercase letters, numbers, and most punctuation characters. They cannot include spaces. The underscore character is useful for simulating a space, as in "inventory_expenses."

3 Press **Enter**.

Select a Named Range

- Click in **name box**, then click name to select.

27

Open Workbooks

The Open command lets you open workbook files stored on disk. When you click the Open button on the toolbar or select Open from the File menu, Excel presents a dialog box with tools for listing, finding, and opening workbook files. *(Also see Find Workbooks.)*

Open button

File ➡ Open...

Notes:

- Use the following **folder pane** buttons to locate documents:

  History — recently opened documents

  My Documents — default location for Office documents

  Desktop — root folder on your computer

  Favorites — shortcuts to documents. *(See Tip on next page.)*

  Web Folders — documents saved on Web sites.

Open a Workbook

1 Click the Open button on the Standard toolbar.

2 To Locate the workbook, click desired button in the folder pane to select starting folder.

   To navigate folders in the folder workspace:
   - Double-click a folder to open it.
   - Click the **Up One Level** button to open parent folder.
   - Click the **Previous** button to return to previously opened folder.

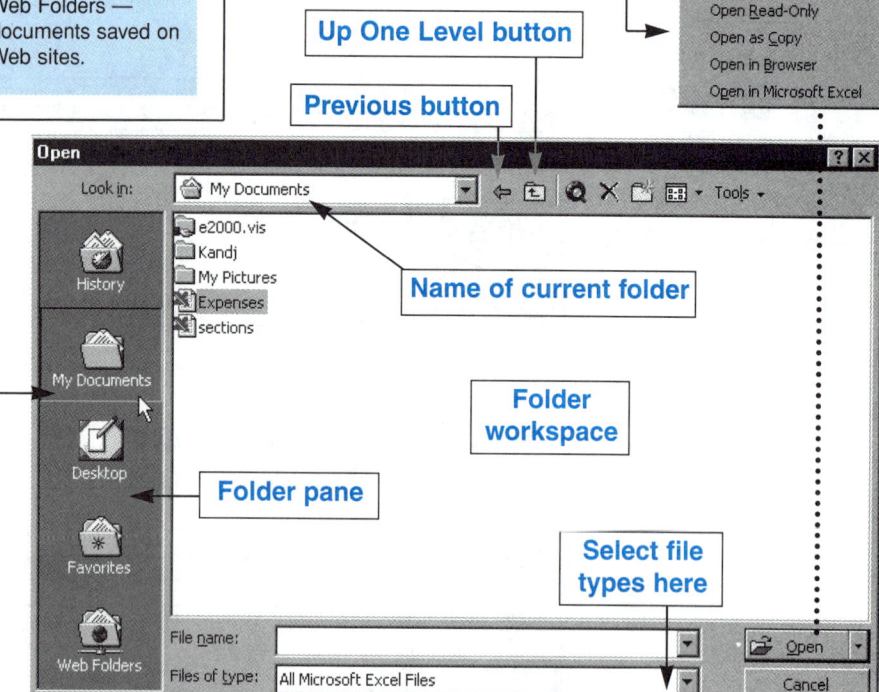

3 Click desired workbook, then click **Open**.

   You can also click the Open arrow to choose from additional open options.

Up One Level button

Previous button

Name of current folder

Folder workspace

Folder pane

Select file types here

Open Dialog Box in List View

28

Notes:
- Folders in the **Look in** box are displayed in a hierarchical order, starting with the root folder:

  The Desktop
  My Computer
  Drive C
  My Documents
  and so on.

- You cannot open subfolders from the **Look in** box list. Instead, select a folder, then double-click that folder's subfolder in the folder workspace.

Use the Look in Box to Select Source Folder

1. Click the **Look in** box arrow.
2. Click desired folder name.

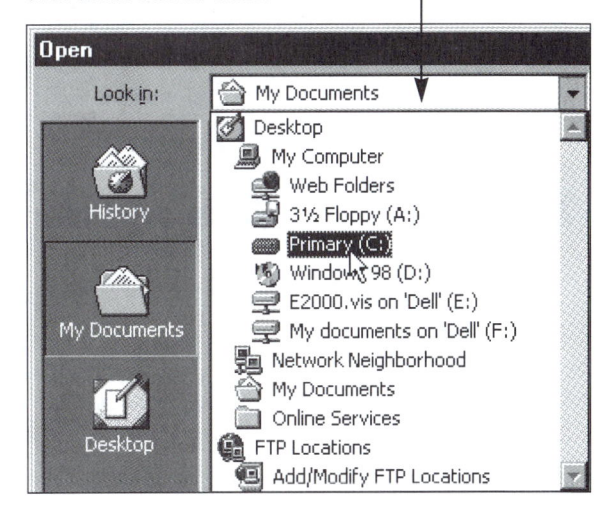

Look in list with Drive C Selected

Notes:
- Sorting items in the folder workspace can help you to locate workbooks efficiently.
- Each time you click a column heading, Excel reverses the sort order for the column.
- While in Details view, you can drag column heading borders to change their sizes.

Sort Items in Folder Workspace

1. Click the **Views** button arrow, then click **Details**.
2. Click the column heading to sort by.

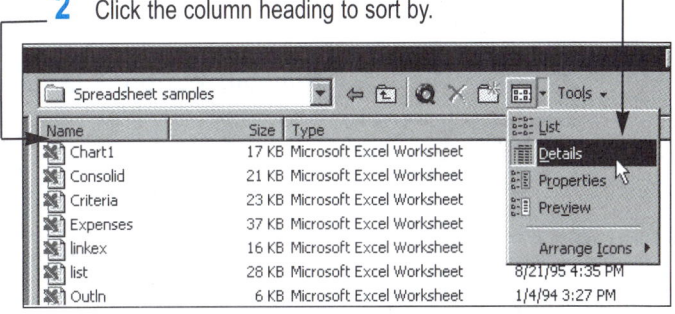

Folders and Files in Name Order

TIP: You can add folders (or documents) to the Favorites folder. Select the folder or document icon, click the Tools button, then click Add to F<u>a</u>vorites.

You can then click the Favorites button in the folder pane to locate a shortcut to the item.

29

Save Workbooks

The Save command lets you store workbooks to be opened in future sessions. When saving a file for the first time, or saving and renaming a file, Excel displays a dialog box containing controls for naming the workbook and changing the destination folder. Additionally, you can now save (publish) Excel documents on the Web.

Save button

File → **Save** / **Save As...**

Notes:

- Use the following **folder pane** buttons to locate documents:

  History — recently opened documents.

  My Documents — default location for Office documents.

  Desktop — root folder on your computer

  Favorites — shortcuts to documents. *(See Tip on next page.)*

  Web Folders — documents saved on Web sites.

Save and Name Workbook

1. Click **File** menu, then **Save As**.

   NOTE: To save a file again quickly, without renaming it, click the Save button on the Standard toolbar, or click **File** menu, then **Save**.

2. To locate the destination folder, click desired button in folder pane to select starting folder.

   To navigate folders in folder workspace:
   - Double-click a folder to open it.
   - Click the **Up One Level** button to open parent folder.
   - Click the **Previous** button to open the previously opened folder.

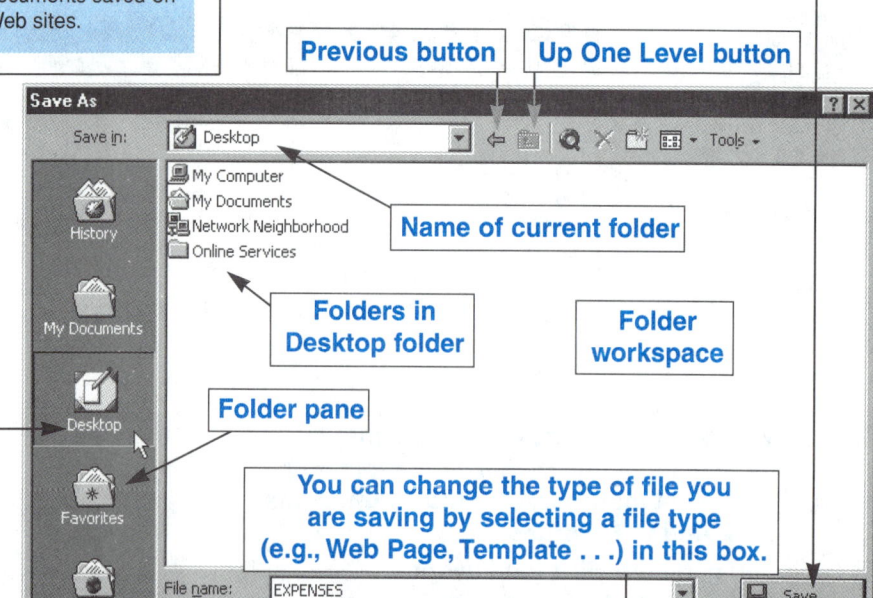

3. Type name in **File name** box, then click **Save**.

Previous button

Up One Level button

Name of current folder

Folders in Desktop folder

Folder workspace

Folder pane

You can change the type of file you are saving by selecting a file type (e.g., Web Page, Template . . .) in this box.

Save As Dialog Box

30

Notes:

- The shortcut menu options will vary between folders and files.

- You can also right-click the workspace to access comands. For example, you can move a document to a different folder with this procedure:

  Right-click document and select **Cut**, navigate to destination folder, right-click that folder's workspace and click **Paste**.

Manage Documents and Folders

1 Right-click desired file or folder icon.

2 Click desired command on the shortcut menu that appears.

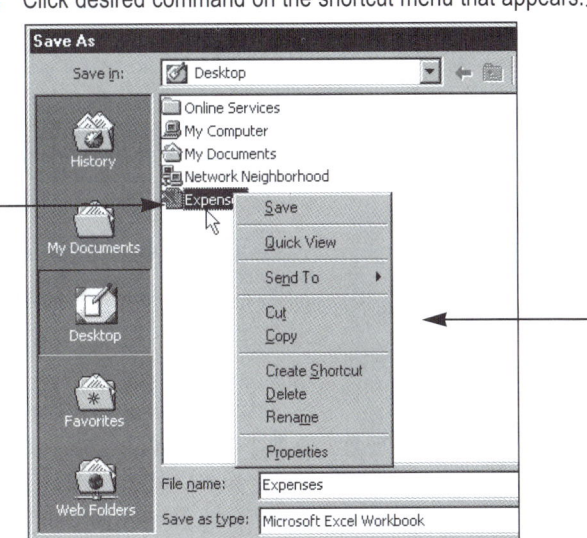

Notes:

- Excel creates the new folder in the current folder. It opens the new folder after you name it.

- Folder names may contain spaces and can be up to 255 characters long.

Create a New Folder

1 Click the **Create New Folder** button on toolbar.

2 Type folder name in **Name** box, then click **OK**.

3 Double-click the new folder to open it.

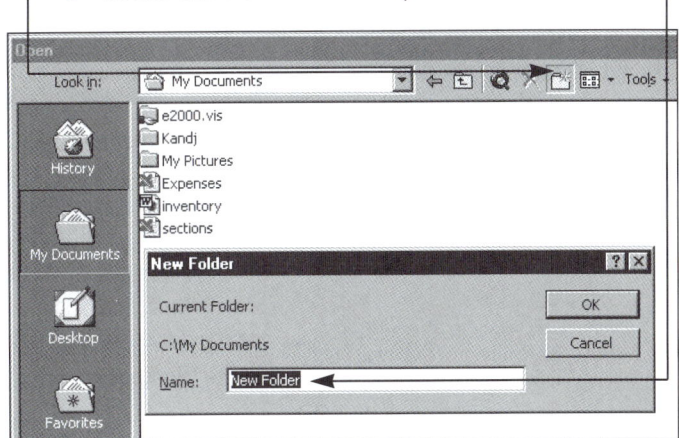

New Folder Dialog Box

Continued . . .

31

Save Workbooks (continued)

[File] → [Save as Web Page...]

Notes:

- You can preview how the Web document will look in a Web browser before publishing it: Click **File** menu, then click **Web Page Preview**. Excel will launch Internet Explorer and display the entire workbook.

Save as Web Page

You can save Excel workbooks (which may contain worksheet data, charts, PivotTables, and PivotCharts) to local (intranet) or Web (Internet) folders. Interactive settings will let users who browse your Web pages with Internet Explorer 4.0 or greater modify or change the view of the data you publish.

1. If you wish to save part of the worksheet as a Web Page, select desired cells.

2. Click **File** menu, then **Save as Web Page**.

   The Save As dialog box opens. It contains additional options as shown below.

Web Publishing Options at the Bottom of the Save As Dialog Box

3. Select folder or FTP site on which to store the document.

   NOTE: For information about browsing local folders, see Save and Name Workbook on page 30. For information about adding an FTP site, refer to the procedure on the next page.

4. Select **Entire Workbook**

   OR

   Select **Selection: selection name**

   OR

   Select **Republish: item name**

5. Click **Publish**.

   The Publish as Web Page dialog box appears.

continued . . .

Notes:

- In **step 6**, if you select **Previously published items**, you may need to select a specific item in the list below it, as shown.

- In **step 7**, the **Add interactivity with** options will vary depending on the item you chose to publish in step 6.

- In **step 8**, if you click **Change**, you will be prompted to choose a Web page title for the document.

- In **step 9**, you can click **Browse** to locate the folder. Internet access is required if the folder is located at an FTP site.

Save as Web Page (continued)

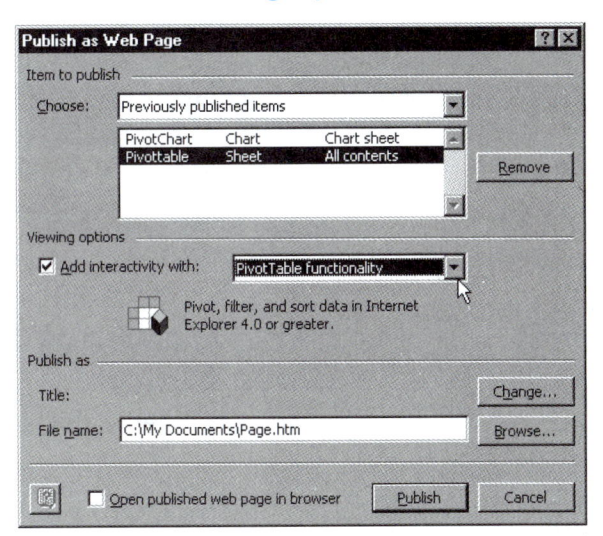

6 Select item to publish in the **Choose** list box.

7 Select **Add interactivity with** and choose an option from list box.

8 To specify a title, click the **Change** button.

9 In the File name box, type the location and Web document name, then click **Publish**.

Notes:

- In **step 2**, FTP (File Transfer Protocol) sites are folder locations that store Web documents. Private FTP sites often require a user name and password. Ask the administrator of the FTP site to supply these, if necessary. If the site allows for anonymous visitors, it may or may not require a password.

- You can add multiple FTP sites by repeating steps 1 and 2 without clicking **OK**.

Add an FTP Site to the Save or Open Dialog Box

FROM THE SAVE OR OPEN DIALOG BOX:

1 Open the **Look in** box, and click **Add/Modify FTP Locations**.

2 Specify the FTP site information, click **Add**, then click **OK** to close the dialog box.

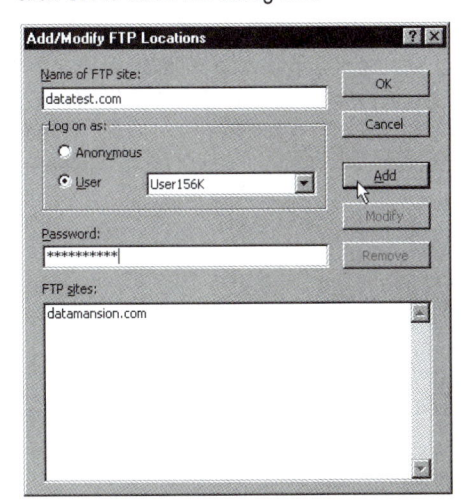

33

Close Workbooks and Quit Excel

When you close a workbook, Excel continues to run in computer memory. When you close Excel, all open workbooks close, and Excel is removed from computer memory. Excel will prompt you to save open workbooks when closing.

close button

File → Close / Exit

Notes:

- **Caution:** Be sure to click the **close** button for the *workbook*, not the close button for the Excel application window.

  When the workbook window is maximized, its window controls appear just below the Excel window, as shown below.

- When prompted to save changes, you can click **Cancel** to undo the close command.

- You can close without saving changes to retain the previously saved version of the workbook file. *(See Save Workbooks and Open Workbooks.)*

- **Other ways to close a workbook:**

  Press **Ctrl+W**.
  or
  Double-click the **workbook control** icon in the workbook title bar.
  or
  Click the **File** menu, then click **Close**.

Close Workbook Using Close Button

- Click **close** button on workbook window.

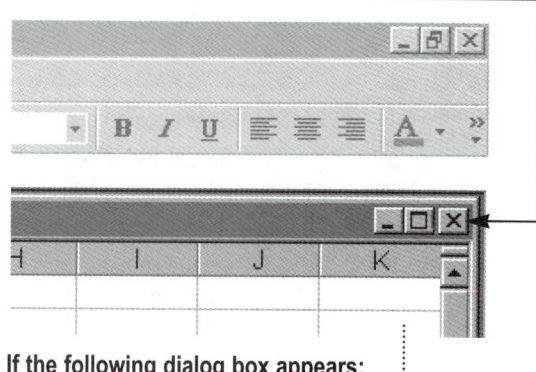

If the following dialog box appears:

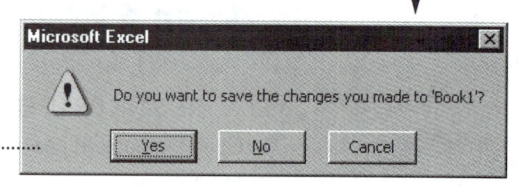

Microsoft Excel — Do you want to save the changes you made to 'Book1'? Yes / No / Cancel

- Click **Yes** to save changes made to the file.
  (See Save Workbooks.)
  OR
  Click **No** to close without saving.

  CAUTION: If you close without saving a workbook, you cannot use the Undo command to retrieve the unsaved file.

34

Notes:

- **Caution:** Be sure to click the **close** button for the *Excel window*, not the close button for the workbook.

  When the workbook window is maximized, the Excel window controls appear just above the workbook window as shown below.

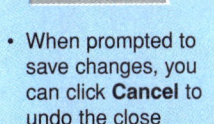

- When prompted to save changes, you can click **Cancel** to undo the close command.

- When prompted to save changes, you can click **Cancel** to undo the close command.

- **Other ways to close Excel:**

  Press **Alt+F4**.
  or
  Double-click **Excel control** icon in the Excel title bar.
  or
  Click the **File** menu, then click **Exit**.
  or
  Right-click **Excel** button on Windows taskbar, then click **Close**.

Close Excel Using Close Button

- Click **close** button on Excel window.

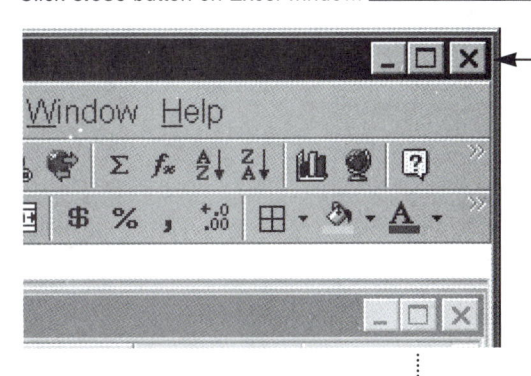

  If the following dialog box appears:

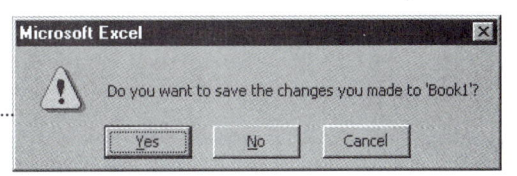

- Click **Yes** to save the changes made to the file.
  (See Save Workbooks.)
  OR
  Click **No** to close without saving.

  CAUTION: If you close without saving a workbook, you cannot use the Undo command to retrieve the unsaved file.

  NOTE: The prompt to save open Excel workbooks will look like the illustration below, if the Office Assistant is active.

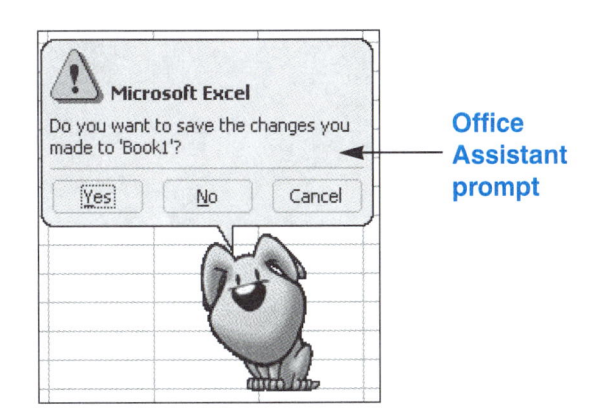

Office Assistant prompt

35

Basic Skills

This section contains illustrated procedures arranged in alphabetical order, covering a variety of basic workbook skills.

Adjust and Hide Columns

Data appears in cells defined, in part, by the column width. You can control the width of columns or hide them. You can also adjust columns while print previewing your workbook *(see Print Preview).*

Format ➡ Column

Notes:

- In **step 2**, the pointer's shape indicates when you can perform the action. It must be a cross with left- and right-facing arrows, as shown in the illustration.

- Column width is measured by the number of characters of the standard font.

Change Column Width Using the Mouse

1 **To set width of multiple columns:**

Drag through column headings of columns to change.

OR

Press **Ctrl** and click each column heading to change.

2 Rest pointer on right border of any selected column heading.

Pointer becomes ↔ .

3 Drag pointer left or right to decrease or increase the column size.

If you have selected nonadjacent column headings, press Ctrl while dragging pointer to uniformly change all selected columns.

Excel displays width in a pop-up box as you drag.

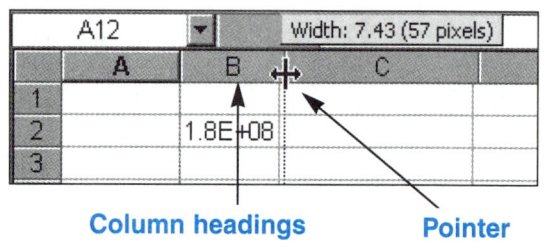

Column headings   **Pointer**

Notes:

- In **step 1**, you can select multiple columns.

Automatically Size Column to Fit Largest Entry

1 Rest pointer on right border of column heading.

Pointer becomes a cross with arrows facing left and right.

2 Double-click.

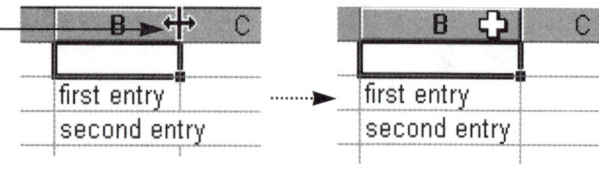

Before double-click   **After**

Notes:

- In **step 1**, you can drag through column headings to hide multiple columns.
- You can hide columns to prevent others from seeing the data, or to temporarily display columns of data next to each other for charting or other purposes.

Hide Columns by Dragging

1 Click column heading, then rest pointer on right border of selected column heading.
   Pointer becomes a ↔.

2 Drag pointer left beyond its own left border to hide the column.

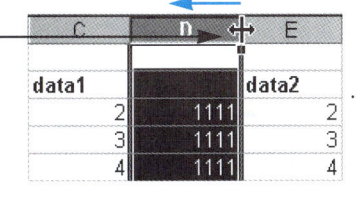

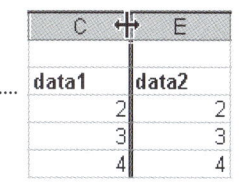

Before   After

Notes:

- In **step 1**, when the pointer is a cross with double vertical line and left- and right-facing arrows, you can perform the action.

Display Hidden Columns by Dragging

1 Rest pointer just to the right of column heading border.
   Pointer becomes a ↔.

2 Drag pointer right to display the hidden column.

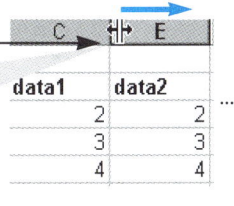

Before   After

Notes:

- Use the menu commands when you find it difficult to adjust columns with the mouse.
- In **step 1**, when using the menu to unhide columns, select the columns to the left and right of the hidden columns.

Adjust Columns Using the Menu

1 Select column(s) to adjust.
2 Click **Format** menu, then point to **Column**.
3 Click desired column command.

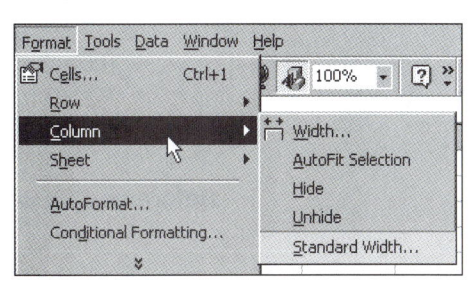

39

Adjust and Hide Rows

Data appears in cells defined, in part, by row height. You can control the height of rows and also hide rows.

Format → Rows

Notes:

- In **step 2**, the pointer indicates when you can perform the action. It must be a cross with up- and down-facing arrows, as shown in the illustration to the right.
- The height of the row is measured in *points* — there are 72 points in an inch. If you set the row height to zero, the row is hidden.

Change Row Height Using the Mouse

1 **To set width of multiple rows:**

Drag through consecutive row headings of rows to change.

OR

Press **Ctrl** and click row headings to change.

2 Rest pointer on lower border of any selected row heading.

Pointer becomes a ✢.

3 Drag pointer up or down to increase or decrease row height.

Excel displays height in a pop-up box.

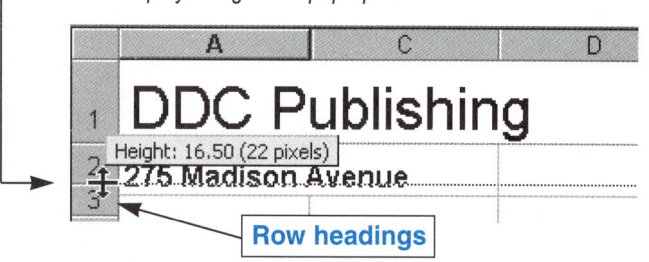

Row headings

Notes:

- In **step 1**, you can select multiple rows, but each row will adjust to the same size.
- In **step 2**, the pointer indicates when you can perform the action. It must be a cross with up- and down-facing arrows, as shown in the illustration to the right.

Automatically Size Row to Fit Largest Entry

1 Rest pointer on lower border of row heading.

Pointer becomes a ✢.

2 Double-click.

Before double-click   After

40

Notes:

- In **step 1**, to hide multiple rows, drag through row headings to hide.
- You can hide rows to prevent others from seeing the data they contain, or to temporarily display rows of data next to each other for charting or other purposes.

Hide Rows by Dragging

1 Click row heading to select row to hide.

2 Rest pointer on lower border of row heading to hide.
Pointer becomes a ✛ .

3 Drag pointer **up** beyond its own upper border.

	A	B	C
1	Date	Expenses	Amount
2	1/6/97	inventory	$16,000
3	1/7/97	inventory	$20,000
4	1/8/97	inventory	$16,000
5	Totals		$52,000

	A	B	C
1	Date	Expenses	Amount
5	Totals		$52,000
6			
7			

Notes:

- In **step 1**, the pointer indicates when you can perform the action. It must be a cross with double horizontal line and up- and down-facing arrows.

Display Hidden Rows by Dragging

1 Rest pointer just below row heading border.
Pointer becomes a ✛ .

2 Drag pointer down to display hidden row(s).

	A	B	C
1	Date	Expenses	Amount
5	Totals		$52,000
6			

	A	B	C
1	Date	Expenses	Amount
2	1/6/97	inventory	$16,000
3	1/7/97	inventory	$20,000
4	1/8/97	inventory	$16,000
5	Totals		$52,000
6			

Notes:

- In **step 1**, when unhiding rows using the menu, select the rows above and below hidden rows.

Adjust Rows Using the Menu

1 Select row(s) to adjust.

2 Click **Format** menu, then point to **Row**.

3 Click desired row command.

```
Height...
AutoFit
Hide
Unhide
```

41

Align Data in Cells

Align cell data horizontally and vertically; apply text controls (wrap text in cells, shrink text to fit, merge cells); orient text in a variety of angles.

Format → Cells... | Alignment

Notes:

- In **step 2**, if the desired alignment button is not visible, click the More Buttons arrow on the right side of the toolbar to view additional buttons.

- If no alignment is set, Excel applies the **General alignment** which left-aligns text and right-aligns values.

- If text does not fit in a cell, you can increase the column width or select the **Shrink to fit** option *(see next page)*.

Align Cell Data Using Toolbar

1 Select cell(s) to align.

   NOTE: To select cells that are nonadjacent, you can press **Ctrl** and click or drag through cells.

2 Click desired alignment button on the Formatting toolbar:

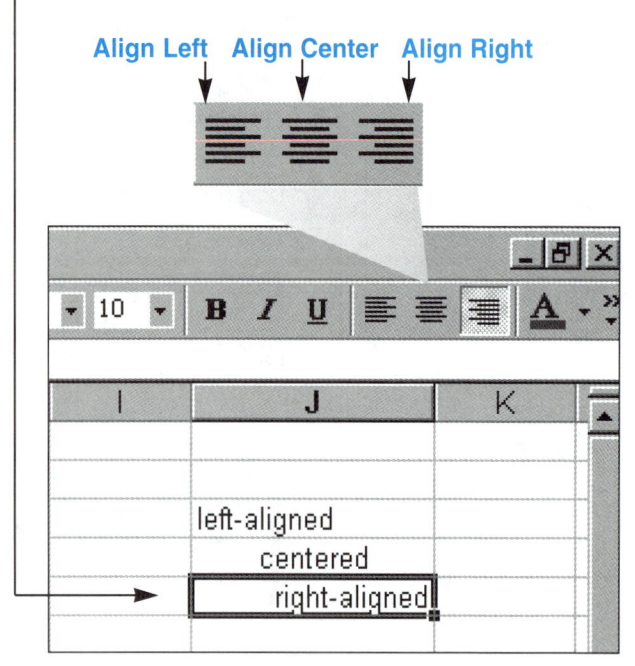

Align Left   Align Center   Align Right

left-aligned
centered
right-aligned

Horizontal Alignment Examples

42

Notes:

- In **step 1**, if Merge and Center button is not visible, click the More Buttons ›› arrow to view additional buttons.

- A merged cell is one or more consecutive cells combined into one cell address.

- When you merge cells, only the contents of the upper-left cell are retained. That cell becomes the cell reference.

Merge and Center

1 Select cell containing data and drag to extend selection to include cells in which data will be centered.

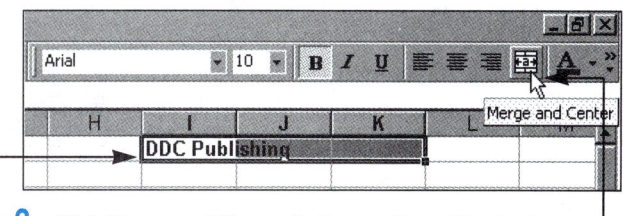

2 Click **Merge and Center** button on Formatting toolbar.

Merge and Center Example

Notes:

- Alignment options:

  Horizontal and **Vertical** — sets alignment of text in cells.

  Wrap text — inserts line breaks when needed and increases row height to fit text.

  Shrink to fit — shrinks characters to fit the column width.

  Merge cells — joins selected cells. The contents of the upper-left cell are retained. That cell becomes the cell reference.

  Indent — offsets data from left side of cell. Increments are measured in widths of characters.

  Orientation — sets the rotation of text. Increments are measured in degrees.

Menu Alignment Options

Set alignment options from a dialog box.

1 Select cells.
2 Click **Format** menu, then click **Cells**.
3 Click the **Alignment** tab.
4 Select desired options and click **OK**.

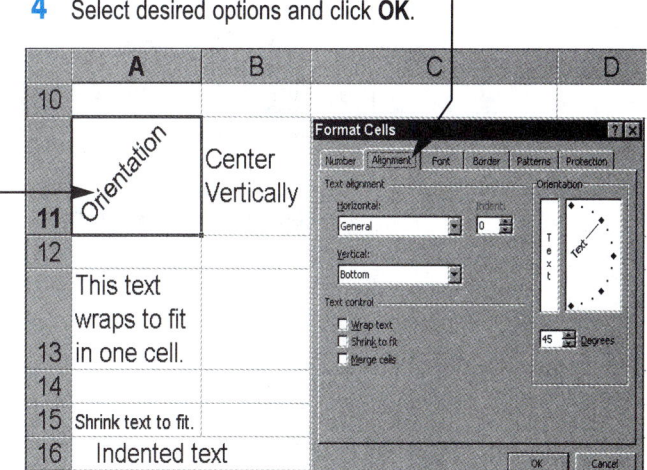

Menu Alignment Examples

43

AutoCalculate

AutoCalculate automatically provides the Average, Count, Count Nums, Max, Min, or Sum for a selected range. This result cannot be transferred to the worksheet.

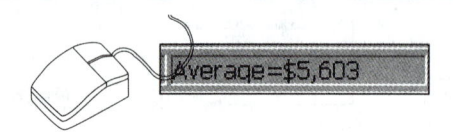

Notes:
- After selecting the range to be calculated, you can right-click the mouse on the AutoCalculate section of the Status Bar and select any function from the pop-up list.
- After you have selected the desired function, the answer will appear on the Status Bar.

Change AutoCalculate Function

1 Right-click on Status bar AutoCalculate area.

A pop-up list of functions appears.

2 Click desired function.

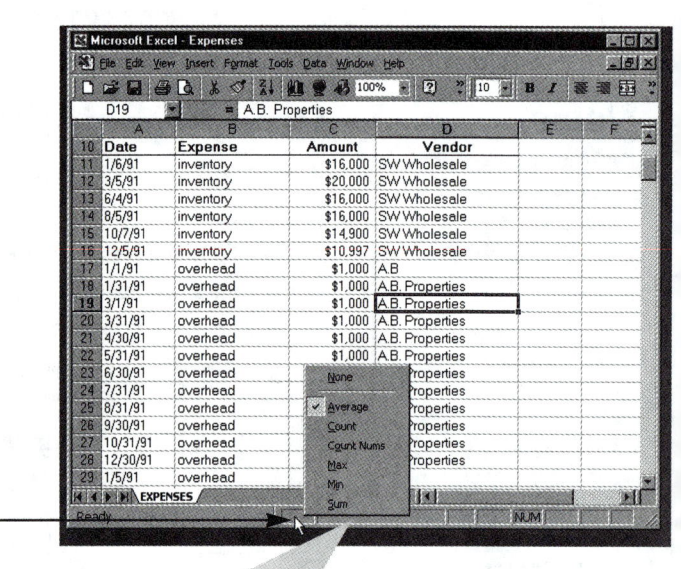

AutoCalculate Functions

44

Notes:

- AutoCalculate functions perform the following calculations on the selected range:

  None — no calculation is performed.

  Average — finds average of numbers selected.

  Count — counts all entries.

  Count Nums — counts numbers selected.

  Max — indicates highest value.

  Min — indicates lowest value.

  Sum — finds total of all values.

Use AutoCalculate to Find Results

1 Set desired AutoCalculate function.
2 Select cells to calculate.

Result appears on the AutoCalculate area of the status bar.

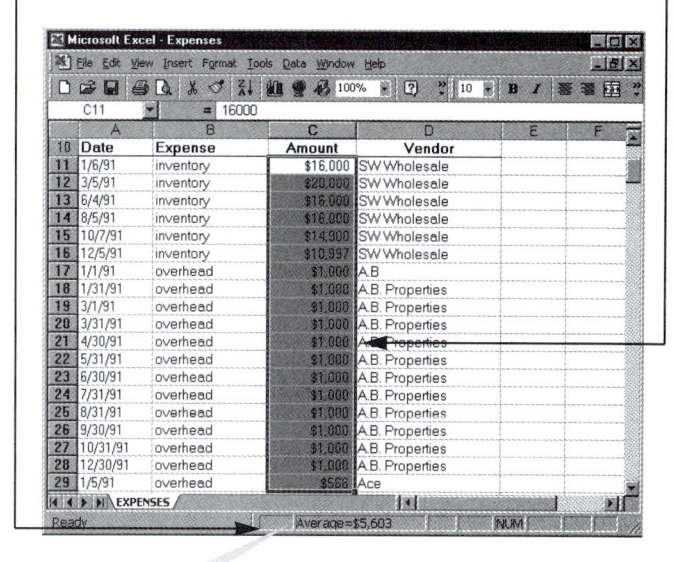

AutoCalculate Result

45

AutoCorrect

The AutoCorrect feature replaces misspelled words or abbreviations automatically as you type. You can change AutoCorrect options to meet your needs.

Tools → AutoCorrect...

How AutoCorrect Works

1 Select cell to receive text.
2 Type abbreviation or misspelling.
3 Press **Space** or **Enter**.

Excel replaces the text.

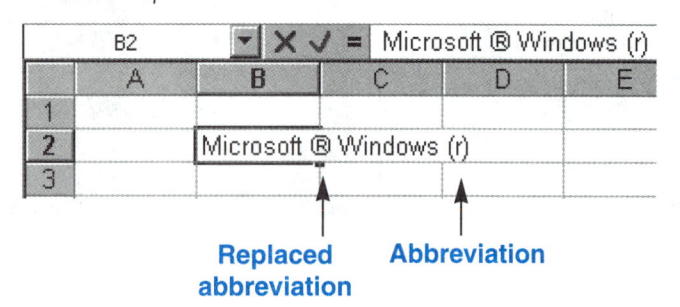

Notes:
- You can add abbreviations and misspellings to the AutoCorrect list, or you can disable AutoCorrect.

Replaced abbreviation

Abbreviation

Disable AutoCorrect

1 Click **Tools** menu, then click **AutoCorrect**.
2 Deselect **Replace text as you type** (uncheck it).
3 Click **OK**.

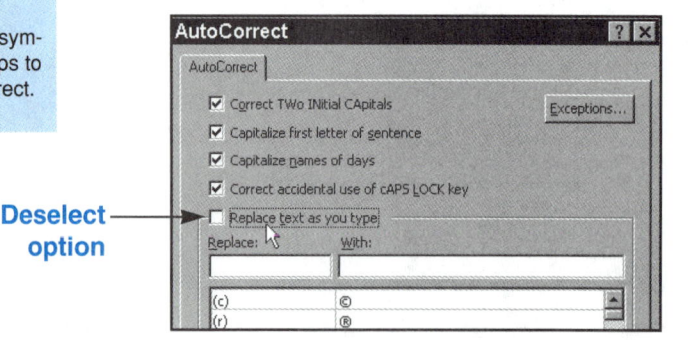

Notes:
- Use this procedure to temporarily disable AutoCorrect, for example, when you don't want an abbreviation replaced with a symbol. Repeat steps to enable AutoCorrect.

Deselect option

Notes:

- In **step 2**, you may have to click the button at the bottom of the menu to view **AutoCorrect**.

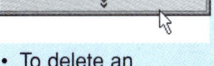

- To delete an abbreviation or misspelling from the AutoCorrect list, scroll to the item in the list, click the item, then click **Delete**.

- By default, AutoCorrect will:

    Correct two initial capital letters in a word.

    Capitalize first letter of a sentence.

    Capitalize names of days.

    Correct accidental use of **Caps Lock** key.

Other corrections AutoCorrect will make.

Add Abbreviations or Misspellings to AutoCorrect List

1 Click **Tools** menu, then click **AutoCorrect**.

The AutoCorrect dialog box appears.

2 Type text to be replaced in **Replace** box.

3 Type replacement text in **With** box.

4 Click **Add**.

5 To add more items, repeat steps 2-4.

6 Click **OK** when done.

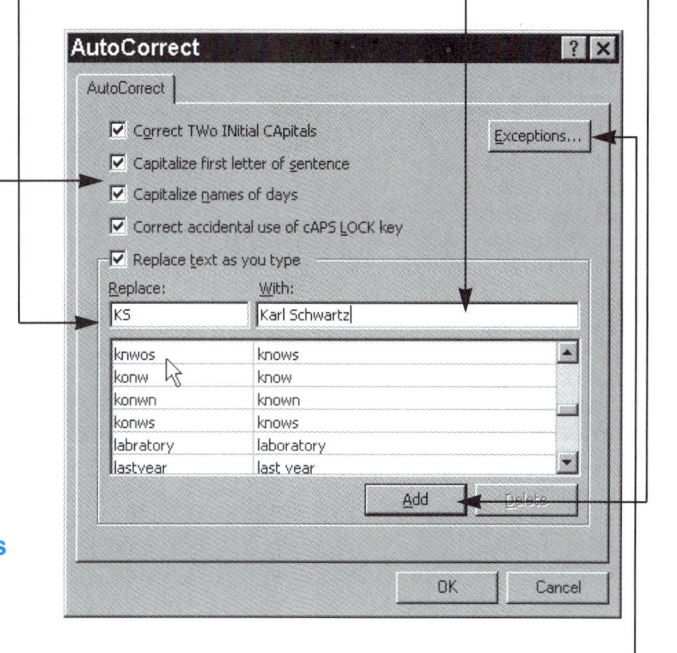

TIP: Click **Exceptions** to add to Excel's list of First Letter and Initial Caps exceptions. For example, Excel might consider an unknown abbreviation as the end of a sentence. To fix this, just add the abbreviation to the "Don't capitalize after" list.

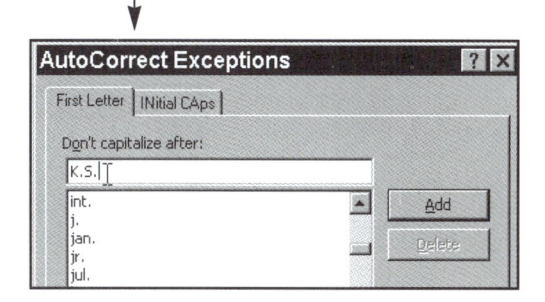

47

Clear Cell Contents

Using menu commands, you can clear either cell formats, contents, or comments, or clear all of these items.

Edit → Clear

Notes:

- In **step 1**, Excel will perform the clear command on all selected cells in one step.
- After you clear cells, you can the click **Edit** menu, then **Undo** to reverse the operation.
- Notice that after the **Clear Contents** command has been applied, the surrounding cells do not change position.
- When you clear a cell, the format of the cell, such as bolding or alignment, is retained.

Clear Cell Contents

Removes the contents (data and formulas) and leaves the cells blank in the worksheet without removing formats or comments.

1 Select cells to clear.

    NOTE: To select cells that are nonadjacent, you can press **Ctrl** and click or drag through cells to include in the selection.

2 Press **Delete**.

    OR

- Right-click any selected cell.
- Click **Clear Contents**.

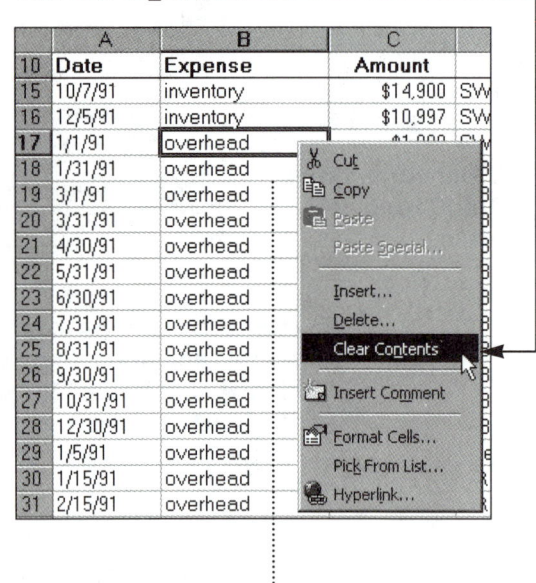

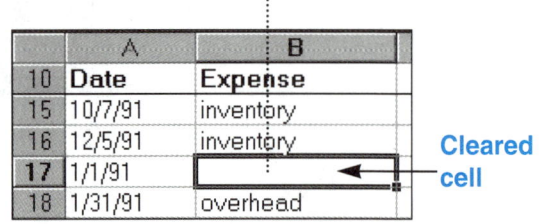

Cleared cell

48

Notes:

- In **step 2**, you can point to the **Clear** command on the menu without clicking to open a submenu.

- **Comments** are notes inserted into a cell. Excel displays comments when you rest the pointer on a cell containing a comment. A red triangle in the upper-right corner of a cell indicates the cell contains a comment. *(See Insert and Remove Comments.)*

Clear Cell Options Using Menu

Clears cell formats, contents, comments, or all of these items.

1 Select cells to clear.

   NOTE: To select cells that are nonadjacent, you can press **Ctrl** and click or drag through cells to include in the selection.

2 Click **Edit** menu, then **Clear**.

3 Click one of the following:

All	to clear formats, contents, and comments.
Formats	to clear only formats, such as border styles and font attributes.
Contents	to clear just the contents of the cell.
Comments	to clear just the comment attached to the cell.

   Excel clears the cells as directed by your command.

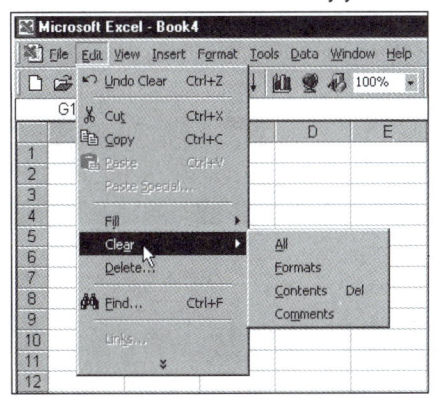

Clear Options on Edit Menu

TIP: You can also clear cell contents by dragging the fill handle in a selection over the selected cells.

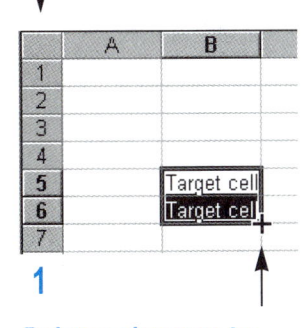

1 Pointer changes to a cross when resting on fill handle.

2 Drag fill handle up.

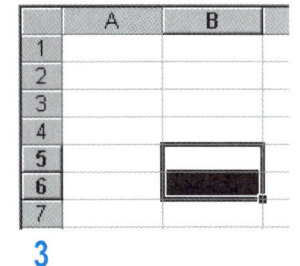

3 Release mouse to clear the cells.

49

Copy and Paste Special

You can use the Paste Special feature to apply the copied data in a variety of ways. For example, the Values option lets you copy only the result of a formula; the Add operation lets you copy the value and add it to existing data in the destination cell.

Edit ➡ Copy / Paste Special...

Notes:

- The **Paste Special** command includes a variety of paste options.
- **Paste** options copy all or an aspect of the source data:

  All – copies all cell contents and formatting.

  Formulas – copies only the formulas.

  Values – copies only the displayed value.

  Formats – copies only the cell formats.

  Comments – copies only comments that are attached to the cells.

  Validation – copies validation rules (see Validate Cell Entries).

  All except borders – copies all cell contents except border formatting.

  Column widths - copies only column widths.

Copy and Paste Cell Data in Special Ways

1. Select cells to copy.
2. Click **Edit** menu, then click **Copy**.
   A flashing dashed outline appears around selected cells.
3. Select destination cell.
4. Click **Edit** menu, then click **Paste Special**.
   The Paste Special dialog box appears.

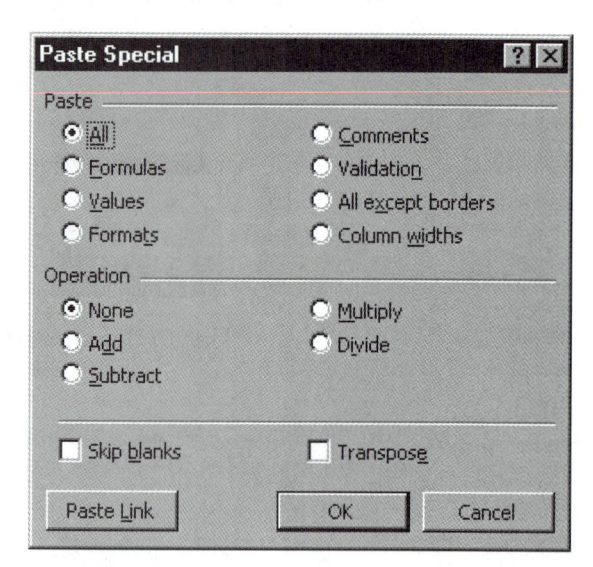

5. Select desired options.
6. Click **OK**.
   OR
   Click **Paste Link** to establish a reference to the source data.

   NOTE: **Paste Link** *is often used to insert a reference to values stored in other workbooks.*

   Excel pastes data as specified by selected options.

50

- **Operation** options, located in the **Paste Special** dialog box, let you combine source and destination data. These options are only available when **All**, **Values**, **Formulas**, or **All except borders** is selected.

  Mathematical operations include: **None**, **Add**, **Subtract**, **Multiply**, and **Divide**.

- Other Paste Special options:

  Skip blanks — tells Excel not to overwrite data in destination cells when source cells are blank.

  Transpose — changes orientation of range you are copying to a row or a column.

  Paste Link — establishes a connection to the source data that causes the destination cells to show changes made to source cells. Paste Link is often used to link data from different workbooks or worksheets.

  The **Paste Link** command is only available when **All** or **All except Borders** is selected.

Link Data on Different Worksheets Using Paste Special

1 Select cell in sheet to copy.
2 Click **Edit** menu, then click **Copy**.

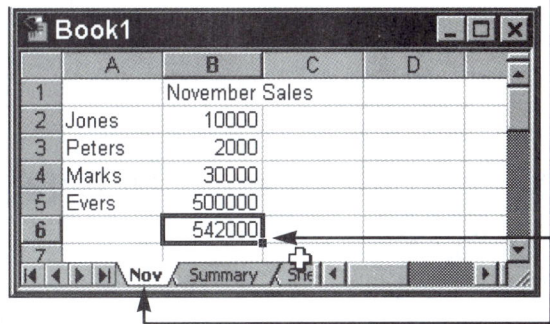

[Book1 spreadsheet showing November Sales: Jones 10000, Peters 2000, Marks 30000, Evers 500000, total 542000, on Nov sheet]

3 Select sheet, then cell in sheet to receive the link.
4 Click **Edit** menu, then click **Paste Special**.
5 Click **Paste Link**.

Excel creates linked reference to cell in source sheet.

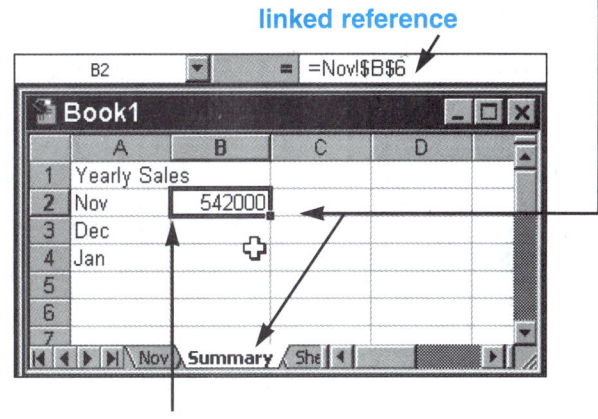

linked reference

B2   =Nov!$B$6

[Book1 spreadsheet showing Yearly Sales: Nov 542000, Dec, Jan, on Summary sheet]

This value will change if value in Nov sheet in cell E6 changes.

Tip: In steps 2 and 4, you can right-click the selection to access the Copy and Paste Special commands from a shortcut menu.

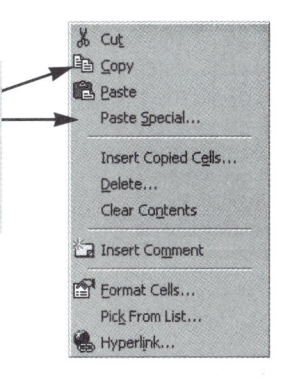

[Shortcut menu showing: Cut, Copy, Paste, Paste Special..., Insert Copied Cells..., Delete..., Clear Contents, Insert Comment, Format Cells..., Pick From List..., Hyperlink...]

51

Copy Cell Contents

You can copy data from one cell to another cell in a variety of ways. The method you choose often depends upon the location of the source and the destination.

Edit ➔ Copy / Paste

Notes:

- Using menu commands to copy cells is must useful when both the source and destination cells are *not* in the same viewing area.

- In **step 2**, the flashing dashed outline remains until you press **Esc**, press **Enter**, or add input to another cell. The flashing outline indicates you can repeat the paste operation.

- In **step 2** and **step 4**, you can also right-click the selected cells to access the **Copy** and **Paste** commands from a shortcut menu.

- **Caution:** When you paste data, existing data in the destination cells will be replaced. Click **Edit** menu, then **Undo** to reverse the paste operation.

- In **step 4**, to avoid overwriting data, click **Insert** menu, then click **Copied Cells**. The Insert Paste dialog box appears from which you can choose a direction to shift the existing cells.

Copy Cell Data Using Menu Commands

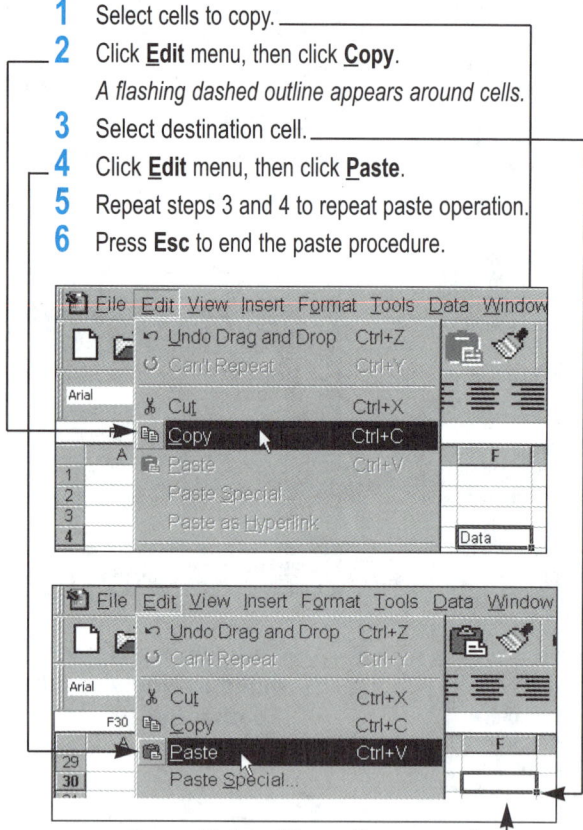

1. Select cells to copy.
2. Click **Edit** menu, then click **Copy**.
   A flashing dashed outline appears around cells.
3. Select destination cell.
4. Click **Edit** menu, then click **Paste**.
5. Repeat steps 3 and 4 to repeat paste operation.
6. Press **Esc** to end the paste procedure.

Copy Using Menu Commands

> Tip: If you intend to paste the data only once, you can bypass steps 4-6 and just press Enter.

52

Notes:

- The drag cell border method is best when the source and destination cells are near each other.

- In **step 3**, press **Ctrl** and **Shift** to copy data and *insert* it between destination cells. Otherwise data in the destination cells will be overwritten.

Copy Cell Contents by Dragging Cell Border

1. Select cell(s) to copy.
2. Point to any border of selected cell(s).

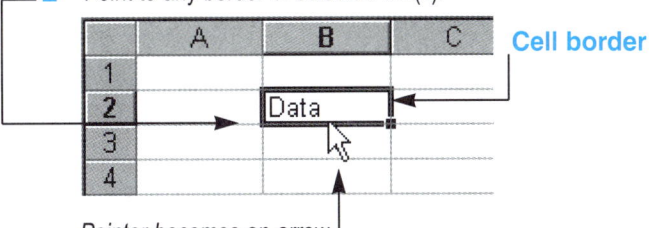

Cell border

Pointer becomes an arrow.

3. Press **Ctrl** and drag border outline to new location.
4. Release mouse button.

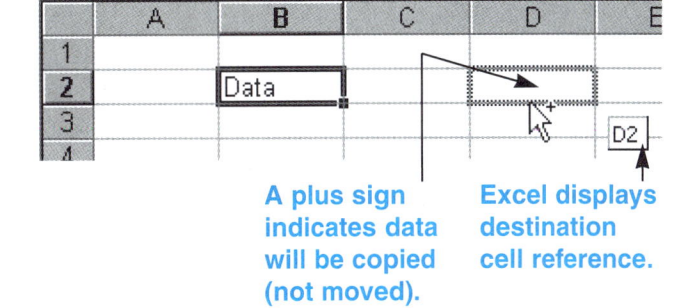

A plus sign indicates data will be copied (not moved).

Excel displays destination cell reference.

Notes:

- The drag fill handle method can only be used to copy and fill adjacent cells.

- In **step 1**, if you select more than one cell, press **Ctrl** while dragging to suppress creating a series—a set of related numbers or text. *(See Fill Cells with a Series.)*

Copy Cell Contents by Dragging Fill Handle

Crosshair appears when pointer rests on fill handle.

1. Select cell(s) to copy then point to fill handle.

   A crosshair appears.

2. Drag crosshair to extend border over adjacent cells to fill.

3. Release mouse button.

   Excel copies data into all cells within extended border.

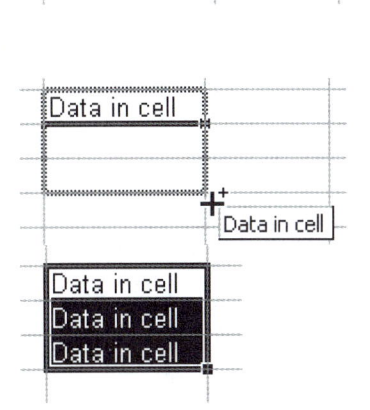

53

Collect and Paste Multiple Items

When you collect (copy or cut) successive items, the Office Clipboard automatically stores each item to be pasted into a sheet, chart, or another Microsoft Office document.

Copy | Paste All | Clear Clipboard | Close

Notes:

- The last item you cut or copy is also placed in the Windows clipboard, so you can paste that data into non-Microsoft Office applications.

- In previous versions of Excel (and Microsoft Office), each time you used the Cut or Copy command, the item replaced what was previously stored in the Windows clipboard.

Automatically Store Multiple Items in the Office Clipboard

Items are stored in the Office Clipboard when you do one of the following:

- Copy or cut distinct items consecutively while in Excel or another Microsoft Office application.
- Copy one item, paste the item, then copy another item while staying in Excel or another Microsoft Office application.
- Copy the same item twice in succession.

The Office Clipboard appears.

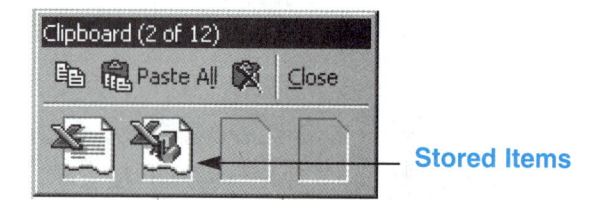

Stored Items

The Office Clipboard

Notes:

- When the Office Clipboard toolbar is in view, pressing **Ctrl+C** (copy) or **Ctrl+X** (cut) automatically adds the selected item to the Office Clipboard.

Copy an Item Using the Office Clipboard toolbar

1 Select item to copy.
2 Click the Copy button on the Office Clipboard toolbar.

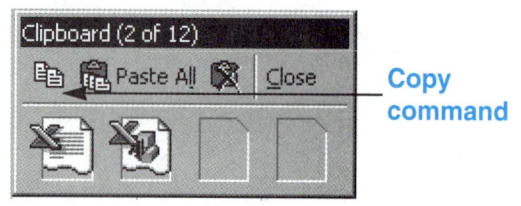

Copy command

54

Notes:

- The Office Clipboard will show some of the data the item contains, or for objects such as pictures, indicate the object type and number it. For example, Picture 1 and Picture 2.
- The source application is identified by the icon.
- Rest the pointer on the Office Clipboard toolbar buttons to identify them.

Identify Items in the Office Clipboard

- Rest pointer on the item you wish to identify.
  A description of the item appears in a pop-up window.

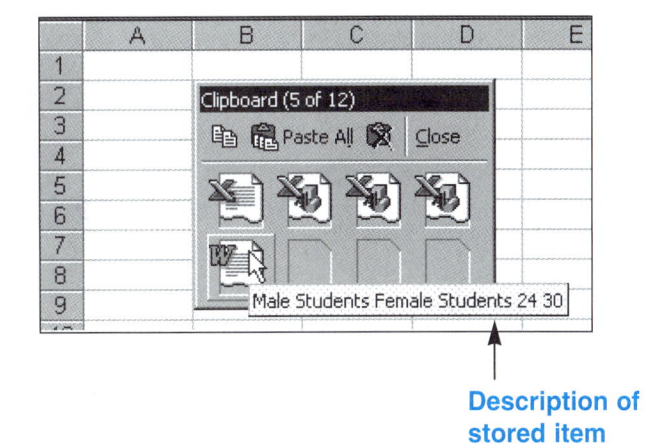

Description of stored item

Notes:

- When you use the **Paste** command on the **Edit** menu, Excel pastes the contents stored in the Windows clipboard (the most recent item you copied or cut) into your document.

Paste Data Stored in the Office Clipboard

1 Select destination cell, object, or area of document where you want item inserted.
2 Click item in the Office Clipboard you wish to insert.
   OR
   Click the Paste All command to paste all items into the document.

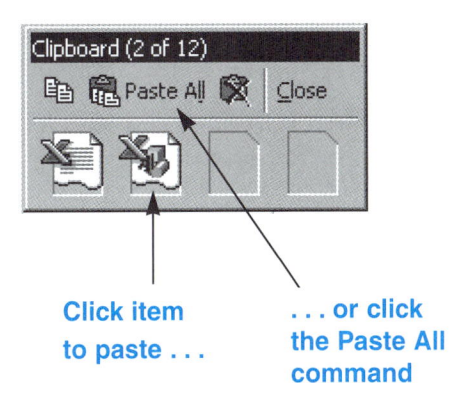

Click item to paste . . .

. . . or click the Paste All command

55

Customize Excel

The Customize command lets you customize toolbars, toolbar buttons, menu commands, and shortcut keys.

Tools → Customize...

Notes:

- Other Toolbar options:

  You can restore original settings for a toolbar by selecting it and clicking **Reset**.

  You can create a new toolbar by clicking the **New** button. *(See procedures that follow.)*

  You can **Rename** and **Delete** toolbars. If a built-in toolbar is selected, however, these options will not be available.

  You can use the **Attach** command to make sure that a custom toolbar is always available with a specific workbook.

Show or Hide Toolbars

1 Click **Tools** menu, then click **Customize**.

The Customize dialog box appears.

2 Click the **Toolbars** tab.

3 Click the name of the toolbar to hide or show.

4 Click **Close** when done.

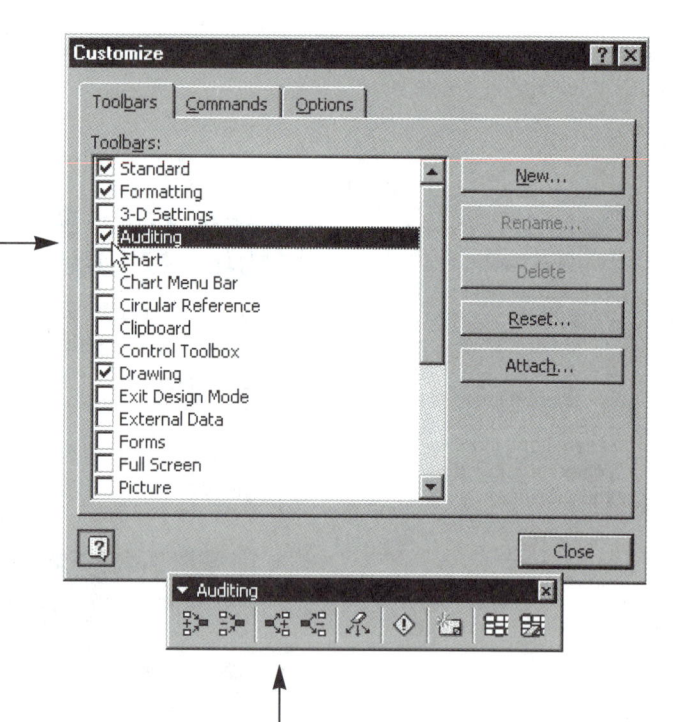

Excel displays toolbar when you check the option.

Notes:

- In **step 4**, the custom toolbar that appears will be small, and its full name may not fit in the title bar. The size of the custom toolbar will increase as you drag commands onto it (step 7). You can also drag the toolbar borders to change its shape and size, or dock it on one of the borders of the Excel application window.

Create a Custom Toolbar and Add Command Buttons To It

1. Click **Tools** menu, then click **Customize**.

    The Customize dialog box appears.

2. If necessary, click the **Toolbars** tab (see illustration on previous page).

3. Click **New**.

4. Type name for toolbar in **New Toolbar** dialog box, then click **OK**.

    New floating toolbar appears.

5. Click the **Commands** tab.

6. Select the command category in the **Categories** box.

7. Drag desired commands in **Commands** list onto custom toolbar.

8. Click **Close** when done.

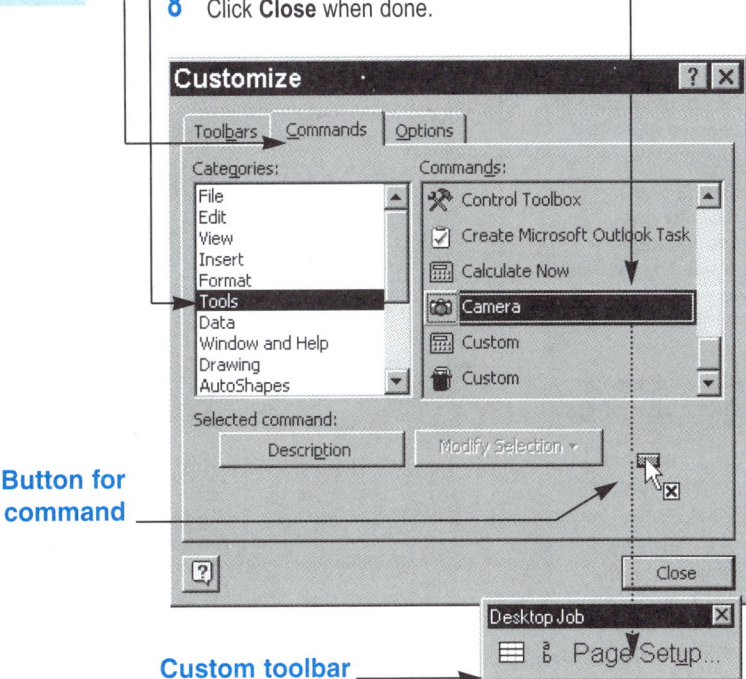

Button for command

Custom toolbar

TIP: In step 7, you can also drag commands onto the Excel application menu bar. When you do, Excel will open the menu and indicate where on the menu it will be inserted as you move the mouse.

Continued . . .   **57**

Customize Excel (continued)

Notes:

- Personalized Menu and Toolbar options include:

  Standard and Formatting toolbars share one row — this setting increases visible workspace in the Excel window. However, because it hides buttons used less often, it often requires additional mouse clicks.

  Menus show recently used commands first — this setting makes it easier to access commands you use often.

  Show full menu after a short delay — this setting anticipates that you need the full command list.

  Reset my usage data — restores toolbar and menu usage to default setting, deleting the record of commands you have used recently.

  continued...

Set Menu and Toolbar Options

1 Click **Tools** menu, then click **Customize**.

The Customize dialog box appears.

2 Click the **Options** tab.

To delete record of commands you have used:

- Click **Reset my usage data**.

3 Select or deselect options as desired.

4 Click **Close** when done.

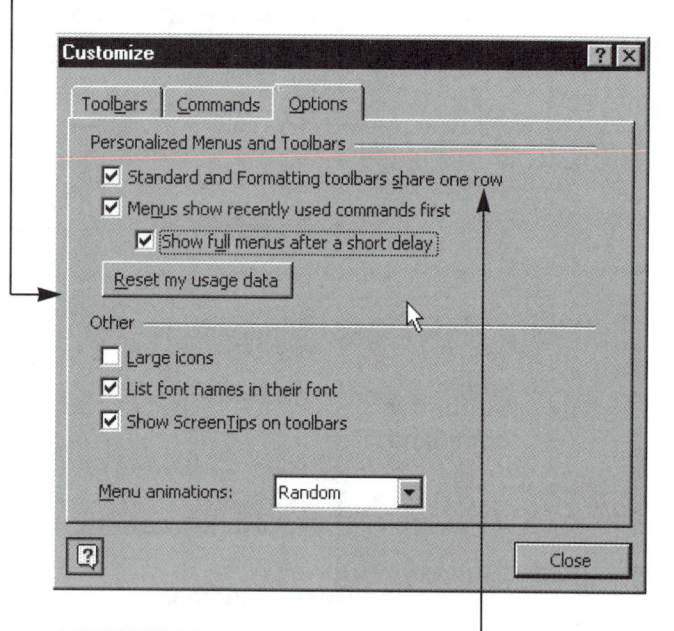

> **TIP:** If you often find it difficult to locate a toolbar button, deselect this option so all toolbars will be visible and their location on the toolbar will be predictable.

58

Menu and Toolbar Options (continued)

Other options include:

Large icons — use this setting if your vision or display resolution makes it necessary.

List font names in their own font — this setting shows a sample of the font you are selecting in the Font box on the Formatting toolbar (see Format Font).

Show ScreenTips on toolbars — this setting displays the name of a toolbar button when you rest the mouse pointer on it.

Menu animations — this setting lets you pick from the following animations:

None
Random
Unfold
Slide

Hide or Show Toolbar Buttons

1 Click down arrow on left side of toolbar.
 The Add or Remove Buttons item appears.

2 Click Add or Remove Buttons.
 A menu of buttons appears.

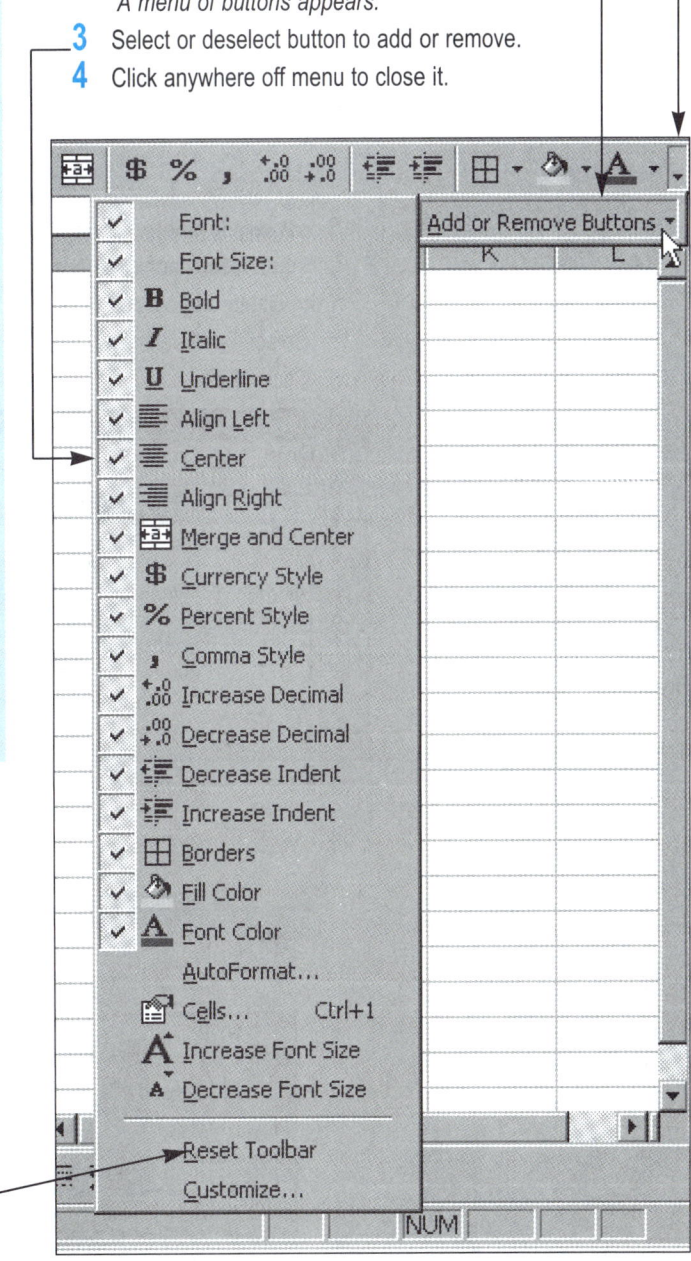

3 Select or deselect button to add or remove.

4 Click anywhere off menu to close it.

Click to reset toolbar to show default buttons.

59

Delete Cells, Columns, or Rows

You can delete cells, rows, or entire columns, from a worksheet. Existing cells adjust to take the place of the removed cells.

Edit → Delete...

Notes:

- In **step 1**, to select nonadjacent cells, you can press **Ctrl** and click or drag through cells to include in the selection.

- If deleted cells are used in formulas, the formulas will display #REF! error messages. If there are references to adjusted cells in formulas, Excel adjusts the formulas, even absolute references.

- **Caution:** You can lose data with the delete action. However, you can click **Edit** menu, then **Undo** to reverse the action.

- Do not confuse Delete with Clear. Clearing cells removes only the data, while deleting cells removes the cells from the worksheet.

TIP: In step 2, you can also right-click any selected cell, then click **Delete** from the shortcut menu.

Delete Cells Using Menu

1 Select cells to delete.
2 Click **Edit** menu, then click **Delete**.

If the Delete dialog box appears:
- Select the direction you want existing cells to shift.
- Click **OK**.

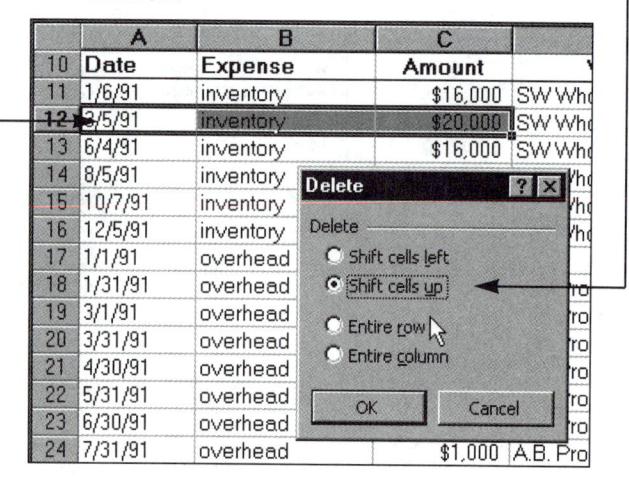

Shortcut Menu

60

Notes:

- To select multiple columns or rows to be deleted, drag through row or column headings, or press **Ctrl** and click nonadjacent headings to select. You cannot delete columns and rows at the same time, however.

Delete Entire Column or Row

1. Click row or column heading to select.
2. Click **Edit** menu, then click **Delete**.

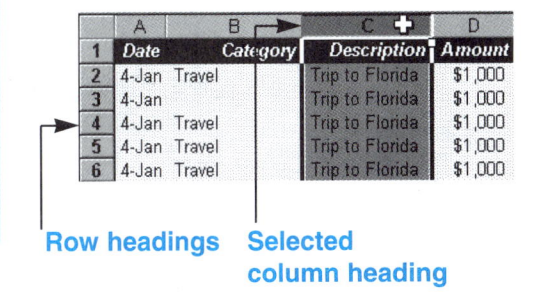

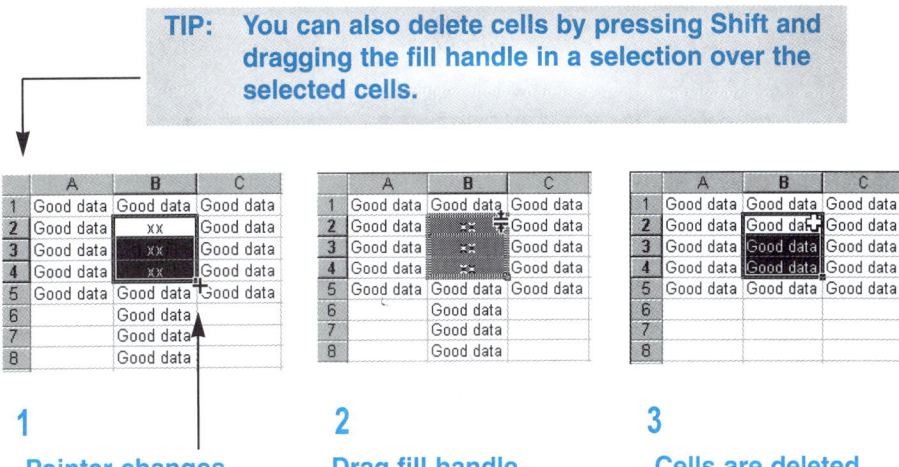

Row headings   Selected column heading

TIP: You can also delete cells by pressing Shift and dragging the fill handle in a selection over the selected cells.

1
Pointer changes to a cross when you rest it on fill handle.

2
Drag fill handle up over cells while holding the Shift key.

3
Cells are deleted and cells shifts up in this example.

61

Draw Objects

This topic will introduce you to drawing objects using Microsoft Excel.

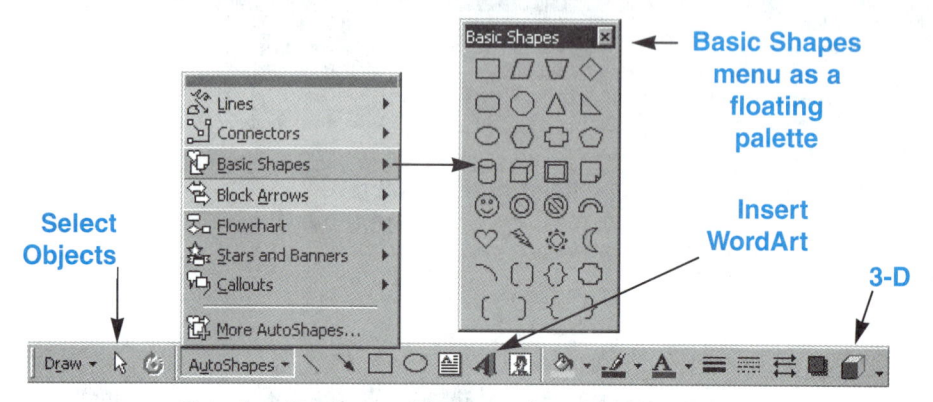

Drawing Toolbar with Open AutoShapes Menu

Notes:

- The illustration contains three graphic objects:

  WordArt — 3D Text objects.

  AutoShape — a shaded callout with text.

  Rectangle — basic AutoShape with a fill texture applied.

- Notice that the WordArt is in front of the rectangle. To change the order of any graphic object, right-click the object; click **Order**, then select an option such as **Bring to Front**.

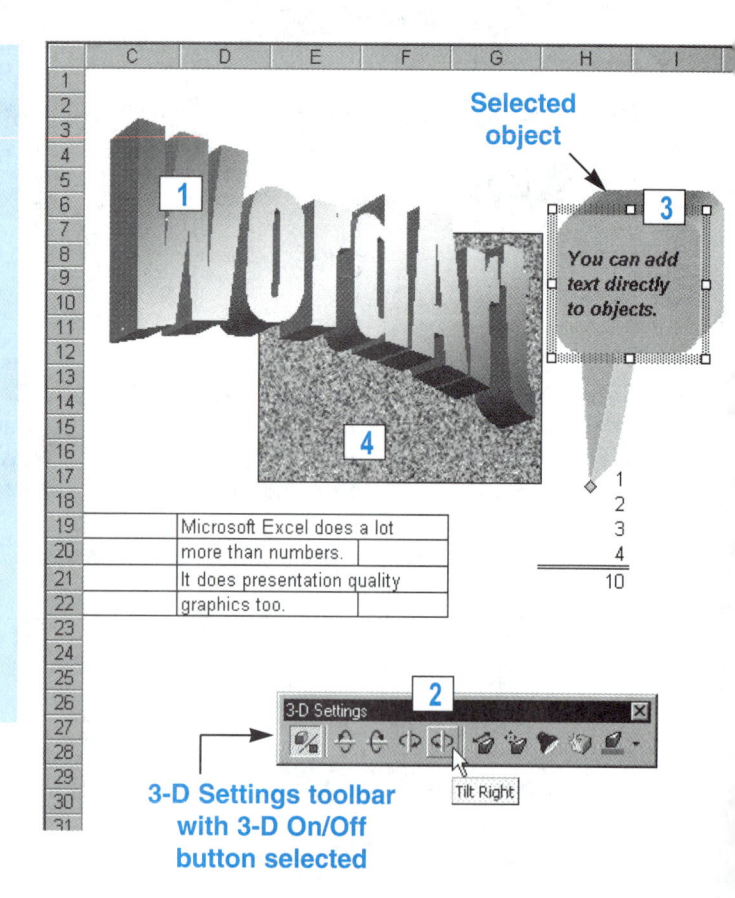

Drawing Objects and 3-D Settings Toolbar

62

Notes:

- **WordArt**:

  Rest your pointer on each button on the WordArt toolbar to identify its purpose. Notice that you can edit the text of the selected WordArt object by clicking the **Edit Te̱xt** button.

- **3-D toolbar**:

  Rest your pointer on each button on the **3-D Settings** toolbar. Select an object and use each of the buttons to change it.

  If you use the **3-D Settings** toolbar on an object that is not 3-D, Excel converts it to a 3-D object.

- **AutoShapes**:

  Basic shapes, such as Line, Arrow, Rectangle, and Oval, on the Drawing toolbar are considered AutoShapes.

  You can change the selected AutoShape object: Click the **Draw** button on Drawing toolbar; click **Change AutoShape** and select a shape from the menus that appear. Excel redraws the object, while maintaining formats.

  You can change the font format for text in an object: Drag through the text; right-click the selection, then click **Format Auto̱Shape**.

Introduction to Drawing, by Example

- If necessary, click the **Drawing** button on the Standard toolbar to display the Drawing toolbar.

Create WordArt 1

1. Click the **Insert WordArt** button on Drawing toolbar.

    The WordArt Gallery dialog box appears.

2. Double-click the desired design box.
3. Type the text: **WordArt**, then click **OK**.

    WordArt graphic appears with sizing boxes. WordArt toolbar also appears.

4. Drag the sizing boxes to change the object size.
5. Drag within the object to change the object position.

Open the 3-D Toolbar 2

1. Click the **3-D** button on Drawing toolbar.
2. Click **3̱-D Settings**.
3. With WordArt object selected (click it), use **Tilt** tools on 3-D Setting toolbar to change object angle.

Create Bubble Callout (AutoShape) 3

1. Click **Au̱toShapes** button on Drawing toolbar, point to **Callouts**, then click a bubble shaped callout in the menu.

    Pointer changes to a small crosshair.

2. Drag pointer to adjust size and shape of callout.
3. Click the **3-D** button on Drawing toolbar, then click the sample shape in upper-left corner of menu.
4. Type the text: **You can add text directly to objects.**
5. Size and position the callout object as you did the WordArt.

Create a Simple Rectangle and Fill Effect

1. Click the **Rectangle** button on Drawing toolbar. 4

    Pointer changes to a small crosshair.

2. Drag pointer to adjust the size of object.
3. Right-click the object, then click **Format Auto̱Shape**.
4. From the **Colors and Lines** tab, click **C̱olor** box, then click **Fi̱ll Effects**.
5. From the **Texture** tab, click desired effect, then click **OK** to close all dialog boxes.

63

Edit Cell Data

A cell entry can be changed (edited) with a variety of techniques. When cell editing is enabled, the formula bar gains extra controls (buttons) and displays the cell contents both in the cell and in the formula bar.

Notes:

- There are three ways to edit a cell entry:

  Double-click the cell.

  Click the cell, then click in the formula bar.

  Click the cell, then press **F2**.

- When editing:

  Excel displays a flashing cursor where new input will be inserted.

  You can press the **Ins** key to toggle between insert and overwrite mode.

  The formula bar changes to include **Cancel**, **Enter** and **Edit Formula** buttons.

  When editing a cell, you can insert text stored from the Clipboard, by pressing **Ctrl+V**.

Edit a Cell Entry by Double-Clicking

1 Double-click cell containing data to edit.

   Excel displays a flashing insertion pointer in the entry and extra controls next to the formula bar.

   Insertion pointer

2 Click in the entry to place the insertion pointer.
   OR
   Drag through characters to select (the next action will replace or delete your selection).

3 Edit the entry as needed:
   - Type characters to insert.
   - Press **Del** to delete characters to the right of insertion pointer or to delete the selection.
   - Press **Backspace** to delete character to the left of the insertion pointer or to delete the selection.

4 Press **Enter**.
   OR
   Click ✓ on formula bar.

64

Notes:

- Replacing cell data by typing over it is best when little or none of the original cell data will be retained.

Replace a Cell Entry

1. Select cell containing data to replace.
2. Type new data.
3. Press **Enter**.

   OR

   Click ✓ on formula bar.

Notes:

- Use **Esc** to undo your changes prior to completing it.
- If you have already entered the change, you can click the **Edit** menu, then **Undo**.

Cancel Changes to a Cell Entry

Prior to entering the change:

- Press **Esc**.

  OR

  Click ✗ on formula bar.

Notes:

- By default, Excel lets you edit cell contents directly in the cell. To set this option, click **Tools** menu, then **Options**; select the **Edit** tab; then select **Edit directly in cell**.

Formula Bar and Related Controls

Name box . . . . Displays cell reference of the data you are editing.

Cancel button ✗ . . . . Lets you cancel a revision before completing it.

Enter button ✓ . . . . Lets you complete the revision.

Edit Formula button . . . . . Provides help when editing formulas.

Formula bar . . . . Lets you edit the cell content.

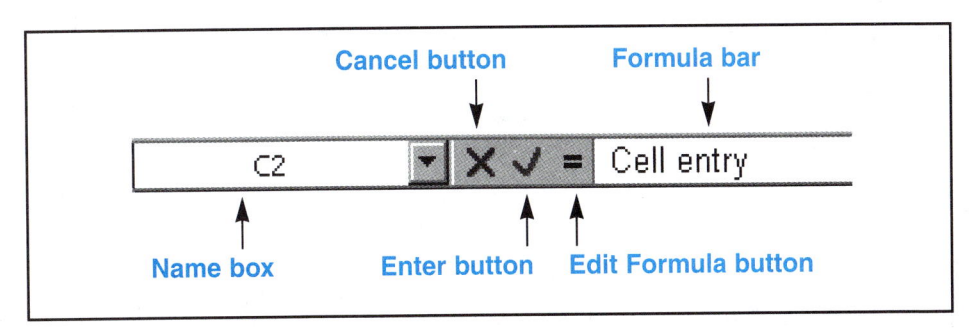

Formula Bar and Related Controls

65

Enter Cell Data

Entering data is very straightforward. There are, however, many techniques for entering data of different types, such as dates, times, fractions, percents, and formulas.

Notes:

- In **step 2**, to wrap text within the cell, press **Alt+Enter**.

- In **step 2**, if what you type matches a previous entry in the current column, Excel's Auto-Complete feature fills in the text of the previous entry as you type.

- In **step 3**, you can also press an **arrow key** in the direction of the next cell you want to select, or click any other cell.

- In **step 3**, if what you enter matches an abbreviation in the AutoCorrect feature, Excel replaces the abbreviation with the specified replacement text.

- If no alignment is chosen, Excel applies the **General alignment** which automatically left-aligns text and right-aligns values (including dates and times).

- If your entry does not fit in the column, it overlaps into the next column, unless the next column cell also contains data.

Enter Text or Whole Numbers

1 Select cell to receive entry.

2 Type the text or whole number.

A flashing insertion pointer appears after the data you type. The formula bar also displays your entry.

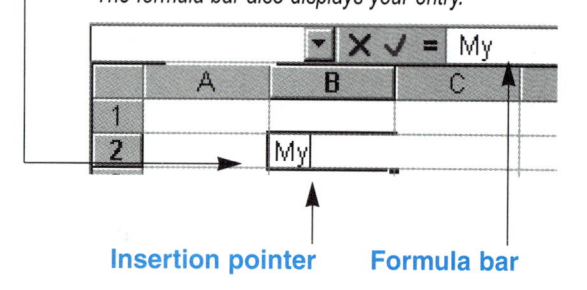

Insertion pointer **Formula bar**

3 Press **Enter**.

OR

Click ✓ on formula bar.

Excel completes the entry and selects the cell below it.

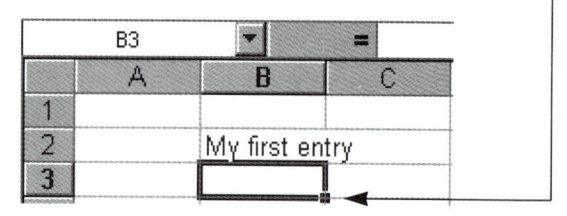

To cancel the entry before completing it:

- Press **Esc**.

OR

Click ✗ on formula bar.

Tip:	To enter identical data in multiple cells, select cells, type data, then press Ctrl+Enter.

Notes:

- Excel automatically applies special number formats when you enter a value in a specific order, or when you enter a value with special characters, such as a comma. For example, if you type a zero, a space, and a fraction, Excel will automatically apply the fraction format and display the value as a fraction.

- Dates and times may be displayed as a combination of text and numbers. However, Excel stores dates and times as serial values and right-aligns them.

- Excel formats large numbers that do not fit within a column as Scientific. For example: 9E+14.

Enter Special Kinds of Data

1 Select cell to receive entry.

2 Type the data as shown in the table below.

A flashing insertion pointer appears after the data you type. The formula bar also displays your entry.

3 Press **Enter**.

Category:	Example of what to type:
Currency	$25,000.25
Date	6/24/97
	24-Jun
	24-Jun-97
	Jun-97
Date and time	6/24/97 10 AM
Fraction	0 1/2
Label	text
Mixed number	1 1/2
Number	25
Number as label	="25"
Percent	25%
Time	10 AM
Formula (simple)	=A1+B1

Tip: To enter today's date, press Ctrl + ; (semicolon).

Notes:

- AutoComplete will not assist in entering numbers.

- Another way to use AutoComplete is to right-click the cell to receive the data, click **Pick from List**, then select the data you want to enter. This method lets you input data using only the mouse.

How AutoComplete Works

The AutoComplete feature assists you when entering repeating text in a column.

1 Select cell to receive text.

2 Type beginning of text.

Excel automatically completes the entry (see highlighted text in illustration below) based on data previously entered in the column.

Categories
vegetable
stone
ve**getable**

NOTE: Type over the highlighted text to change it.

3 Press **Enter**.

67

Fill Cells with a Series

The Fill Series feature extends the values in existing cells to selected adjacent cells. This time-saving feature lets you project future values (such as trends), or extend dates or special lists—such as text indicating the days of the week.

Edit → Fill → Series...

Notes:

- In **step 1**, **series data** may include numbers, dates, and special lists.

- In **step 2**, the **fill handle** is a small box in the lower-right corner of the selection. The pointer changes to a crosshair when positioned over the fill handle.

- In **step 3**, you can use the **left** mouse button to fill the series with the default values for your data.

- In **step 5**, the fill options available will depend on the kind of data selected.

Fill Cells with a Series by Dragging

1 Select cells containing series data.

2 Point to fill handle.

   A crosshair appears.

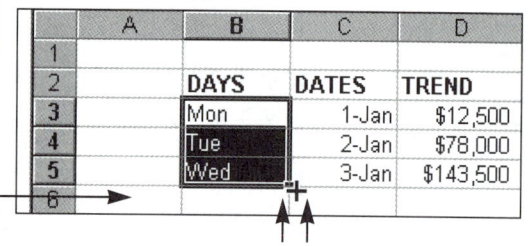

Fill handle **Crosshair pointer**

3 Press and hold **right** mouse button and drag crosshair to extend border over adjacent cells to fill.

   Excel displays default fill value in a pop-up box.

4 Release mouse button.

   Excel displays fill options on a shortcut menu.

5 Click fill option appropriate to your data.

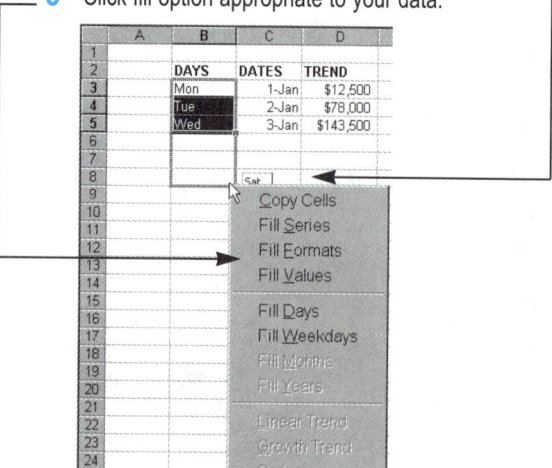

68

Notes:

- In **step 1**, your selection determines where the series will end, although setting a **Stop value** setting in **step 4** can override the selection method.

- In **step 4**, the Series dialog box offers the following options:

  Series in (Rows or Columns) lets you change the orientation of the series.

  Type lets you specify the type of calculation that will determine the series. Available options will depend on the data in your selection.

  Date unit lets you specify the kind of date units to apply.

  Trend lets you calculate future values (Linear or Growth).

  Step value lets you specify increments by which the series will increase.

  Stop value lets you set the value at which the series will end.

Use Menu to Fill Cells with a Series

Use this method to control exactly how the series is calculated.

1. Select cells containing existing series data and extend selection to adjacent cells to fill.
2. Click **Edit** menu, then point to **Fill**.
3. Click **Series**.

   The Series dialog box appears.

4. Select options appropriate to your data.
5. Click **OK** when done.

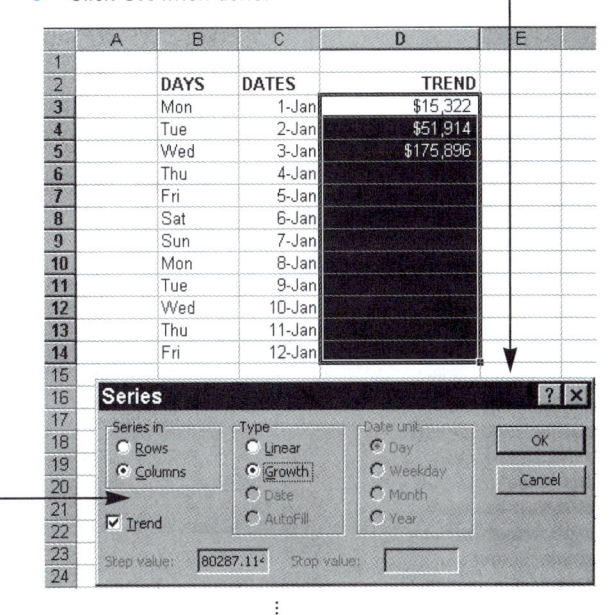

Trend Calculated By Setting in Series Dialog Box

69

Find and Replace

The Find and Replace feature will find information in one or more spreadsheets and give you the option of replacing it with new information that you specify.

Notes:

- In **step 1**, to select multiple sheets, press **Ctrl** and click desired sheet tabs.
- In **step 2**, you can also press **Ctrl+F**.
- In **step 3**, you can search for specific formulas or data, results of calculations, and comments.
- In **step 4**, the **Look in** box provides options for where to find data. For example, if you want to find the result of a formula, select **Values**. If you want to find a specific formula, select **Formulas**.
- Other Find options:

  Select the **Match case** option to find only data that matches the case of your search string.

  Select the **Find entire cells only**, to find only cells containing an exact and complete match of characters in your search string.

  You can change the direction that Excel searches (By Rows, or By Columns) in the **Search** box.

Find Data in Worksheets

Finds contents of cells (formulas, data), results of calculations (values), and comments.

1 Select any cell to search all of the current worksheet.

OR

Select sheets to search.

OR

Select range of cells to search.

2 Click **Edit** menu, then click **Find**.

The Find dialog box appears.

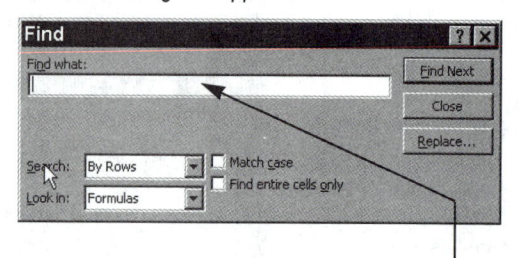

3 Type data to search for in the **Find what** box.

> NOTE: You can use the ? (question mark) in place of any single character. Use * (asterisk) in place of any group of consecutive characters.

4 Select the data's location in the **Look in** box.

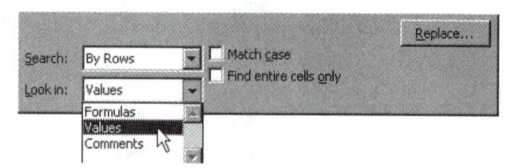

5 Change other options as needed.

6 Click **Find Next**.

Excel selects first cell containing the data specified.

7 Click **Find Next** again, or click **Close** when done.

Notes:

- In **step 1**, to select multiple sheets, press **Ctrl** and click each sheet you want to select.

- In **step 2**, you may have to click the double arrow on the **Edit** menu to view the **Replace** option.

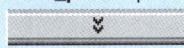

- In **step 2**, you can also press **Ctrl+H**.

- In **step 3**, you can search for specific formulas or data, results of calculations, and comments.

- In **step 5**, select the **Match case** option to find only data that matches the case of your search string. Select the **Find entire cells only** to find only cells containing an exact and complete match of characters in your search string.

- **Caution:** Be careful when using the **Replace All** command, because it is easy to obtain unexpected results. For example, if you replace all instances of AND with JOIN, Excel will change words like BAND to read BJOIN. To avoid this type of error, consider using space characters in the **Find what** and **Replace with** text boxes. That is, find spaceANDspace and replace it with spaceJOINspace.

- To undo Replace actions click the **Edit** menu, then **Undo**.

Replace Data in Worksheets

Finds and replaces data in worksheet; does not search for comments or results of calculations.

1 Select any cell to search all of the current worksheet.
   OR
   Select sheets to search.
   OR
   Select range of cells to search.

2 Click **Edit** menu, then click **Replace**.
   The Replace dialog box appears.

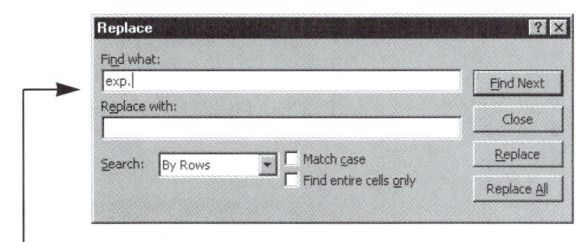

3 Type the data to find in the **Find what** box.

   NOTE: You can use the ? (question mark) in place of any single character. Use * (asterisk) in place of any group of consecutive characters.

4 Click in the **Replace with** box and type replacement text.

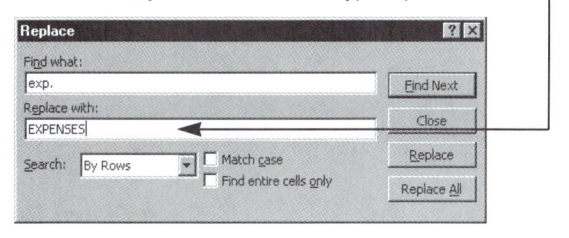

5 Set options as needed.

6 Click **Find Next** to find the first occurrence of the data.
   Excel selects first cell containing data.

7 Click **Find Next** again to retain data in current selection and to find the next instance.
   OR
   Click **Replace** to replace data in current selection.
   OR
   Click **Replace All** to replace data in all instances.

8 Repeat step 7 as needed, then click **Close** when done.

71

Find Workbooks

It can be difficult to remember just where or in what file your work is stored. From the Open dialog box, the Find command on the Tools menu can make this task easier.

Open button

File → Open... → Tools ▾

Notes:

- From the **Find** dialog box consider the following when adding search criteria, as described on the next page:

- In **step 5a**, all **And** criteria are evaluated together; all criteria must be met. Add **Or** criteria when adding criteria that is evaluated independently.

- In **step 5b**, consider choosing the following Property items when trying to locate Excel documents:

    Creation date
    File name
    Last modified
    Text or property

- In **steps 5c** and **5d**, use the **Condition** and **Value** boxes to specify the characteristics of each criteria you add.

Find Workbooks

1 Click the **Open** button on Standard toolbar.
2 Click the **Tools** button on the toolbar.
3 Click **Find**.

Excel opens the Find dialog box (next page).

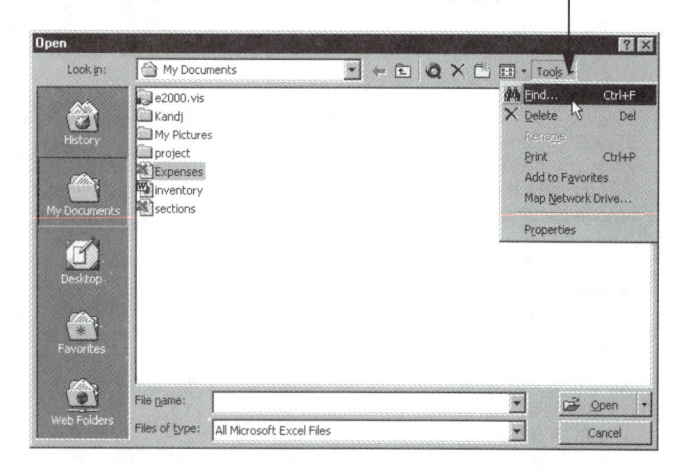

Open Dialog Box With Open Tools Menu

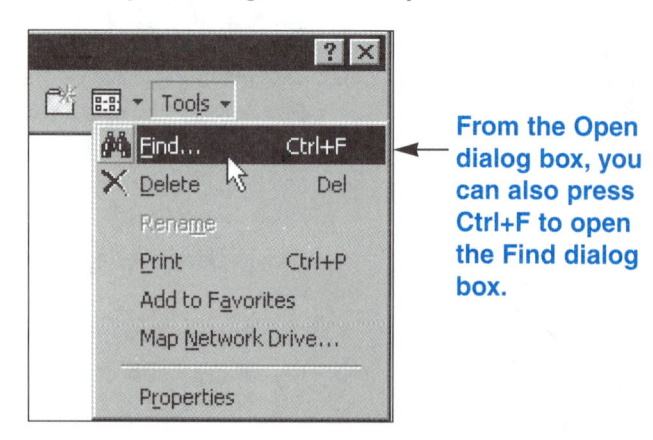

From the Open dialog box, you can also press Ctrl+F to open the Find dialog box.

Continued . . .

72

Notes:

- Other Find options:

  Match case — finds only workbooks containing text that matches cases as you entered them.

  Delete — removes selected criteria from list.

  New Search — removes all criteria.

  Save Search — lets you save the criteria for future use.

  Open Search — lets you open a search criteria saved earlier.

Find Workbooks (continued)

4. Select starting directory in **Look in** box.
5. If desired, select **Search subfolders**.

   The Advanced Find dialog box appears.

   ### Add search criteria:
   a. Select **And** or **Or**.
   b. Select desired property in **Property** box.
   c. Select desired condition in **Condition** box.
   d. If available, select desired value in **Value** box.
   e. Click **Add to List**.
   f. Repeat steps to add additional criteria.
6. Click **Find Now** to begin search.

   Excel displays only folders and files containing files that meet your criteria.

Criteria list

The Open dialog box displays found files.

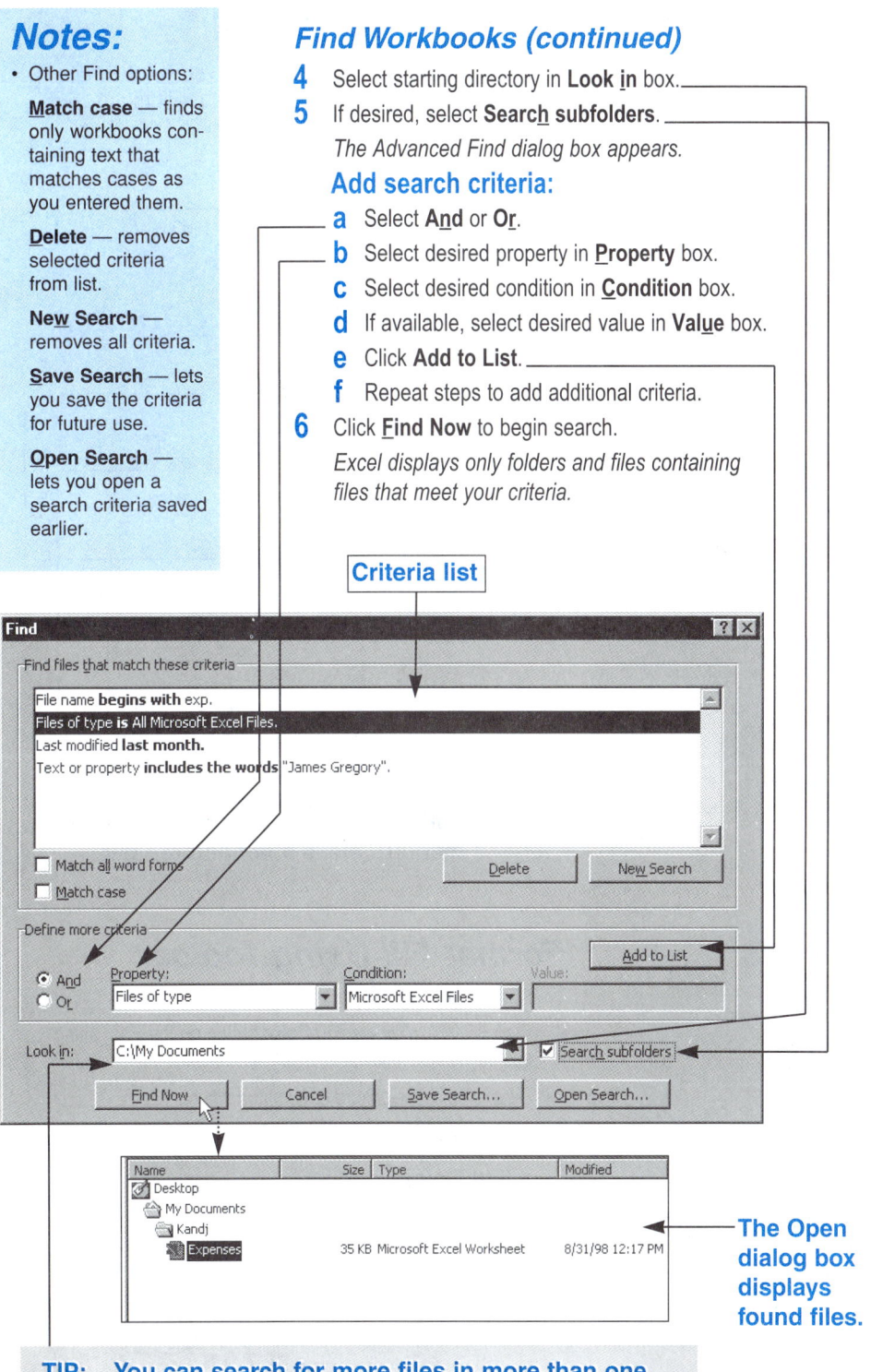

TIP: You can search for more files in more than one location at a time: In the Look in box, type each location name, separated by a semicolon (for example, type c:\;d:\).

73

Format Cell Borders and Fill

Cells borders and fill areas can be formatted to emphasize data in your worksheet. You can apply formats using toolbar buttons, or you can use the F<u>o</u>rmat C<u>e</u>lls menu command to add formats of your own making.

F<u>o</u>rmat ➔ C<u>e</u>lls... ➔ Border/Patterns

Notes:

- In **step 2**, if the Borders button is not visible, click the More Buttons » arrow on the right side of the toolbar to view additional buttons.

- In **step 2**, you can click the button (not the arrow) to apply the last border used to the current cell selection.

- Click the **Edit** menu, then **Undo** to reverse the border command.

Format Borders Using Toolbar

1 Select cells to format.

2 Click the arrow on the **Borders** button on the Formatting toolbar.

Excel displays a palette of common borders.

3 Click desired border.

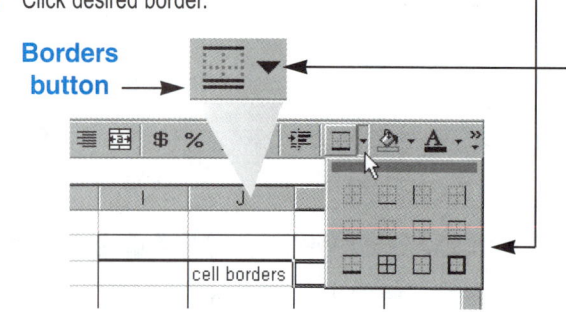

Borders button

Tip: You can drag the title bar of the palette menu to make a floating toolbar.

Notes:

- In **step 2**, if the Fill Color button is not visible, click the More Buttons » arrow on the right side of the toolbar to view additional buttons.

- In **step 2**, you can click the button (not the arrow) to apply the last fill used to the current cell selection.

- Click the **Edit** menu, then **Undo** to reverse the fill command.

Format Fill Using Toolbar

1 Select cells to format.

2 Click the arrow on the **Fill Color** button on the Formatting toolbar.

Excel displays a palette of common fill colors.

3 Click desired fill color.

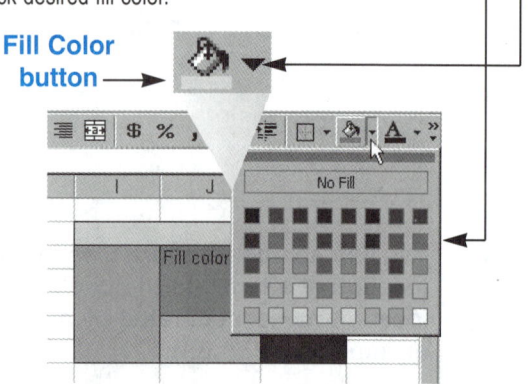

Fill Color button

74

Notes:

- Shortcuts to open the Format Cells dialog box:

  Press **Ctrl+1**

  OR

  Right-click selection, then click **Format Cells**.

- To quickly remove all cell borders: Select the cells, then press **Ctrl+Shift+-** (minus).

- **Border option:** To change the color of borders, select a color in the **Color** box on the Border tab prior to applying the border.

- The preview area represents the cell(s) you've selected. Click borders in the preview area to apply the selected line style to a corresponding border.

Format Borders and Fill Using Menu

1 Select cell(s) to format.

2 Click the **Format** menu, then click **Cells**.

The Format Cells dialog box opens.

To apply borders:

a Click the **Border** tab.

b Click the desired line style in **Style** box.

c Click **Outline** or **Inside** button (in Presets section).

   OR

   Click specific border in preview area.

d Repeat steps b and c as desired.

To remove borders:

- Click the **None** button (in Presets section).

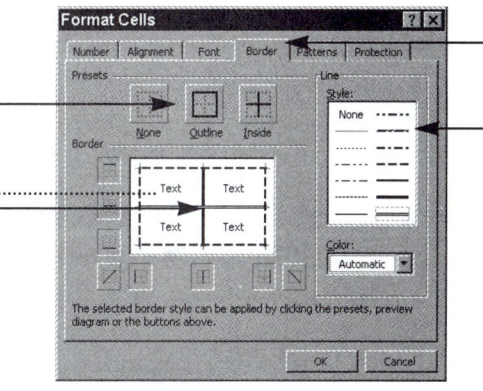

To apply fill colors:

a Click the **Patterns** tab.

b Click desired **Color** for foreground and background.

   AND/OR

   Click **Pattern** box, then select desired pattern.

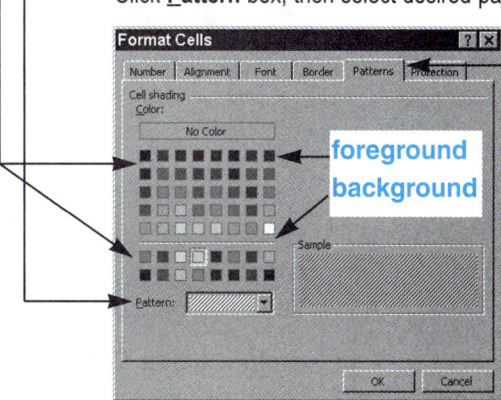

foreground
background

3 Click **OK** when done.

75

Format Cells Conditionally

This feature lets you set formats for cells and data based on their content. You can set up to three conditional formats for a given cell or range. For example, you could set up a range of cells to display negative values as red italic text with a cell border and values over $10,000 in bold blue text.

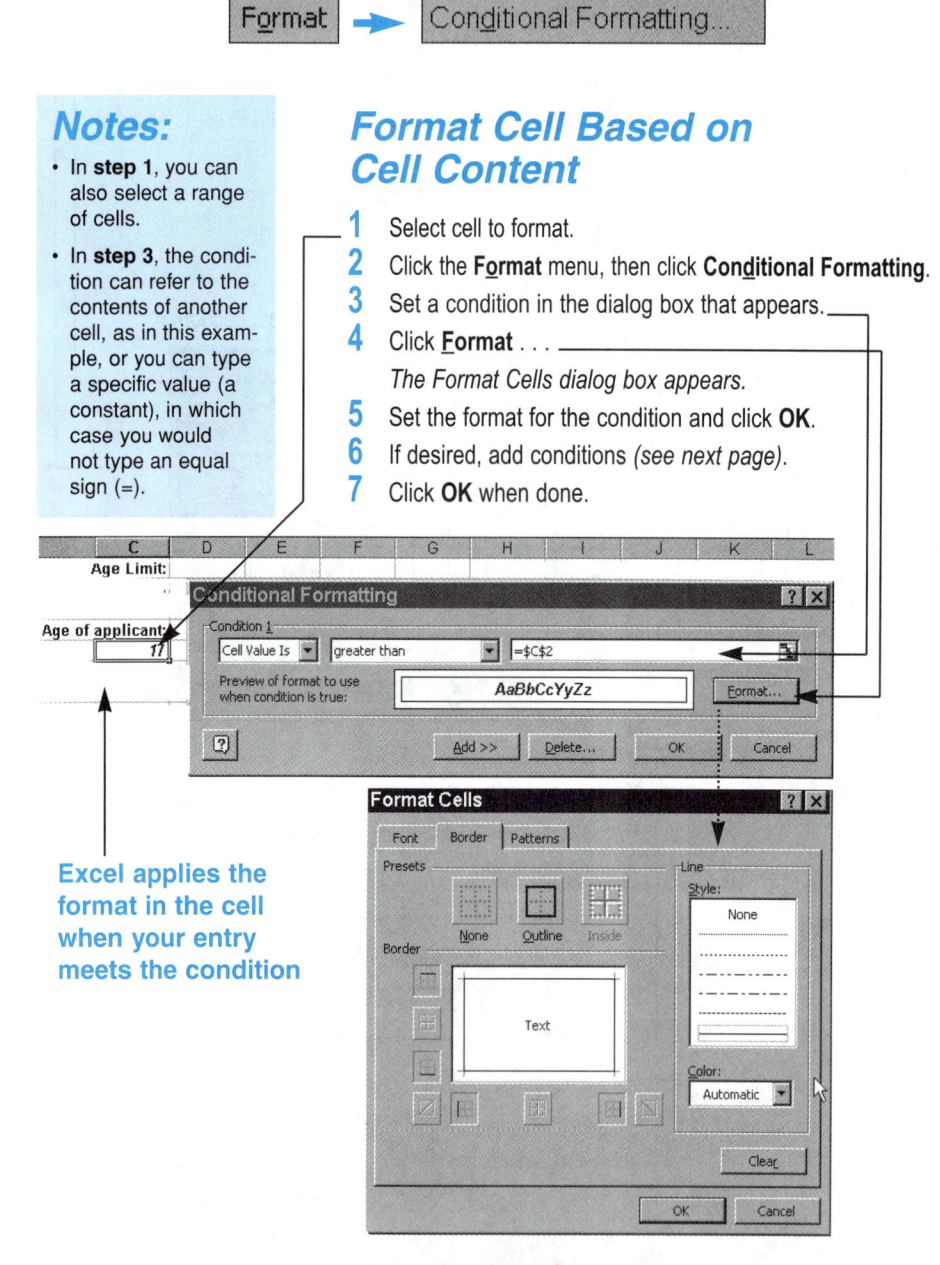

Format → Conditional Formatting...

Notes:
- In **step 1**, you can also select a range of cells.
- In **step 3**, the condition can refer to the contents of another cell, as in this example, or you can type a specific value (a constant), in which case you would not type an equal sign (=).

Format Cell Based on Cell Content

1. Select cell to format.
2. Click the **Format** menu, then click **Conditional Formatting**.
3. Set a condition in the dialog box that appears.
4. Click **Format** . . .
   The Format Cells dialog box appears.
5. Set the format for the condition and click **OK**.
6. If desired, add conditions *(see next page)*.
7. Click **OK** when done.

Excel applies the format in the cell when your entry meets the condition

Example Using Cell Value Is Condition

76

Notes:

- You can add up to three conditional formats for a cell. They can be **Cell Value Is** and/or **Formula Is** conditions.

- Conditional formats remain in effect until you delete them.

- You can search for cells containing conditional formats: Click the **Edit** menu, then **Go To**; click **Special**, then select **Conditional Formats**).

Add and Delete Conditions

From the **Conditional Formatting** dialog box:

- Click the **Add** or **Delete** buttons.

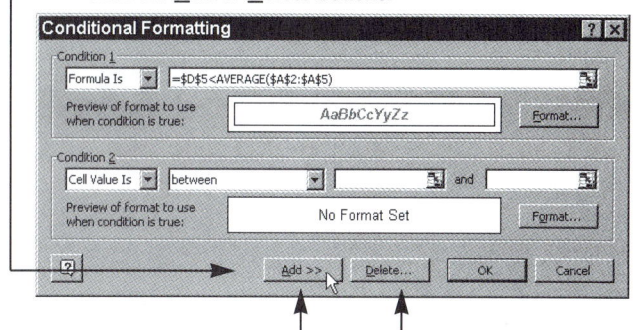

When you click **Add**, the dialog box expands, and you can define a second or third condition.

If you click **Delete**, Excel will prompt you for the condition to be removed.

Notes:

- The **Formula Is** condition can evaluate cells other than the cell to which the format is applied.

- The **Formula Is** condition requires a logical formula that can be evaluated as True or False.

- You can enter a cell reference in a formula by clicking the desired cell in the worksheet.

- If a reference in a formula is located in another workbook or worksheet, you must define a name *(see Name Cells)* for the reference in the active worksheet, then use that name.

Format Cell Based on Formula

1. Follow steps in **Format Cell Based on Cell Content** *(see previous page)*.
2. Set the condition for **Formula Is**.

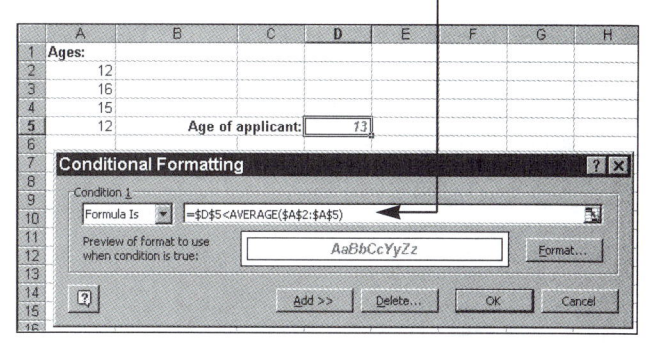

Example Using Formula Is Criteria

77

Format Cells Using Format Painter

The Format Painter button lets you copy all the formats from one cell to another in one step.

Notes:

- In **step 2**, if the Format Painter button is not visible, click the More Buttons arrow >> on the right side of the toolbar to view additional buttons.

- Format Painter copies the following formats:
  - Number
  - Alignment
  - Font
  - Border
  - Patterns
  - Protection

  It will include column widths and row heights if you first click a column or row headings, click the **Format Painter** button, then click the column or row heading to receive the formats.

- After you click the **Format Painter** button, the pointer becomes a paint brush, and source cells are outlined with dashes.

- If you make a mistake with Format Painter, click the **Edit** menu, then **Undo** to reverse the action.

Copy Formats Using Format Painter

1 Select cells containing formats to copy.
2 Click **Format Painter** button on Standard toolbar.
3 Click on cell or drag through cell range to receive the formats.

Format Painter

Paintbrush pointer

78

Notes:

- In **step 2**, if the Format Painter button is not visible, click the More Buttons arrow ⏵⏵ on the right side of the toolbar to view additional buttons.

- The source and destination cells do not have to be the same size or shape.

Copy Formats Multiple Times Using Format Painter

1 Select cells containing formats to copy.

2 Double-click **Format Painter** button on Standard toolbar.

3 Click on cell or drag through cell range to receive the formats.

Format Painter remains active.

4 Click or drag through other cell ranges as needed.

5 Click **Format Painter** button again to end process.

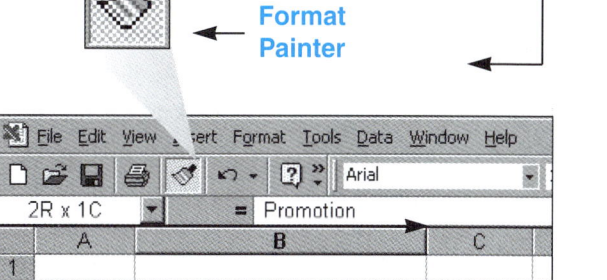

Active Format Painter

Dashed outline

TIP: You can use Format Painter to remove all formats from cells: Just use the procedures above to copy unformatted areas of your worksheet to the cells containing the formats you want removed.

79

Format Data Tables Automatically

AutoFormats are combinations of formats, such as lines and fills, that you can apply to a range of cells. You can pick the premade style you like from a list of samples.

Format → AutoFormat...

Notes:

- In **step 1**, Excel will automatically select the surrounding cells in the table to format. You can also manually select the range.

- In **step 3**, consider the kind of printer you have when making your selection.

- You may want to omit a format, such as the **Number** format, when you have already applied a format to your data.

- You cannot apply an AutoFormat if the worksheet is protected.

- You can click the **Edit** menu, then **Undo** to undo the AutoFormat.

Format a Table Automatically

1 Select any cell in table.

2 Click the **Format** menu, then click **AutoFormat**.

The AutoFormat dialog box appears.

3 Click desired Autoformat style.

You can click scroll arrows to view additional styles.

To omit specific formats:

a Click **Options**.

b Click formats to remove in **Formats to apply** area.

4 Click **OK** when done.

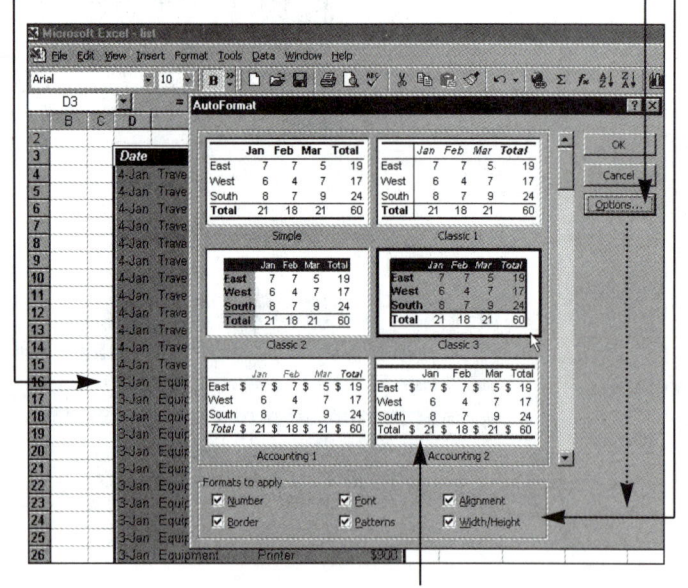

AutoFormat styles

AutoFormat Dialog Box

80

Notes:

- A **PivotTable** lets you evaluate data stored in a list interactively (see Create PivotTable).

- In the example below, the PivotTable changes shape and the AutoFormat is retained when the Category field is dragged up into the Page position; it readjusts when the Description and Category fields change places.

Format a PivotTable® Automatically

For these steps, refer to illustration on previous page. Sample results for a PivotTable are shown below.

1 Select any cell in PivotTable.

2 Click the **Format** menu, then click **AutoFormat**.

  The AutoFormat dialog box appears.

3 Click desired Autoformat style.

  You can click scroll arrows to view additional styles.

To omit specific formats:

  a Click **Options**.

  b Click formats to remove in **Formats to apply** area.

4 Click **OK** when done.

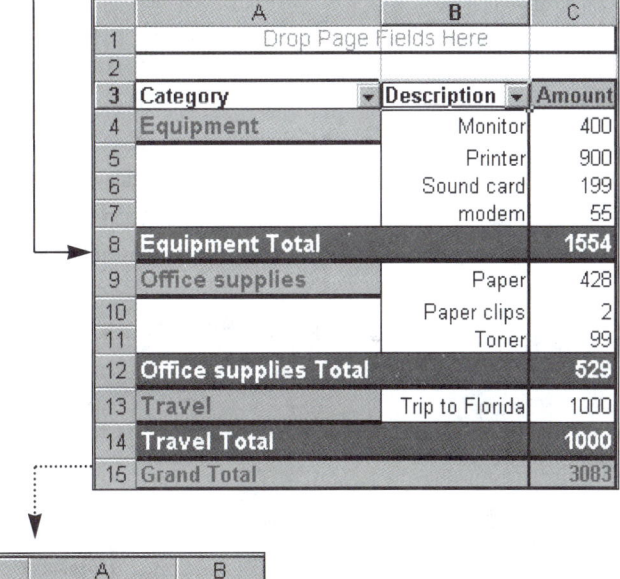

The AutoFormat is Retained as PivotTable Field Positions Change

81

Format Font

You can emphasize particular data by formatting the text — choosing fonts and font attributes. A font is a set of characters that share style characteristics. You can also apply, for example, bold or italic attributes to a given font.

Format → Cells... | Font

Notes:

- In **step 1**, press **Ctrl** while you click to select each cell to format.

- In **step 2**, if the desired format button is not visible, click the More Buttons arrow » on the right side of the Formatting toolbar to view additional buttons.

- In **step 2**, you can apply any combination of font and font attributes. For example, you can both bold and underline data.

- In **step 2**, click anywhere on the **Font** or **Font Size** boxes, then click the desired option from the drop-down list.

- Font size is measured in points. There are 72 points in an inch.

- When you select a cell, Excel displays its font settings on the Formatting toolbar. For example, in the illustration following step 2, cell B3 is formatted as Arial Black, bold.

Format Font Using Toolbar

1 Select cell(s) to format.

OR

To format only part of the text in a cell:

  a Double-click cell containing text to format.

  b Drag through desired text. → Cell entry

2 Select desired options on the Formatting toolbar:

- Select desired font in **Font** box.
- Select or type desired font size in **Font Size** box.
- Click the **Bold** button to apply the bold attribute.
- Click the **Italic** button to apply the italic attribute.
- Click the **Underline** button to apply the underline attribute.

Formatting toolbar

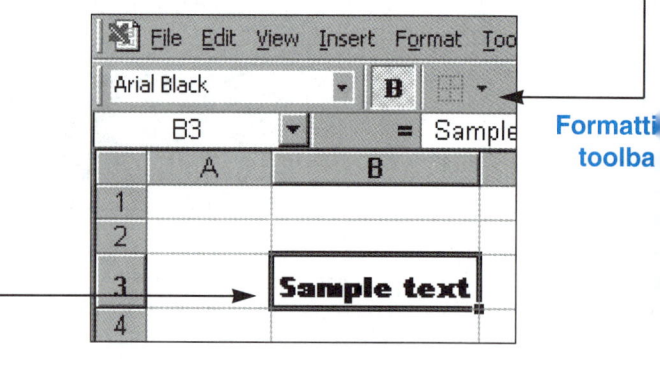

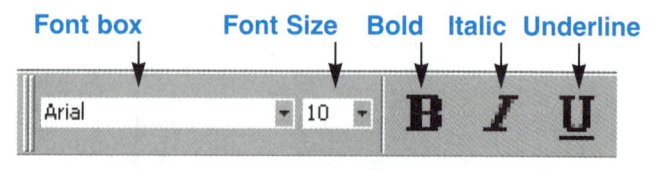

Font box | **Font Size** | **Bold** | **Italic** | **Underline**

Font Controls on the Formatting Toolbar

82

Notes:

- In **step 1**, press **Ctrl** while you click each cell to select multiple cells to format.

- Font options:

  Select desired font in the **Font** list box.

  Select desired font style in **Font style** list box.

  Select desired font size in **Size** box.

  Select underline style in **Underline** box.

  Select font color in **Color** box.

  Select desired effect in **Effects** group.

  Click the **Normal font** check box to remove all font attributes.

- The **Preview** window shows a sample of the font and font attributes you have selected.

Format Font Using Menu

1 Select cell(s) to format.

   OR

   To format only part of the text in a cell:

   a   Double-click cell containing text to format.

   b   Drag through desired text.   ⟶   Cell entry

2 Click **Format** menu, then click **Cells**.

   The Format Cells dialog box appears.

3 Click the **Font** tab.

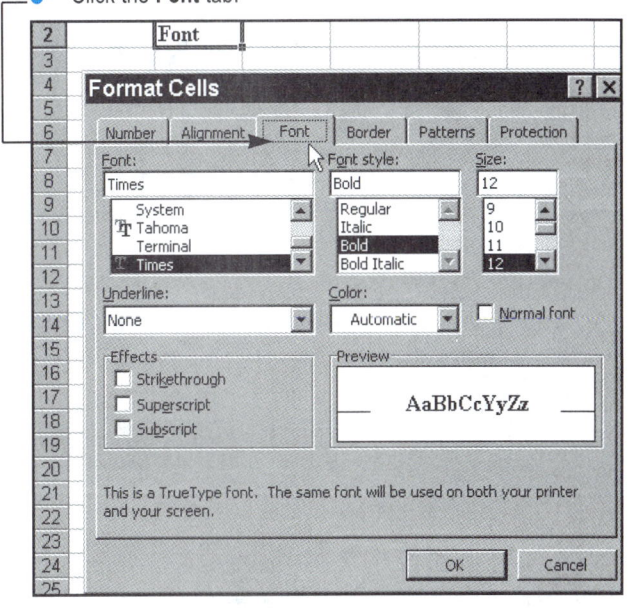

4 Select desired options.

5 Click **OK** when done.

Font	Size
Century Gothic	14pt
Effects	
~~Strikethrough~~	superscript subscript
Font styles	
Regular	*Italic* **bold** ***Bold Italic***
Color	**Normal** **Mixed**
Blue	no font attributes See Jane₂ Run ™
Underline	
Single	Double Single Accounting Double Accounting

Sample Font and Font Attributes

83

Format Numbers

When you enter a value, Excel applies the format it thinks appropriate to your entry *(see Enter Cell Data)*. You can also apply common number formats from the Formatting toolbar, such as Currency and Percentage; or you can select specific number formats using menu commands and the Format Cells dialog box.

F__o__rmat → Cells... | Number

Notes:

- In **step 2**, if the desired number format button is not visible, click the More Buttons » arrow on the right side of the toolbar to view additional buttons.

- When you change a number format, Excel does not change the value.

- If the number does not fit in the cell after you change the number format, Excel displays ####### (pound signs) in the cell. To fix this problem, increase the column width *(see Adjust and Hide Columns)*, or select the **Shrink to fit** option *(see Align Data in Cells)*.

- You can format a number when you enter it by typing specific symbols, such as a $ or %.

Format Numbers Using Toolbar

1 Select cell(s) containing values to format.

  NOTE: *To select cells that are nonadjacent, press* **Ctrl** *and click or drag through cells to include.*

2 Click desired number format button on the Formatting toolbar:

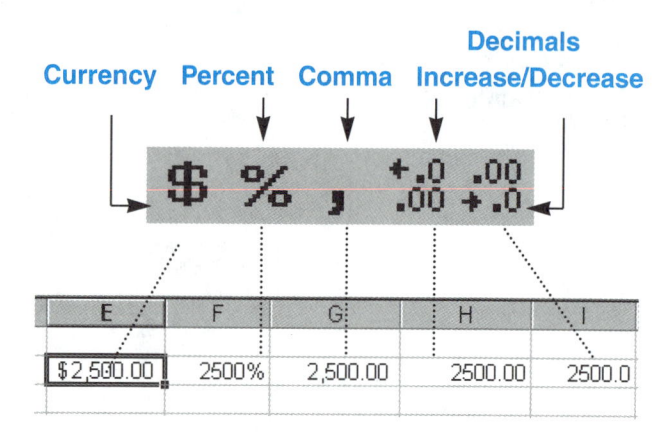

Currency   Percent   Comma   Decimals Increase/Decrease

$ %   ,   +.0 .00 / .00 +.0

E	F	G	H	I
$2,500.00	2500%	2,500.00	2500.00	2500.0

Sample Results Using Buttons on the Formatting Toolbar

84

Notes:

- In most cases, Excel applies the General number format, unless you include special characters (see Enter Cell Data).

- In **step 4**, the selected category indicates the current number format of the selected cell. If more than one cell is selected, and they have different number formats, no category will be displayed.

- The **Custom** category contains templates for all the number formats. Select the format that is closest to the desired format, then modify it as needed. In the sample below, the custom format (date and time) shows the full year 1900.

- You can hide data in a cell by applying a custom number format. To create the format:
Select **Custom** in **Category** box, then type three semi-colons (;;;) in the **Type** box that appears.

  Type:
  ;;;
  General
  0
  0.00

- Excel displays descriptions of the selected category near the bottom of the dialog box.

Format Numbers Using Menu Commands

1. Select cell(s) containing values to format.

   NOTE: To select cells that are nonadjacent, **Ctrl** and click or drag through cells to include.

2. Click the **Format** menu, then click **Cells**.

3. Click the **Number** tab.

4. Select category of number format in **Category** list.

   Excel displays options for the selected category.

5. Select options for the category you have selected.

   Excel displays sample in Sample box.

6. Click **OK** when done.

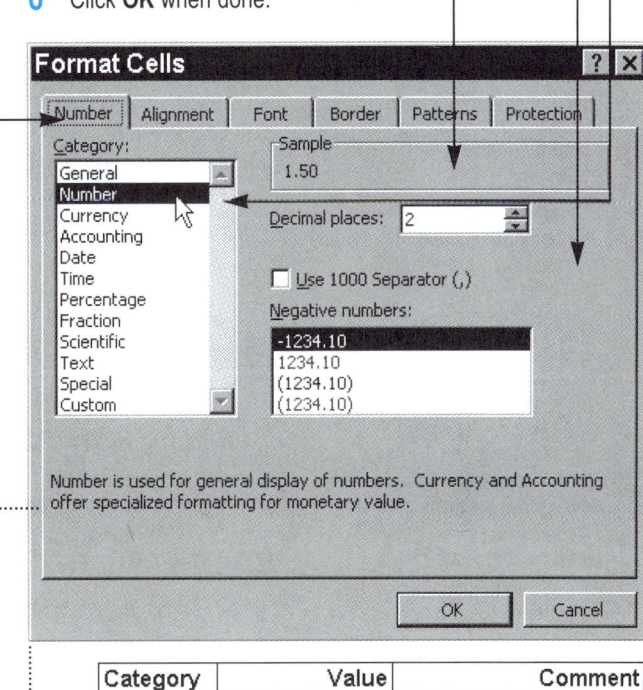

Format Cells

Tabs: Number | Alignment | Font | Border | Patterns | Protection

Category:
General
Number
Currency
Accounting
Date
Time
Percentage
Fraction
Scientific
Text
Special
Custom

Sample: 1.50

Decimal places: 2

☐ Use 1000 Separator (,)

Negative numbers:
-1234.10
1234.10
(1234.10)
(1234.10)

Number is used for general display of numbers. Currency and Accounting offer specialized formatting for monetary value.

OK | Cancel

Category	Value	Comment
General	1.5	
Number	1.50	
Currency	$1.50	
Accounting	$ 1.50	
Date	January 1, 1900	first day of century
Time	1/1/00 12:00 PM	first day and a half of century
Percentage	150.00%	you can set decimal places
Fraction	1 1/2	
Scientific	1.50E+00	
Text	1.5	
Special	00002	zip code
	(718) 980-0999	phone number
	000-00-0002	social security number
Custom	1/1/1900 12:00 PM	customized date and time

Sample Number Formats

85

Insert, Edit, and Remove Comments

You can attach notes to cells by inserting a comment (formerly called cell notes). Comments do not interfere with the data in your worksheet, but they're easy to view: Rest your mouse on the marker and the comment appears.

Insert → Comments

Notes:

- Common uses for comments are to describe the purpose of a formula, to give an operator instruction, or to remind yourself of something still to be done.

- In **step 3** you can use common editing techniques, such as selecting, formatting, deleting, inserting, and pasting text.

- Excel inserts the name of the program's registered user into the comment. To edit the user name, click the **Tools** menu, click **Options**, then select the **General** tab.

Insert a Comment

1. Select cell to receive comment.
2. Click **Insert** menu, then click **Comments**.
   A comment box appears with your name inserted at the top.
3. Type the comment.
4. Drag the sizing handles (small squares) to change the size of the comment box.
5. Drag the border of the comment box to change its position in the worksheet.
6. Click anywhere outside comment box to close it.

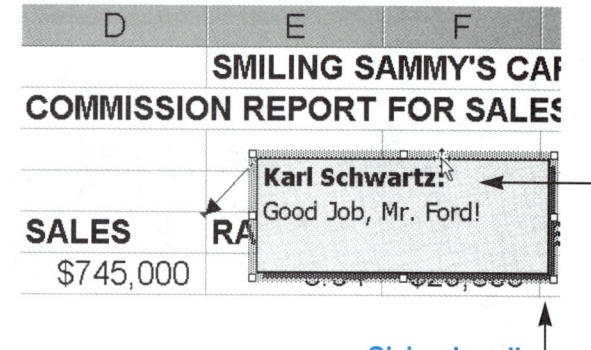

Sizing handle

Notes:

- To set Excel to always show the indicator, or comment and the indicator, click the **Tools** menu, then click **Options**; click the **View** tab, and select the desired Comments option.

View a Comment

- Rest pointer on comment indicator to display the comment.

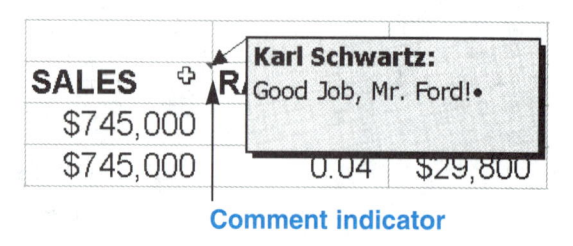

Comment indicator

86

Notes:

- The 3-D drawing tool on the Drawing toolbar can be used to format the comment box. You must first set the **View** option to **Comment & Indicator** (see Set View Options).

- To review all comments, click the **View** menu, then click **Comments**. A **Reviewing** toolbar appears to help you navigate, edit, and create comments.

- To format comment text, select text, right-click selection, then click **Format Comment** on the shortcut menu.

Edit a Comment

1 Right-click cell containing comment to edit.
2 Click **Edit Comment** on shortcut menu that appears.
3 Edit the comment as desired.
4 Drag the sizing handles to change the size of the comment box.
5 Drag the border of the comment box to change its position in the worksheet.
6 Click outside comment box to close it.

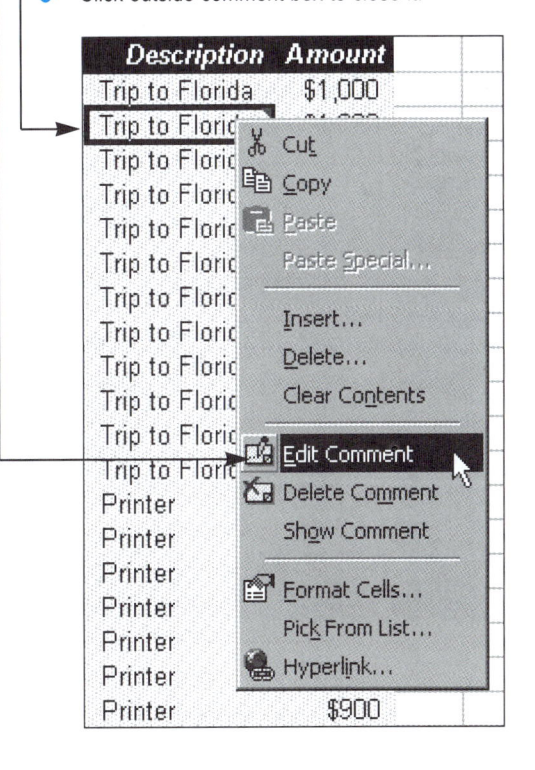

Notes:

- To delete all comments in a large worksheet, select them all, click the **Edit** menu, then **Go To**; click the **Special** command, select **Comments** and click **OK**. To delete the selected comments, click the **Edit** menu, then **Clear**.

Delete a Comment

1 Right-click cell containing comment to delete.
2 Click **Delete Comment** on shortcut menu that appears.

The comment is removed. Undo this action, if needed, from the Edit menu.

TIP: You can also print comments: Click **File** menu, then Page Set**u**p; click the Sheet tab, then select the desired print option in the Co**m**ments box.

87

Insert Cells, Columns or Rows

You can insert cells, rows, or entire columns into a worksheet. Existing cells adjust to accommodate the new cells.

Insert ➜ Cells... / Rows / Columns

Notes:

- In **step 2**, you may have to click the button at the bottom of the menu to view the **Cells** command.

- If there are references to adjusted cells in formulas, Excel adjusts the formulas, even the absolute references.

- In **step 2**, you can also right-click any selected cell, then click **Insert** from the shortcut menu.

Insert Cells Using Menu

1 Select location where new cells will be inserted.

2 Click the **Insert** menu, then click **Cells**.
   The Insert dialog box appears.

3 Select direction you want existing cells to shift.

4 Click **OK**.

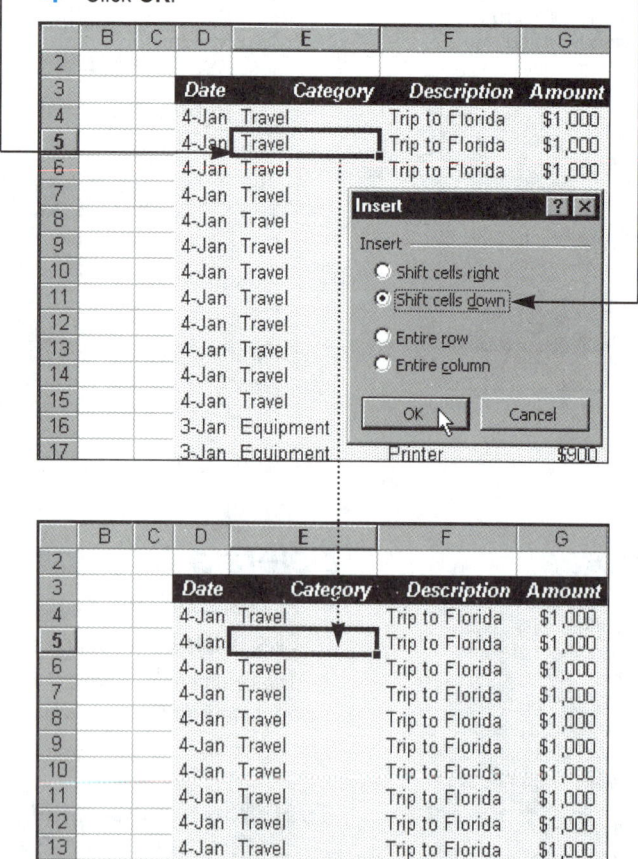

Cells Shift Down

Notes:

- To insert multiple columns or rows, drag through row or column headings to select, or press **Ctrl** and click nonadjacent headings to select before using the **Insert** menu. You cannot insert columns and rows at the same time, however.

Insert Columns or Rows Using Menu

1 Click desired row or column heading.

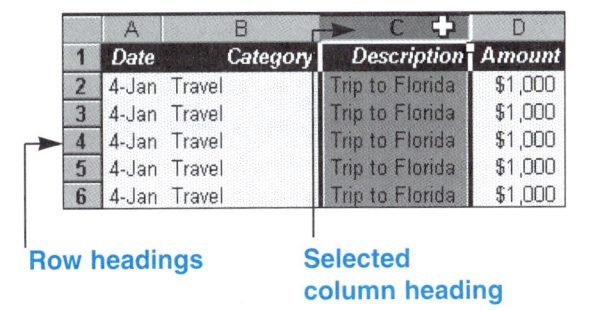

	A	B	C	D
1	Date	Category	Description	Amount
2	4-Jan	Travel	Trip to Florida	$1,000
3	4-Jan	Travel	Trip to Florida	$1,000
4	4-Jan	Travel	Trip to Florida	$1,000
5	4-Jan	Travel	Trip to Florida	$1,000
6	4-Jan	Travel	Trip to Florida	$1,000

Row headings   Selected column heading

2 Click the **Insert** menu, then click **C**olumns or **R**ows.

Notes:

- In **step 1**, Excel may prompt you for the direction to shift existing cells, if it cannot determine it from your selection.

- When you insert cells, columns, or rows, Excel automatically extends references to ranges affected by the insertion.

  For example, the formula =SUM(C2:**C9**) would become =SUM(C2:**C11**) if two rows were inserted above the cell containing the formula.

Insert Cells, Columns, or Rows Using Shortcut Menu

1 Select cells or click or drag through row or column headings.

   NOTE: The number of headings you select tells Excel how many columns or rows to insert.

2 Right-click the selection.
3 Click **Insert** on shortcut menu.

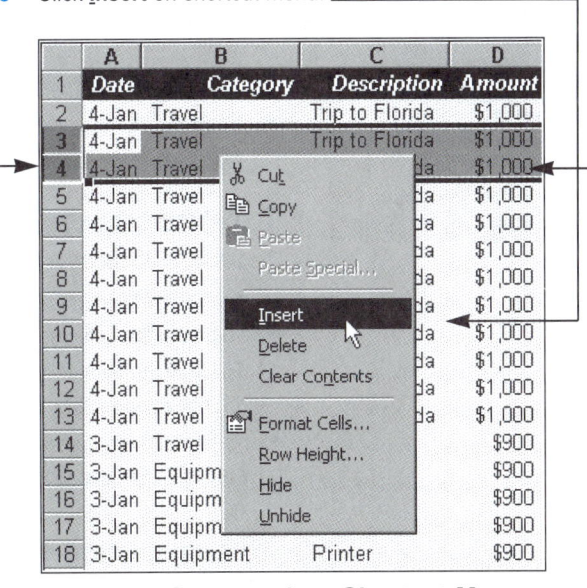

	A	B	C	D
1	Date	Category	Description	Amount
2	4-Jan	Travel		$1,000
3	4-Jan	Travel	Trip to Florida	$1,000
4	4-Jan	Travel		$1,000
5	4-Jan	Travel	Cut	$1,000
6	4-Jan	Travel	Copy	$1,000
7	4-Jan	Travel	Paste	$1,000
8	4-Jan	Travel	Paste Special...	$1,000
9	4-Jan	Travel	Insert	$1,000
10	4-Jan	Travel	Delete	$1,000
11	4-Jan	Travel	Clear Contents	$1,000
12	4-Jan	Travel		$1,000
13	4-Jan	Travel	Format Cells...	$1,000
14	3-Jan	Travel	Row Height...	$900
15	3-Jan	Equipm	Hide	$900
16	3-Jan	Equipm	Unhide	$900
17	3-Jan	Equipm		$900
18	3-Jan	Equipment	Printer	$900

Insert Command on Shortcut Menu

89

Insert OLE Objects

The Insert Object command lets you insert OLE objects — collections of information, such as a Word document into Excel. When activated, OLE objects provide access to the tools of the application in which the file was created. If you insert a linked object, Excel updates it when changes are made to the source file.

Insert ➔ Object...

Notes:

- In **step 1**, selecting a cell will give you a beginning insertion point for the object. You can move the object later by dragging it:

  Drag its border if the object is activated.

  Drag anywhere within it when the object is selected, but not activated.

- In the **Object** dialog box, the **Create from File** tab lets you select a stored file to which Excel will maintain a link. Linked objects automatically update when you make changes to the linked file in its source application.

Insert a New OLE Object

Refer to the next page for illustrations.

1. Select cell where you want to insert the object.
2. Click the **Insert** menu, then click **Object**.

   The Object dialog box appears. [1]

3. Select object type in **Object type** list.
4. Click **OK**.

   The object is inserted. Menus and tools for the application to which it belongs appear in place of the Excel tools. [2]

   - Use the application tools to create the object.
   - Drag the sizing handles (small squares) to change the size and shape of the object.
   - Drag the border of the object to change its position.
   - Click outside the object to return to normal editing.

To activate (edit) object information:

- Double-click the object.

  The source application tools replace Excel's tools. [2]

To select and work on object as a picture:

- Click the object once to select it.

  Sizing handles appear around the object. [3]

- To delete the selected object, press **Delete**.
- To show the Picture toolbar for the object, right-click the object, then click **Show Picture Toolbar**.
- To format the selected object, right-click the object, then click **Format Object**.

  OR

  Use the buttons on the **Picture** toolbar that appears when the object is inserted. Rest the pointer on each button to determine its purpose.

[1] Select object type

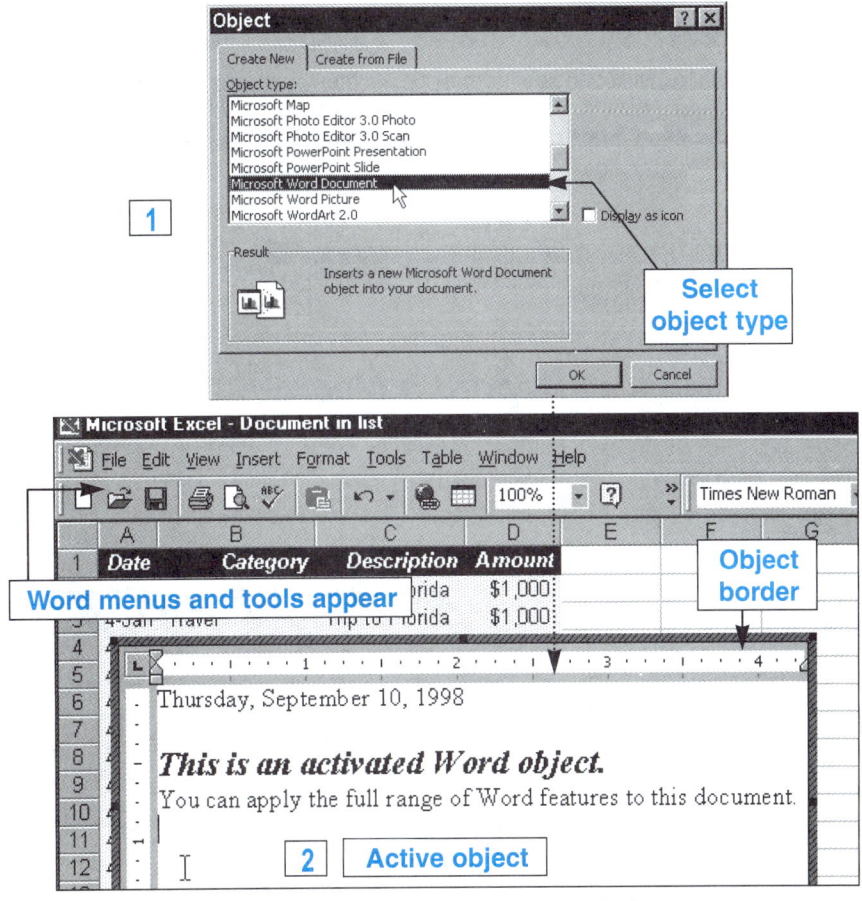

Word menus and tools appear

Object border

[2] Active object

Object Activated in Excel Worksheet

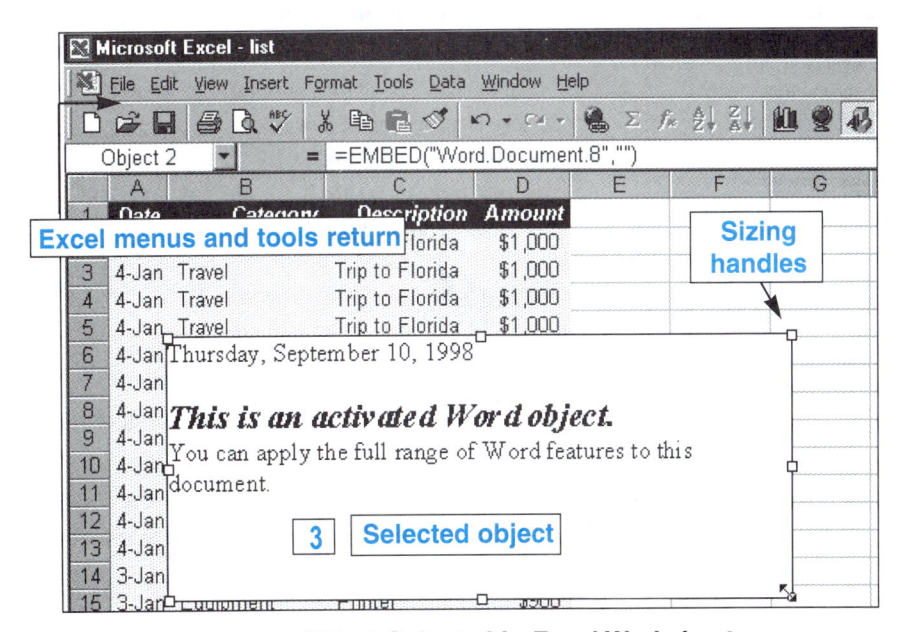

Excel menus and tools return

Sizing handles

[3] Selected object

Object Selected in Excel Worksheet

91

Macros

A macro is a shortcut to a series of commands. When you run a macro, the commands are carried out automatically. You can create macros by recording complex tasks. This topic will show you how to record and play back (run) simple macros.

Tools → Macro

Notes:

- In **step 2**, you may have to click the button at the bottom of the menu to view the **Macro** command.

- In **step 4**, the first character in the macro name must be a letter. Remaining characters may include numbers, letters, or the underscore character. Spaces are not valid.

- In **step 5**, if you store the macro in the **Personal Macro Workbook**, the macro can be used in any workbook.

- In **step 7**, if you select this option, Excel will play back the macro relative to active cell, instead of playing it back in the same cells in which it was recorded. You can turn this feature on and off to achieve different results with the same macro.

Record a Macro

1 Plan the actions you want to record.
2 Click the **Tools** menu, then point to **Macro**.
3 Click **Record New Macro** on the submenu.

The Record Macro dialog box appears.

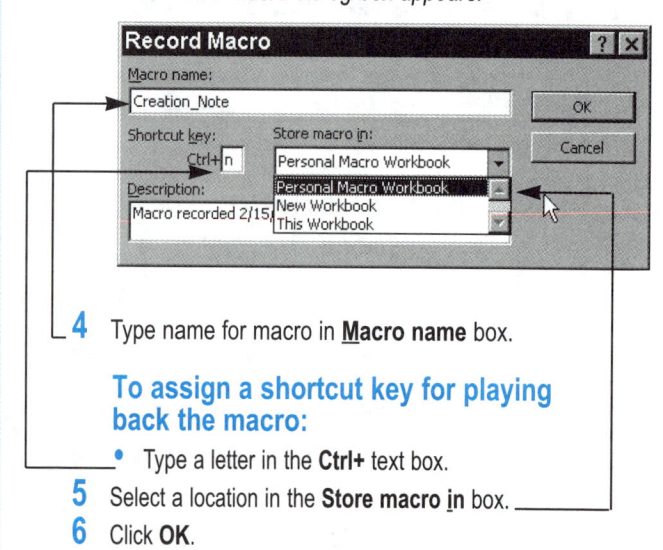

4 Type name for macro in **Macro name** box.

To assign a shortcut key for playing back the macro:

- Type a letter in the **Ctrl+** text box.

5 Select a location in the **Store macro in** box.
6 Click **OK**.

The Stop Recording toolbar appears indicating that you can begin recording the macro.

7 Select or deselect the **Relative Reference** button on the **Stop Recording** toolbar.
8 Perform actions to record.
9 Click **Stop Recording** on the **Stop Recording** toolbar when done.

Notes:

- If you need to select a graphic object without activating the macro assigned to it, first click the **Select Objects** tool on the Drawing toolbar.

Assign Macro to Graphic Object

After you assign a macro to a graphic object, you can run it by clicking the graphic.

1 Right-click graphic object.
2 Click **Assign Macro** on the shortcut menu.
   The Assign Macro dialog box appears.
3 Select macro to assign to graphic in **Macro Name** list.
4 Click **OK**.

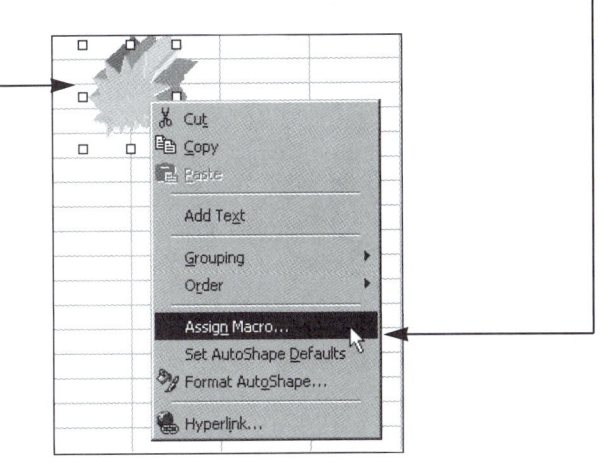

Notes:

- If a macro does not work as expected and you want to delete it, follow the **Using menu** steps below, then click **Delete** instead of **Run**.

- To edit a macro, use the **Visual Basic Editor** and macro language.

  Recording macros, then examining the code, is one way to learn Visual Basic code.

Run (Play Back) a Macro

- If necessary, select cell in which macro will begin.

  ### Using assigned shortcut key:
  - Press key combination assigned when you created the macro, such as **Ctrl+M**.

  ### Using assigned graphic object or picture:
  - Click picture or graphic to which the macro has been assigned (see above).

  ### Using menu:
  a Click the **Tools** menu, then point to **Macro**.
  b Click **Macros** on the submenu.
    The Macro dialog box appears.
  c Select name of macro to run from **Macro Name** list.
  d Click **Run**.

93

Move Cell Contents

You can move data from one cell to other cells in a variety of ways. The best method to choose depends upon the location of the source data and its destination. *(Also see Collect and Paste Multiple Items.)*

Edit ➝ Cut / Paste

Notes:

- Using menu commands to move cells is best when the source and destination cells are *not* in the same viewing area.

- In **step 2** and **step 4**, you can also right-click the selection to select the **Cut** and **Paste** commands from a shortcut menu.

- **Caution:** When you paste data, existing data in the destination cells will be replaced. Click the **Edit** menu, then **Undo** to reverse the paste operation.

- In **step 4**, to avoid overwriting data, you can click the **Insert** menu, then **Cut Cells**. The **Insert Paste** dialog box will appear, from which you can choose the direction to shift the existing cells.

  You may have to click the button at the bottom of the menu to view the **Cut Cells** command.

Move Cell Contents Using Menu Commands

1 Select cell(s) to move.

2 Click the **Edit** menu, then click **Cut**.

   A flashing dashed outline appears around selected cell(s).

3 Select destination cell(s).

4 Click the **Edit** menu, then click **Paste**.

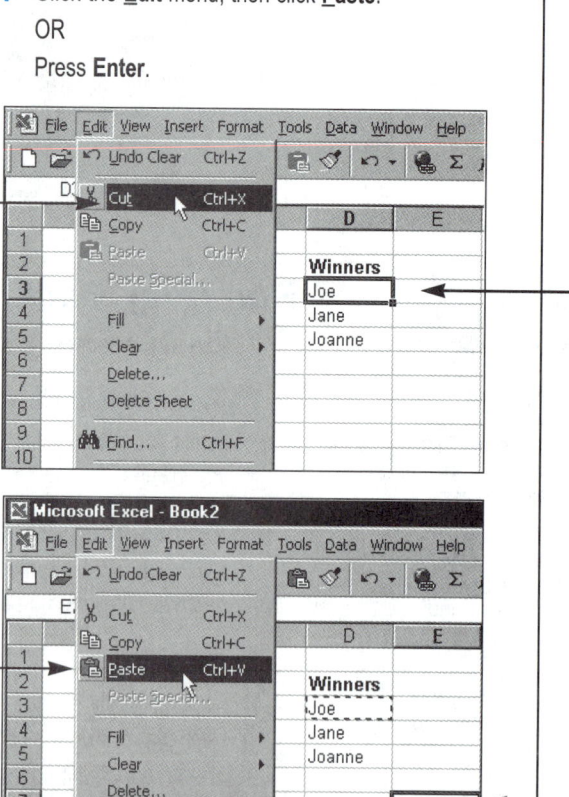

   OR

   Press **Enter**.

Move Using Menu Commands

94

Notes:

- The drag border method is best when the source and destination cells are near each other.

- In **step 3**, "drag" means to press and hold the left mouse button while moving the mouse.

- In **step 3**, to avoid overwriting data in destination cells, press **Ctrl+Shift** while dragging cell border. Existing cells will shift to accommodate new data.

Move Cell Contents by Dragging Cell Border

1 Select cell(s) containing data to move.
2 Point to any border of selected cell(s).

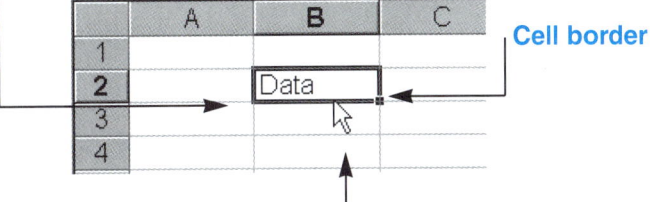

← Cell border

Pointer becomes a solid arrow.

3 Drag border outline to new location.
4 Release mouse button.

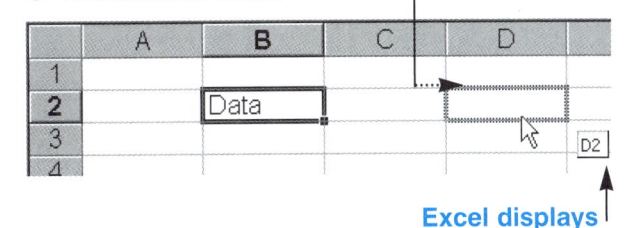

Excel displays reference of destination cell.

Notes:

- You can also use menu commands (**Edit**, **Cut** and **Edit**, **Paste**) to move a cell's content.

- If you make a mistake, you can click the **Edit** menu, then click **Undo**. Excel lets you undo multiple actions, not just the most recent.

Move Part of a Cell's Contents into Another Cell

1 Double-click cell containing data to move.

   A flashing insertion pointer appears.

2 Drag through data to select it. ⟶ Cell entry

3 Press **Ctrl+X** (Cut).

4 Double-click destination cell and click where data will be inserted.

   OR

   Excel highlights data in cell.

5 Select cell to be overwritten by data.
6 Press **Ctrl+V** (Paste).

95

Name Cells

When you name a range of cells, you can use the name (instead of a cell reference) to calculate values in the range. For example, you can create a formula, such as =SUM(Salary), when Salary is a named range of cells containing salary values.

Insert → Name

Notes:

- In **step 2**, when you first click in the Name Box, Excel displays the active cell reference. Type the name over that selection.

Name Cells Using Name Box

1. Select the range to name.
2. Click in the **Name Box** and type a descriptive name.

   NOTE: Named ranges cannot include spaces. They may contain uppercase and lowercase letters, numbers, and most punctuation characters. The underscore character is useful for simulating a space, as in inventory_expenses.

3. Press **Enter**.

Notes:

- You must first convert titles that are numbers into text. Excel converts date values to text automatically. Spaces in titles are replaced with underscore characters in the reference name.
- After creating names, click arrow in Name Box to select/view names.

Name Cells Using Titles

1. Select range containing data and column or row titles.
2. Click the **Insert** menu, then point to **Name**.
3. Click **Create** on the submenu.
4. Select location of titles in the **Create Names** dialog box.
5. Click **OK**.

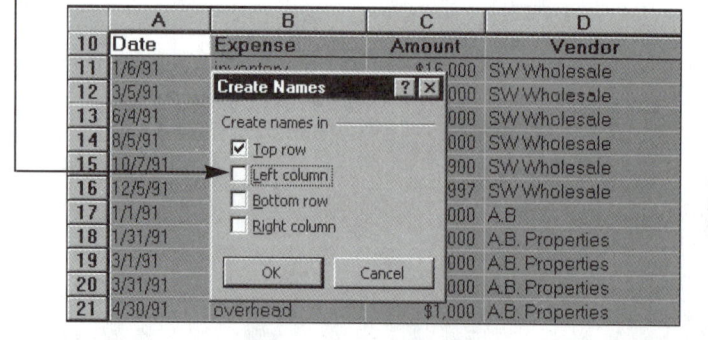

Notes:

- From the **Define Name** dialog box you can also add and delete names, values, and formulas.

- **Add names:**
Type the new name in the **Names in workbook** box; define the range in the **Refers to** box, then click **Add**.

- **Delete names:**
Click the name, then click **Delete**.

  Name formulas or values:
Type the name in the **Names in workbook** box; define the formula or type a value in the **Refers to** box, then click **Add**.

- **Examples:**

  You might name the formula =SUM(C4:C9) as Total_for_Inv. Then you could build another formula in a cell that refers to the result of that calculation by name.

  You might name the value 5280 as Mile. You can then build a formula in a cell that refers to that value, as in =3*Mile.

- In **step 7**, to undo the change, click **Close** instead of **OK**.

Change Name Definition Using Menu

1. Click the **Insert** menu, then point to **Name**.
2. Click **Define** on the submenu.
   The Define Name dialog box appears.
3. Click the name of the reference to change.
4. Click in the **Refers to** box.
   Excel marks range in worksheet with a dashed line.
5. Drag through cells in worksheet to change the reference.
   Excel collapses the dialog box so you can see more of the worksheet.
6. Release the mouse.
   Excel expands dialog box and corrects reference.
7. Click **OK** when done.

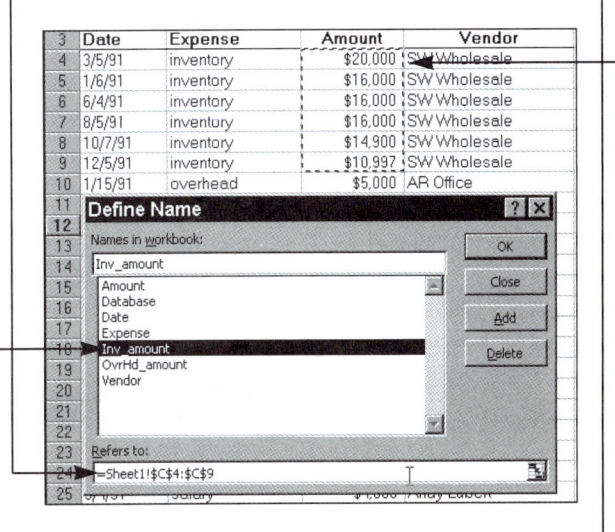

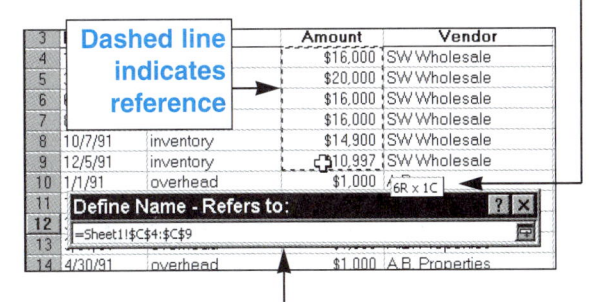

Dashed line indicates reference

Collapsed dialog box

97

Protect Workbooks

The Protect Workbook feature prevents changes to the structure of the workbook, so that its sheets cannot be moved, copied, hidden, renamed, or deleted. You can prevent workbook windows from being moved or sized. You can also set a password when saving a file to restrict the workbook.

Tools → Protection → Protect Workbook...

Notes:

- Before protecting the workbook, check the current workbook structure and/or window arrangement to ensure it is as you want it.
- **Caution:** If you protect the workbook with a password and forget the password, you will not be able to change the workbook structure at a later time.
- The workbook protection password is case sensitive.

Protect Workbook Structure and Windows

1 Click the **Tools** menu, then point to **Protection**.
2 Click **Protect Workbook** on the submenu that appears.
  The Protect Workbook dialog box appears.

To protect the workbook structure:
- Select the **Structure** check box.

To prevent windows from being moved or sized:
- Select the **Windows** check box.

To protect workbook with a password:
- Type password in **Password** box.

3 Click **OK**.

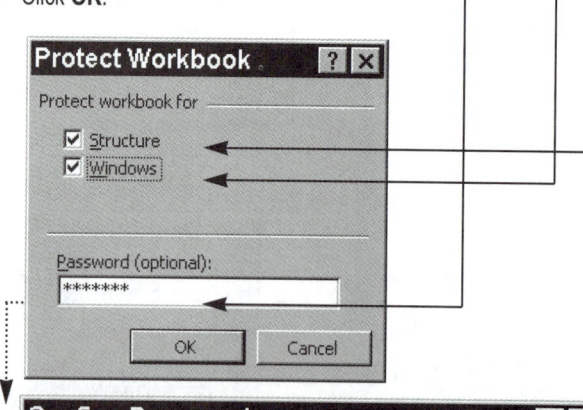

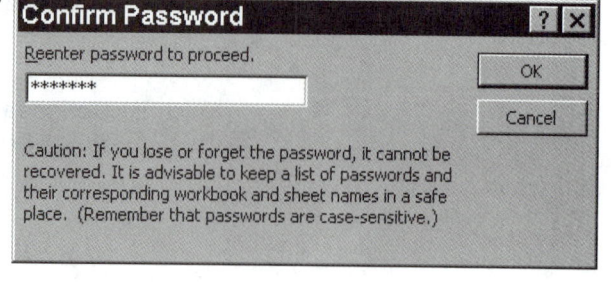

The Confirm Password dialog box appears if you protect the workbook with a password.

Notes:

- To save time, you may not want to assign a password when protecting the workbook until you have finished developing and testing it.

Unprotect a Protected Workbook

1 Click the **Tools** menu, then point to **Protection**.
2 Click **Unprotect Workbook** on the submenu.

If you assigned a password, the Unprotect Workbook dialog box appears:

- Type the password, then click **OK**.

File ➡ Save As... ➡ Tools ▼ ➡ General Options...

Notes:

- Save options:

  Always create backup — creates a backup of the previous version of the workbook each time you save it.

  Password to open — requires a password to open it. If someone supplies the password they can modify and save the changes.

  Password to modify — requires a password to open it. If someone supplies the password the workbook is opened as read-only and changes to the file must be save with a different name.

  Read-only recommended — sets workbook to display a read-only recommendation when opened.

- **Caution:** You can't open the workbook if you lose the password.

Save and Protect Workbook

1 Click the **Save** button on the Standard toolbar.
OR
If you have saved and named the file previously:

- Click the **File** menu, then click **Save As**.

The Save As dialog box appears.

2 Click the **Tools** menu, then click **General Options**.

The Save Options dialog box appears.

3 Select workbook protection options in File Sharing section of dialog box.

4 Click **OK** when done.

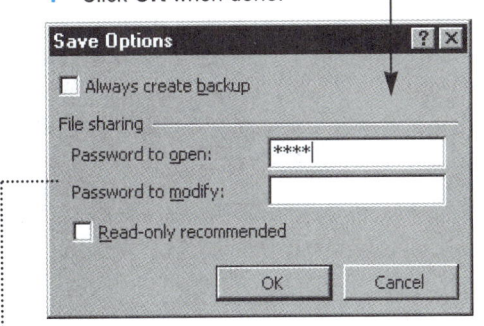

5 Click **Save** in the **Save As** dialog box to save the document with the options you selected.

99

Protect Worksheet Data

The Protect Worksheet feature lets you protect or lock an entire worksheet, individual cells, or a range of cells from accidental or unauthorized use. You can assign a password to a protected worksheet so others cannot unprotect it without supplying the password.

Format → Cells... | Protection

Notes:

- By default, all cells in a worksheet are locked. However, this state is activated only when the worksheet is protected (see below).
- In **step 1**, if the worksheet is protected, first unprotect the worksheet *(next page)*.
- In **step 4**, a grey check in the check box indicates that some of the cells are currently locked, while others are not.

Lock and Unlock Cells in a Worksheet

1. Select cells to unlock or lock.
2. Click the **Format** menu, then click **Cells**.
3. Click the **Protection** tab.
4. Select or deselect **Locked** check box.

   ### To hide formulas for selected cells:
   - Select **Hidden** check box.

   NOTE: Selecting this option prevents Excel from displaying any formulas contained in the selected cells on the formula bar.

5. Click **OK**.
6. To enable your settings, protect the worksheet.

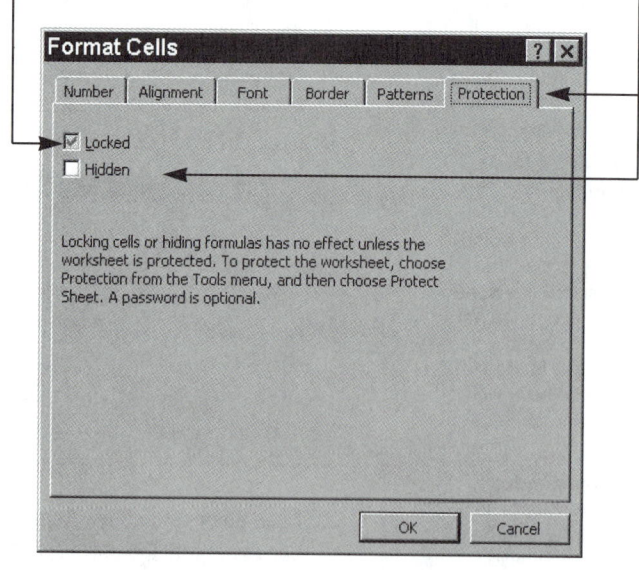

Protection Options for Cells

100

Format → Protection → Protect Sheet...

Notes:

- Before protecting worksheet, be sure to lock or unlock the cells you want to protect. Also, size and position objects if you plan to protect them.
- **Caution:** If you protect a worksheet with a password and lose the password, you will not be able to unprotect it.

Protect a Worksheet

1 Click the **Tools** menu, then point to **Protection**.

2 Click **Protect Sheet** on the submenu.

The Protect Sheet dialog box appears.

3 Click the desired protection options to select or deselect them.

Contents ..... protects data in locked cells.
Objects .... protects pictures, shapes, and charts.
Scenarios ..... protects scenario definitions.

To protect sheet with a password:

a Type password in **Password** box, then click **OK**.

b When prompted, re-enter password, then click **OK**.

4 Click **OK**.

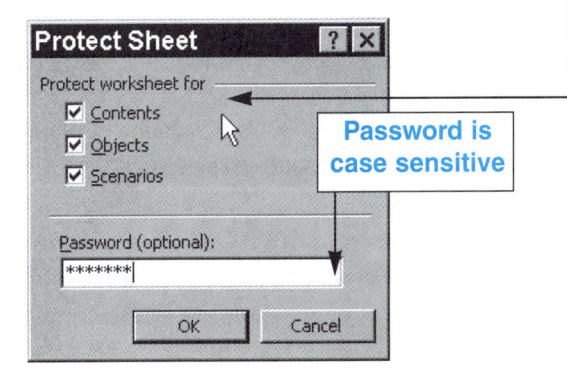

Password is case sensitive

Notes:

- In **step 2**, if you type the password incorrectly, you must redo steps 1 and 2, then retype the password correctly. Remember, passwords are case sensitive.

Unprotect Worksheet

1 Click the **Tools** menu, then point to **Protection**.

2 Click **Unprotect Sheet** on the submenu.

If you assigned a password:

- Type password in **Password** box when prompted.

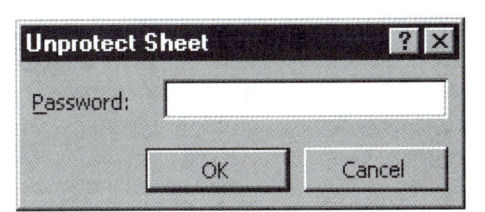

101

Set Calculation Options

The Options dialog box collects related settings in tabs. The Calculation tab lets you set how to perform calculations in your worksheet.

Tools ➡ Options... | Calculation

Notes:

- In **step 2**, you will not have to select **Calculation** tab if it was selected the last time you opened the **Options** dialog box.

Set Calculation Options

1. Click the **Tools** menu, then click **Options**.
   The Options dialog box appears.
2. Click the **Calculation** tab.
3. Select options (described on the next page).
4. Click **OK** when done.

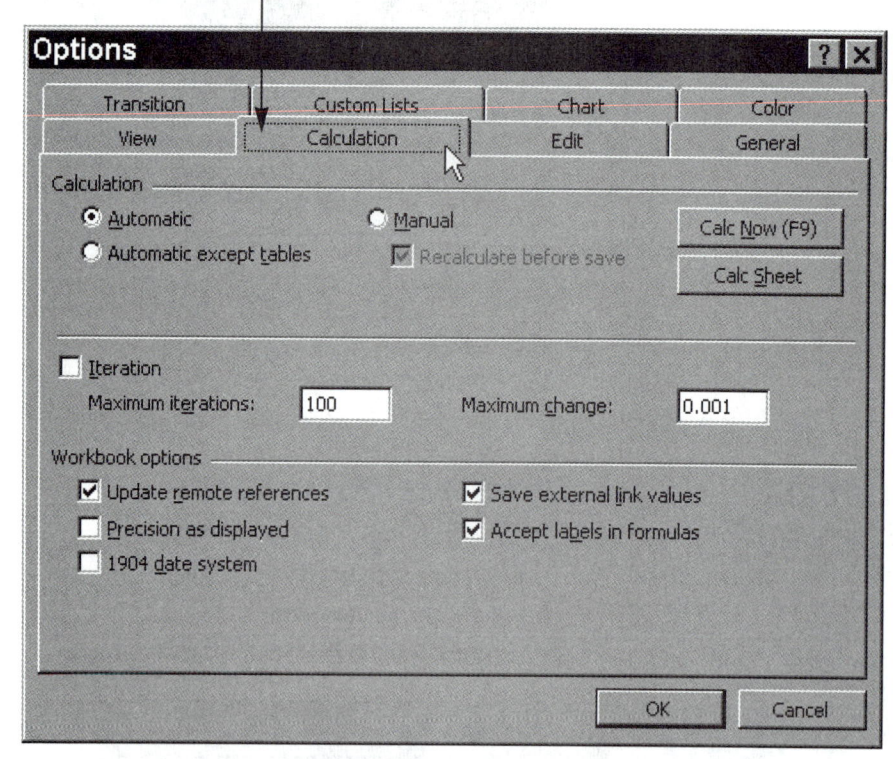

Options Dialog Box with Calculation Tab Selected

Notes:

- The **optimum calculation settings** are best determined by the size and number of calculations performed in your worksheets.
- **Iterations** indicate the number of times Excel will calculate a formula until a specific result or condition is met.
- **Precision** refers to the accuracy of a value as defined by the number of decimal places displayed. For example, .5 and .5002 have two different levels of numeric precision.
- The **Accept la**b**els in formulas** option lets you work more intuitively with values in your worksheet, without specifically naming ranges.

Calculation Options (Grouped)

CALCULATION

Automatic: Automatically calculates formulas when changes are made in worksheet. This is the default calculation setting.

Automatic except **tables:** Automatically calculates formulas, but not data tables, when changes are made in worksheet. When this setting is enabled, you will have to click **Calc **N**ow** or press **F9** to calculate formulas in data tables.

Manual: Turns off automatic calculations. When this setting is enabled, you will have to click **Calc **N**ow** or press **F9** to calculate formulas in your worksheets. Excel automatically selects **Recalc**u**late before save** when you select **Manual**.

Recalcu**late before save:** If **Manual** is selected, deselect this option to prevent calculations before saving the workbook.

Calc **Now (F9):** Calculates all open workbooks and the data tables and charts they contain.

Calc **Sheet:** Calculates only the active worksheet and the data tables and charts linked to it.

ITERATION

Iteration: Limits the number of iterations Excel performs when goal seeking or resolving circular references (formulas that contain references to their own results).

Maximum ite**rations:** Choose the maximum number of iterations to perform before the iteration stops.

Maximum **change**: Choose the maximum change that can result from the iteration before the iteration stops.

WORKBOOK OPTIONS

Update **remote references**: Automatically calculates formulas containing references to other workbooks or applications.

Precision as displayed: Changes the precision stored values in cells to number format displayed in cells.

1904 **date system:** Changes the January 1, 1900 starting date, from which all dates are calculated, to January 2, 1904 (Macintosh date system).

Save external **link values:** Automatically saves copies of values from external documents to which the workbook is linked. Clear this setting to reduce the time it takes to load workbooks containing links to other workbooks.

Accept lab**els in formulas:** Enables use of label names in formulas for titled ranges of values.

103

Set Edit Options

The Options dialog box collects related settings in tabs. The Edit tab lets you establish the editing environment, such as allowing direct editing in cells, and applies the settings to all worksheets in the workbook.

Tools → Options... → Edit

Notes:

- In **step 2**, you will not have to select **Edit** tab if it was selected the last time you opened the **Options** dialog box.

Set Edit Options

1. Click the **Tools** menu, then click **Options**.
   The Options dialog box appears.
2. Click the **Edit** tab.
3. Select options described on the next page.
4. Click **OK** when done.

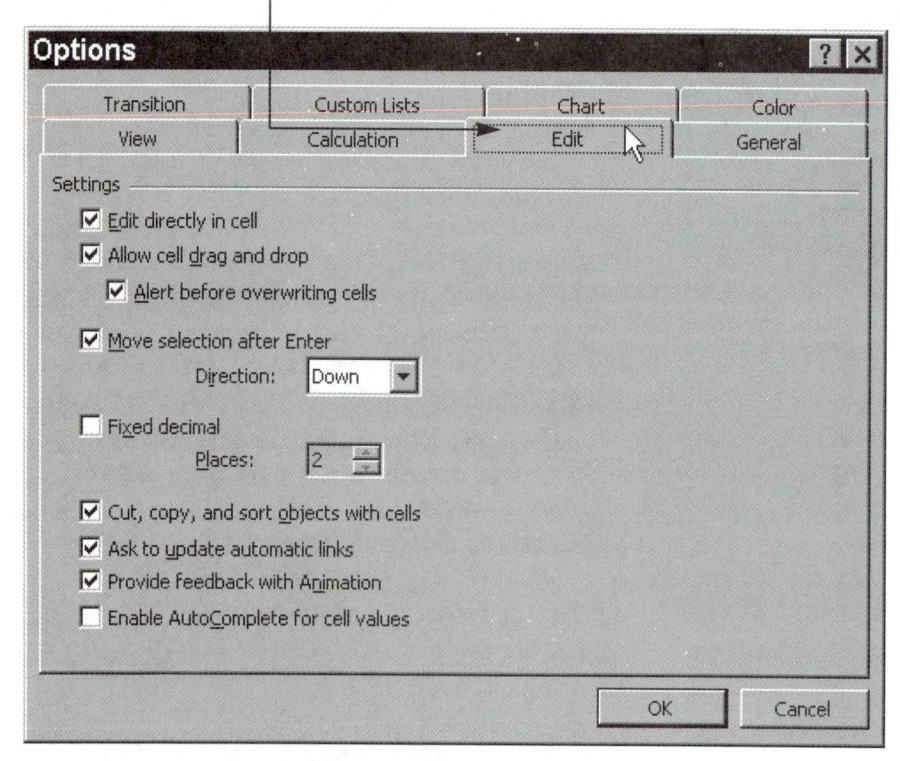

Options Dialog Box with Edit Tab Selected

104

Notes:

- The default Edit options will work well in most instances. If your system does not have a lot of memory and is slow, however, consider disabling the **Provide feedback with A**n**imation** option to improve performance.

- The **Fi**x**ed decimal Places** option can save you a great deal of time. For example, if you need to enter many decimal values like .05, .55, 3.12, select **Fixed decimal** and set **P**laces to 2. Then, in your worksheet, you need only type 05, 55, 312, and Excel will change the values you typed by moving the decimal left two places when you press **Enter**.

Edit Options (Alphabetical)

Allow cell d**rag and drop:** Allows you to move and copy cell contents by dragging the cell border. This option also allows you to copy data into adjacent cells, or to create a series by dragging a cell's fill handle.

Alert **before overwriting cells:** Alerts you that existing data will be replaced when you are using drag-and-drop editing.

Ask to u**pdate automatic links:** Displays a confirmation message before updating linked items.

Cut, copy, and sort o**bjects with cells:** Keeps objects with cells in which they were inserted when you cut, copy, filter, or sort cells.

Edit **directly in cell:** Lets you edit cell entries in the cells by double-clicking them. If deselected, you must work with the entries in the formula bar.

Enable AutoComplete **for cell values:** Enables the AutoComplete feature to complete your entries based on existing entries in a column.

Fix**ed decimal:** Moves the decimal place to the left or right automatically. This setting changes the values you enter in cells. To override this setting, type the decimal point when you enter a number.

Places: Choose the number of places to move the decimal point in your entries. Positive numbers decrease the value you type, moving the decimal two places to the left.

Move **selection after Enter:** Select the direction of the next active cell after you complete an entry.

Di**rection:** Select the direction in which Excel will move to activate the next cell after each entry is completed.

Provide feedback with An**imation:** Animates worksheet changes, such as inserted cells or columns.

105

Set General Options

The Options dialog box collects related settings in tabs. The General tab lets you set a variety of working defaults, such as the number of recently used files to display on the File menu. New to this version of Excel is the Web Options dialog box that contains settings for publishing Excel documents on the Internet.

Tools → Options... → General

Notes:

- In **step 2**, you will not have to select **General** tab if it was selected the last time you opened the **Options** dialog box.

Set General Options

1. Click the **Tools** menu, then click **Options**.
   The Options dialog box appears.
2. Click the **General** tab.
3. Select options (described on the next page).
4. Click **OK** when done.

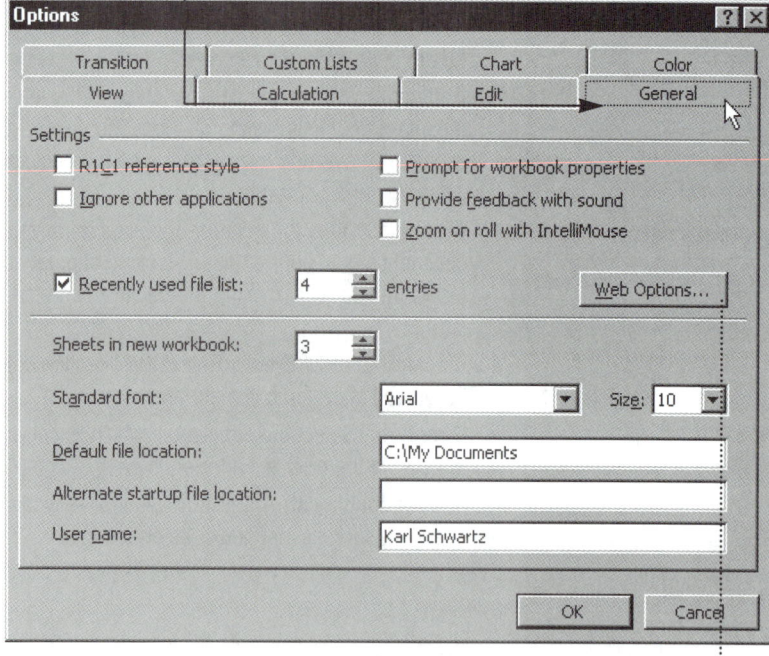

Options Dialog Box with General Tab Selected

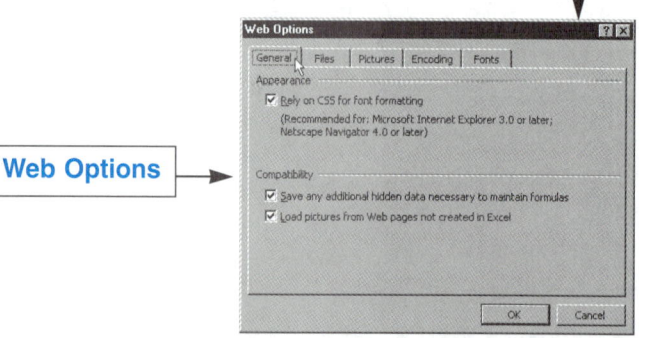

Web Options

Notes:

- The default General options will work well in most instances. If you find that you are consistently adding worksheets, consider changing the **Sheets in new workbook** option.

- Change the **Default file location** if you consistently need to change the current folder when opening or saving files.

General Options (Alphabetical)

Alternate startup file location: Type directory path to indicate location of workbooks or other files you want to open automatically when you first run Excel. Files in this folder will open in addition to files stored in the XLstart folder, a folder created when Excel is installed.

Default file location: Type directory path to indicate the default location of files you save or open. You must restart Excel for this change to take effect.

Ignore other applications: Prevents the exchange of data with other applications using the DDE protocol.

Prompt for workbook properties: Sets Excel to prompt for workbook properties (such as title, keywords, author) each time you save a new workbook file.

Provide feedback with sound: Plays sounds associated with Office 97 events.

R1C1: Changes reference style of row and column headings from letter-numbers to number-numbers, and designates references in formulas as relative to the current cell position.

Recently used file list: Lists recently used files at the bottom of the File menu. You can select from the list to open a file quickly.

entries — select number of recently opened files to list.

Sheets in new workbook: Type number of blank worksheets to include in new workbooks.

Standard font: Select desired default font to use for new worksheets. You must restart Excel for this change to take effect.

Size: Select size of default font.

User name: Type your name here. Excel uses this information to address a comment and identify the user of a shared workbook.

Web Options: Specify Web publishing options such as appearance and compatibility settings, file names and locations, default editor of Web pages created with Office, Office controls, file formats, target monitor, pixels per inch, encoding settings, and default fonts.

Zoom on roll with IntelliMouse: Enables use of Microsoft's IntelliMouse.

107

Set View Options

The Options dialog box collects related settings in tabs. The View tab lets you set a variety of working defaults, such as whether or not to show gridlines, row and column headings, and zero values.

Tools → Options... | View

Notes:

- In **step 2**, you will not have to click the **View** tab if it was selected the last time you opened the **Options** dialog box.

Set View Options

1 Click the **Tools** menu, then click **Options**.

 The Options dialog box appears.

2 Click the **View** tab.

3 Select options described on the next page.

4 Click **OK** when done.

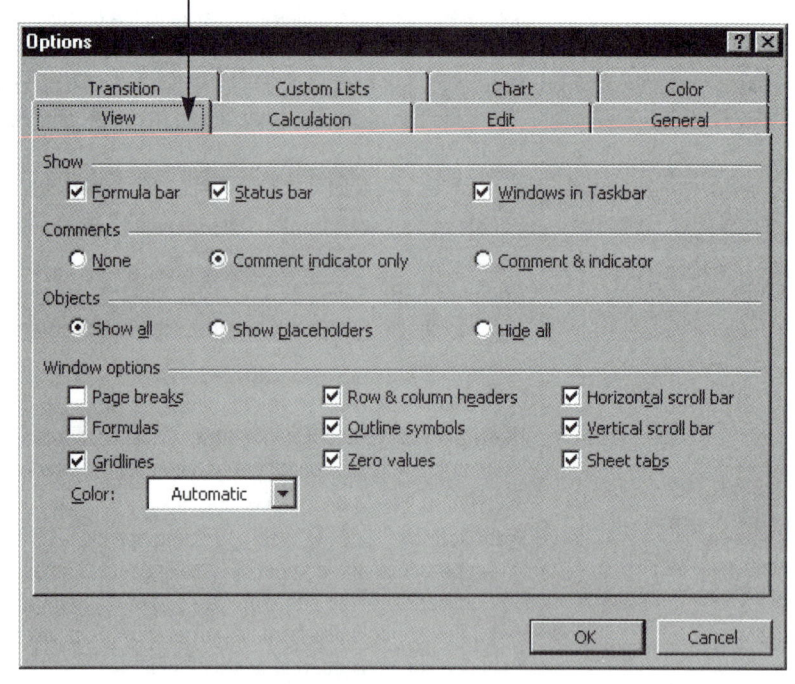

Options Dialog Box with View Tab Selected

Notes:

- The **Hi_d_e all** option will hide comments even if you have enabled the **Co_m_ment & Indicator** option.

- You can deselect **_Z_ero value** to hide the results of formulas that result in zero.

View Options (Grouped)

_F_ormula bar: Displays Formula bar at the top of the worksheet.

_S_tatus bar: Displays Status bar at the bottom of the Excel window.

_W_indows in Taskbar: Displays an icon on the taskbar for each open workbook or window.

_N_one: Hides comments and comment indicators in cells containing comments.

Comment _i_ndicator only: Shows only the comment indicator in cells containing comments. The comment itself will appear only when you rest the pointer on the indicator.

Co_m_ment & indicator: Shows both the comment and comment indicator in cells containing comments.

Show _a_ll: Shows all graphic objects and embedded charts in worksheet.

Show _p_laceholders: Shows only placeholders for graphic objects and embedded charts in worksheet.

Hi_d_e all: Hides all graphic objects and embedded charts in worksheet.

Page brea_k_s: Displays automatic page breaks.

Fo_r_mulas: Displays formulas in cells, instead of formula results.

_G_ridlines: Displays cell gridlines. This setting does not affect print gridlines, which are set in the Sheet tab of the Page Setup dialog box.

_C_olor: Select a color for worksheet gridlines.

Row & column h_e_aders: Shows row and column headings.

_O_utline symbols: Shows outline symbols when outline mode is on.

_Z_ero values: Shows zeros when cells contain them.

Horizon_t_al scroll bar: Shows Horizontal scroll bar.

_V_ertical scroll bar: Shows Vertical scroll bar.

Sheet ta_b_s: Shows sheet tabs so that you can select worksheets with the mouse.

109

Sheet Tabs

Sheet tabs let you work with multiple worksheets within a single workbook file. You can select, group, insert, rename, delete, move, and copy sheet tabs. Also see *Navigate Worksheets* for information about scrolling and selecting sheet tabs.

Notes:

- In **step 2**, you can also press **Shift** and click to select consecutive sheets.

  Grouped sheets appear highlighted (white), while ungrouped sheets appear grey. When sheets are grouped, "[Group]" appears after the workbook name on the title bar.

- You can also ungroup sheets by clicking any sheet tab that is not currently grouped.

Group and Ungroup Sheet Tabs

When you group sheets, data and formatting changes made to the active sheet are repeated in the grouped sheets.

1. Click first sheet tab in group.
2. Press **Ctrl** and click each sheet tab to add to group.

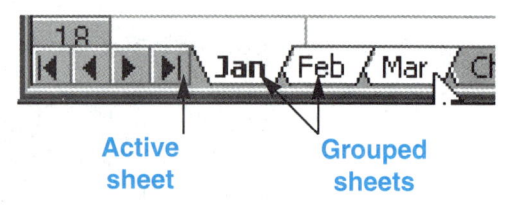

   Active sheet **Grouped sheets**

3. Click any grouped sheet tab to make it active.

   ### To ungroup sheet tabs:
   - Right-click any grouped sheet tab, then click **Ungroup Sheets** on the shortcut menu.

Notes:

- **Caution:** Be careful when deleting worksheets, because you cannot undo this action.

Delete Sheet Tabs

1. Right-click sheet tab to delete, then click **Delete** on the shortcut menu.
2. Click **OK** to confirm the action.

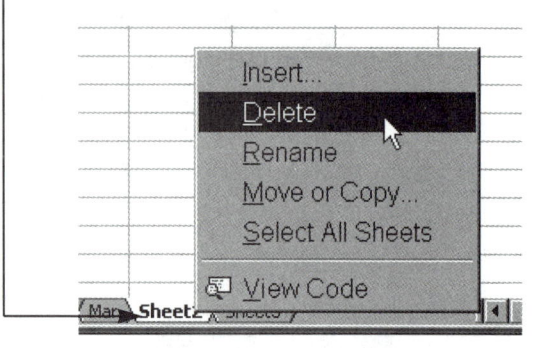

110

Notes:
- In **step 1**, you can insert multiple worksheets by first selecting (grouping) the number of sheets you want to insert, then right-clicking on that group.
- In **step 2**, you can also insert special items, such as chart and macro sheets.
- From the **Spreadsheet Solutions** tab, you can select a custom template to insert.

Insert a New Sheet

1. Right-click any sheet tab, then click **Insert** on the shortcut menu.
   The Insert dialog box appears.
2. Click **Worksheet** icon, then click **OK**.
3. Move and rename sheet tab as desired.

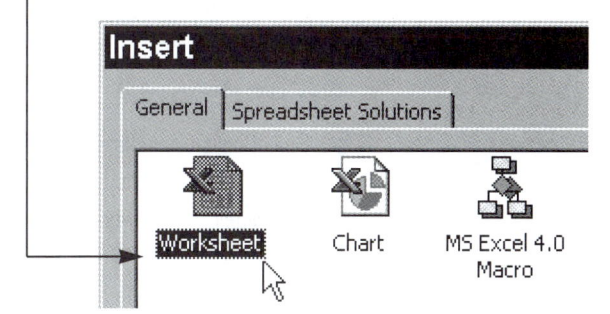

Notes:
- In **step 1**, you can also right-click the tab to rename, then click **Rename** from the shortcut menu.
- Worksheet names may contain spaces and punctuation.

Rename a Sheet

1. Double-click sheet tab to rename.
   Excel highlights the sheet tab name.
2. Type new name, then click anywhere in worksheet.

Notes:
- When you copy a sheet, Excel renames the new sheet by adding a number to it. For example, a copy of **Sheet1** may be named **Sheet1 (2)**. You can, of course, rename the sheet.

Move and Copy Sheets

1. Select sheet(s) to move or copy.
   Excel highlights sheet tab names.
2. To move sheets, drag selection to desired location.

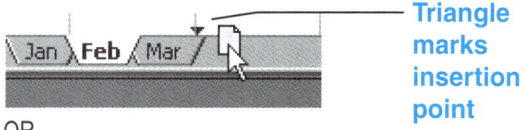

   Triangle marks insertion point

   OR

   To copy sheets, press **Ctrl** and drag selection to desired location.

   Plus sign indicates copy

111

Spell Check

The Spell Check feature helps you find and correct misspelled words in your worksheets and charts. If words you use often are not in Excel's main dictionary, you can add them during the Spell Check operation. See *AutoCorrect* for information about correcting spelling errors as you type.

Tools → Spelling...

Notes:

- In **step 1**, if you are checking a worksheet, select cell A1 to check the entire worksheet.
  You can select multiple sheet tabs (see Sheet Tabs) to spell check multiple sheets.
- The **Ignore All** command tells Excel to ignore all matching words.
- The **Change All** command tells Excel to change all matching words to the word in the **Change to** box.
- Once you add a word to the custom dictionary, Excel uses both the main and custom dictionaries to spell check words.

Spell Check

1 Select cells or worksheets to spell check.

2 Click the **Tools** menu, then click **Spelling**.

   The Spelling dialog box appears when the first word not listed in Excel's main dictionary is found.

   The **Suggestions** box lists suggested replacements, and the first suggestion is placed in the **Change to** box.

   ### To leave word unchanged:
   - Click **Ignore** or click **Ignore All**.

   ### To change the word:
   - If necessary, click desired word in **Suggestions** list.
   - Click **Change** or **Change All**.

   ### To leave word unchanged, and add it to custom dictionary:
   - Click **Add**.

   ### To leave word unchanged and add it to the AutoCorrect list:
   - Click **AutoCorrect**.

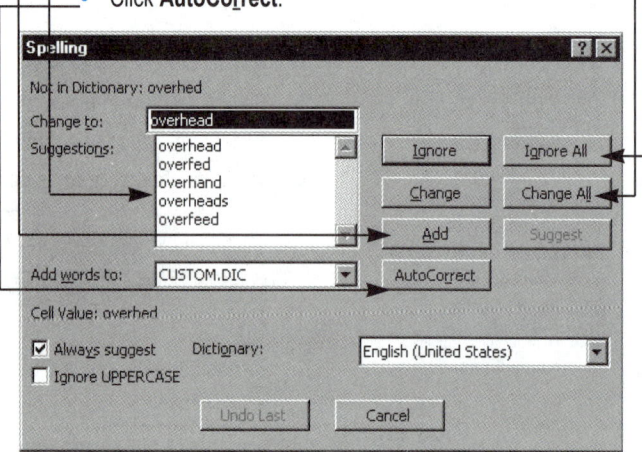

3 Click **OK** when notified that Spell Check is complete.

Notes:

- Sometimes when Excel finds a misspelled word, you will realize that a completely different word would be more appropriate. Type the word you want in the **Change to** box.

Look Up Words While Spell Checking

1. Select cells or worksheets to spell check.
2. Click the **Tools** menu, then click **Spelling**.

   The Spelling dialog box appears when the first word not listed in Excel's main dictionary is found.

   The **Suggestions** box lists suggested replacements, and the first suggestion is placed in the **Change to** box.

3. Type word to lookup in **Change to** box.
4. Click **Suggest**.

   *Excel displays possible spellings for typed word in **Suggestions** list.*

Type word, then click **Suggest**

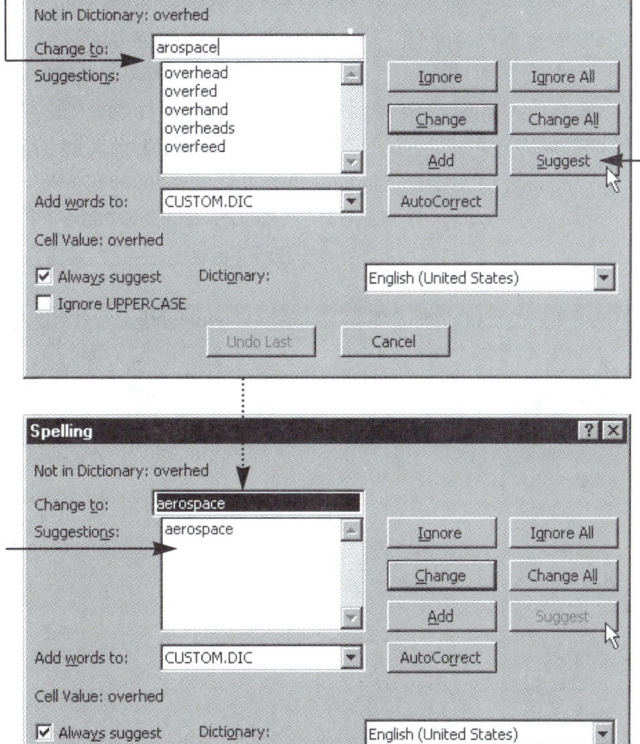

Excel displays suggestions here

TIP: You can type any replacement text you want in the **Change to** box and click **Change**.

113

Templates

Each time you create or insert a new workbook, you are opening a plain template. You can create custom templates for special purposes — templates containing special headings, formatting, and page setups — so that you do not have to recreate from scratch work that you repeat often.

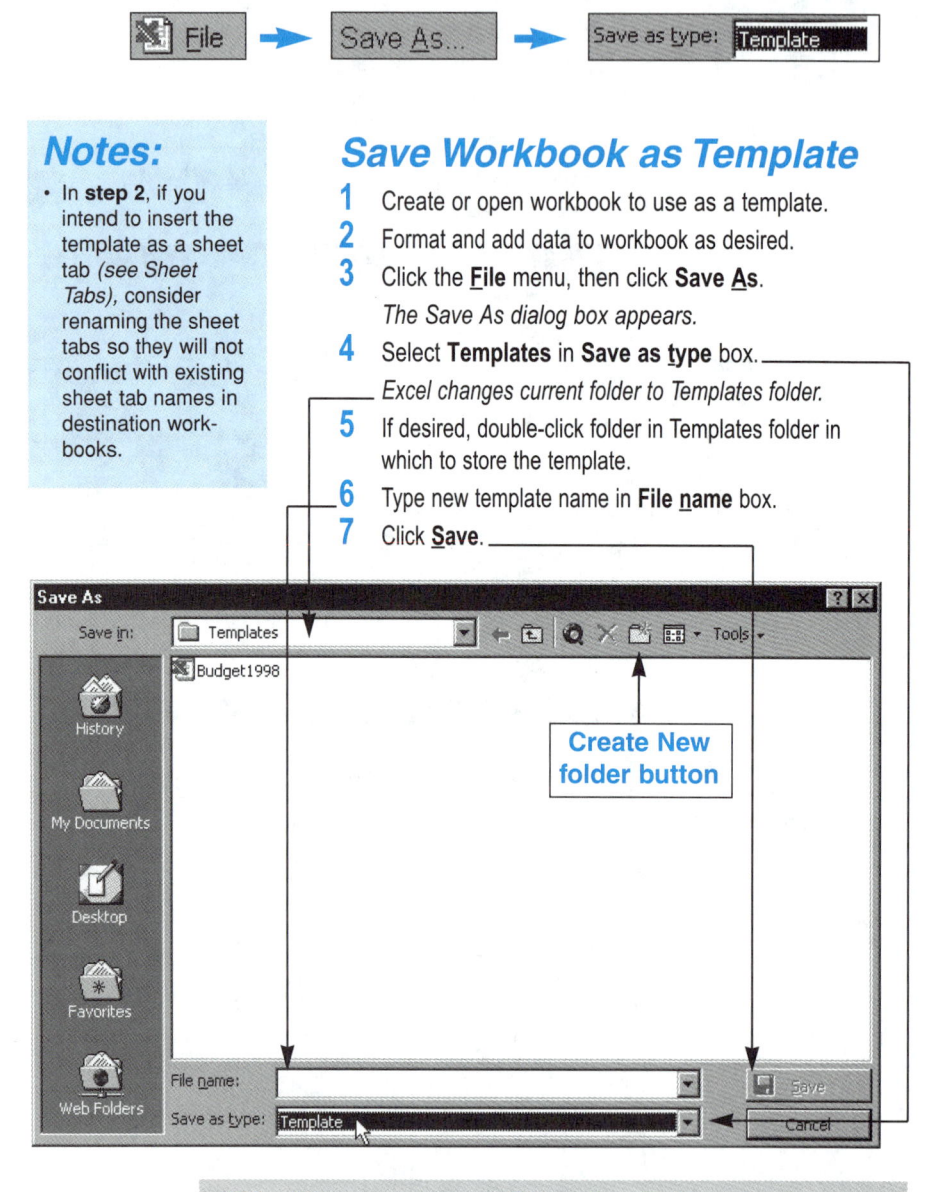

File → **Save As...** → **Save as type: Template**

Notes:

- In **step 2**, if you intend to insert the template as a sheet tab *(see Sheet Tabs)*, consider renaming the sheet tabs so they will not conflict with existing sheet tab names in destination workbooks.

Save Workbook as Template

1 Create or open workbook to use as a template.
2 Format and add data to workbook as desired.
3 Click the **File** menu, then click **Save As**.
   The Save As dialog box appears.
4 Select **Templates** in **Save as type** box.
   Excel changes current folder to Templates folder.
5 If desired, double-click folder in Templates folder in which to store the template.
6 Type new template name in **File name** box.
7 Click **Save**.

Create New folder button

TIP: You can create a folder by clicking the Create New Folder button on the Save As toolbar. The new folder name will appear as a tab in the New dialog box when you create a new file.

Notes:

- By default, Excel stores templates in the **Windows\ Application Data\ Microsoft\ Templates** folder. This folder can be hard to find. Consider adding it to your list of favorites by clicking the **Add to Favorites** button on the **Open** dialog box toolbar.

Edit Template File

1. Click the **File** menu, then click **Open**.
2. Select **Templates (*.xlt)** in **Files of type** box.
3. Open folder containing the template.
4. Click the file, then click **Open**.
5. Make changes as desired, then save the template.

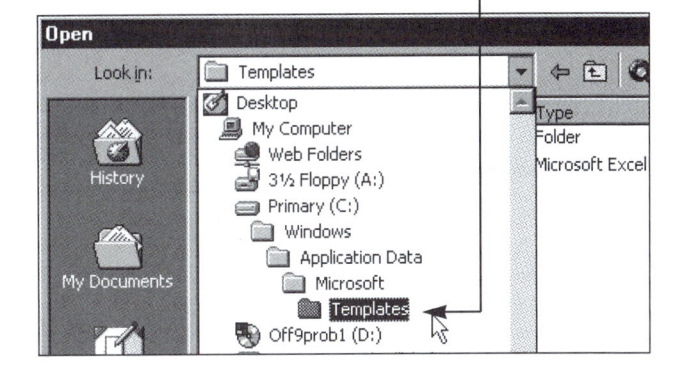

Notes:

- The **New** dialog box also appears when you insert a worksheet tab *(see Sheet Tabs)*.

Create New File Based on Custom Template

1. Click **File** menu, then click **New**.

   The New dialog box appears.

2. If you created a folder for the template, click the tab for the folder name.
3. Select the template name, then click **OK**.

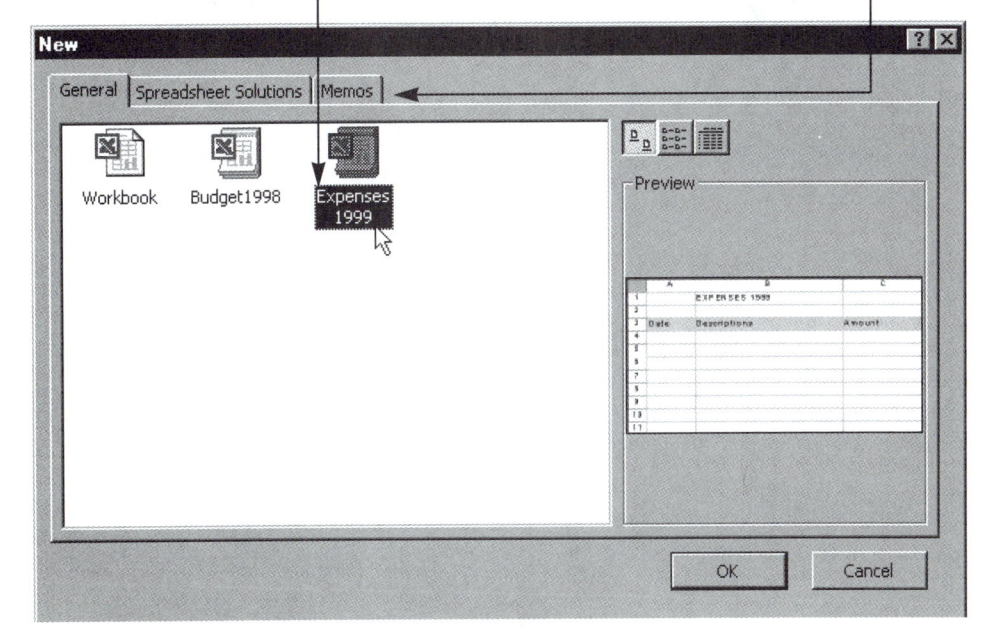

115

Workbook Properties

Workbook file properties can help you identify and find a file. These properties include statistics on the file size and when it was created and changed last. In addition, you can fill in standard fields, such as S‾ubject and A‾uthor. For help with future searches for the file, you can select the "Sa‾ve preview picture" option.

File ➜ Properties

Notes:

- To open the **Properties** dialog box when you save a workbook for the first time, click **Tools** menu, then click **Options**. From the General tab, select **Prompt for workbook properties**.

- You can use information listed in the **Properties** dialog box to help locate workbooks from the **Open** dialog box: Click **Tools** menu, then click **Find**. From the **Find** dialog box, select desired file property from the **Property** list box (such as Comment or Subject), select a value, and add it to the list of criteria.

Set Workbook File Properties

1 Click the **File** menu, then click **Properties**.

   The Properties dialog box appears.

2 On the **Summary** tab, type information you want saved with the file in the field boxes provided.

   ### To save preview of workbook:
   - Select **Sa‾ve preview picture**.

3 Click the following tabs to display file information:

   General file type, location, size, attributes, dates.
   Statistics file modification information, including user names.
   Contents worksheet names.

4 To set custom properties, see next page.
5 Click **OK** when done.

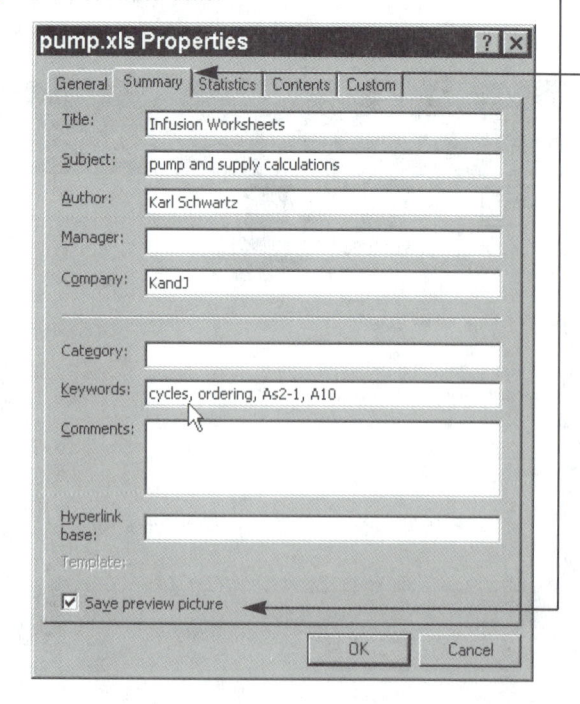

116

Notes:

- In **step 1**, to name a selected cell, click in the **Name Box** and enter a descriptive name *(see Name Cells)*.

- A linked property will change to show the value in the named cell when it was last saved. You can review this value without opening the file from the **Open** dialog box.

Create a Custom Property Linked to Data in Workbook

1 Name the cells in the worksheet to which you want to create a link.

2 Click **File** menu, then click **Properties**.
  The Properties dialog box appears.

3 Click the **Custom** tab.

4 Type property name in **Name** box or select ready-made names from list.

5 Select type of property in **Type** list.

6 Select **Link to content**.

7 Select named range in **Source** box, then click **Add**.
  Excel adds custom property to Properties list.

8 Click **OK** when done.

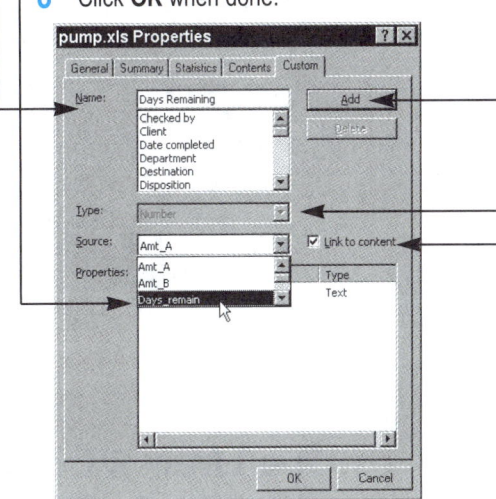

Notes:

- From the **Open** dialog box, click the View button, then select **Preview** to show the preview of the selected file. You must have previously selected the **Save preview picture** property for the file.

View Properties from the Open Dialog Box

1 Open a new file *(see Open Workbooks)*.

2 Click **Tools** button on Open toolbar.

3 Click **Properties** on menu.
  The Properties dialog box appears.

4 Click desired tab in **Properties** dialog box.

5 Click **OK** when done.

117

Workbook Window Commands

You can open several workbooks simultaneously. You can view all open workbooks at one time, or you can hide one or more workbooks, while still keeping their information accessible to formulas.

Window → **Arrange...** , **New Window** , **Hide** / **Unhide**

Notes:
- A check mark appears next to the currently selected workbook window as shown.
- Hidden workbooks do not appear on the Window menu.

Select a Workbook Window

- Click the **Window** menu, then click name of workbook.
  Excel brings selected workbook to the front.

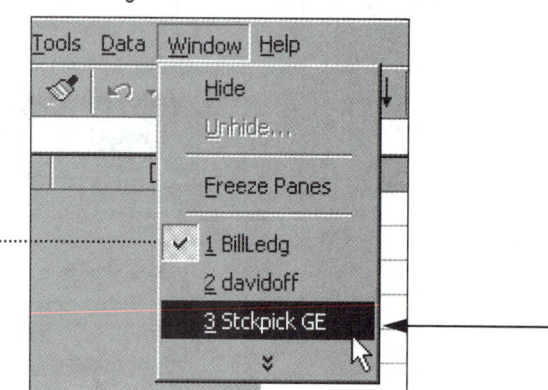

Notes:
- You may have to click the button at the bottom of the menu to view the **New Window** command. 
- The **New Window** command lets you maintain different views for a single workbook. You can use this feature to view two worksheets in the same workbook side-by-side.

Open New Window for Current Workbook

- Click **Window** menu, then click **New Window**.
  Excel brings the selected workbook to the front and adds a number to the end of its name in the title bar.

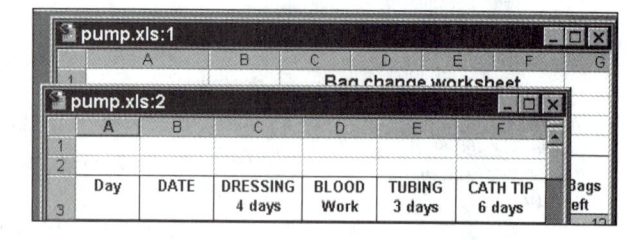

118

Notes:

- In **step 1**, you may have to click the button at the bottom of the menu to view the **Arrange** command.

- **Arrange** options:

  Tiled — arrange windows in side-by-side grid order.

  Horizontal and **Vertical** — arrange windows one below or to the right of the other.

  Cascade — arrange windows in an overlapping order.

  Window of active Workbook — arrange duplicate windows only (created with **New Window** command).

Arrange Workbook Windows

1 Click the **Window** menu, then click **Arrange**.
2 Select desired option on **Arrange Windows** dialog box.
3 Click **OK**.

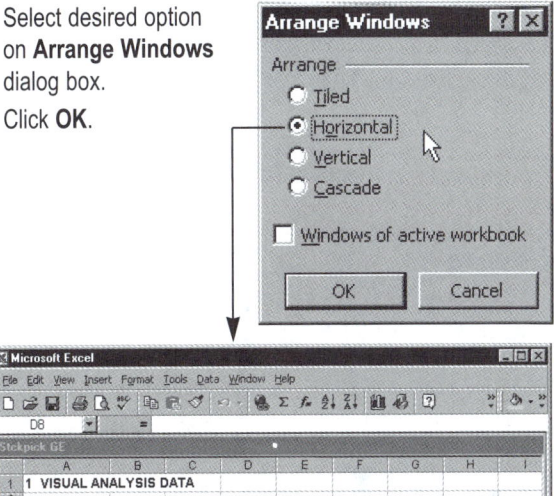

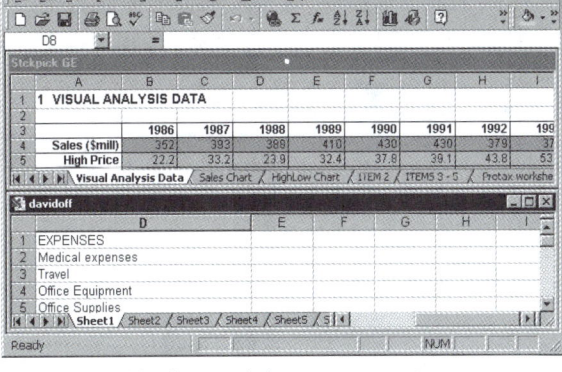

Horizontal Arrangement

Notes:

- In **step 1**, you may have to click the button at the bottom of the menu to view the **Hide** or **Unhide** command.

- A hidden workbook is still open. Formulas with references to the hidden workbook will work as before.

- By default, the Personal Macro workbook is hidden.

Hide Workbook Windows

1 Select workbook window to hide.
2 Click the **Window** menu, then click **Hide**.
   The workbook window disappears from view.

Unhide Workbook Window

1 Click the **Window** menu, then click **Unhide**.
   The Unhide dialog box appears.
2 Select workbook to unhide, then click **OK**.

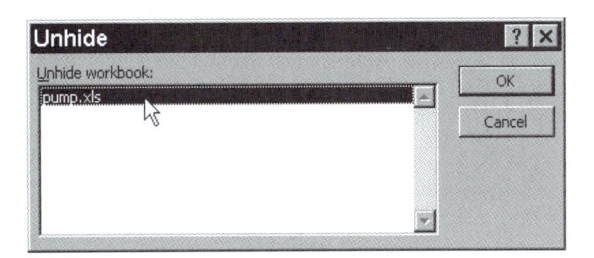

Worksheet Window Commands

To view and work with different parts of a large worksheet simultaneously, use the Split command to create separate panes. To keep headings or titles in view as you scroll down or across a worksheet, use the Freeze Panes command.

Window → Split / Freeze Panes

Notes:

- In **step 1**, the split occurs above and to the left of the selected cell.
- In **step 2**, you may have to click the button at the bottom of the menu to view the **Split** command.

- To split worksheet horizontally, select a cell in column A other than the first cell.

  When you split a window horizontally, the panes scroll together when you scroll left and right, but move independently when you scroll up and down.
- To split worksheet vertically, select a cell in row 1 other than the first cell.

  When you split a window vertically, the panes scroll together when you scroll up or down, but move independently when you scroll left and right.

Split Worksheet Window Into Panes

1 Select cell to indicate where row and column will be split.

2 Click the **Window** menu, then click **Split**.

Excel divides worksheet into two or four panes. Each pane includes a scroll bar.

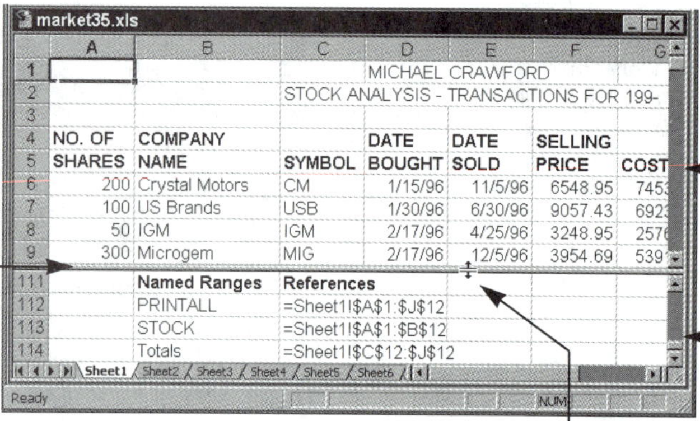

Adjust or Remove Panes

1 Point to split bar.

Pointer becomes a .

2 Drag split bar to move it.

To remove the split bar:

- Drag spilt bar onto row or column headings.

  OR

  Click the **Window** menu, then click **Remove Split**.

Notes:

- In **step 1**, the split will occur above and to the left of the selected cell.

- When you freeze panes, you cannot change their location by dragging a split bar. Unfreeze the panes, then reset them by either dragging a split bar, or selecting a new starting cell.

Freeze Panes

Locks top and/or upper-left pane(s) at selected location. Also locks panes created by split procedure (see previous page).

1 Select cell to indicate where split will be.

   NOTE: Skip step 1, if you have already split the window into panes.

2 Click the **Window** menu, then click **Freeze Panes**.

   Excel divides worksheet into two or four panes. The top and/or left panes are frozen and will remain visible (frozen) when you scroll down or left.

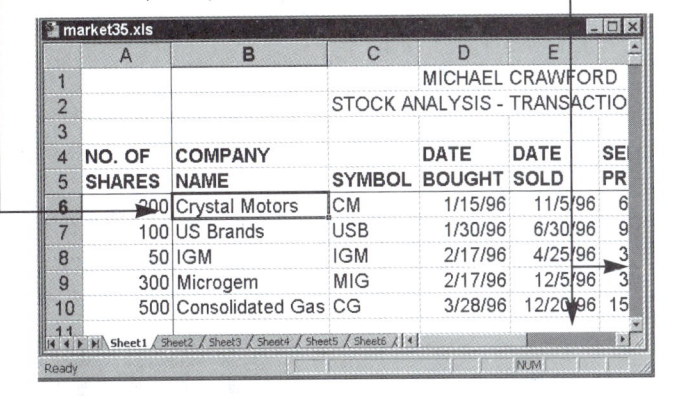

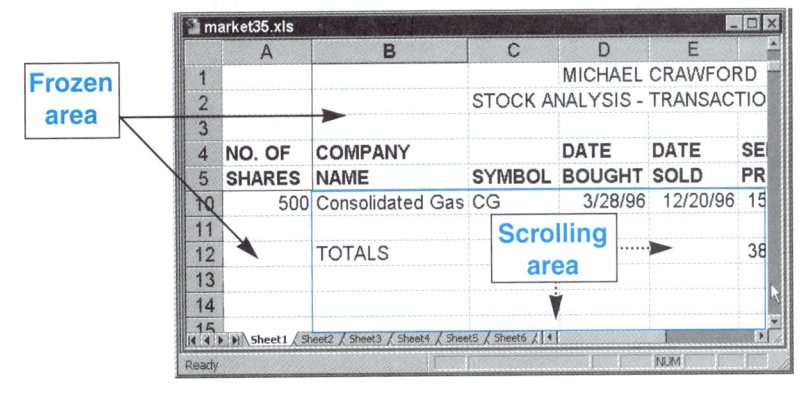

Notes:

- Unfreezing panes returns your worksheet to normal scrolling. It does not remove split bars.

Unfreeze Panes

- Click the **Window** menu, then click **Unfreeze Panes**.

121

Undo and Repeat Actions

Excel lets you undo not only your last action but a series of actions. Excel also lets you repeat actions you have undone.

Edit → Undo / Repeat

Notes:

- In **step 2**, you may have to click the button at the bottom of the menu to view the **Repeat** command.

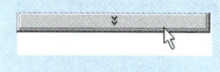

- Keyboard shortcuts:

    Press **Ctrl+Z** to undo your last action.

    Press **Ctrl+Y** to repeat your last action.

- Excel records a history of actions and repeated actions for all open workbooks.

Undo or Repeat Last Action Using Menu

1 Click the **Edit** menu.

   The edit menu displays possible undo and repeat actions.

2 Click **Undo** *action* to undo the last action.

   OR

   Click **Repeat** *action* to repeat the last action.

   NOTE: Repeat actions do not have to be carried out on the same cell or object.

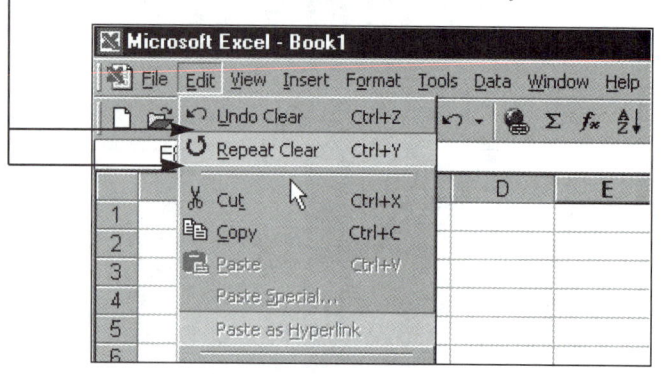

Undo and Redo Commands on Edit Menu

Tip: To undo a cell entry before completing it, press Esc. If you have already completed the entry, press Ctrl+Z (Undo).

122

Notes:

- In **step 1**, if you click the **Undo** button, and not the arrow, Excel will undo the last action.

- In **step 2**, Excel highlights actions as you point to them. You can only select actions from the top of the list, down.

Undo Last Actions Using Toolbar

1 Click arrow on **Undo** button on Standard toolbar.

Excel opens a drop-down list of past actions.

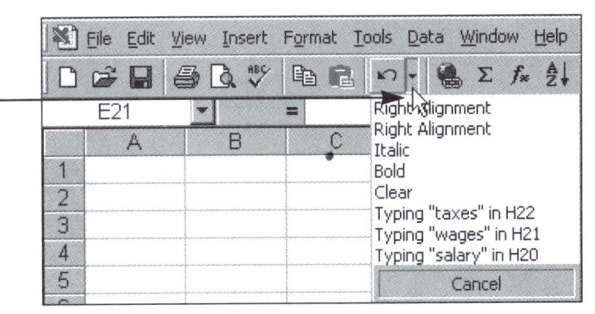

2 Click first action on list.

OR

Move pointer through series of actions to undo, then click.

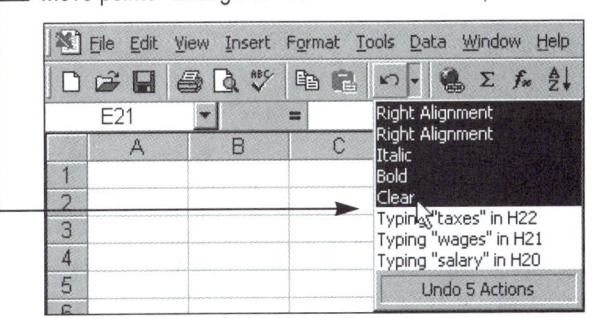

Notes:

- To redo a series of actions using a keystroke, press **Ctrl+Y** repeatedly.

- In **step 1**, if the Redo button is not visible, click the More Buttons arrow on the right side of the toolbar to view additional buttons.

Redo Last Actions Using Toolbar

1 Click arrow on **Redo** button on Standard toolbar.

Excel opens a drop-down list of undone actions.

2 Click first action on list.

OR

Move pointer through series of actions to redo, then click.

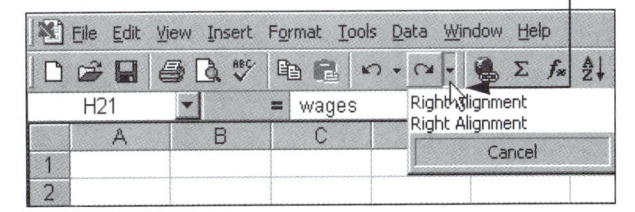

123

Validate Cell Entries

Use the Validation feature to ensure that only correct data is entered in a worksheet. For example, you can restrict the entry in a cell to a whole number and provide prompts for the user. When an incorrect entry is made, you can display an error message.

Data → Validation...

Notes:

- In **step 1**, select multiple cells only if the restriction will apply equally to all the cells.

- In **step 5**, comparison operators include: *between, not between, equal to, not equal to, greater than, less than, greater than or equal to, less than or equal to.*

- Select **Ignore blank** so referenced cells (step 6) can be blank.

- In **step 4**, data validation options in the **Allow** box include:

    Any value — the cell accepts any value.

    Whole number — restricts entries to non-decimal numbers.

    Decimal — restricts entries to decimal numbers.

    continued...

Restrict Cell Entries of Numbers, Dates, or Times

1. Select cell(s) to restrict.
2. Click the **Data** menu, then click **Validation**.
   The Data Validation dialog box appears.
3. Click **Settings** tab.
4. Select one of the following data types in the **Allow** box: *Whole Number, Decimal, Date, Time.*
5. Select desired comparison operator in **Data** box.
6. Set data restriction in the **Value**, **Minimum**, **Maximum** boxes. *You can enter values, cell references, or formulas in these boxes.*

    NOTE: *The boxes available depend on the comparison operator you select in step 5.*

7. Set **Input Message** for restricted cells (see illustration on next page).
8. Set **Error Message** for restricted cells (see illustration on next page).
9. Set other options, then click **OK**.

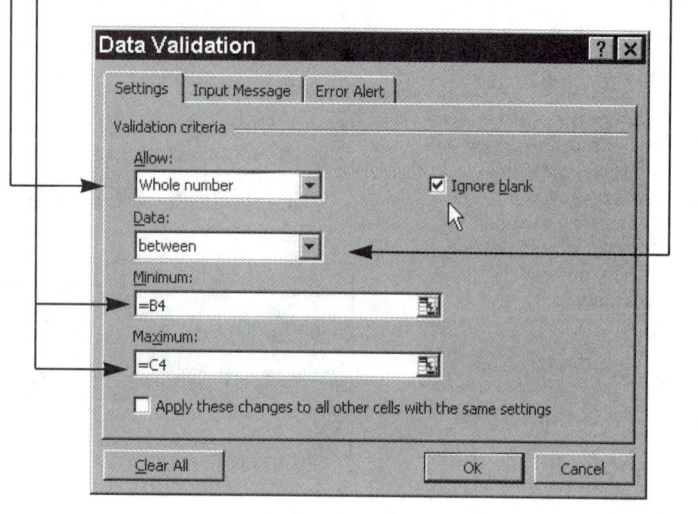

124

List — restricts entries to items in a list (a range of cells containing text or numbers).

Date — restricts entries to a date or range of dates.

Time — restricts entries to a time or range of times.

Text length — specifies the number of characters possible in an entry.

Custom — restricts entries to those that cause a formula to evaluate True. For example, you can specify that an entry in A1 is equal to an entry in B3 as in this logical formula: =A1=B3.

- To edit cell restrictions, repeat steps 1–9 on the previous page. If other cells in your workbook contain the same restrictions, select **Apply these changes to all other cells with same settings**.

Set Input and Error Message for Restricted Cells

1. Click the **Input Message** tab, and type the title and an input message as shown in the example below.
2. Click the **Error Alert** tab, and type title and message, as shown below.
3. Click **OK** when done.

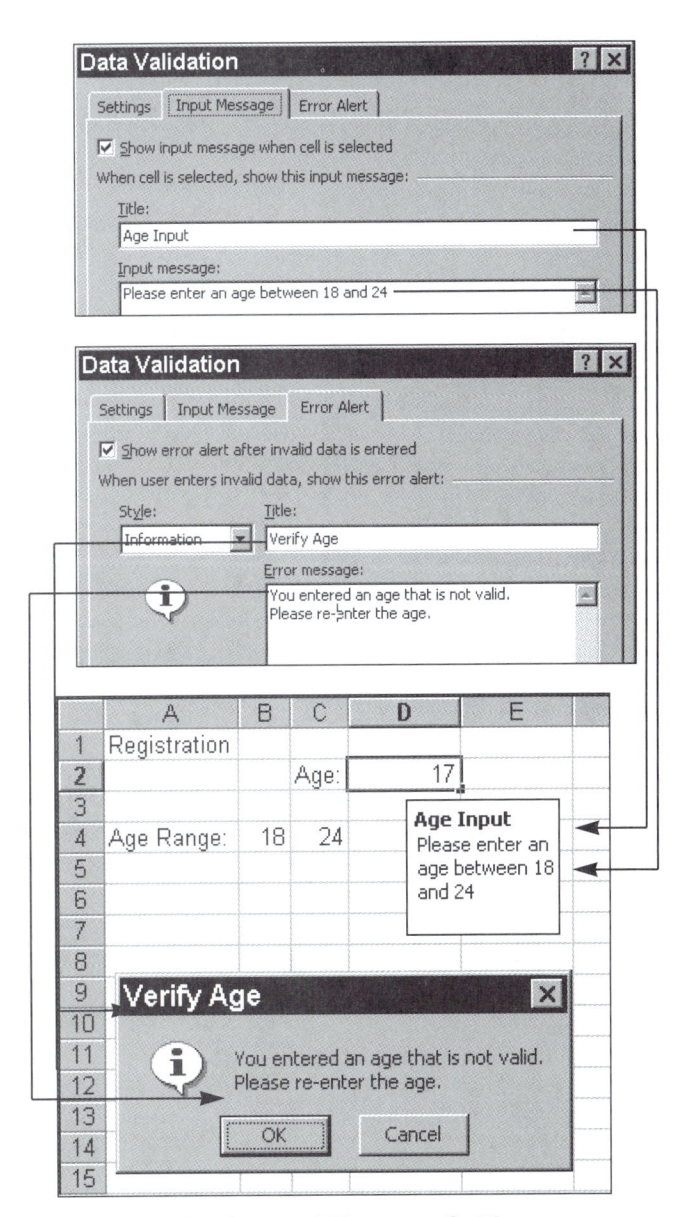

Validation and Message Settings

125

Formulas, Lists, and Data Tables

This section contains illustrated procedures arranged in alphabetical order for creating and working with formulas, lists, and data tables.

About Formulas

You will use formulas to calculate values stored in your worksheet. This topic explains basic information about formulas — formula location, formula parts, controlling the order of operation, and formula examples. (For additional information, see *About References, Create Formulas, Create Functions*, and *Edit Formulas*.)

Notes:

- A **formula** is an instruction to calculate numbers.
- You can display formulas in cells by pressing **Ctrl** + ~ (tilde). Press the key again to return worksheet to normal.

Formula Location

Enter a formula in the cell where the result should appear. As you type the formula, it will appear in the cell and in the formula bar. After you enter a formula, the result is displayed in the cell, and the formula is displayed in the formula bar. *(See Create Formulas.)*

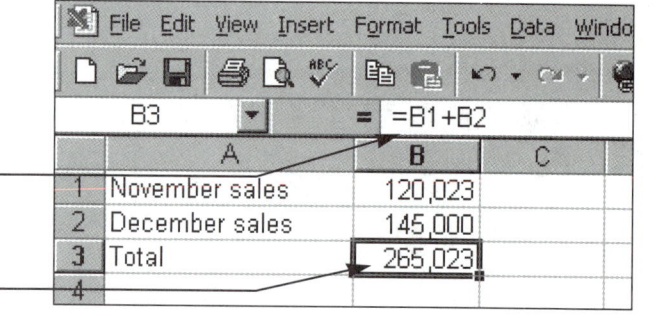

Notes:

- **Cell references** and **reference names** indicate the location of cells in a worksheet.
- **Functions** are predefined formulas.
- **Operators** tell Excel the kind of calculation to perform.
- **Parentheses** affect the order of operations. They must be used in pairs.

Formula Parts

Formulas always begin with an equal sign (**=**) and often contain elements such as those shown in bold type in the following sample formulas:

numbers	=A1+**25**
cell references	=**A1**-25
reference names	=A1***Salary**
functions	=**Sum(A1:A10)**+Salary
operators	=A1**/**2**+**25***22**-**3
parentheses	=**(**24+A1**)**/2%

128

Notes:

- When a formula contains both an multiplication and division operator, Excel performs the operations from left to right.

- When a formula contains both an addition and subtraction operator, Excel performs the operations from left to right.

Control the Order of Operations in Formulas

It is important to consider the order of mathematical operations when preparing formulas. Excel will perform the operation in your formulas in the following order:

- operations enclosed in parentheses ( )
- percentage %
- exponential ^
- multiplication and division * /
- addition and subtraction + -
- concatenation (connection of text strings) &
- comparisons = < > <= >= <>

Notes:

- Some of the examples contain named ranges. You must name a range before you can refer to it in a formula. However, Excel will let you use names when labels exist next to numbers in your worksheet.

Formula Examples

This is a list of common formulas with a brief explanations:

=A1+25 — adds the contents of cell A1 to the constant 25.

=A1-25 — subtracts 25 from the content of cell A1.

=A1*TotalSalary — multiplies the content of cell A1 by the content of the cell named TotalSalary.

=Sum(A1:A10)+TotalSalary — adds the content of the cell named TotalSalary to the sum of cells A1 through A10.

=A10+(25*TotalSalary) — multiplies the content of the cell named TotalSalary by 25, then adds that result to the content of cell A10.

=A10^3 — multiplies the content of A10 by itself 3 times (exponentially).

=2%*A10 — two percent of the content of cell A10.

=(Min(Salary)+Max(Salary))/2 — adds the minimum value in the range of cells named Salary to the maximum value in that range, and divides the result by 2.

=A10 & " " & A11 — combines the text in cells A10 and A11 with a space between them. If A10 contains HELLO and A11 contains THERE, the result would be HELLO THERE.

=IF(A1<>0,A1*B10," ") — if the value in cell A1 is not zero, multiplies A1 by the value in B10, otherwise displays blank text.

129

About References in Formulas

References in formulas indicate the locations of values you want the formula to use in calculations. (For additional information, see *About Formulas*, *Create Formulas*, *Create Functions*, and *Edit Formulas*.)

```
B13        ▼    =   =A10
```

Notes:

- A **reference** is a notation that identifies the location of a cell in a workbook.

  External references require the drive and folder locations. Quotation marks are used if file names contain spaces.

- A **range** is a group of consecutive cells.

- A **union** combines multiple references into one reference.

- An **intersection** of ranges indicates where two ranges meet.

- A **named reference** indicates a cell or range to which you have assigned a name.

- A **reference to other worksheets** requires an exclamation point to separate the sheet name from the cell reference. Quotation marks are used if worksheet names contain spaces.

- **3-D references** identify a range of cells in different worksheets that are in the same position on each sheet.

References — Cell Locations

Following is a list of the kinds of references you can use. Range operators in example references are bolded.

REFERENCE TYPE	EXAMPLE
range	A1**:**A10
union of cells	C5**,**E5
intersection (space)	C5:C10 ** ** A7:E7
entire column	C**:**C
entire row	3**:**3
range of columns	A**:**C
range of rows	3**:**5
named reference	TotalSalary
cells in another worksheet	Sheet2!A10
3-D range of cells	Sheet1**:**Sheet3!A10
external reference (link) to cells in another workbook	'c:\my docs\[sales.xls]!Sheet1'!A10

130

Notes:

- The type of reference is important when you copy or move formulas.

  For example, it is common to copy formulas down a column with references to cells in the same row. In this case, the relative references will adjust appropriately. If the same formula contains a reference to a value that is not moved, errors will occur after you copy the formulas unless you have created an absolute reference to that cell.

Reference Types

Relative Cell Reference

A **relative cell reference** (such as A2) describes a cell location that changes when the formula is moved or copied.

Formula example: =A2*10

If this cell is copied one cell down, the reference A2 would become A3. Thus the copied formula would be =A3*10

Absolute Cell Reference

An **absolute cell reference** (such as $A$2) describes a cell that will not change when the formula is moved or copied. Use a dollar sign ($) before both the column letter and the row number to specify an absolute cell reference.

Formula example: =$A$2*10

If this cell is copied one cell down, the reference A2 would remain $A$2. Thus the copied formula would remain =$A$2*10

Mixed Cell Reference

A mixed cell reference (such as $A2) describes a cell location with both relative and absolute parts. The dollar sign ($) marks the absolute part of the reference (A), while the unmarked part (2) defines the relative part of the reference.

Formula example: =$A2*10

If this cell is copied one cell down and one cell position to the right, only the relative part of the reference will adjust. Thus the copied formula is =$A3*10

Notes:

- In **step 3**, when you press **F4**, Excel selects the entire reference and changes it simultaneously.

Change Reference Type

1 Double-click formula containing reference to change.
2 Click on reference in formula to change.
3 Press **F4** until desired reference type appears.
4 Press **Enter**.

=+C6+E6+G6   ◄──── relative (E6)

=+C6+$E$6+G6 ◄──── absolute ($E$6)

=+C6+E$6+G6   ◄──── mixed (E$6)

131

Audit Formulas in Worksheets

If you have an unexpected result in a formula, you can audit, or trace, the formula to determine the problem. For this purpose, Excel provides the Auditing toolbar. Also see *Insert and Remove Comments* for information about adding comments to cells, and *Validate Cell Entries* for information about ensuring that valid entries are made.

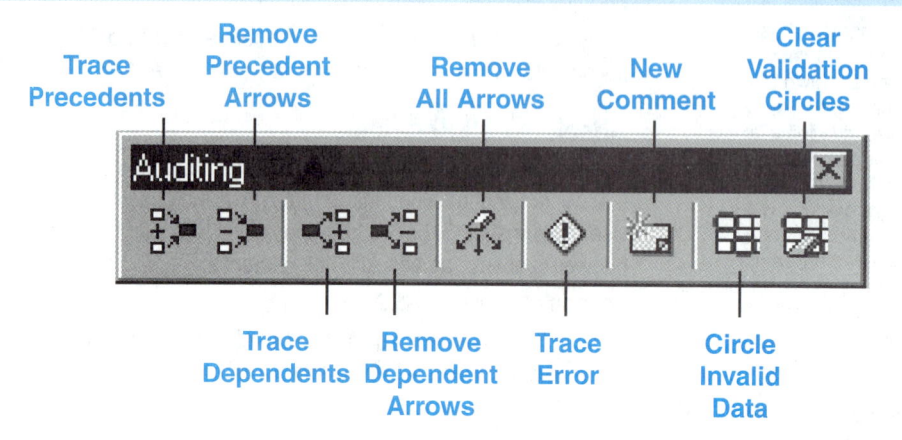

Trace Precedents — Remove Precedent Arrows — Remove All Arrows — New Comment — Clear Validation Circles

Trace Dependents — Remove Dependent Arrows — Trace Error — Circle Invalid Data

Notes:
- You can dock the Auditing toolbar by dragging it to any border of the Excel window.

Display Auditing Toolbar

1. Click the **Tools** menu, then point to **Auditing**.
2. Click **Show Auditing Toolbar** on the submenu.

Notes:
- **Dependents** are cells containing formulas that refer to the audited cell. The value in C4 (72) is referenced by four formulas in the worksheet. Each formula "depends" on that value.

Trace Dependents

1. Select cell to trace.
2. Click **Trace Dependents** button on Auditing toolbar.

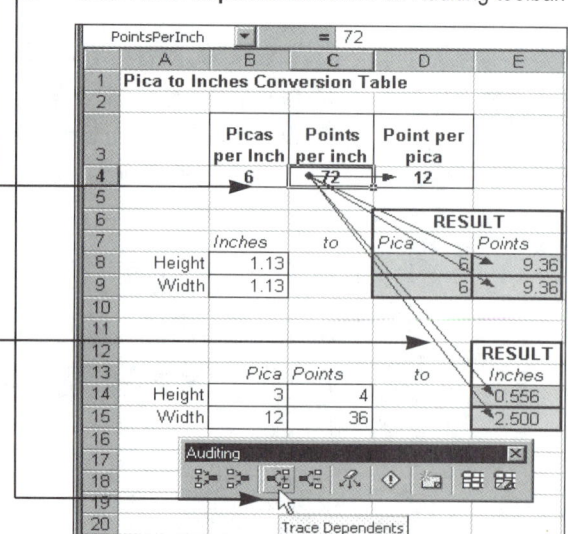

Excel draws arrows to formulas that refer to audited cell.

132

Notes:

- **Precedents** are the cells to which a formula refers. The formula in D8 refers to values in B8 and B4.

Trace Precedents

1. Select cell containing formula to analyze.
2. Click **Trace Precedents** button on Auditing toolbar.

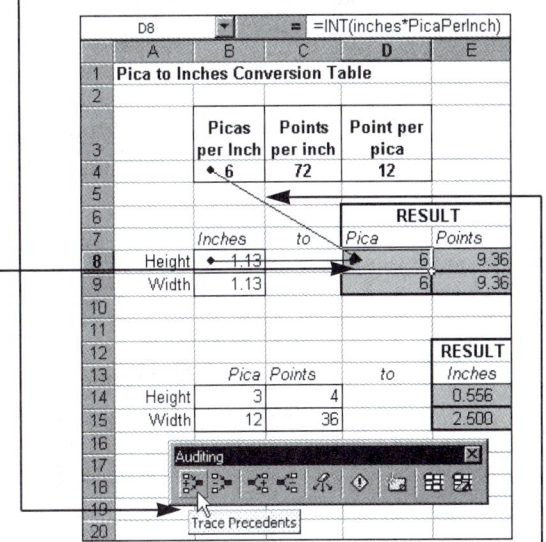

Excel draws arrows to cells formula refers to.

Notes:

- See *Help Overview* for information about common error messages in formulas.
- The formula in B7 refers to values in B4-B6, and A1 — which does not contain a value.

Trace Errors

1. Select cells containing error to analyze.
2. Click **Trace Errors** button on Auditing toolbar.

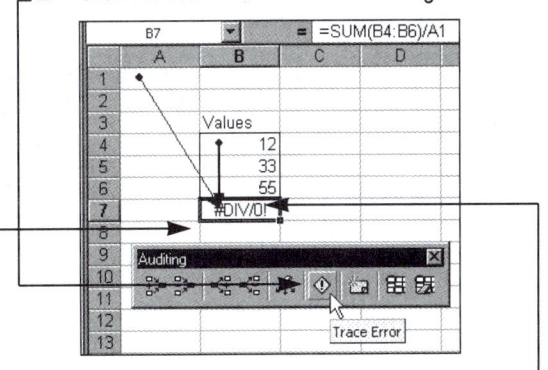

Excel draws arrows to source of error.

133

Create Formulas (Simple)

Enter and build formulas to calculate values stored in your worksheet. This section includes basic information about building formulas, pasting names into a formula, and inserting references in formulas. For additional information, see *About References*, *Create Formulas (Complex)*, *Create Functions*, and *Edit Formulas*.

Notes:

- In **step 1**, select a cell in which you want to enter the result of the calculation.
- In **step 2**, when you type the equal sign, controls appear on the formula bar.
- In the illustration, the simple formula =25*A1 multiplies the value in A1 by 25.
- You can insert references until all the cells you want to calculate are included in the formula. For information about changing a formula, see *Edit Formulas*.
- If you decide to cancel the entry, press **Esc**.

Build Formula (Add References)

1 Select cell to receive formula.

2 Type an equal sign (=).

   The equal sign displays in the cell and in the formula bar.

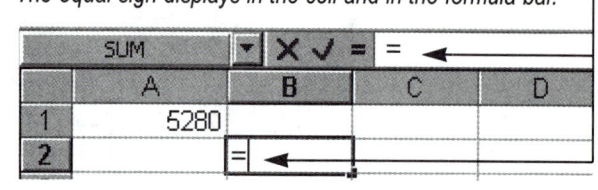

3 Type the formula *(for example, see About Formulas)*.

To insert a reference in formula by pointing with the mouse:

- Click cell to reference.

   A dashed line appears around the cell, and Excel inserts the cell reference in your formula.

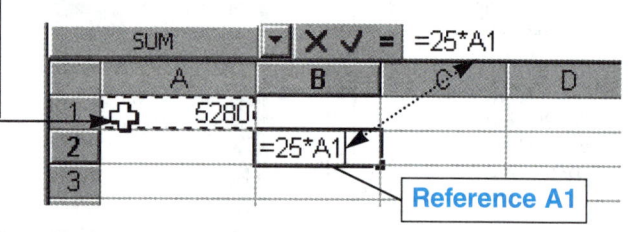

4 Type next part of formula. If formula is complete, go to step 5, below.

   Excel removes dashed outline, and your entry appears in cell and formula bar.

5 Press **Enter**.

   OR

   Click ✓ on formula bar.

   Excel calculates the formula and displays the result in the cell.

134

Notes:

- For information about how to create names, see *Name Cells*.

- In **step 2**, you can also type the name of a range, instead of pasting it.

Paste a Named Range into a Formula

1 Place insertion point in formula.
2 Click the **Insert** menu, then click or point to **Name**.
3 Click **Paste** on the submenu.
4 Click name to paste in formula, then click **OK**.

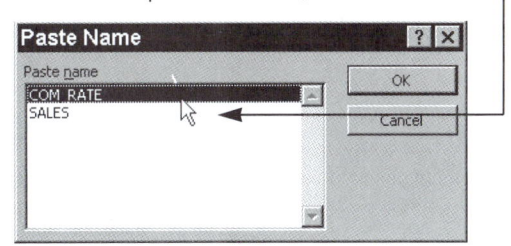

Notes:

- This procedure explains the steps needed to build a typical formula. References to the illustration appear in parentheses.

- When creating a formula, each time you point to a cell, Excel inserts it in the formula and outlines the cell.

- In **step 4**, each time you press **F4**, Excel changes the reference type.

- **Illustration result:** Formula in C7 should display 1360.

Create Formula, Insert Cell References, and Change Reference Type

1 Type the data in a new worksheet, as shown in the illustration below. Then create the formula in C7 to calculate the commission (=$B$2*C5).

	A	B	C	D
1		SALES COMMISSION		
2	COM RATE	4.00%		
3				
4		ELMHURST	CADDY	WUILLS
5	SALES	640000	340000	540000
6	BONUS	2000	1000	2000
7	COMMISSION	25600		
8	TOTAL COMP	27600		

2 Select cell to receive formula (C7).
3 Type **=** to start the formula.
4 Click cell for reference in formula (B2).

To change the inserted reference to absolute:

- Press **F4**.

  Reference changes to absolute (B2 becomes $B$2).

5 Type desired operator (*) .
6 Click next cell for reference in formula (C5).
7 Press **Enter** to complete the formula.

135

Create Formulas (Complex)

In this topic you will learn skills needed to create complex formulas — formulas that use functions with references to a range of cells, cells in other worksheets, cells in other workbooks, and cells that span consecutive worksheets.

Notes:

- **Functions** are pre-defined formulas that perform specific kinds of calculations. This topic will introduce you to the **SUM function** which adds all numbers in a range of cells. See *Create Functions* for more information about functions.

- In **step 2**, the SUM function requires a pair of parentheses: SUM( ). Within the parentheses, type or insert the cells to total. This element of a function is called the **argument**. You can use the SUM function to calculate references, not just a range, as in this example: SUM(A1, B3, B4:B10). See *About References* for additional information.

Create SUM Function and Insert a Range by Dragging

1 Select cells to receive formula.

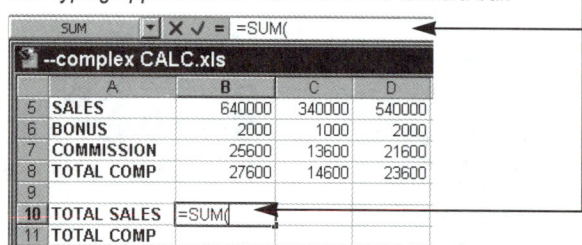

2 Type an equal sign (=), then type **SUM(**.
Your typing appears in the cell and in the formula bar.

To insert a range in formula by dragging:

- Drag through cells containing values to calculate.

  A dashed line surrounds the range, and Excel inserts the reference in your formula.

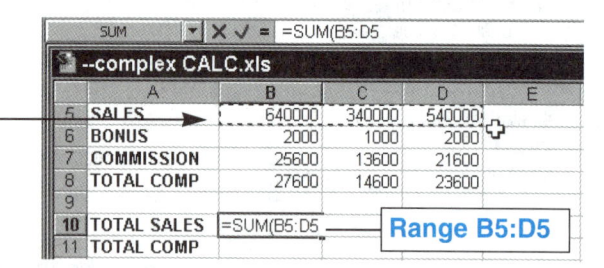

  Range B5:D5

3 Type closing parenthesis.
Excel removes dashed outline.

4 Press **Enter**.
OR
Click ✓ on formula bar.
Excel calculates the formula and displays the result in the cell.

Notes:
- In the illustration, the external reference (or link) includes the name of the workbook and the sheet name, followed by the cell range. If you close the source workbook, the reference will also include the folder in which the workbook has been saved.

External references link workbooks.

Insert an External Reference into a Formula

1 Open workbook containing cells to reference.

2 In destination worksheet, create the formula, then place insertion point in formula where external reference will appear.

3 Select source workbook, then worksheet, then cell or range to insert.

Excel inserts external reference in formula.

4 Type the rest of the formula.

`= =SUM([YEAREND.xls]Sheet1!$A$1:$B$1)`

Notes:
- A reference to a cell or range on another worksheet includes the sheet name, separated from the cell reference by an exclamation point, as in these examples:

=SUM(Sheet2!B1)

=SUM(Sheet2!B1:B5)

- A reference to a range of cells that spans multiple sheets is a **3-D reference**.

3-D references link consecutive cells in sheets.

Insert a Reference to Cells in Another Sheet or 3-D Range

1 In destination worksheet, create the formula, then place insertion point in formula where reference will appear.

To insert a cell or range reference on another sheet:
- Click source worksheet tab, then click cell or range to insert.

Excel inserts worksheet reference in formula.

To insert a 3-D reference to cells in a range of worksheets:
a Click first worksheet tab in range.

b Click cell or range on that sheet to insert.

c Press **Shift** and click last sheet tab in range of sheets.

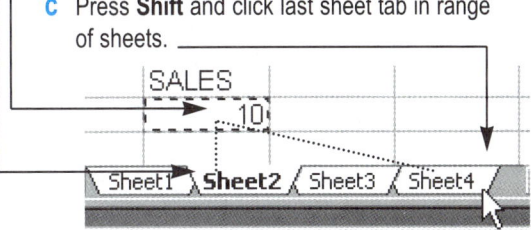

```
         SALES
          10

\ Sheet1 \Sheet2 / Sheet3 / Sheet4 /
```

Excel inserts 3-D worksheet reference.

`= =SUM('Sheet2:Sheet4'!B19`

2 Type next part of formula.

137

Create Functions

Functions are predefined formulas that perform specific calculations, such as finding an average or future value. Functions require arguments — the data to be calculated. To make it easy to create a function, Excel provides the Paste Function Wizard.

Paste Function button

Functions list on formula bar

Notes:

- In **step 2**, you can also click the **Insert** menu, then click **Function**.

- You can also click the **Paste Function** button when you want to insert a function in a formula you have already started to create.

- When creating a formula, you can click the **Function list** on the formula bar to insert frequently used functions and access the **Paste Function Wizard**.

- The **Paste Function Wizard** may insert a suggested range in a **Number** box. Delete this range if it is not appropriate.

- As you click in a **Number** box, the Paste Function Wizard may add more boxes.

Dialog Collapse button

Insert a Function Using Function Wizard

1. Select cell in which to create the function.

2. Click **Paste Function** button on Standard toolbar.

   The Paste Function dialog box appears.

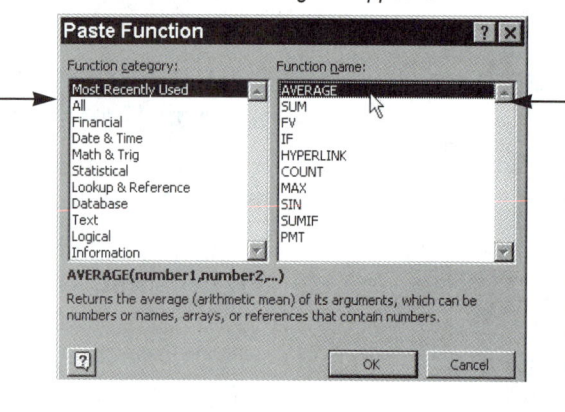

3. Select desired category in **Function category** list.

4. Select desired function in **Function name** list, then click **OK**.

   A dialog box for the function you selected appears.

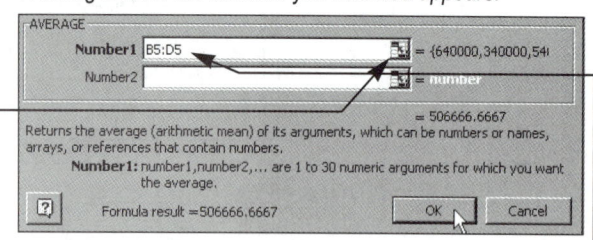

5. Insert cell references or values in **Number** boxes.

   NOTE: You can click the **Collapse Dialog** button on the right side of the **Number** box, then select cells directly from the worksheet. (See Use Dialog Box Controls.)

6. Click **OK** when done.

Notes:

- In **step 1**, if you double-click the cell, then click the **Paste Function** button, you will insert a new function.

- In **step 3**, refer to illustration on bottom of previous page.

Edit a Function

1 Select cell containing the function to edit.

NOTE: Do not double-click the cell.

2 Click the **Paste Function** button on Standard toolbar.

3 Change arguments in **Number** boxes, then click **OK**.

Notes:

- For this procedure, refer to illustrations on the previous page.

- A **nested function** is a function that contains a function as an argument.

Combine (Nest) Functions

1 Double-click cell containing function(s).

2 Place insertion point where new function will appear, or select argument to replace with a function.

3 Click the **Paste Function** button on Standard toolbar.

4 Select desired category in **Function category**.

5 Select desired function in **Function name** list, then click **OK**.

6 Insert cell references or values in **Number** boxes.

7 Click **OK** when done.

=AVERAGE(B5:B9,SUM(B6:D6))

Nested Functions

Notes:

- If Excel detects subtotals within a range of values, it may suggest to add just those totals to obtain a grand total. When this occurs, Excel applies dashed outlines only to cells containing subtotals in the immediate column or row.

Use AutoSum Function

1 Click cell in which function will be entered.

2 Click **AutoSum** button on Standard toolbar.

Excel surrounds suggested cells to add with dashed outline.

3 To change the range, drag through desired cells.

4 Press **Enter** when done.

	A	B	C	D	E
4		ELMHURST	CADDY	TOTALS	
5	SALES	640000	340000	=SUM(B5:C5)	
6	BONUS		2000	1000	

139

Create Lookup Tables

You can create a table, then use Excel's lookup functions, VLOOKUP and HLOOKUP, to find particular values in the table and display them in a cell. For example, you can use VLOOKUP to look up the status of a flight by simply typing in the flight number.

`VLOOKUP  ▼ X ✓ =  =VLOOKUP($A$4,TABLE,2)`

Notes:

- In **step 1**, when creating your list:

    Do not include blank rows.

    Use the first column for lookup values, which may be text or values.

    Sort the left-most column in ascending order.

- **Step 2** is optional, but recommended. To name the table, select it (including headings), then click the Name Box and type the desired name. For additional information, see *Name Cells*.

- In **step 3**, it is best to set up labels above the table, to avoid having to move them when the table of information grows.

- Use VLOOKUP when records in table are organized in rows.

- Use HLOOKUP when records in table are organized in columns. This organization is unusual for data in lists.

Use VLOOKUP to Return Information Stored in a Table

Refer to the illustrations on the next page when executing these steps.

1. Create the table of information, such as the list of flights shown in the illustration.
2. Give the table a name, such as TABLE.
3. Type labels to identify where information returned by VLOOKUP will appear.
4. Type initial value to be found (212 in example) in blank cell under appropriate label, (Flight No.).
5. Select cell to return information (B5).
6. Type **=VLOOKUP(**
7. Select cell in which you typed the value to find to insert its cell reference in the formula (A5).
8. Type the remainder of the function: **,TABLE,2, False)**

    =VLOOKUP(*A4,TABLE,2,False***)**

    A4 . . . . Indicates cell containing value to look up.

    , (comma) . . . . Separate each argument.

    TABLE . . . . . . Refers to name of range containing information.

    2 . . . . Indicates column number in table containing information to return.

    False . . . . An optional argument that tells Excel to find an exact match.

9. Press **Enter**.

> **TIP:** In the example on the next page, you could create VLOOKUP functions under the Fare and Status labels to return information in columns 3 and 4, respectively, for lookup values in cell A5.

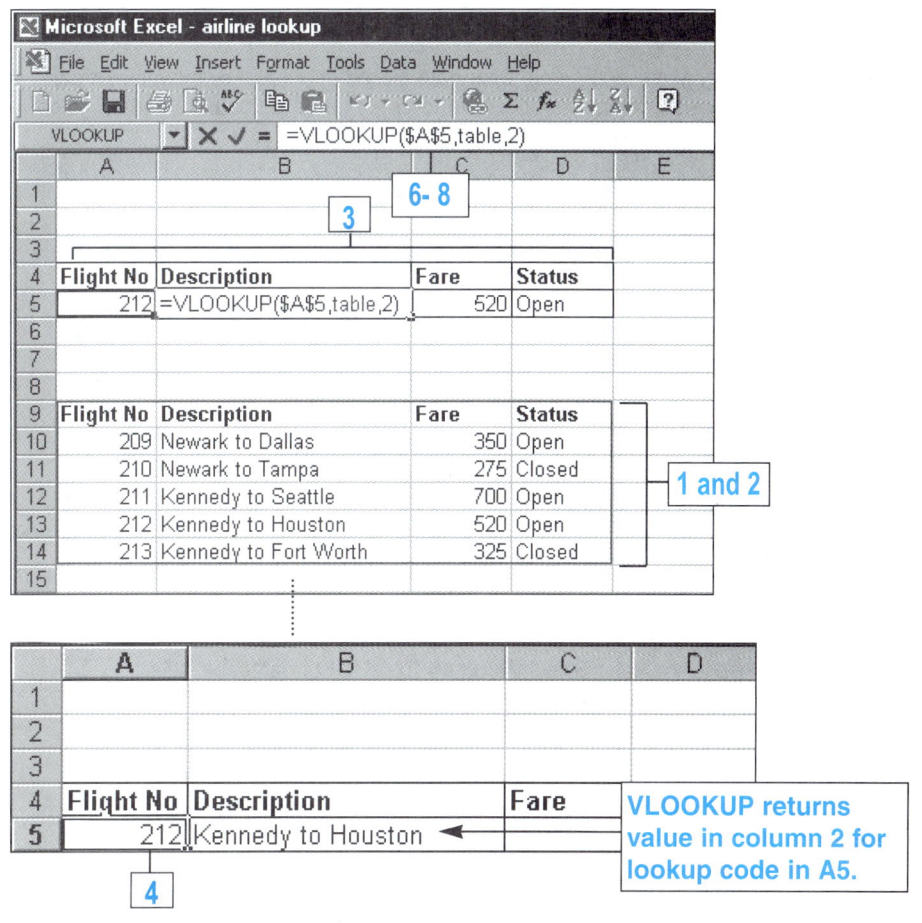

Look Up Flight Information Using VLOOKUP

In the example above, a #NA error will result in B5, if A5 does not contain a found value — a flight number.

TIP: You can also use the Function Wizard to create a VLOOKUP formula. *(See Create Functions.)*

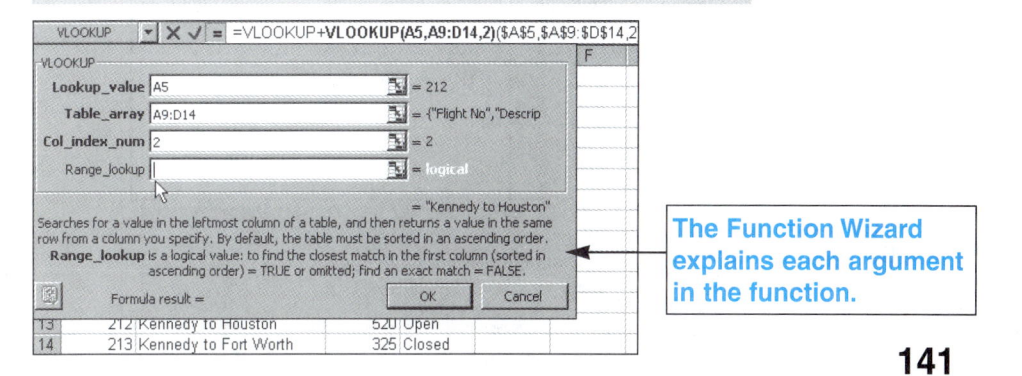

The Function Wizard explains each argument in the function.

141

Create PivotTable

A PivotTable lets you analyze and summarize data stored in a list. For example, it can show subtotals for expense categories for all vendors, or just a particular vendor. *(Also see Edit PivotTable and Create PivotChart.)*

Data → PivotTable and PivotChart Report...

Notes:

- In **step 1**, a **list** must contain **field names** so Excel can determine the list categories *(see Lists)*. Consider naming the list range if the data is likely to expand.

- In **step 4**, Excel selects the range based on the cell you selected in step 1. For information about selecting a range in a dialog box, see *Use Dialog Box Controls*.

Create a PivotTable from a List

1. If necessary, create a list, then click any cell in list, as shown below.

	A	B	C	D
10	Date	Expense	Amount	Vendor
11	1/6/91	inventory	$16,000	SW Wholesale
12	3/5/91	inventory	$20,000	SW Wholesale
13	6/4/91	inventory	$16,000	SW Wholesale

2. Click the **Data** menu, then click **PivotTable and PivotChart Report**.

   Wizard - Step 1 of 3 dialog box appears.

3. Select **Microsoft Excel list or database**, select **PivotTable**, then click **Next >**.

   Wizard - Step 2 of 3 dialog box appears.

4. - If the suggested range is not correct, select a new range or named range in **Range** box.
   - Click **Next >**.

   PivotTable Wizard - Step 3 of 3 dialog box appears.

5. Select **New worksheet** or **Existing Worksheet** to place the PivotTable.
   - If you selected **Existing Worksheet**, type or select the desired cell location in worksheet.
   - Click **Finish**.

   Excel creates a framework for the PivotTable on the worksheet and the PivotTable toolbar appears.

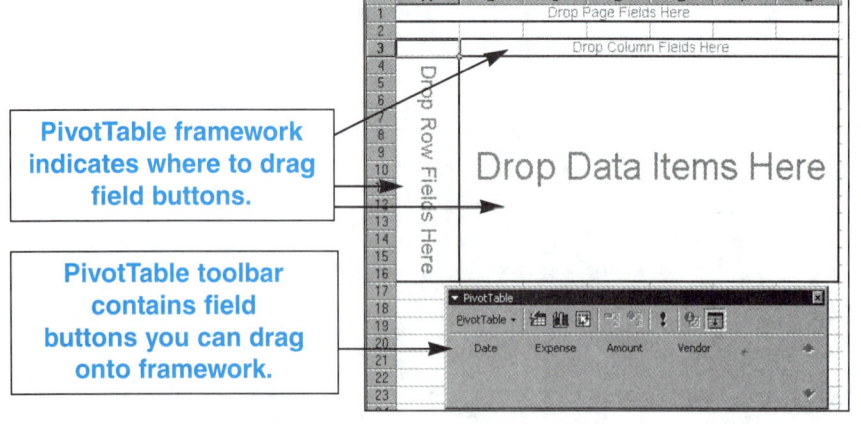

PivotTable framework indicates where to drag field buttons.

PivotTable toolbar contains field buttons you can drag onto framework.

142

Notes:

- In **step 6**, the framework shows the following field areas to help you construct the PivotTable:

  Page — lets you filter the completed PivotTable by an item in the field.

  Row — creates row labels for each unique item in field.

  Column — creates column labels for each unique item in field (Not used in the illustration.)

  Data — summarizes data in field by a function. You must include at least one field in the Data area.

- You drag field items to new positions (on or off the PivotTable) to get a different report for your list. *(See Edit PivotTable).*

You can use the Page field (Expenses, in this example) to filter the report. See *Edit Pivot-Tables* for details.

Create a PivotTable from a List (continued)

6 Drag field buttons onto appropriate areas of PivotTable framework.

Excel activates the PivotTable when you drag a field to the Data area, so consider dragging that item last to maintain the the framework prompts.

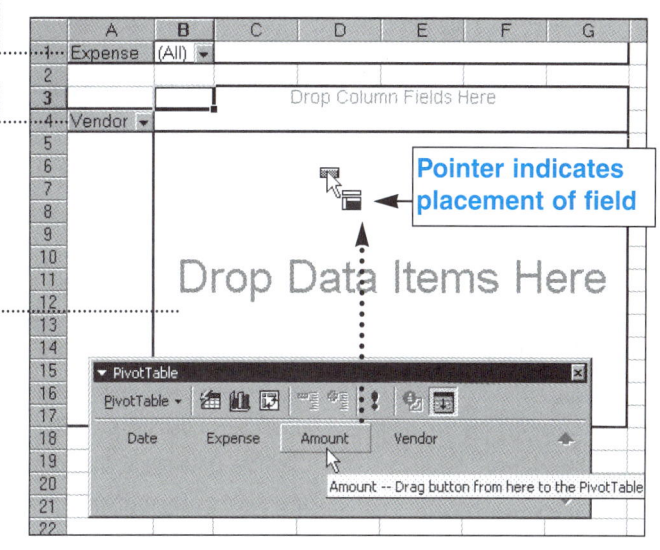

Pointer indicates placement of field

Build Your PivotTable by Dragging Fields

	A	B
1	Expense	overhead
2		
3	Sum of Amount	
4	Vendor	Total
5	A.B	1000
6	A.B. Properties	11000
7	Ace	566
8	AR Office	60000
9	City	440
10	City of Franklin	9234
11	Cook	200
12	Ralph J Cook Garbage	2200
13	Wheelin's Gas Co.	6600
14	Wheeln	600
15	Grand Total	91840

PivotTable Result Showing Overhead Expenses Only

143

Create One-Variable Data Tables

Create a data table to generate answers for a set of values organized in a column or row. You might use this feature to generate a table that converts fahrenheit to centigrade, or meters to feet. Data tables achieve results from a single formula that calculates an array, thus conserving memory.

Data ➡ Table...

Notes:

- In **step 1**, you can type the first two values, then fill the remaining cells by dragging the fill handle.

- In **step 3**, the formula must refer to the first column input cell.

- In **step 4**, select the substitution values and the cells in which the results will appear. Do not include labels that describe the values.

- In **step 6**, select the **Column input cell** box if your substitution values are organized in a column. If your substitution values are organized in a row, choose the **Row input cell** box instead.

Create a One-Variable Data Table

Refers to the illustration on the next page.

1 Type substitution values (values to substitute in formula) in a column.

2 Select cell where first result will appear (D4).

3 Enter formula that refers to first substitution value (=0.3937*C4).

4 Select entire data table, including first column input cell, substitution values, and result cells (C4:D13).

5 Click the **Data** menu, then click **Table**.

The Table dialog box appears.

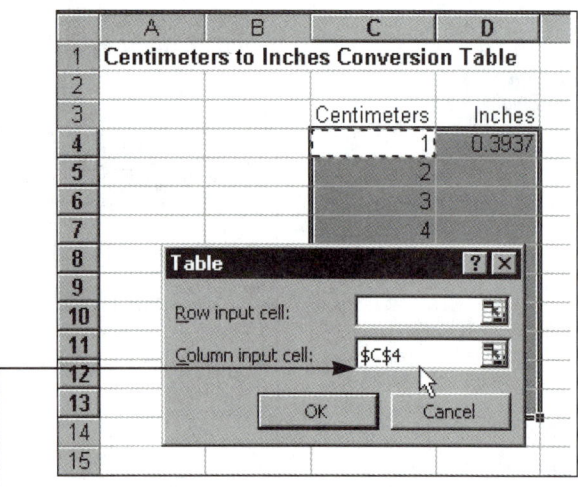

6 Click in **Column input cell** box, then click cell containing column input value (C4) to insert reference in box.

   NOTE: The column input cell refers to the data the formula created in step 3.

7 Click **OK**.

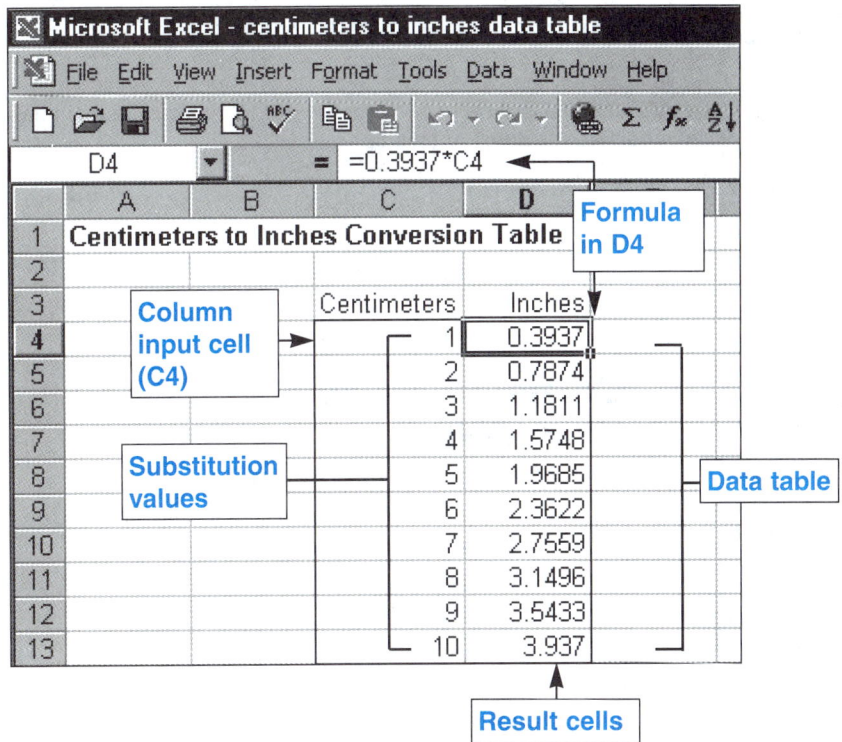

One-Variable Data Table Example

TIP: You can extend a data table: Add substitution values and select the entire table (include new substitution values and result cells). Then repeat steps 5-7.

Notes:
- In **step 1**, you do not have to select the cell containing the formula.

Delete Results in a Data Table

If you attempt to delete part of the results in a data table, you will receive this message: Cannot change part of a table.

1 Select all result cells.

2 Press **Delete** key.

145

Create Two-Variable Data Tables

You can create a data table to generate answers from two sets of values organized in a column and a row. You might use this feature to generate a table that calculates monthly payments for principles over different lengths of time.

Data → Table...

Notes:

- In **step 1**, the **row** and **column input cells** refer to initial values used in the formula that correspond to substitution values in the table.

- In **step 4**, just select the substitution values and the cells in which the results will appear. Do not include labels in your selection that you may have typed to describe the values.

- In **step 6**, you can insert a cell reference by clicking the desired cell in the worksheet.

Create a Two-Variable Data Table

Refer to the illustration on the next page.

1 Enter table substitution values (values to substitute in formulas) in a column and row (principle values and years in the example).

Enter row and column input values outside of the table (B16 and B17).

2 Select cell where substitution values intersect (B5).

3 Enter formula. The formula must refer to row and column input cells (bolded).

=PMT(B3/12,**B16***12,-**B17**)

4 Select entire data table, including the cell containing the formula (B5:F13).

5 Click the **Data** menu, then click **Table**.

The Table dialog box appears.

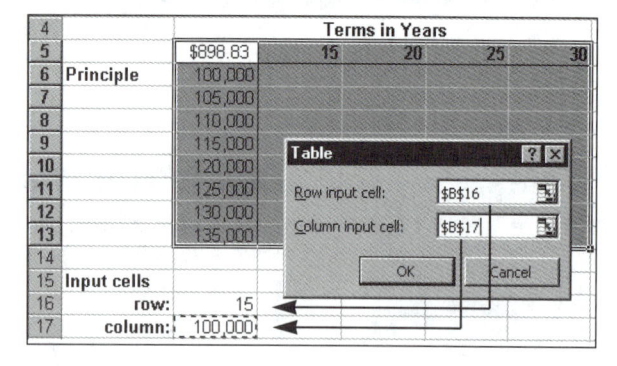

6 In **Row input cell** and **Column input cell** boxes, insert references to row and column input cells, respectively.

7 Click **OK**.

146

Mortgage Payment Table Example

	A	B	C	D	E	F
1	Mortgage Payment Table			Formula		Row substitution values
2						
3	Rate:	7%				
4				Terms in Years		
5		$898.83	15	20	25	30
6	Principle	100,000	$ 898.83	$ 775.30	$ 706.78	$ 665.30
7		105,000	$ 943.77	$ 814.06	$ 742.12	$ 698.57
8		110,000	$ 988.71	$ 852.83	$ 777.46	$ 731.83
9	Column substitution values	115,000	$1,033.65	$ 891.59	$ 812.80	$ 765.10
10		120,000	$1,078.59	$ 930.36	$ 848.14	$ 798.36
11		125,000	$1,123.54	$ 969.12	$ 883.47	$ 831.63
12		130,000	$1,168.48	$1,007.89	$ 918.81	$ 864.89
13		135,000	$1,213.42	$1,046.65	$ 954.15	$ 898.16
14						
15	Input cells			Data table		
16	row:	15				
17	column:	100,000				

B5 = =PMT(B3/12,B16*12,-B17)

Use values that exist in the row and column substitution values

Row (B16) and column (B17) input cells

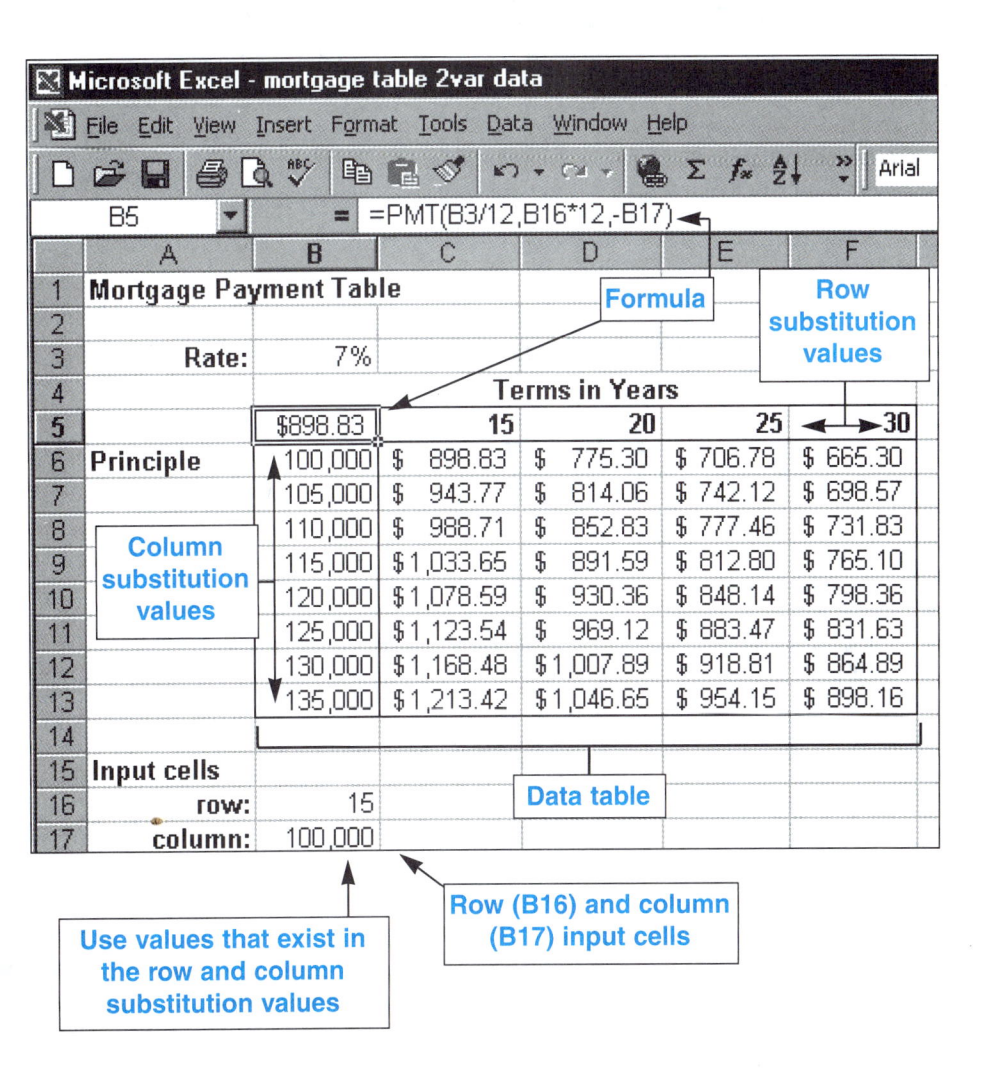

TIP: When possible, create formulas that refer to values in cells, instead of typing a value in the formula. This makes it easier to change the value. In the example, you only need to change cell B3 (7%) to obtain a new set of results.

Notes:

- In **step 1**, you do not have to select the cell containing the formula.

Delete Results in a Data Table

If you attempt to delete part of the results in a data table, you will receive this message: Cannot change part of a table.

1 Select all result cells.
2 Press **Delete** key.

147

Edit Formulas

You will sometimes need to change a formula — perhaps replace an operator, add a set of parentheses, or change the cell or range to which the formula refers.

Notes:

- After you double-click the cell, Excel displays the formula in the cell and on the formula bar.

- To insert a function, click desired location in formula, then click the **Functions** button to the right of the formula bar (it shows the last function selected). Follow the prompts to insert the function.

- In **step 2**, if you drag through characters, your next action, such as typing, will replace the selection.

- If the edited formula displays an incorrect result, click the **Edit** menu, then **Undo Typing** to undo your change.

Edit Formulas

1. Double-click the cell containing the formula to change.

   Excel displays a flashing insertion pointer in the formula. Cell references in the formula are colored. Cell outlines indicate locations of references in worksheet.

2. Click in the entry to position the insertion pointer.

   OR

   Drag through characters to select.

3. Edit the entry as needed:
   - Type characters to insert.
   - Press **Del** to delete characters to the right of insertion pointer or to delete the selection.
   - Press **Backspace** to delete characters to the left of the insertion pointer or to delete the selection.
   - Follow steps described on the next page to change reference or extend a cell range.

4. Press **Enter** or click ✓ on formula bar.

   OR

   To cancel the change:

   Press **Esc**, or click ✗ on formula bar.

Notes:

- Excel assigns a different color to each border and reference to help you identify them.

Change Reference in Formula

1. Double-click the formula to edit.
   Excel outlines references in worksheet with colored borders.
2. Point to border of outlined reference in worksheet.
   Pointer becomes an ⇖ when positioned on border.
3. Drag border to desired cell or range.

Action:

Drag border to cell containing new value to calculate.

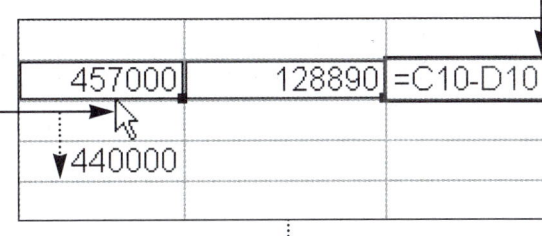

457000	128890	=C10-D10
440000		

Result:

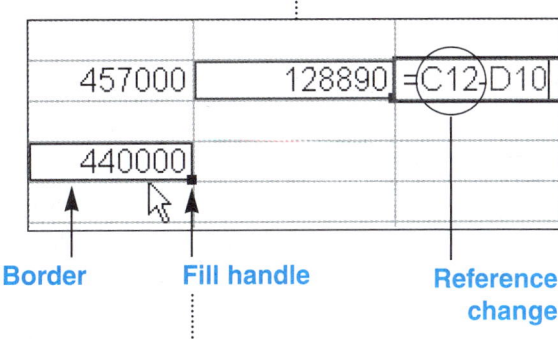

457000	128890	=C12-D10
440000		

Border — Fill handle — Reference change

Notes:

- In **step 2**, the **fill handle** is a small square in the lower-right corner of the outlined reference.

Extend Cell Range in Formula

1. Double-click the formula to edit.
   Excel outlines references in worksheet with colored borders.
2. Point to fill handle of outlined reference in worksheet.
   Pointer becomes a + when positioned on fill handle.
3. Drag fill handle in direction to extend the range.

40000	20000
300000	15000
35000	33000
39000	25890
43000	35000

=SUM(C4:C8)

40000	20000
300000	15000
35000	33000
39000	25890
43000	35000

=SUM(C4:D8) — Reference change

In this example, range C4:C8 becomes ... C4:D8

149

Edit PivotTable

Once you create a PivotTable *(see Create PivotTable)*, you can use controls, such as the Page button to filter and summarize data, or you can drag fields and items to reorganize the view of the data. You can also use tools on the PivotTable toolbar.

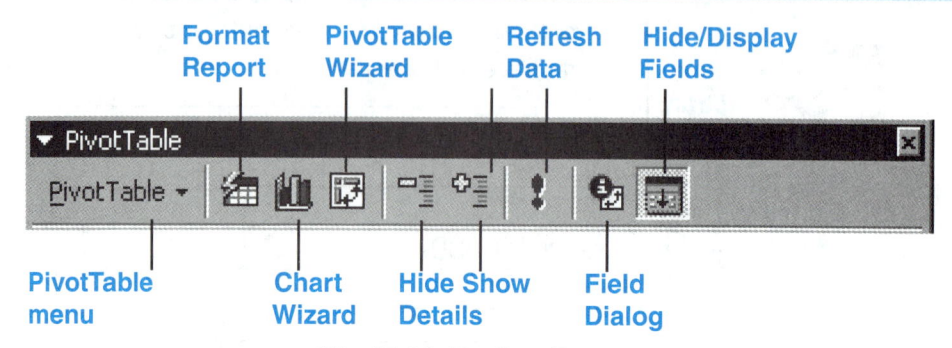

PivotTable Toolbar Buttons

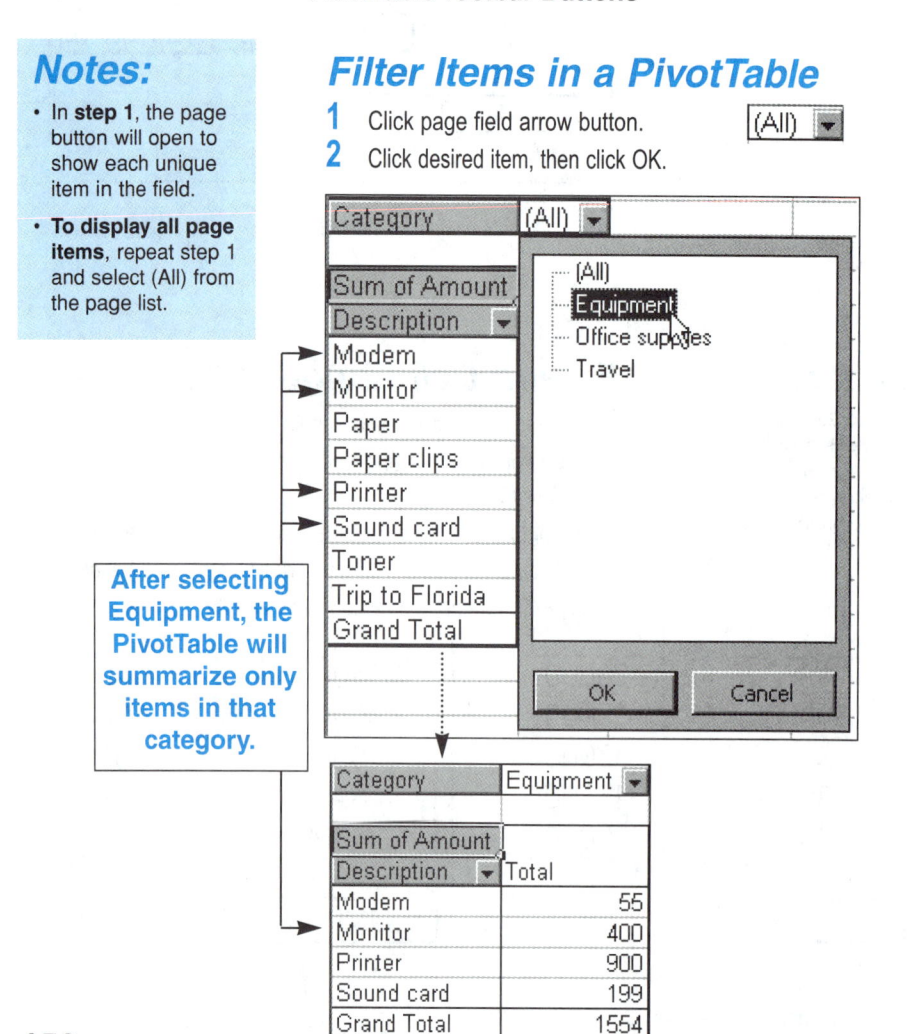

Toolbar labels:
- Format Report
- PivotTable Wizard
- Refresh Data
- Hide/Display Fields
- PivotTable menu
- Chart Wizard
- Hide Show Details
- Field Dialog

Notes:

- In **step 1**, the page button will open to show each unique item in the field.
- **To display all page items**, repeat step 1 and select (All) from the page list.

Filter Items in a PivotTable

1. Click page field arrow button.
2. Click desired item, then click OK.

After selecting Equipment, the PivotTable will summarize only items in that category.

Category	Equipment
Sum of Amount Description	Total
Modem	55
Monitor	400
Printer	900
Sound card	199
Grand Total	1554

150

Notes:

- In **step 1**, you can identify cells containing summary names by words like "Sum of" and "Count of."

- In **step 1**, you can also modify a summary field by selecting the field button and clicking **PivotTable Wizard** on the PivotTable toolbar.

- In **step 2**, to format the number style click **Number**.

- In **step 2** to change the name of the summary field, type a new name in the **Name** box.

- After **step 2**, you can undo actions performed on the PivotTable: Click the **Edit** menu, then click **Undo** *action name*.

Modify Summary (Data) Fields

1 Double-click any cell containing summary name.

Sum of Amount

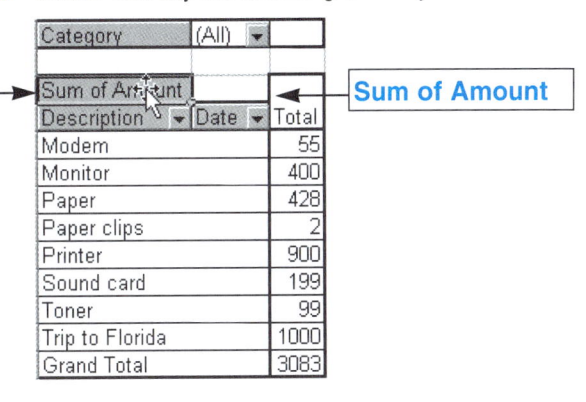

Category	(All)		
Sum of Amount			
Description	Date	Total	
Modem		55	
Monitor		400	
Paper		428	
Paper clips		2	
Printer		900	
Sound card		199	
Toner		99	
Trip to Florida		1000	
Grand Total		3083	

The PivotTable Field dialog box appears.

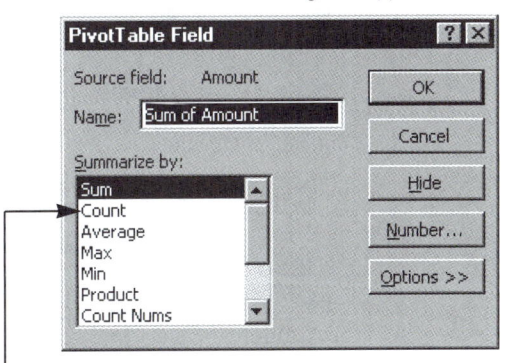

PivotTable Field

Source field: Amount
Name: Sum of Amount

Summarize by:
- Sum
- Count
- Average
- Max
- Min
- Product
- Count Nums

Buttons: OK, Cancel, Hide, Number..., Options >>

2 Select desired function in the **Summarize by** list, then click **OK**.

The PivotTable summarizes items by the selected function.

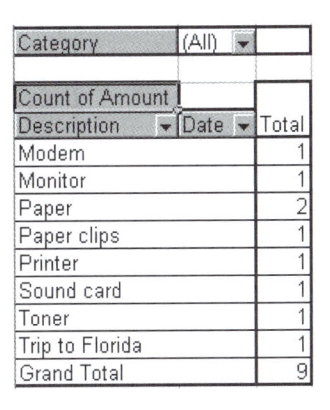

Category	(All)	
Count of Amount		
Description	Date	Total
Modem		1
Monitor		1
Paper		2
Paper clips		1
Printer		1
Sound card		1
Toner		1
Trip to Florida		1
Grand Total		9

Count of Amount

Continued . . .

Edit PivotTable *(continued)*

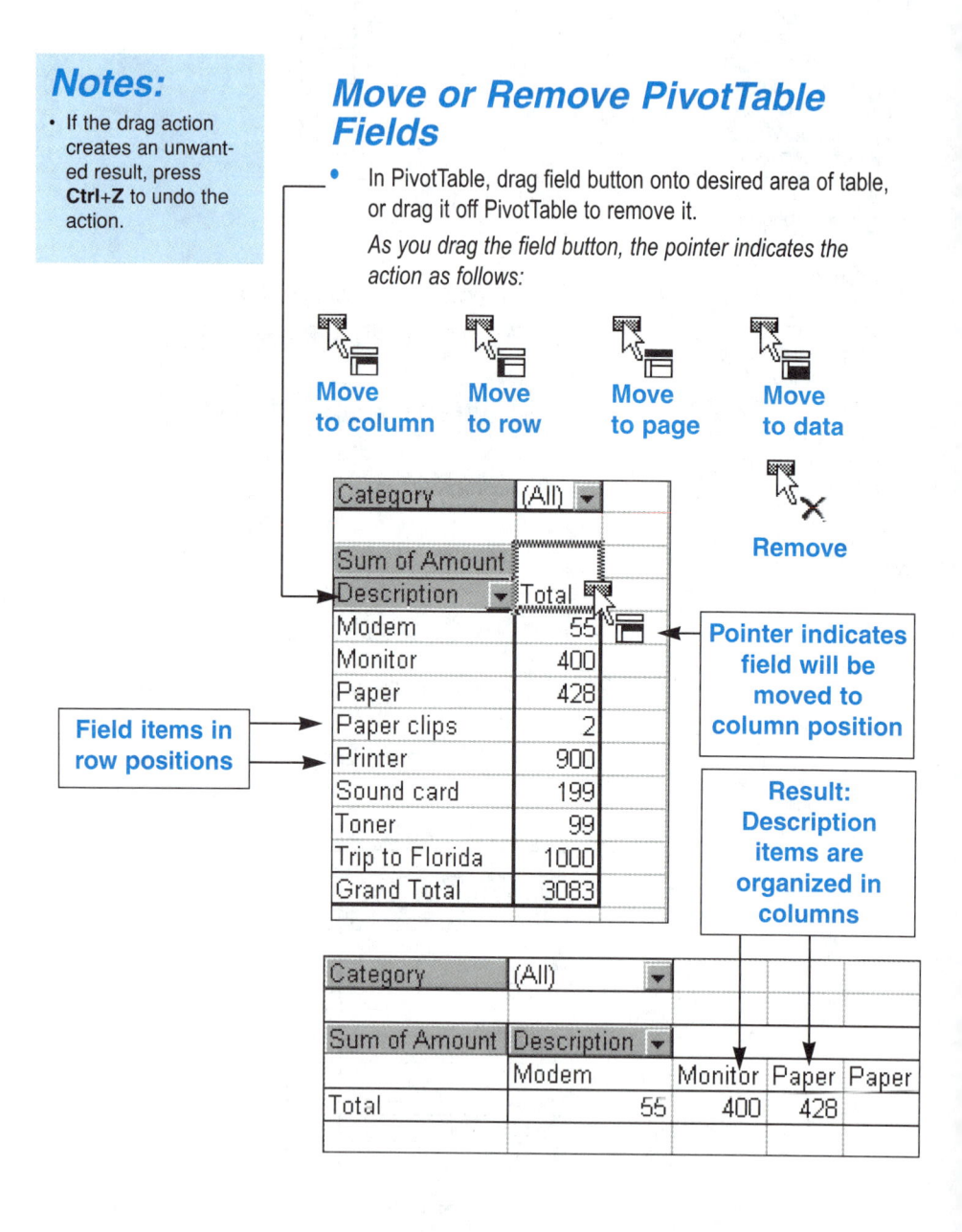

Notes:
- If the drag action creates an unwanted result, press **Ctrl+Z** to undo the action.

Move or Remove PivotTable Fields

- In PivotTable, drag field button onto desired area of table, or drag it off PivotTable to remove it.

  As you drag the field button, the pointer indicates the action as follows:

  Move to column   **Move to row**   **Move to page**   **Move to data**

  Remove

  Field items in row positions

  Pointer indicates field will be moved to column position

  Result: Description items are organized in columns

Category	(All)			
Sum of Amount	Description			
	Modem	Monitor	Paper	Paper
Total	55	400	428	

152

Notes:

- In **step 1** and **step a**, if clicking the top border does not select the item, click the **PivotTable** button on the PivotTable toolbar, point to **Select**, then click **Enable Selection**.

- In **step 1**, you can also show details for specific items by double-clicking the item, then selecting a field.

- In **step a**, you can hide details for specific items by selecting the item, and clicking the Hide Detail button on the PivotTable toolbar

- You can also remove a detail by dragging the detail field button off the table area.

Show or Hide PivotTable Details

Use this procedure when you want to show additional information about items in a PivotTable report, such as dates, as in the example below.

1 Select the entire field by clicking the top border of the field button.

The pointer appears as a ↓ when positioned on the border.

Pointer position   **Selected items.**

Excel highlights selected items, as shown above.

2 Click the Show Detail button on the PivotTable toolbar.

The Show Detail dialog box appears.

3 Select field to show and click **OK**.

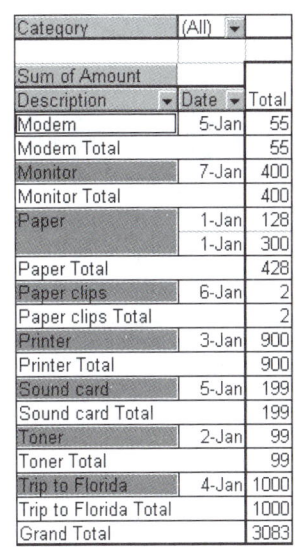

Result includes subtotals for detail field.

To hide details:

a Select the entire field by clicking the top border of the field button.

b Click the Hide Detail button on the PivotTable toolbar.

Continued . . .   **153**

Edit PivotTable *(continued)*

Notes:

- When you add records (rows) to the source list, the PivotTable will not summarize that data unless you have named the range and added the record using the Data Form. (See *Name Cells*, and *Use Data Forms with Lists*.)

Update a PivotTable

Update a PivotTable when the list on which it is based changes.

- Select any item in the PivotTable, then click the **Refresh Data** button on the PivotTable toolbar.

  Excel updates the PivotTable to reflect changes to the source list.

Notes:

- For more information, see *About Toolbars*.

View the PivotTable Toolbar

- Right-click any toolbar, then click **PivotTable** on the shortcut menu.

Notes:

- These new autoformats, designed specifically for PivotTables, include indented formatting, which improves the readability of the report.

Format a PivotTable Report

1. Select any item in the PivotTable, then click the **PivotTable** menu button on the PivotTable toolbar.

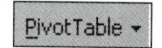

2. Click **Format Report**, select desired report format, and click **OK**.

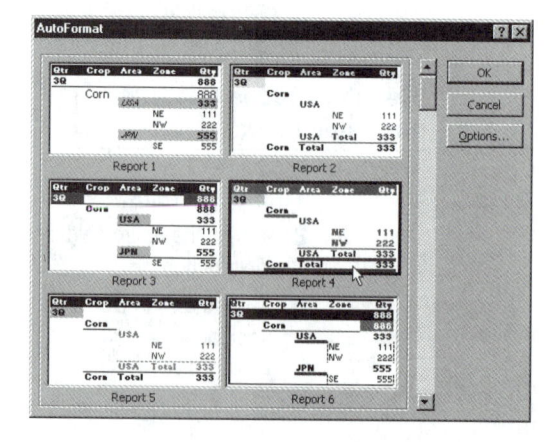

154

Notes:

- To read about a setting, click the **Help button**, then a setting you want help on. When you click the **Help button**, the pointer becomes an arrow with a question mark.

Set PivotTable Options

1. Select any item in the PivotTable, then click the **P**ivotTable menu button on PivotTable toolbar.

2. Click Table **O**ptions, select desired options, and click **OK**.

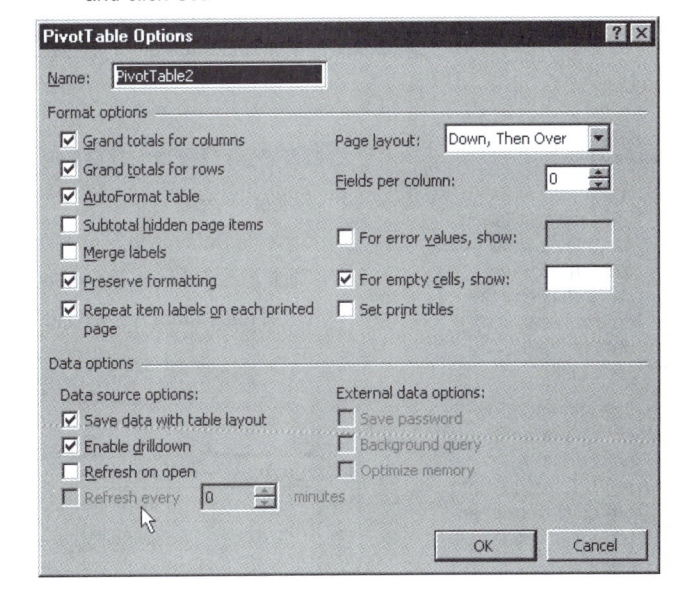

Notes:

- Wizard options include:

  Layout — use to place field items as in previous versions of Excel.

  Options — use to set various options.

  Back — use to change or adjust list reference (Wizard step 2), and specify location of data source (Wizard step 1).

Use the PivotTable Wizard to Change the Layout and Source Reference

1. Select any item in the PivotTable, then click the **PivotTable Wizard** button on the PivotTable toolbar.

   The PivotTable and ChartTable Wizard Step 3 of 3 appears.

2. Select desired option.

155

Filter Lists Automatically

With the AutoFilter feature you can instantly display just the information you want in a list. For example, in a list of all your company's expenses, you can show just salary or office expenses. For information on setting up a list, see *Lists*.

Data → Filter → AutoFilter

Notes:

- A **list** (or database) must contain labels that define **field names** so Excel can determine the categories of the data in the list (see Lists).

- In a list, each row of information is considered a **record**. All records are displayed when you initially start AutoFilter.

- You can use AutoFilter with only one list in a worksheet at a time. To filter multiple lists simultaneously, set up each list on a separate worksheet.

- End AutoFilter if you wish to add records to your list.

Start AutoFilter

1. Select any cell in list.
2. Click the **Data** menu, then point to **Filter**.
3. Click **AutoFilter** on the submenu.

   Excel adds AutoFilter arrows to each field name in your list.

	A	B	C
1			
2			
3	Date ▼	Expense ▼	Amount ▼
4	1/6/97	inventory	$16,000
5	3/5/97	inventory	$20,000
6	4/4/96	inventory	$16,000
7	8/5/96	inventory	$16,000
8	10/7/96	inventory	$14,900
9	12/5/96	inventory	$10,997
10	1/1/97	overhead	$1,000
11	1/5/96	overhead	$1,000
12	3/1/97	overhead	$1,000
13	3/31/97	overhead	$1,000
14	4/30/91	overhead	$1,000
15	5/31/91	overhead	$1,000
16	6/30/96	overhead	$1,000

List with AutoFilter Enabled

Notes:

- When you end AutoFilter, Excel displays all records that were hidden by any filters.

End AutoFilter

1. Click the **Data** menu, then point to **Filter**.
3. Click **AutoFilter** on the submenu.

   Excel removes AutoFilter arrows from each field name in your list.

Notes:

- A **criterion** identifies a condition that must be met. With AutoFilter you need only select criteria from items in your list.

  For example, if you select "salary" in the Expenses field, you are selecting the criteria: Show only records that include "salary" in the Expense field.

- The **Custom** option lets you set complex criteria like: Expenses *equals* "inventory" OR Expenses *does not equal* "salary."

- The **Blanks** and **NonBlanks** options appear only if the column contains one or more blank cells.

- When you set filters for multiple columns only records meeting all criteria are displayed.

Filter a List

1 Start AutoFilter.

2 Click **AutoFilter arrow** of field where you will set the criteria.

Excel displays a list of valid criteria.

3	Date	Expense	Amount
4	1/6/97	(All)	$16.0(
5	3/5/97	(Top 10...)	$20.0(
6	4/4/96	(Custom...)	$16.0(
7	8/5/96	inventory	$16.0(
8	10/7/96	office furniture	$14.9(
9	12/5/96	overhead salary	$10.9(
10	1/1/97	(Blanks)	$1.0(
11	1/5/96	(NonBlanks)	$1.0(
12	3/1/97	overhead	$1.0(

3 Click desired automatic filter option.

All: Displays all items for this field.

Top 10: Select Top/Bottom items or percent of numeric items to display.

Custom: Selects two criteria using AND or OR comparison operators.

item: Displays only records containing item you select in this field.

Blanks: Displays only records containing blank items for this field.

NonBlanks: Displays only records containing nonblank items for this field.

3	Date	Expense	Amount	Vendor
26	4/14/97	office furniture	$5,000	AR Office
27	5/14/91	office furniture	$4,000	AR Office
250				

Blue AutoFilter arrow indicates a filter has been set for column.

Filter Shows Records with Expenses that equal "office furniture" AND Amounts greater than $3,000

157

Filter Lists (Advanced)

Advanced Filter lets you display only rows in a list that meet predefined criteria that you enter in a range of cells called the *criteria range*. For information about setting up a list, see *Lists*.

Data ➔ Filter ➔ Advanced Filter...

Notes:

- A **list** (or database) must contain labels that define **field names** so Excel can determine categories of the data in the list (see Lists).

- A **criterion** identifies a condition that must be met. A **criteria range** tells Excel where the criteria you entered are located.

Set Up a Criteria Range for Comparison Criteria

The criteria range you set prior to using Advanced Filter tells Excel how to filter a list.

1. Insert blank rows above list you want to filter.
2. Copy column labels in the list to blank rows above the list.

   NOTE: These labels are called **comparison labels**. They must be identical to the labels in the list you want to filter.

3. Enter criteria below criteria labels using these guidelines:
   - The criteria range cannot contain empty columns.
   - To show records meeting *all* of the criteria in the criteria range, enter criteria in same row.
   - To show records meeting *any* of the criteria in the criteria range, enter criteria in different rows.
   - To show records meeting different criteria for the same column, set up duplicate criteria labels.

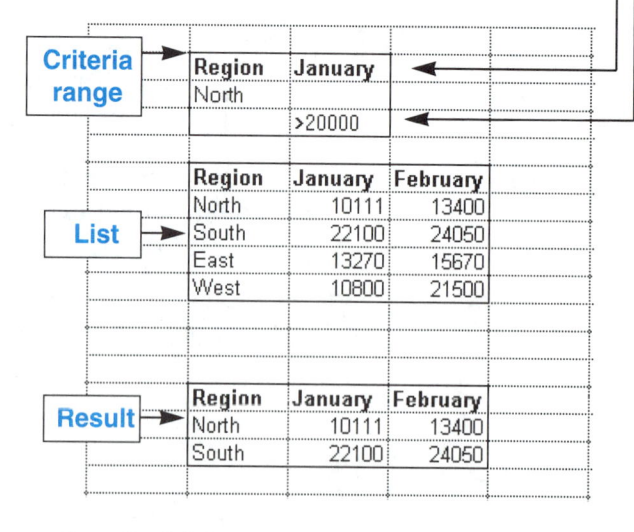

Criteria range

Region	January
North	
	>20000

List

Region	January	February
North	10111	13400
South	22100	24050
East	13270	15670
West	10800	21500

Result

Region	January	February
North	10111	13400
South	22100	24050

Result of Advanced Filter Criteria Copied to Another Location

Notes:

- These examples include typical criteria you can use to set up a criteria range.

Criteria Examples

TO FIND:	EXAMPLE:
an exact text match	="=text to find"
any character in a specific position	Topic?
consecutive characters in a specific position	Sa*y
a question mark, asterisk, or tilde	What is that~?
a value greater than another value	>1000

Notes:

- You must set up the criteria range before filtering a list.

- In **steps 4** and **5**, you can insert references in the dialog boxes by clicking in the box, then dragging through cells in worksheet.

  To change a reference in a dialog box, first select the existing reference and press **Delete**.

- When a list is filtered in-place:

  The status line reports the number of records (rows) found.

  You can use the following features to work with the visible cells: AutoSum, Chart, Clear, Copy, Delete, Format, Print, Sort, Subtotal.

Filter a List with Advanced Filtering

1 Set up criteria range *(see previous page)*.
2 Click the **Data** menu, then point to **Filter**.
3 Click **Advanced Filter** on the submenu.
   The Advanced Filter dialog box appears.

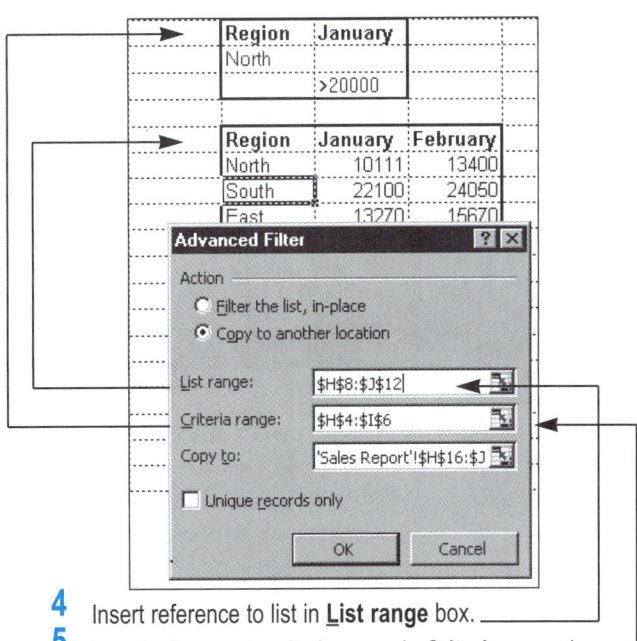

4 Insert reference to list in **List range** box.
5 Insert reference to criteria range in **Criteria range** box.
6 Select **Filter the list, in-place**.
   OR
   Select **Copy to another location**, then insert destination reference in **Copy to** box.
7 Click **OK**.

To end in-place filtering:

- Click the **Data** menu, point to **Filter**, then click **Show All**.

159

Goal Seek

The Goal Seek feature adjusts a value in a specified cell until a dependent formula achieves the desired goal. For example, you can use Goal Seek to find the sales needed for a sales person to achieve a total compensation of $100,000.

Tools → Goal Seek...

Notes:

- In **step 1**, **dependent values** are cells to which a formula refers.

- In **step 2**, you may have to click the button at the bottom of the menu to view the **Goal Seek** command.

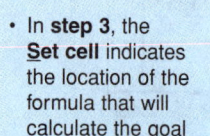

- In **step 3**, the **Set cell** indicates the location of the formula that will calculate the goal specified in the **To value** box.

- In **step 5**, the **By changing cell** box identifies the value to change in order to obtain the desired goal.

Find a Specific Solution to a Formula with Goal Seek

1. Enter data, formula, and dependent values.
2. Click **Tools** menu, then click **Goal Seek**.

   The Goal Seek dialog box appears.

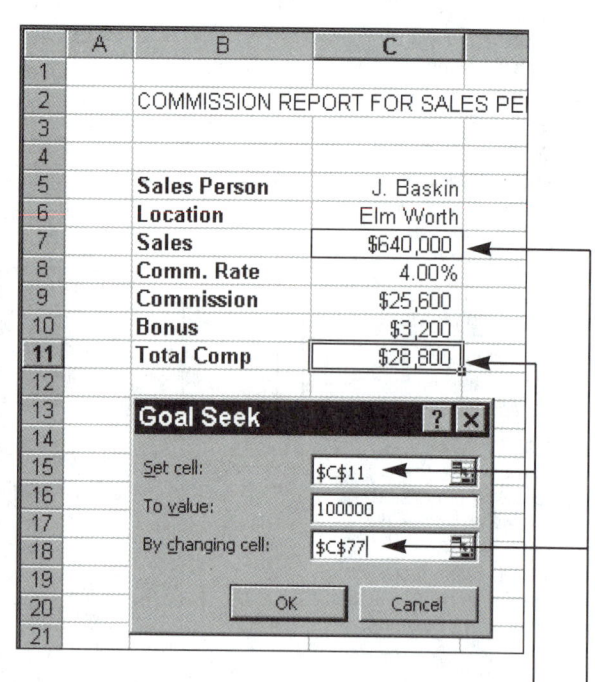

3. Insert reference to cell containing formula in **Set cell** box.
4. In the **To value** box type the goal for the formula.
5. Insert reference to cell containing value to change in the **By changing cell** box.
6. Click **OK** when done.

continued . . .

160

Notes:

- In **step 7**, click the **Step** command to move through the goal-seeking iterations one step at a time. This option will not be available if your computer performs the calculations quickly.

- **Iterations** are the number of times Excel will calculate a formula until a specific result or condition is met. To set limits for iterations refer to *Set Calculation Options*.

Find a Specific Solution to a Formula with Goal Seek (continued)

The Goal Seek Status dialog box appears.

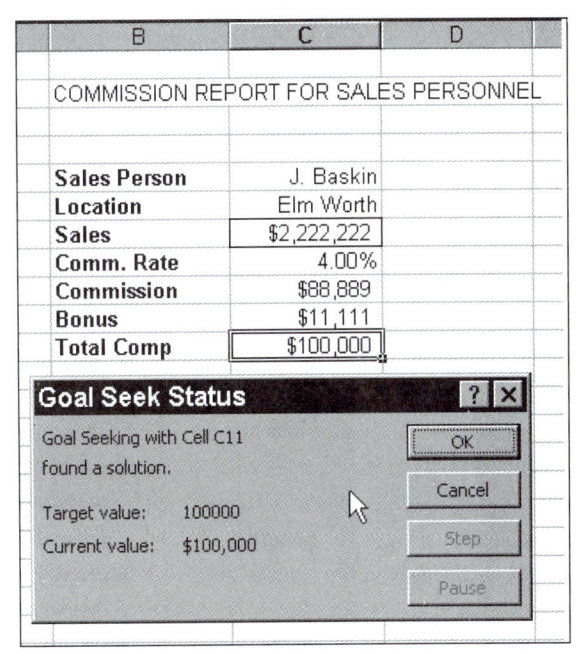

	B	C	D
	COMMISSION REPORT FOR SALES PERSONNEL		
	Sales Person	J. Baskin	
	Location	Elm Worth	
	Sales	$2,222,222	
	Comm. Rate	4.00%	
	Commission	$88,889	
	Bonus	$11,111	
	Total Comp	$100,000	

Goal Seek Status

Goal Seeking with Cell C11 found a solution.

Target value: 100000
Current value: $100,000

[OK] [Cancel] [Step] [Pause]

7 Click **OK** to change current value to the Goal Seek solution.

OR

Click **Cancel** to retain original values.

TIP: Excel provides a custom program (or add-in) called Solver to solve complex what-if problems. Solver's methods are similar to that of Goal Seek. If you installed Solver, you can click the **T**ools menu, then Sol**v**er, to run it.

To install Solver: Click the **T**ools menu, click Add-**I**ns, select Solver Add-in, then click OK.

Lists

Excel recognizes information organized in rows with column labels as a list (or database). Excel treats each row in a list as a record and each column as a field. Field names are derived from the column labels. Once you create a list, you can perform database tasks, such as sorting and filtering, and generate subtotals or PivotTables.

Date	Expense	Amount	Vendor
2/5/91	taxes	$440	City of Franklin
3/1/91	taxes	$440	City of Franklin

Notes:

- You should format **field names** differently from the records in your list.
- If field names must contain two lines, keep them in one cell by pressing **Alt+Enter** to create a line break.
- Do not leave a blank row between the field names and the first record.
- The data entered in each record of a field should be of a consistent type. That is, the data should be all values or all text. This will produce better results when performing database operations like sorting.

Parts of a List

A list, or database, consists of records organized in rows and columns as follows:

Field names ..... Identify categories of information. Indicate the field names by typing column labels.
Example: Expense, Amount

Records .... Each row, except the first row of labels, is a record in the list.
Example: 2/5/91, taxes, $440, City of ...

Fields .... Each column is a field in the list.
Example: The Expense field, the Amount field

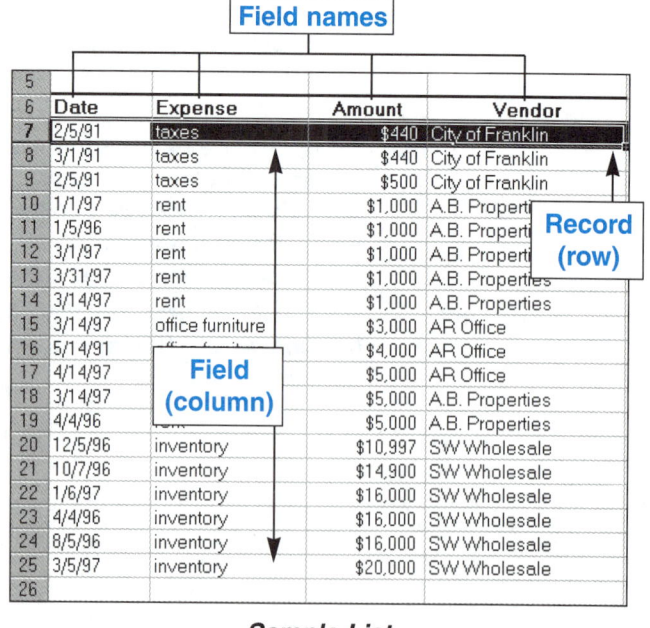

	Date	Expense	Amount	Vendor
7	2/5/91	taxes	$440	City of Franklin
8	3/1/91	taxes	$440	City of Franklin
9	2/5/91	taxes	$500	City of Franklin
10	1/1/97	rent	$1,000	A.B. Properties
11	1/5/96	rent	$1,000	A.B. Properties
12	3/1/97	rent	$1,000	A.B. Properties
13	3/31/97	rent	$1,000	A.B. Properties
14	3/14/97	rent	$1,000	A.B. Properties
15	3/14/97	office furniture	$3,000	AR Office
16	5/14/91		$4,000	AR Office
17	4/14/97		$5,000	AR Office
18	3/14/97		$5,000	A.B. Properties
19	4/4/96		$5,000	A.B. Properties
20	12/5/96	inventory	$10,997	SW Wholesale
21	10/7/96	inventory	$14,900	SW Wholesale
22	1/6/97	inventory	$16,000	SW Wholesale
23	4/4/96	inventory	$16,000	SW Wholesale
24	8/5/96	inventory	$16,000	SW Wholesale
25	3/5/97	inventory	$20,000	SW Wholesale

Sample List

Notes:

- When possible, store lists below data in a worksheet. This way, as the list grows it will not overlap your data. Place list summary labels and formulas above the list for the same reason.

Where to Place Lists

Keep the following guidelines in mind when placing a list:

- If you need to store more than one list in a workbook, it is best to store each on its own worksheet.

  *Reason: The **AutoFilter** command can only process one list in a worksheet at a time.*

- Do not store other data in cells adjacent to list data.

  Reason: It is hard to distinguish where the list ends and other data begins.

- Avoid storing data to the left or right of a list.

  Reason: When you filter records in a list, Excel hides entire rows, including data outside the list.

Notes:

- When you insert records, Excel extends references to ranges affected by the insertion.

  For example, the formula =SUM(C10:C100) would become =SUM(C10:C102) after you insert records as shown in the example to the right.

- To add a record to the end of a list: Enter new record below last record in list.

Insert Records in a List

1 Select records where new records will be inserted.

  NOTE: The number of records (rows) you select tells Excel how many cells to insert.

2 Right-click the selection.

3 Click **Insert** on shortcut menu.

  The Insert dialog box appears.

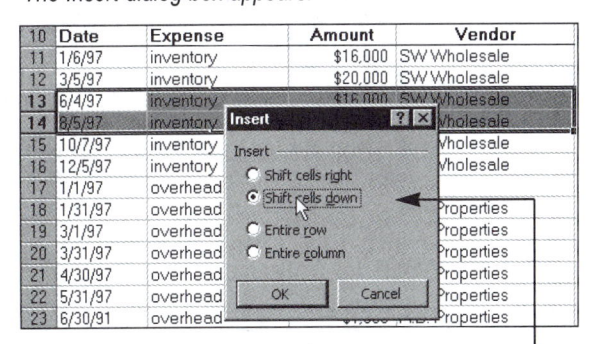

4 If prompted, click **Shift cells down**, then click **OK**.

5 Enter new records in inserted cells.

Notes:

- In **step 1**, you can select the entire row, if you are sure that any data to the left or right of the list will not be affected. Also see *Insert Cells, Columns, and Rows*.

Delete Records in a List

1 Select entire record.

2 Right-click the selection, then click **Delete** on shortcut menu.

  The Delete dialog box appears.

3 Click **Shift cells up**, then click **OK**.

163

Outlines

To use the Outline feature, you must have a list containing detailed data and summary rows consistently placed below the details. Once you outline a list, you can expand and collapse information levels to work with the data.

Data → **Group and Outline** → **Auto Outline**

Notes:

- To clear an outline: Click the **Data** menu and click **Group and Outline**, then click **Clear Outline**.
- Excel automatically outlines lists when you use the SubTotals feature. *(See Subtotal Lists Automatically.)*

Outline a List

1. Create and organize list so that related information is grouped together and summary rows (which must contain formulas) appear consistently below the details.
2. Select any cell in the list.
3. Click the **Data** menu, then point to **Group and Outline**.

   *You may have to click the button at the bottom of the menu to view the **Group and Outline** command.*

4. Click **Auto Outline** on the submenu.

   Outline controls appear to the left of row headings.

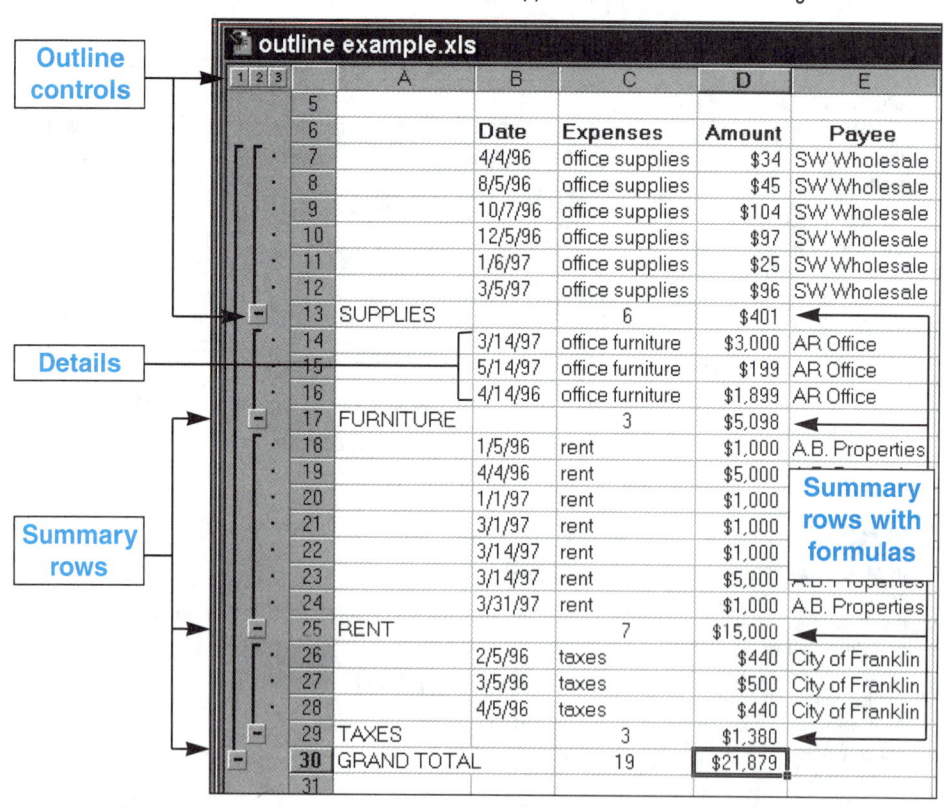

Outline controls →

Details →

Summary rows →

	A	B	C	D	E
5					
6		Date	Expenses	Amount	Payee
7		4/4/96	office supplies	$34	SW Wholesale
8		8/5/96	office supplies	$45	SW Wholesale
9		10/7/96	office supplies	$104	SW Wholesale
10		12/5/96	office supplies	$97	SW Wholesale
11		1/6/97	office supplies	$25	SW Wholesale
12		3/5/97	office supplies	$96	SW Wholesale
13	SUPPLIES		6	$401	
14		3/14/97	office furniture	$3,000	AR Office
15		5/14/97	office furniture	$199	AR Office
16		4/14/96	office furniture	$1,899	AR Office
17	FURNITURE		3	$5,098	
18		1/5/96	rent	$1,000	A.B. Properties
19		4/4/96	rent	$5,000	A.B. Properties
20		1/1/97	rent	$1,000	
21		3/1/97	rent	$1,000	**Summary rows with formulas**
22		3/14/97	rent	$1,000	
23		3/14/97	rent	$5,000	
24		3/31/97	rent	$1,000	A.B. Properties
25	RENT		7	$15,000	
26		2/5/96	taxes	$440	City of Franklin
27		3/5/96	taxes	$500	City of Franklin
28		4/5/96	taxes	$440	City of Franklin
29	TAXES		3	$1,380	
30	GRAND TOTAL		19	$21,879	
31					

Outlined List

164

Notes:

- After you click the **Hide Detail** button, Excel hides the group. Only the summary information appears (SUPPLIES, in the illustration).

Collapse and Expand Outline Levels

To collapse an outline group:
- Click **Hide Detail** button.

To expand an outline group:
- Click **Show Detail** button.

To show all outline groups for a specific level:
- Click **level** button for lowest level to show.

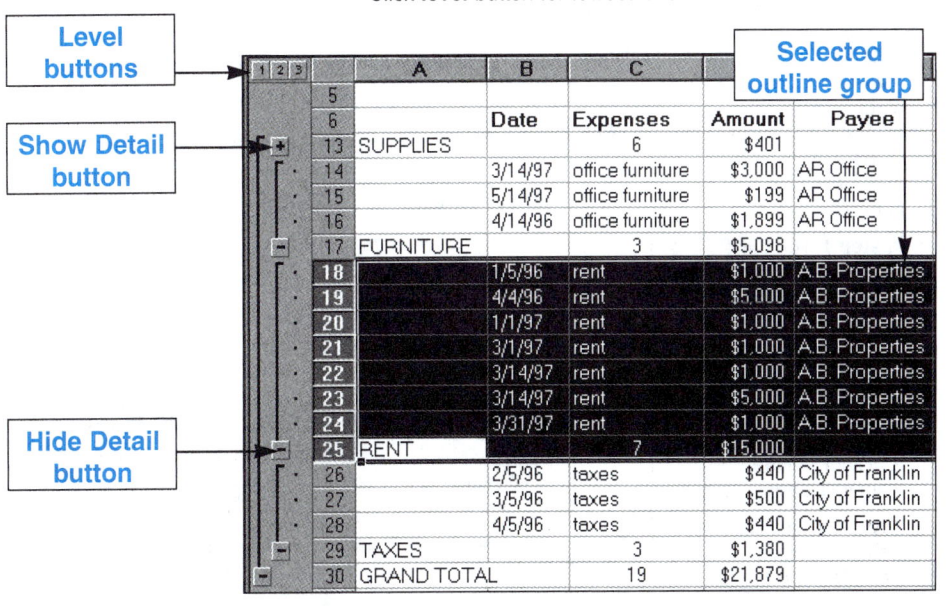

Level buttons

Show Detail button

Hide Detail button

Selected outline group

	A	B	C	
5				
6		Date	Expenses	Amount	Payee
13	SUPPLIES		6	$401
14		3/14/97	office furniture	$3,000	AR Office
15		5/14/97	office furniture	$199	AR Office
16		4/14/96	office furniture	$1,899	AR Office
17	FURNITURE		3	$5,098
18		1/5/96	rent	$1,000	A.B. Properties
19		4/4/96	rent	$5,000	A.B. Properties
20		1/1/97	rent	$1,000	A.B. Properties
21		3/1/97	rent	$1,000	A.B. Properties
22		3/14/97	rent	$1,000	A.B. Properties
23		3/14/97	rent	$5,000	A.B. Properties
24		3/31/97	rent	$1,000	A.B. Properties
25	RENT		7	$15,000
26		2/5/96	taxes	$440	City of Franklin
27		3/5/96	taxes	$500	City of Franklin
28		4/5/96	taxes	$440	City of Franklin
29	TAXES		3	$1,380
30	GRAND TOTAL		19	$21,879

Example: level 2 result

	A	B	C	D	E
5					
6		Date	Expenses	Amount	Payee
13	SUPPLIES		6	$401	
17	FURNITURE		3	$5,098	
25	RENT		7	$15,000	
29	TAXES		3	$1,380	
30	GRAND TOTAL		19	$21,879	

TIP: To quickly select an outline group, press Shift and click the Hide Detail button.

TIP: After collapsing outline levels, you can select and chart only the visible cells.

165

Sort Lists

You can sort a list to arrange rows (records) in alphabetical or numerical order. Sorting groups equivalent items (such as customers from Chicago). You can arrange information in reverse alphabetical or numerical order and sort by more than one column (field), such as by Lastname, then Firstname, then State.

Data ➡ A↓ Sort...

Notes:

- A **list** is a set of rows and columns that contain related data. Excel uses the labels in the first row of a list as field names.
- In **step 1**, you must select a cell within the list that you are sorting and the column you want to sort by.
- Excel automatically detects field names. It will not include them in the sort.
- You can click the **Edit** menu, then **Undo** to undo the sort.
- You can sort selected cells. Excel sorts only the cells in the selection and uses the active cell as the primary **sort key** — the field Excel sorts by.

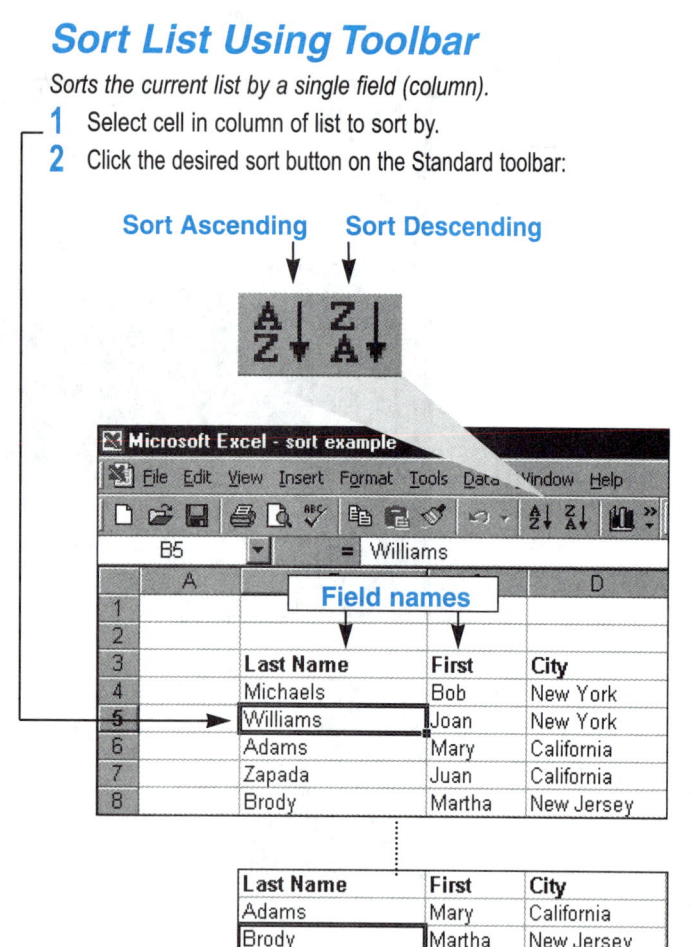

Sort List Using Toolbar

Sorts the current list by a single field (column).

1 Select cell in column of list to sort by.
2 Click the desired sort button on the Standard toolbar:

Sort Ascending   Sort Descending

A↓   Z↓
Z   A

Field names

Last Name	First	City
Michaels	Bob	New York
Williams	Joan	New York
Adams	Mary	California
Zapada	Juan	California
Brody	Martha	New Jersey

Last Name	First	City
Adams	Mary	California
Brody	Martha	New Jersey
Michaels	Bob	New York
Williams	Joan	New York
Zapada	Juan	California

List Sorted (by Last Name) Using Sort Ascending Button

166

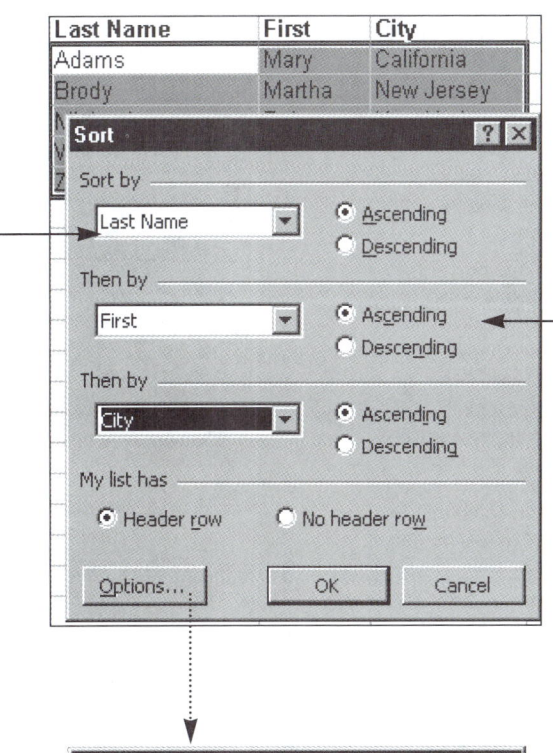

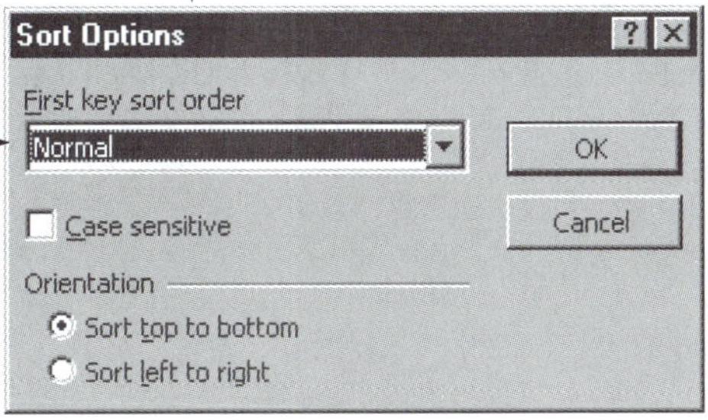

Notes:

- In **step 3**, the **Sort by** field is the first field (column) by which the sets of related data will be arranged. You can select two additional sort fields so that rows containing identical primary field information can be sorted further.

- To sort by more than three columns, sort the list using the least important columns. Then do a second sort using the most important columns.

- When you sort rows that are part of an outline, Excel will keep outline families together.

TIP: Click **Options** to select custom sort orders, change the sort orientation, or to create a case-sensitive sort order.

Sort List Using Menu

1 Select any cell in list.

2 Click the **Data** menu, then click **Sort**.
The Sort dialog box appears.

3 Select primary field to sort by in **Sort by** box.

4 Select **Ascending** or **Descending** order.

To sort by multiple fields:

a Select secondary fields to sort by in **Then by** boxes.

b Select **Ascending** or **Descending** order for each field.

5 If your list does not contain field names (header row), select **No header row**.

6 Click **OK** when done.

167

Subtotal Lists Automatically

The Subtotals feature generates summary information and grand totals for information organized in a list. When you complete the Subtotals operation, Excel outlines the list and provides controls for collapsing and expanding detail levels. See *Outlines* for information about using outline controls.

Data → Subtotals...

Notes:

- A **list** (or database) must contain labels that define **field names**.
- **Field names** identify categories of information in a list.
- In a list, each row of information is considered a **record**.
- Other Subtotal options:

    Replace current subtotals — select when you do not want to create additional subtotal levels.

    Page break between groups — inserts page breaks between each group so you can print groups on separate pages.

    Summary below data — sets location of summary rows.

- You can click the **Edit** menu, then **Undo Subtotals** to quickly undo the Subtotal operation.

Subtotal a List Automatically

1 Sort columns to subtotal *(see Sort Lists)*, then select any cell in list.

   NOTE: *Sort list by all fields you intend to subtotal.*

2 Click **Data** menu, then click **Subtotals**.

   The Subtotal dialog box appears.

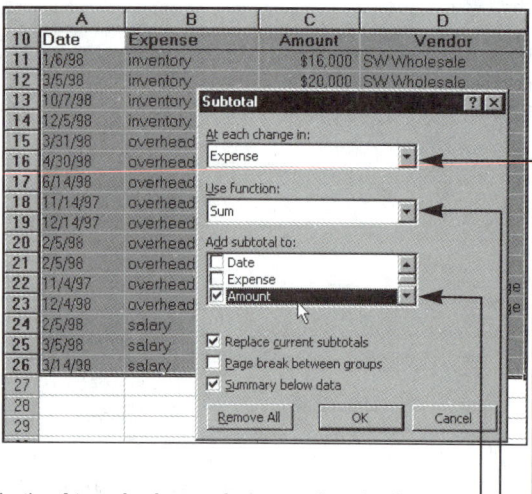

3 In the **At each change in** box, select the field you want to subtotal.

4 In the **Use function** box, select desired function.

5 In the **Add subtotal to** box, click the field name to calculate.

6 Select other applicable options *(see Notes)*.

7 Click **OK** when done.

continued . . .

Notes:

- You can press **Ctrl+8** to hide or show outline controls.

Subtotal a List Automatically (continued)

After you select subtotal options, Excel generates the summary rows and automatically outlines the list. (For information about outlines and outline controls see Outlines.)

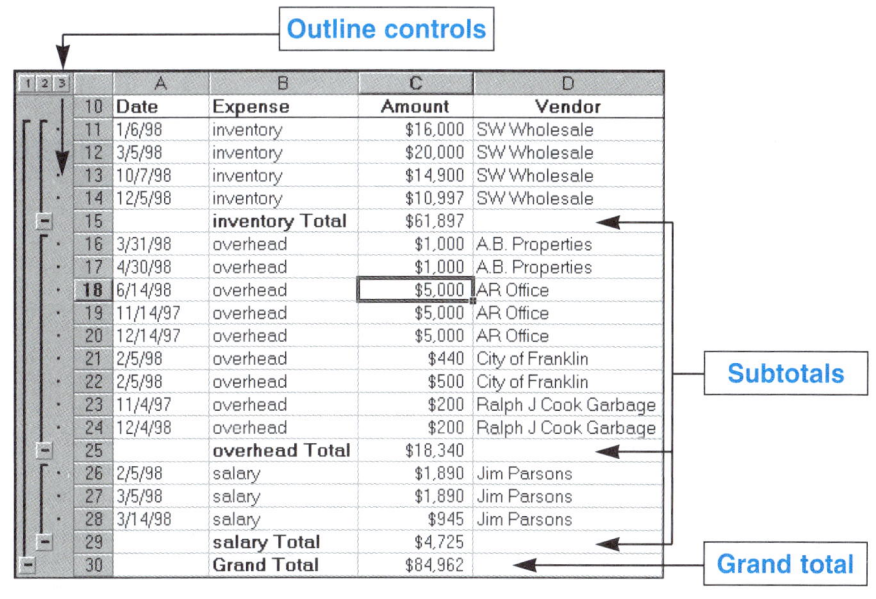

Outline controls

	A	B	C	D
10	Date	Expense	Amount	Vendor
11	1/6/98	inventory	$16,000	SW Wholesale
12	3/5/98	inventory	$20,000	SW Wholesale
13	10/7/98	inventory	$14,900	SW Wholesale
14	12/5/98	inventory	$10,997	SW Wholesale
15		inventory Total	$61,897	
16	3/31/98	overhead	$1,000	A.B. Properties
17	4/30/98	overhead	$1,000	A.B. Properties
18	6/14/98	overhead	$5,000	AR Office
19	11/14/97	overhead	$5,000	AR Office
20	12/14/97	overhead	$5,000	AR Office
21	2/5/98	overhead	$440	City of Franklin
22	2/5/98	overhead	$500	City of Franklin
23	11/4/97	overhead	$200	Ralph J Cook Garbage
24	12/4/98	overhead	$200	Ralph J Cook Garbage
25		overhead Total	$18,340	
26	2/5/98	salary	$1,890	Jim Parsons
27	3/5/98	salary	$1,890	Jim Parsons
28	3/14/98	salary	$945	Jim Parsons
29		salary Total	$4,725	
30		Grand Total	$84,962	

Subtotals

Grand total

Subtotaled List

TIP: To subtotal other fields, repeat steps to Subtotal a List Automatically, select the field and functions, then deselect the Replace current subtotals option.

Notes:

- When you remove subtotals from a list, Excel also removes the Outline controls.
- You cannot undo the **Remove All** command.

Remove Subtotals from a List

1. Select any cell in list.
2. Click the **Data** menu, then click **Subtotals**.
   The Subtotal dialog box appears.
3. Click **Remove All**.

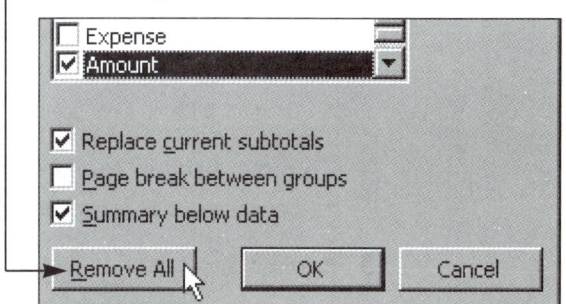

169

Use Data Forms with Lists

The Data Form feature lets you work with list information one record at a time. From a data form you can view, change, add, delete, and find records stored in the current list.

Notes:

- A **list** (or database) must contain labels that define **field names**, so Excel can determine the categories of the data *(see Lists)*.

- In a list, each row of information is considered a **record**.

- In **step 2**, you may have to click the button at the bottom of the menu to view the **Form** command.

- A data form is particularly useful when your records span many columns. It also simplifies the process of inserting or adding records to a list.

- You can also use the **up** and **down** arrow keys to find the previous or next record.

Open Data Form and Navigate

1 Select any cell in list.
2 Click the **Data** menu, then click **Form**.

   The Data form dialog box appears.

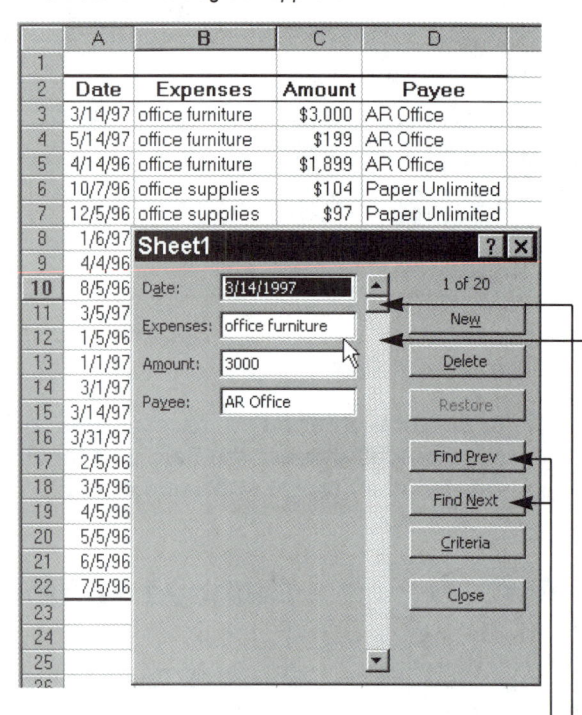

To view next or previous record:

- Click **Find Next** or **Find Prev**.

To scroll to a record:

- Drag **scroll box** up or down.

To move back or forward ten records:

- Click above or below **scroll box** on scroll bar.

3 To close the data form, click **Close** button.

Notes:

- In **step 1**, to open data form, click the **Data** menu, then click **Form**.

- In **step 2**, you can press **Tab** to quickly move to the next field and select its contents.

- Once you move to another record, you cannot restore a change made to the previous record.

- The **Restore** option is only available when a change has been made to the record.

Edit Records in a Data Form

1. Open the data form, then navigate to record to change.
2. Click in field box of record to change.
3. Use the usual editing techniques to change the record, such as selecting data to delete, overwriting selected data, and inserting data from the Clipboard.

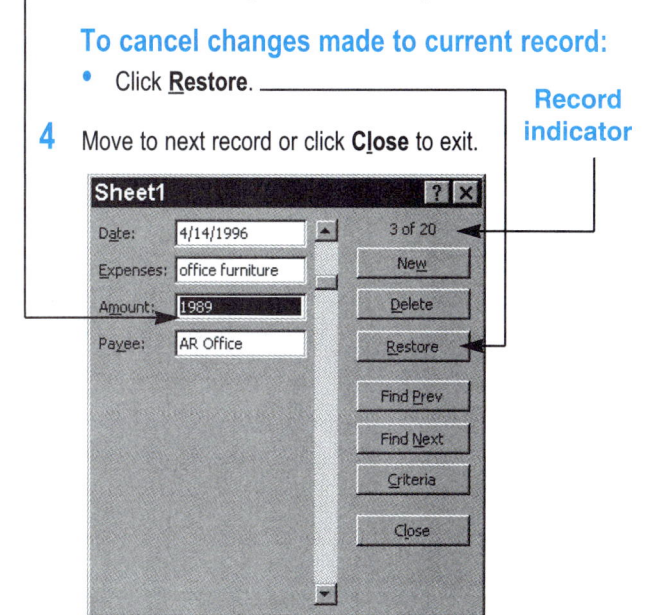

To cancel changes made to current record:

- Click **Restore**.

4. Move to next record or click **Close** to exit.

Record indicator

```
Sheet1                        ? X
Date:     4/14/1996        3 of 20
Expenses: office furniture    New
Amount:   1989                Delete
Payee:    AR Office           Restore
                              Find Prev
                              Find Next
                              Criteria
                              Close
```

Notes:

- In **step 3**, if you type criteria (conditions) in multiple fields, Excel will find only records meeting all conditions.

- In **step 4**, repeat this step to view all records that meet your criteria.

- Your criteria may contain wild cards and comparison operators, as shown in the illustration.

- To end filtering records, click **Criteria**, then **Clear**, then **Form**.

Find Specific Records in a List

1. Open the data form.
2. Click **Criteria**.
3. Type criteria in field boxes.
4. Click **Find Next** or **Find Prev**.

Criteria indicator

```
Sheet1                        ? X
Date:     2/5/96           Criteria
Expenses:                     New
Amount:   >1000               Clear
Payee:    A?                  Restore
                              Find Prev
                              Find Next
                              Form
                              Close
```

171

Printing and Page Setup

This section contains illustrated procedures arranged in alphabetical order, covering printing and page setup skills.

Page Breaks

Page breaks determine where worksheet pages begin and end when printing. Excel automatically creates page breaks as you work, based on the size of your worksheet, margins, scale, and other settings. However, you can insert and move page breaks to control your print results.

Insert → Page Break / Remove Page Break

Notes:
- The location of automatic page breaks is determined by:
  - Paper size and orientation
  - Margins
  - Headers and footers
  - Print scale
  - Manual page breaks

View Automatic Page Breaks

1. Click the **Tools** menu, then click **Options**.
   The Options dialog box appears.
2. Click the **View** tab.
3. Select **Page breaks**, then click **OK**.
   Dashed lines appear where page breaks will occur when printing.

Notes:
- In **step one**, to insert or remove:

  horizontal and vertical page break, select cell where new pages will start.

  horizontal page break, select row where new page will start.

  vertical page break, select column where new page will start.

Insert Manual Page Breaks

1. Select cell, column, or row to indicate placement of page breaks.
2. Click the **Insert** menu, then click **Page Break**.
   Dashed lines appear where pages will break when printed, and Excel recalculates automatic page breaks for worksheet data below and to the right of the manual page breaks.

Remove Manual Page Breaks

1. Select cell immediately to the right or below page break to remove.

   OR

   To remove all manual page breaks, click **Select All** button where row and column headings meet.
2. Click the **Insert** menu, then click **Remove Page Break** or **Reset All Page Breaks** (if entire worksheet was selected).
   Excel recalculates automatic page breaks for specified worksheet data.

View → 🔲 Page Break Preview / 🔲 Normal

Notes:
- While in Page Break mode, you can edit your worksheet as usual.

Open Page Break Preview

This view lets you adjust page breaks with the mouse.

From Page Preview:
- Click **Page Break Preview** on **Page Preview** toolbar.

From the worksheet:
- Click the **View** menu, then click **Page Break Preview**.

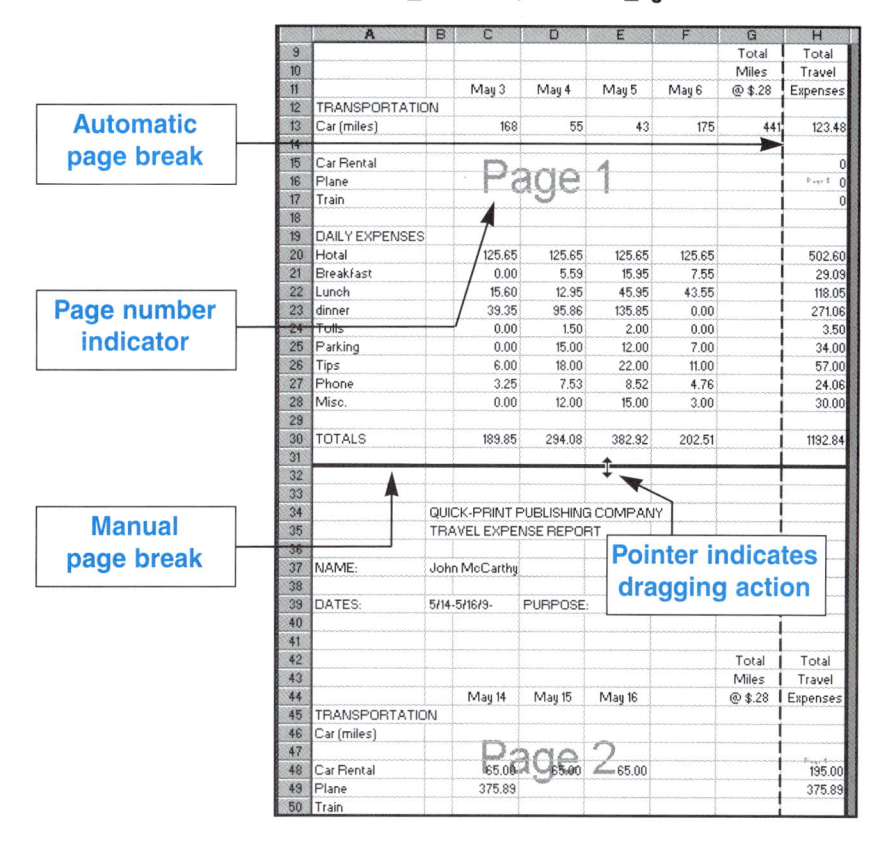

Automatic page break

Page number indicator

Manual page break

Pointer indicates dragging action

Notes:
- When you increase the area of a page by dragging a page break, Excel adjusts the scale of the printed page. *(See Set Scale and Orientation.)*

Change Page Breaks

To move a page break:
- Drag page break to desired location.

To remove a page break:
- Drag page break up or left off the print area.

175

Print Preview

The Print Preview feature lets you see how your worksheet will look when it's printed. From the Print Preview window you can zoom in and out, adjust margins, access the Page Setup dialog box to change settings, view other pages to print, and print your document.

Print Preview button

File → Print Preview

Notes:
- The document preview will be affected by the capabilities of the current printer.

Preview Your Document Before Printing It

1. Select worksheets, worksheet cells, or chart object that you intend to print.

   OR

   Select any cell to preview active worksheet.

2. Click **Print Preview** button on Standard toolbar.

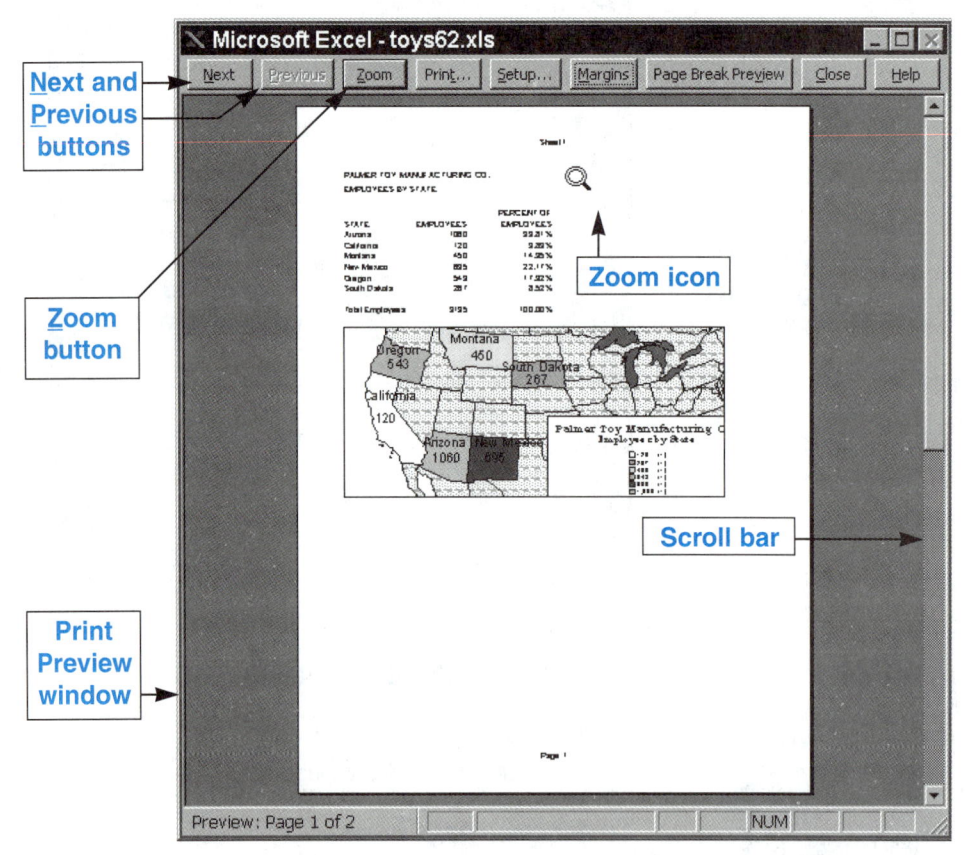

Next and Previous buttons

Zoom button

Zoom icon

Scroll bar

Print Preview window

3. Click **Zoom**, then click the pointer to zoom in and out.
4. Click **Next** or **Previous** to preview other pages.
5. Click **Close** when done.

Notes:

- For information about setting margins from Print Preview see *Set Margins*.

Adjust Columns While Previewing Workbook Data

1. Click **Margins** button on Print Preview toolbar.

   Margin and column handles appear in preview screen.

2. Drag a column handle to change a column dimension.

   As you drag the column handle, the status bar displays the column dimension.

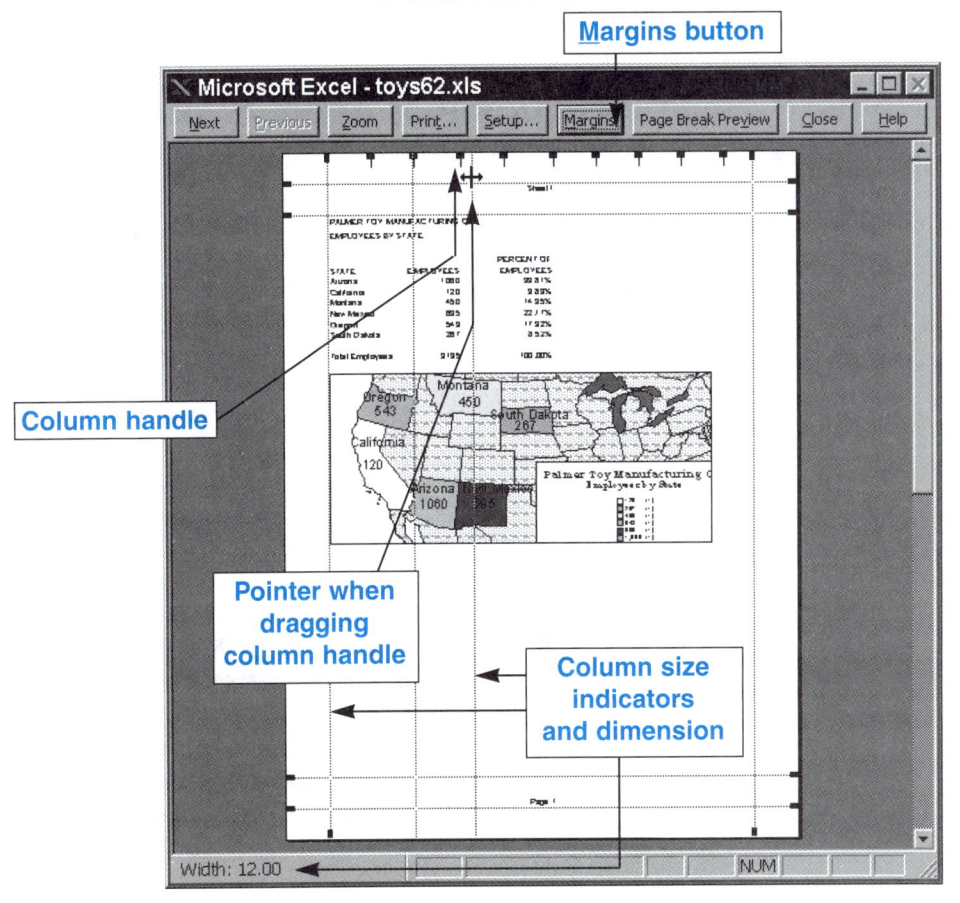

Margins button

Column handle

Pointer when dragging column handle

Column size indicators and dimension

Notes:

- When you are done making changes from **Page Setup**, Excel will return you to the **Print Preview** window.

Change Print Settings While Previewing Workbook

1. Click **Setup** button on Print Preview toolbar.

   The Page Setup dialog box appears.

2. Change settings as described in other **Page Setup** topics:

   Set Headers and Footers, Set Margins, Set Print Area, Set Repeating Print Titles, Set Scale and Orientation, Set Sheet Print Options.

177

Print Workbook Data

The Print feature lets you print the current worksheet, a selection in a worksheet, or an entire workbook. Additionally, you can specify which pages to print, collate printed pages, print multiple copies, and print to a file.

Print button

File → Print...

Notes:
- Consider using **Print Preview** to check how the worksheet will print prior to printing it *(see Print Preview).*

Settings that Affect Print Results

Before printing a worksheet or workbook, consider this checklist of settings that will affect print results:

Headers and footers: Prints repeating information at the top and bottom of each page. *(See Set Headers and Footers.)*

Page breaks: Determines locations in worksheet where printed pages end and new pages begin. *(See Page Breaks.)*

Margins: Determines free space around printed page.
(See Set Margins.)

Orientation: Determines whether the page prints in portrait or landscape orientation.
(See Set Scale and Orientation.)

Print area: Prints a specified area of the worksheet.
(See Set Print Area.)

Repeating print titles: Prints column titles at the top or left side of each new printed page. *(See Repeating Print Titles.)*

Scale: Determines the size of the worksheet information will be when printed. *(See Set Scale and Orientation.)*

Sheet options: Sets print options, such as gridlines, page order, draft quality, and black and white printing.
(See Set Sheet Print Options.)

Notes:
- If necessary, to show additional buttons on a toolbar, click More Buttons » on the right side of the toolbar.

Print Using Toolbar

1. Select worksheets, worksheet cells, or chart object to print.
   OR
   Select any cell to print current worksheet.
2. Click **Print** button on Standard toolbar.

Notes:

- In **step 1**, your selection will determine the parts of the workbook to print.

Print Using Menu

1 Select worksheets, worksheet cells, or chart object to print.

OR

Select any cell to print current worksheet.

2 Click the **File** menu, then click **Print**.

The Print dialog box appears.

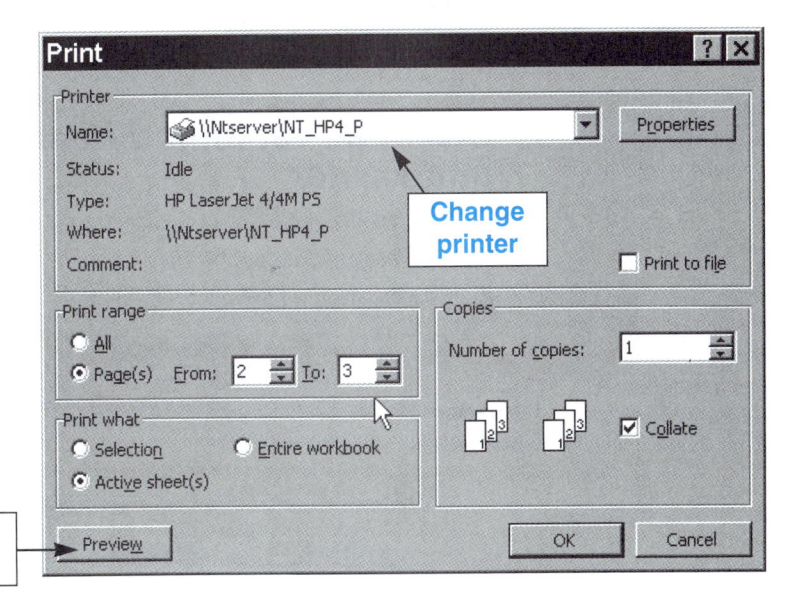

[Print dialog box screenshot with labels: "Change printer" pointing to Name field, "Click to preview" pointing to Preview button]

To indicate what to print:

- Select **Selection**, **Entire workbook**, or **Active sheet(s)**.

To specify pages to print:

- Select **All**, or select pages to print in **From** and **To** boxes.

To disable collating of printed pages:

- Deselect **Collate**.

To print multiple copies:

- Select number of copies in **Number of copies** box.

To print to a file:

- Select **Print to file**.

3 Click **OK** to print.

179

Set Headers and Footers

Headers and footers are text that automatically repeats at the top and bottom of each page when you print. You can select predefined headers and footers or design your own.

File → Page Setup... → Header/Footer

Notes:

- In **step 1**, you can group worksheets (press Ctrl and click sheet tabs), then set the headers and footers for all selected sheets at one time.

- The margins and font size used will determine the number of lines you can include in your headers and footers *(see Set Margins)*.

- Excel maintains a separate header and footer for each worksheet *(see TIP, below)*.

- You can preview your headers and footers before printing *(see Print Preview)*.

Select a Predefined Header and Footer

1 Click the **File** menu, then click **Page Setup**.

   The Page Setup dialog box appears.

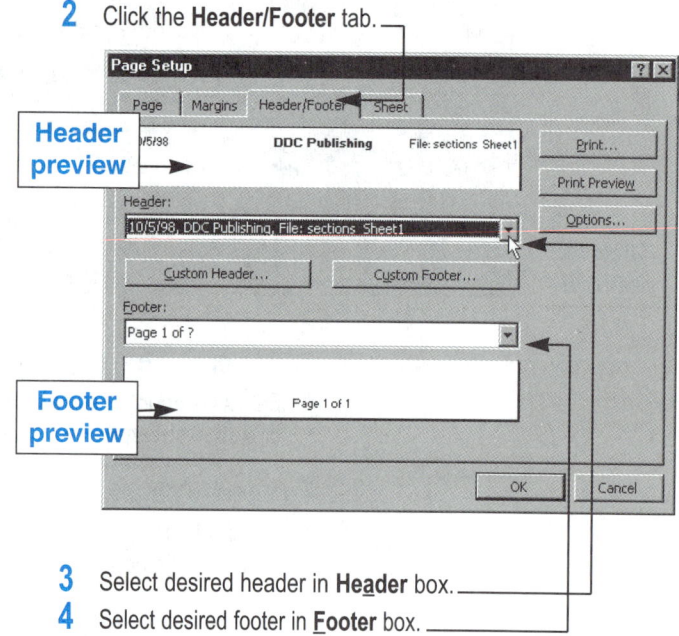

2 Click the **Header/Footer** tab.

3 Select desired header in **Header** box.
4 Select desired footer in **Footer** box.
5 Click **OK** when done.

180

Notes:

- When you click a code button, Excel inserts an ampersand (&), followed by a code, such as [Date]. You can insert the following codes in a header or footer:

Page number — displays current page number.
& [Page]

Total pages — displays total pages that will print.
&[Pages]

Date — displays current date.
&[Date]

Time — displays current time.
&[Time]

Filename — displays workbook name.
&[File]

Sheet name — displays worksheet name.
&[Tab]

Create a Custom Header and Footer

1. Click the **File** menu, then click **Page Setup**.
   The Page Setup dialog box appears.
2. Click the **Header/Footer** tab.
3. Click **Custom Header** or **Custom Footer**.
   The Header or Footer dialog box appears.
4. Click in section to change.
5. Type or edit text.

To format text:
a. Drag through text to format, then click the **Font** button.
b. Select font option, then click **OK**.

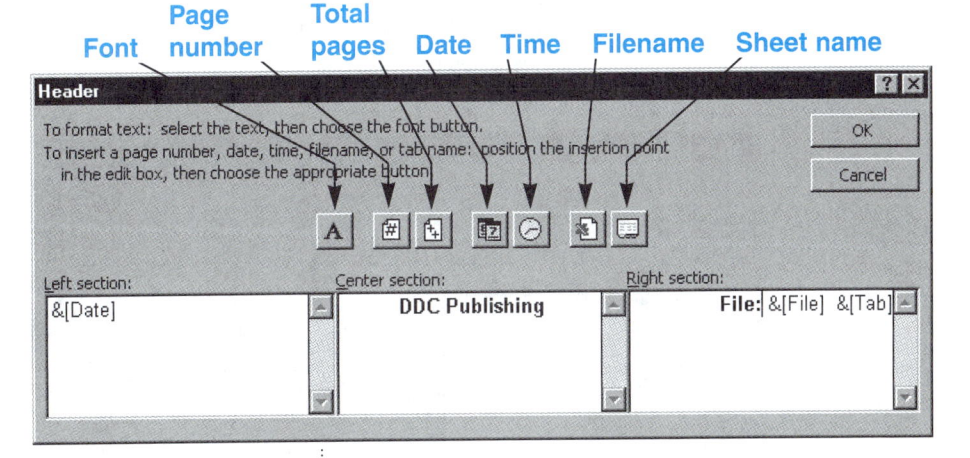

To insert a header or footer code:
a. Place insertion point in section where code will be inserted.
b. Click desired code button *(see Notes)*.
6. Click **OK** when done, then click **OK** to exit Page Setup.

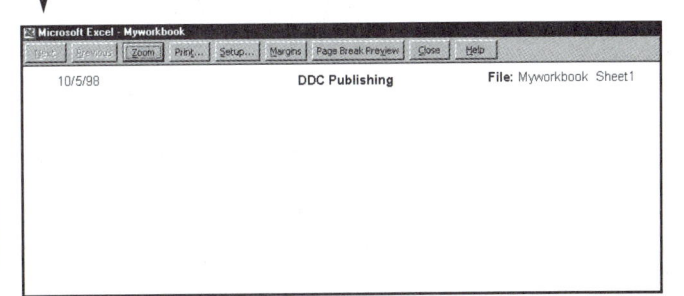

Result of Custom Header Settings

181

Set Margins

Margins determine the amount of blank space between the printed contents of a page and the top, bottom, left and right edges of the page. Header and footer margins are measured from the top and bottom of the page, respectively.

File → **Page Setup...** → **Margins**

Notes:

- If your data does not fit within the margins, you can change the scale. *(See Set Scale and Orientation.)*

Set Page Margins from Page Setup

1. Select sheet or sheets to which you want to apply margin setting.

    NOTE: *To select multiple sheets, press* **Ctrl** *and click each sheet tab you want to select.*

2. Click the **File** menu, then click **Page Setup**.

    The Page Setup dialog box appears.

3. Click the **Margin** tab.

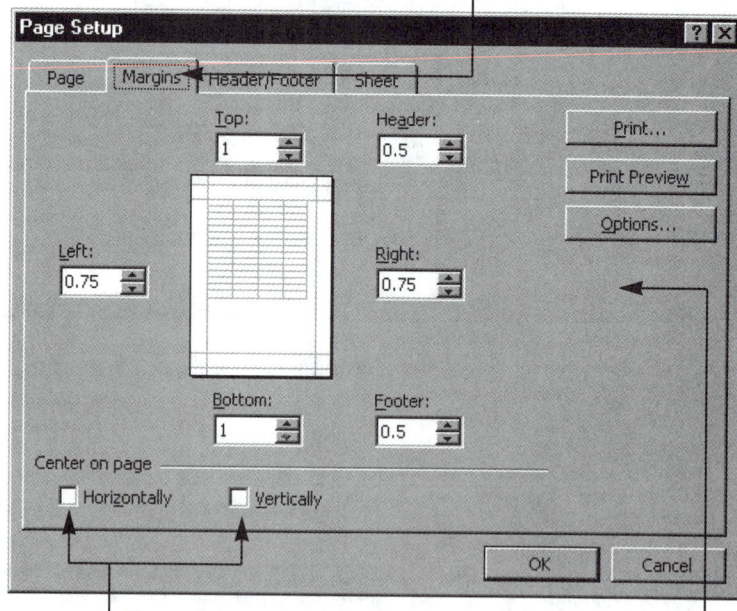

To set page margins:

- Type or select number of inches in **Top**, **Left**, **Right**, **Bottom**, **Header** and **Footer** margin boxes.

To center data within margins:

- Select **Horizontally** and/or **Vertically**.

182

Notes:

- Header and footer margins should be smaller than the top and bottom margin, respectively, to prevent the header and footer from overlapping the worksheet data.

Set Margins From Print Preview

Also see Print Preview.

1 Click **Print Preview button** on Standard toolbar.
2 Click **Margins** button on Print Preview toolbar.
   Margin and column handles appear in preview screen.
3 Drag margin handles to change margin dimensions.

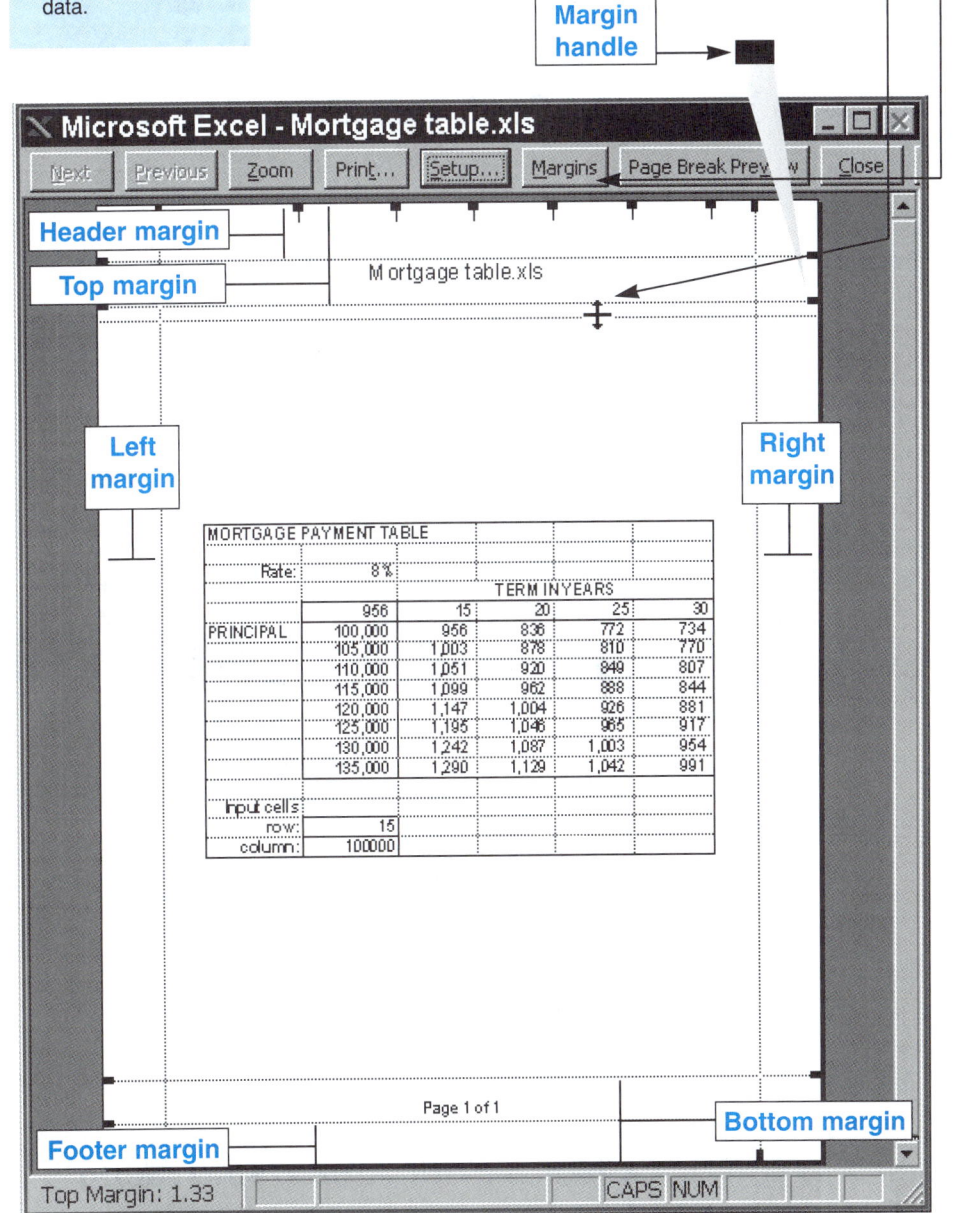

183

Set Print Area

Print area defines the range or ranges of a worksheet that will print when you issue a print command. If you select multiple ranges, each range will print on a separate page.

File ➡ Print Area ➡ Set Print Area

Notes:
- Print areas remain in effect until they are cleared or changed.

Set Print Area Using Menu

1 Select range or multiple ranges to print.

   NOTE: To select multiple ranges, press **Ctrl** while dragging through each range to select. Multiple ranges will print on separate pages.

2 Click the **File** menu, then point to or click **Print Area**.

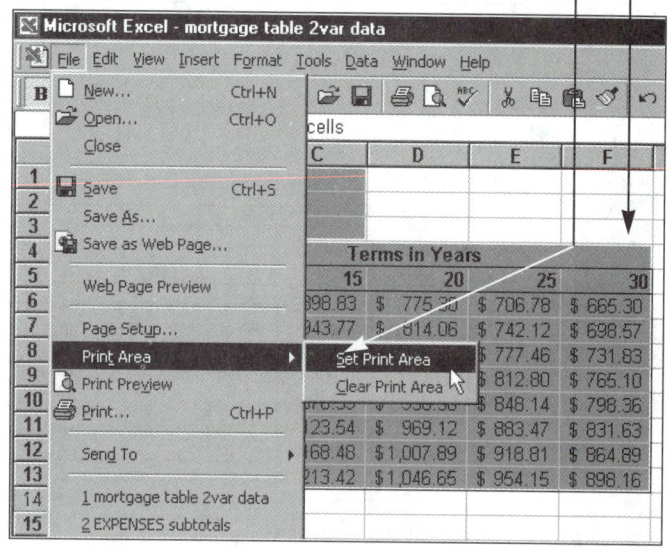

3 Click **Set Print Area** on the submenu.

   Excel outlines print area with a dashed line.

   ### To change the print area:
   - Repeat steps 1-3 above.

Clear a Print Area Using Menu

1 Click **File** menu, then point to **Print Area**.
2 Click **Clear Print Area** on the submenu.

Notes:

- While in Page Break Preview, you can also clear print areas by right-clicking any location in worksheet and clicking **Reset Print Area** on the shortcut menu.

Set Print Area from Page Break Preview

In Page Break Preview, Excel highlights only the defined print areas in your worksheet. The remainder of the worksheet appears grey.

To open Page Break Preview:

FROM PRINT PREVIEW

- Click [Page Break Preview] on Page Preview toolbar.

FROM WORKSHEET

- Click the **View** menu, then click **Page Break Preview**.

To set print area using shortcut menu:

a   Select range of cells to print.

b   Right-click selection.

   A shortcut menu appears.

c   Click **Set Print Area**.

   Excel highlights only the defined print areas in your worksheet.

Excel prints each selection on a separate page and indicates the page numbers.

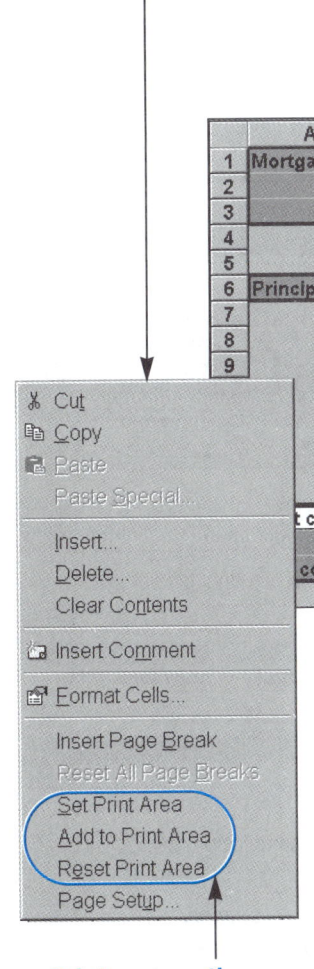

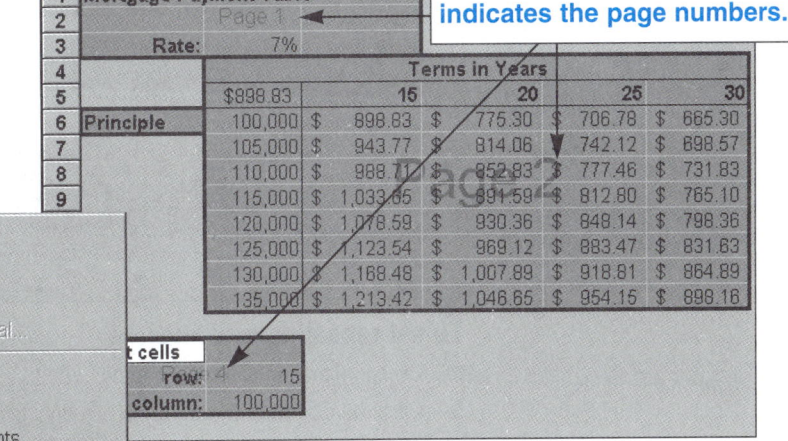

Page Break Preview

Print area options on shortcut menu

To add to print area using shortcut menu:

a   Select additional ranges to print.

b   Right-click selection.

   A shortcut menu appears.

c   Click **Add to Print Area**.

   Excel highlights only the defined print areas in your worksheet.

185

Set Repeating Print Titles

If you are printing a worksheet that spans many pages, you may want your row or column titles to appear on each printed page. Set your worksheet to print in this manner from the Sheet tab on the Page Setup dialog box.

File → **Page Setup...** → **Sheet**

Notes:

- After you set repeating rows and/or repeating columns, you can view the result before printing from Print Preview. (See Print Preview.)

- In most cases, you will set repeating rows or columns, but not both.

Set Titles of Worksheet Data to Print on Every Page

1. Click the **File** menu, then click **Page Setup**.

   The Page Setup dialog box appears.

2. Click the **Sheet** tab.

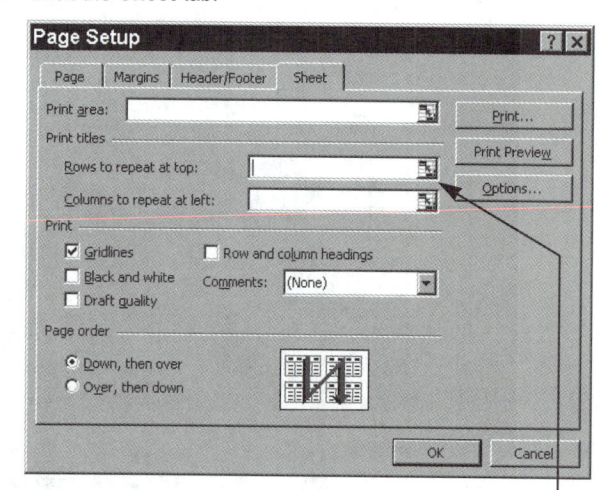

To set repeating row titles:

a. Click in **Rows to repeat at top** box.

b. Click the **Collapse Dialog** button on right side of box.

   The dialog box collapses.

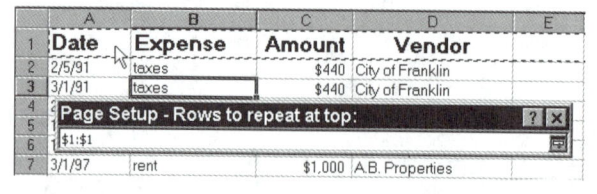

c. In your worksheet, select rows containing titles to repeat when printing.

   Excel inserts the row reference(s) in the box.

d. Click the **Restore Dialog** button to restore dialog box to its previous size.

continued . . .

186

> **Notes:**
> - If you access **Page Setup** from **Print Preview**, the **Sheet** options to set repeating rows and columns will not be available.

Set Titles of Worksheet Data to Print on Every Page (continued)

To set repeating column titles:

a Click in **Columns to repeat at left** box.

b Click the **Collapse Dialog** button on right side of box.

The dialog box collapses.

c In your worksheet, select columns containing titles to repeat when printing.

Excel inserts the column reference(s) in the box.

3 Click the **Restore Dialog** button to restore dialog box to its previous size.

4 Click **OK** when done.

5 Preview your worksheet to check the results.

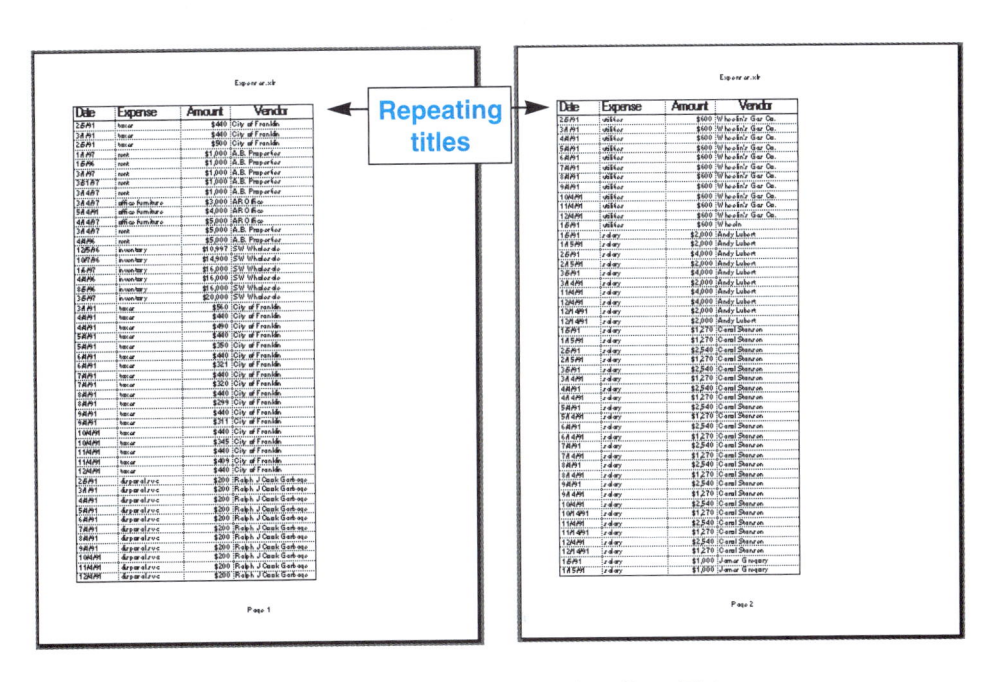

Page 1 and 2 with Repeating Row Titles

187

Set Scale and Orientation

Scale and Orientation are two page settings that determine your print results. Scaling lets you reduce or enlarge printed contents. Orientation lets you specify a portrait or landscape orientation for the printed page.

File → **Page Setup...** | **Page**

Notes:

- Before setting the scale to fit a large amount of data on one page, consider making the margins smaller *(See Set Margins).* This will minimize the amount of scaling necessary.

- Portrait orientation:

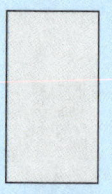

- Landscape orientation:

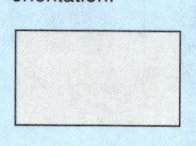

Set Scale, Orientation, and Related Page Settings

1 Click **File** menu, then click **Page Setup**.

The Page Setup dialog box appears.

2 Click the **Page** tab.

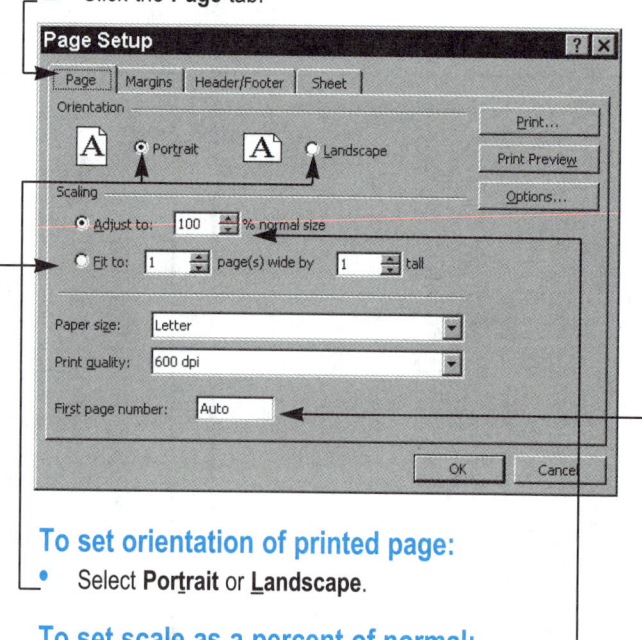

To set orientation of printed page:
- Select **Portrait** or **Landscape**.

To set scale as a percent of normal:
- Select **Adjust to**, then select or type percentage in **% normal size** box.

To scale data to fit on a specific number of pages:
- Select **Fit to**, then select number of **page(s) wide by** and number of pages **tall**.

To change the page number of first printed page:
- Type starting page number in **First page number** box.

continued . . .

188

> **Notes:**
> • **Paper size** and **print quality** options will depend upon the capabilities of your current printer.

Set Scale, Orientation, and Related Page Settings (continued)

To specify a paper size:
• Select paper size in **Paper size** list box.

To set print quality:
• Select desired print quality in **Print quality** box.

3 Click **OK** when done.

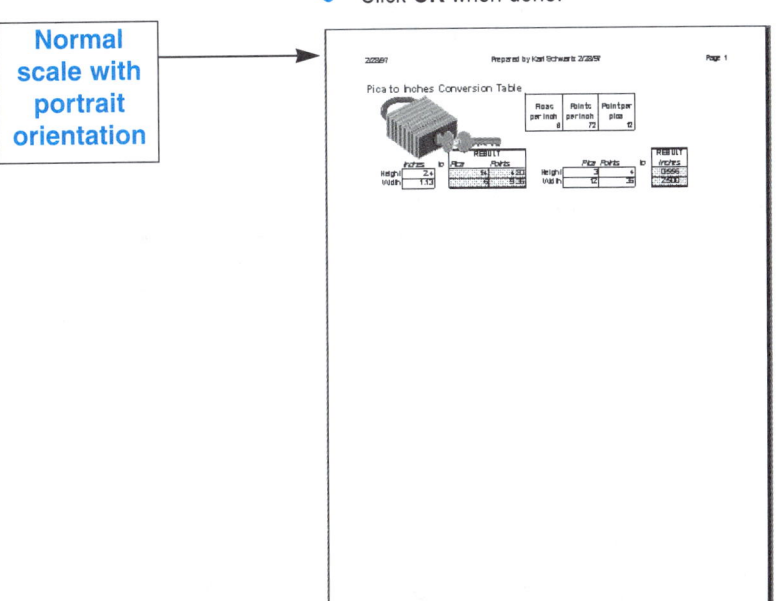

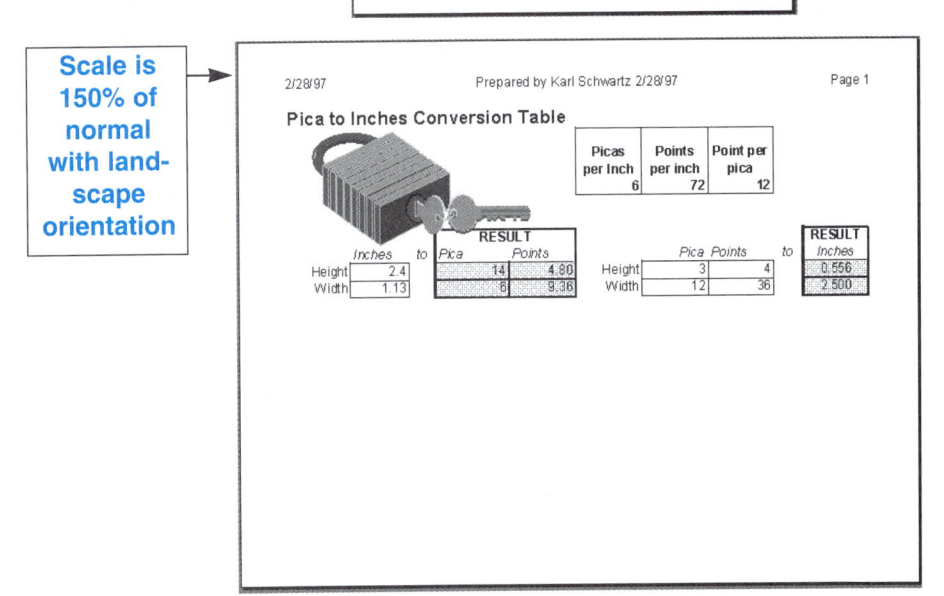

> Normal scale with portrait orientation

> Scale is 150% of normal with landscape orientation

Scaling and Orientation Examples

189

Set Sheet Print Options

You can set a variety of Sheet options prior to printing your worksheet, including gridlines, row and column headings, black and white printing, draft quality printing, printing comments, and the order of worksheets that print on multiple pages.

File → **Page Setup...** → **Sheet**

Notes:

- **Print area** can be set from the **Sheet** tab or from the **File** menu (see Set Print Area).

- For information about **Print titles** see Set Repeating Print Titles.

- The **Gridline** option does not affect how gridlines appear on screen.

- Selecting the **Black and white** option even if you have a color printer will reduce print time.

- Many sheet options, such as **Print area**, **Print titles**, and **Comments**, will not be available if you access Page Setup from the Print Preview window.

Set Sheet Print Options

1 Click the **File** menu, then click **Page Setup**.

The Page Setup dialog box appears.

2 Click the **Sheet** tab.

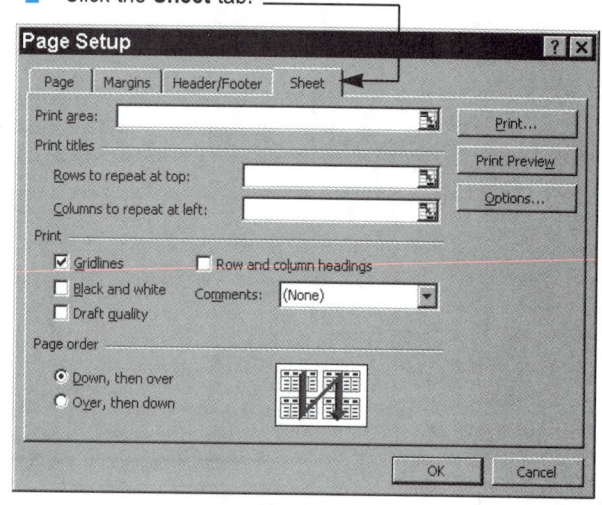

To print cell gridlines:
- Select **Gridlines**.

To print in black and white:
- Select **Black and white**.

To print in draft quality:
- Select **Draft quality**.

To print row and column headings:
- Select **Row and column headings**.

To set the print order:
- Select **Down, then over** or **Over, then down**.

continued . . .

190

Notes:

- For information about comments, see *Insert and Remove Comments*.

Set Sheet Print Options (continued)

To print comments:

- Select **At end of sheet** or **As displayed on sheet** in **Comments** list box.

3 Click **OK** when done.

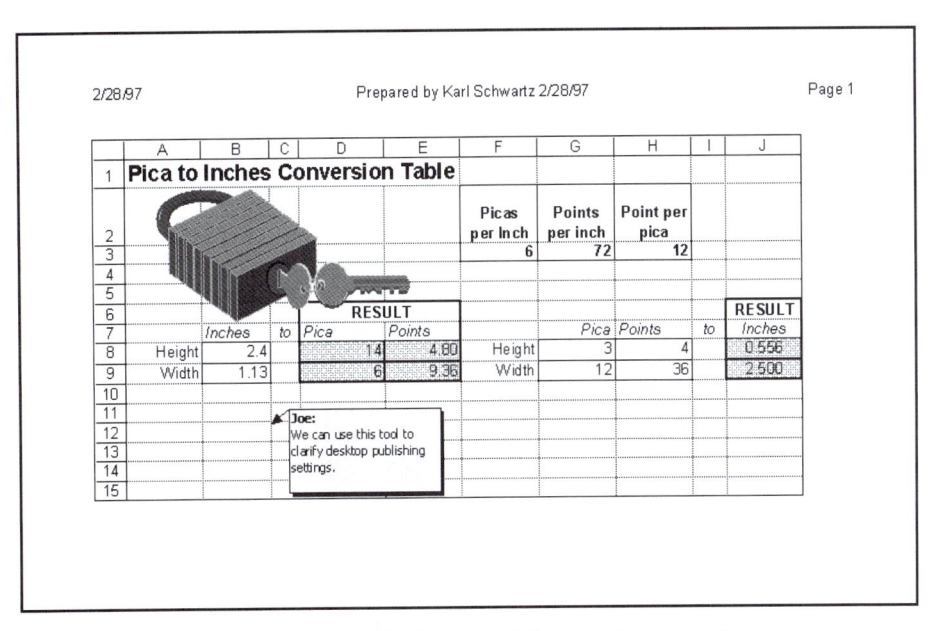

Sheet Options Include Gridlines, Comments, Row and Column Headings

191

Charts

This section contains illustrated procedures arranged in alphabetical order for creating and modifying charts.

About Chart Items

While you create and modify charts, you will be presented with many choices and settings. Understanding the items in a chart and their properties will make it easier for you to design your own.

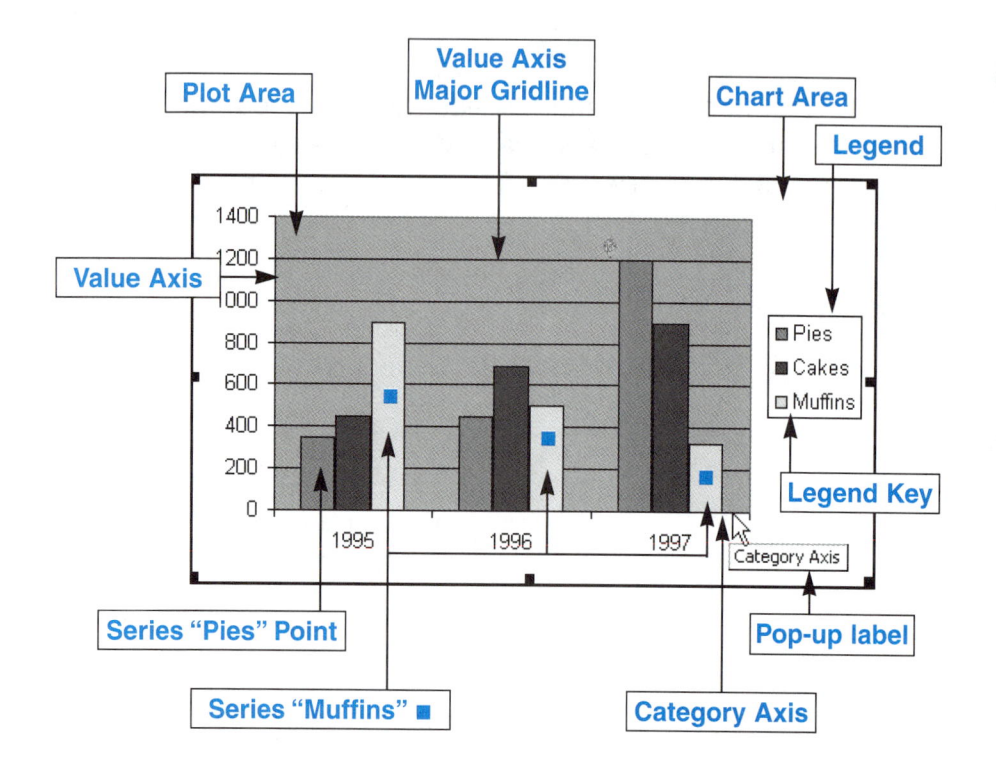

Items in Default Clustered Column Chart

Notes:

- When you rest the pointer on any chart item, Excel displays a pop-up label identifying the name of the item.

Identify Chart Items

The default Clustered Column chart type shown above includes the following items. Item properties are also described.

Category Axis (X Axis) — the horizontal line on which categories of data are usually plotted. Properties include the format and alignment of category names and the scale of names and tick marks.

Chart Area — the space inside the chart. It includes the base properties of the chart, such as font style for chart text, background color, and how the chart moves or sizes when cells around it change.

194

Notes:

- To review the properties of any chart item, rest the pointer on the item. When Excel displays the item name, double-click to display the Format dialog box for the item.

- Charts of different types have items or properties particular to their type. For example, pie charts have properties for a series that describe the angle of the first slice, while line charts have properties such as drop lines and up-down bars.

Legend — a box containing a label and legend key for each series in the chart. Properties include its border, font, and placement.

Legend Key — a graphic in the legend whose color or pattern corresponds to a series in the chart. Legend key properties include border, color, shadow, and fill effects.

Plot Area — the area within which the chart axes and series data is drawn. The properties include its border, area color, and fill effects.

Series — a group of data markers or series points that visually describe the values plotted. For example, the Series "Muffins" describes the number of muffins sold in each category (1995, 1996, and 1997). The properties of data series include borders and colors, plot axes, error bars, data labels, series order, and options such as overlap and gap width.

Series Point — a single item in a data series that visually describes the value for one category. For example, Series "Pies" Point indicates a value of 345 for the category 1995. The properties for series points include border and pattern, data labels, and options such as overlap and gap width.

Value Axis (Y Axis) — the vertical line that describes the values of series points in the chart. Properties include line and tick marks, scale of major and minor values, font for displayed values, number style of values, and text alignment.

Value Axis Major Gridlines — a set of lines that visually define values across the plot area. These gridlines help determine the value of a given series point in the chart. Properties include color, style, pattern, and units of values.

Create a Chart

Chart Wizard provides prompts and options for selecting the chart type, the source data, chart options, and chart location.

Chart Wizard button

Insert → Chart...

Notes:

- Your selection will determine the orientation of the series in your chart. You can change this orientation in **Chart Wizard - Step 2 of 4** on the **Data Range** tab.

- Avoid blank rows and columns when selecting data to chart. Use the **Ctrl** key and drag through ranges to create a multiple selection and omit blank cells.

- You can hide rows and columns that do not pertain to data to be charted.

- In **Chart Wizard**, you can click **Next>** or **<Back** to move forwards or backwards to any step.

- **Chart Wizard - Step 1 of 4:**
  Select the chart type, then the sub-type. Click and hold the **Press and hold to view sample** button to preview how the selected chart type will plot your chart.

Create a Chart

1 Select cells containing labels and values to chart.

    NOTE: You can change this selection as you proceed if you discover that you require different data.

2 Click **Chart Wizard** button on Standard toolbar.

From Chart Wizard - Step 1 of 4 - Chart Type:

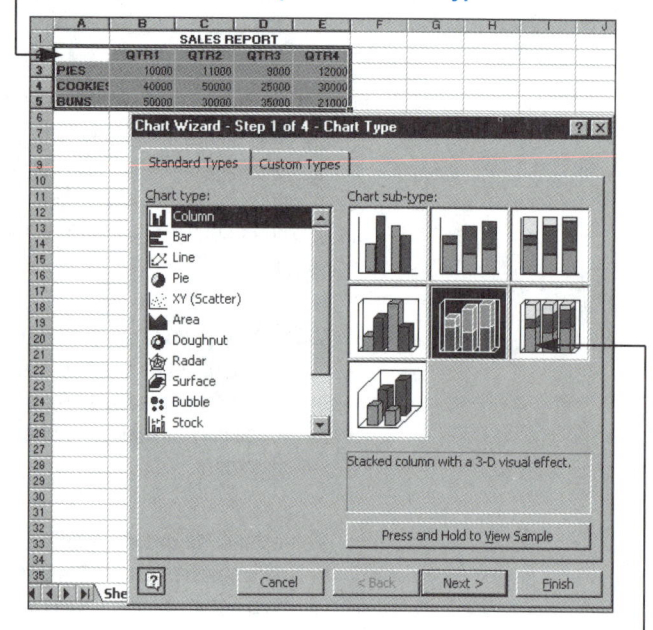

a Select chart type and subtype *(see Select Chart Type).*
b Click **Next >**.

continued . . .

196

Notes:

- **Chart Wizard - Step 2 of 4:**
  From the **Data Range** tab, you can change the range of data to plot, or change the orientation of the data series to columns or rows.

  From the **Series** tab, you can add and remove series and change references to series names, data ranges, and the category (X) axis labels.

- **Chart Wizard - Step 3 of 4:**
  From the **Chart Options** dialog box, you can set options for chart titles, axes, gridlines, legend, data labels, and the data table. You can return to this dialog box after the chart is created *(see Set Chart Options).*

- **Chart Wizard - Step 4 of 4:**
  From the **Chart Location** dialog box, you can change the proposed destination sheet, or the proposed chart sheet name.

  You can click **Finish** from any **Chart Wizard** step to create the chart with default options.

Create a Chart (continued)

From Chart Wizard - Step 2 of 4 - Chart Source Data:

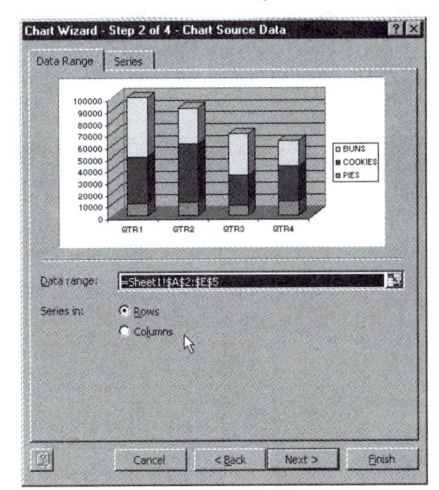

a   Select **Data Range** and **Series** options *(see Set Source of Chart Data).*

b   Click **Next >**.

From Chart Wizard - Step 3 of 4 - Chart Options:

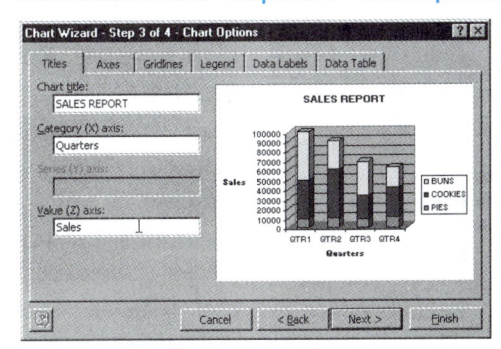

a   Select desired **Chart** options *(see Set Chart Options).*

b   Click **Next >**.

From Chart Wizard - Step 4 of 4 - Chart Location:

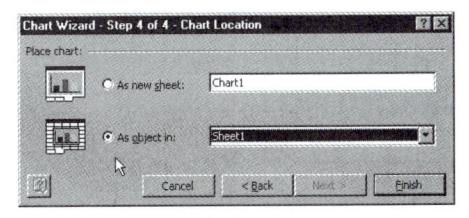

a   Select **As new sheet** or **As object in** *(see Set Location of Chart).*

b   Click **Finish**.

197

Create PivotChart

A PivotChart report lets you interactively and graphically analyze data stored in a list. For example, it can chart subtotals for service categories for all clients, or just a particular client. For information about changing a PivotChart, see *Edit PivotCharts*. For information about PivotTable reports, see *Create PivotTable*.

Data → **PivotTable and PivotChart Report...**

Notes:

- In **step 1**, a list must contain labels that define field names so Excel can determine the list categories (see *Lists*). Consider naming the list range if the data is likely to expand.
- In **step 4**, Excel selects the range automatically. For information about selecting a range from a dialog box, see *Use Dialog Box Controls*.
- Creating a PivotChart automatically creates an associated PivotTable that will reflect all changes you make to the PivotChart, and vice versa.

Create a PivotChart from a List

1. If necessary, create the list to summarize, then click any cell in list.

3	DATE	TYPE	CLIENT	
4	9/1/98	Editing	DDC	Modify
5	9/7/98	Editing	DDC	Global
6	9/9/98	PhonSup	Seaboard Outdoor	Trouble

2. Click the **Data** menu, then click **PivotTable and PivotChart Report**.

   Wizard - Step 1 of 3 dialog box appears.

3. Select **Microsoft Excel list or database**, select **PivotChart (with PivotTable)**, then click **Next >**.

   Wizard - Step 2 of 3 dialog box appears.

4. - If the suggested range is not correct, select a new range in the **Range** box.
   - Click **Next >**.

   PivotTable Wizard - Step 3 of 3 dialog box appears.

5. Select **New worksheet**, or **Existing Worksheet** to place the PivotChart.
   - If you selected **Existing Worksheet**, type or select the desired cell location.
   - Click **Finish**.

   Excel creates a framework for the PivotChart on the sheet as shown and the PivotTable toolbar appears.

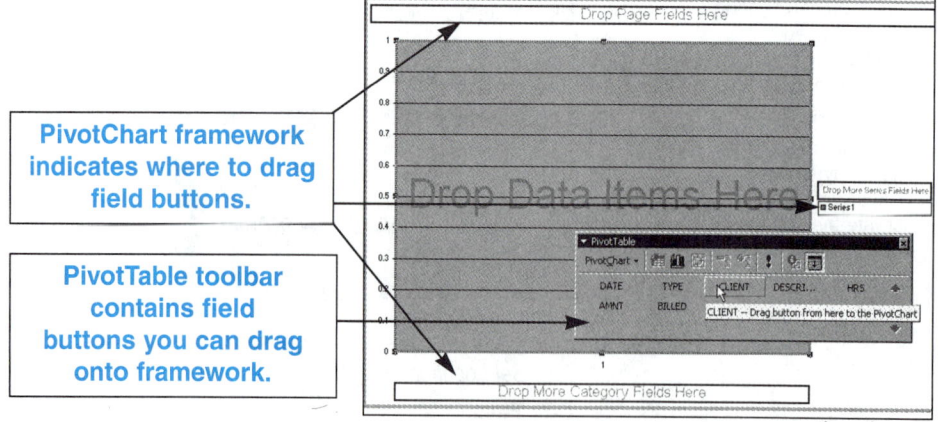

PivotChart framework indicates where to drag field buttons.

PivotTable toolbar contains field buttons you can drag onto framework.

198

continued . . .

Notes:

- In **step 6**, the framework includes the following field areas to help construct the PivotChart:

  Page Fields — drop here to place field on the row axis.

  Data — drop field that contains values to chart. You must include at least one field in the Data area.

  Series Fields — drop field here to place field on series axis.

  Category Fields — drop here to place field on category axis.

- Drag field items to a new position (or off the PivotChart) to get the desired report. You can also modify the associated PivotTable to change the PivotChart (see *Edit PivotTables*).

You can use the Page field to filter the PivotChart report. See *Edit PivotChart* for details.

Create a PivotChart from a List (continued)

6 Drag field buttons onto appropriate areas of PivotChart framework.

Excel activates the PivotChart when you drag a field to the Data area. Therefore, consider dragging a field to that area last to maintain the framework prompts.

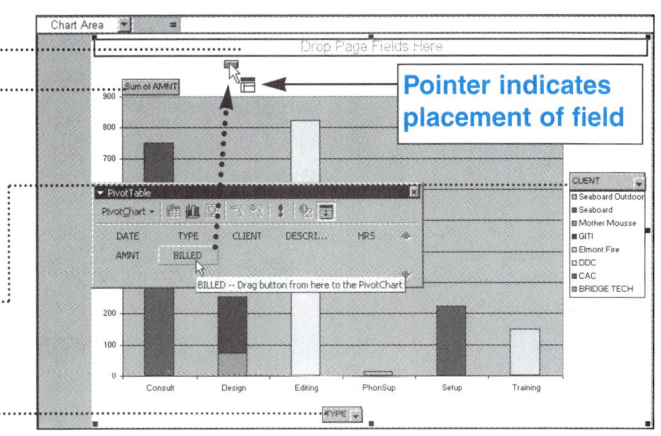

Pointer indicates placement of field

Build Your PivotChart by Dragging Fields

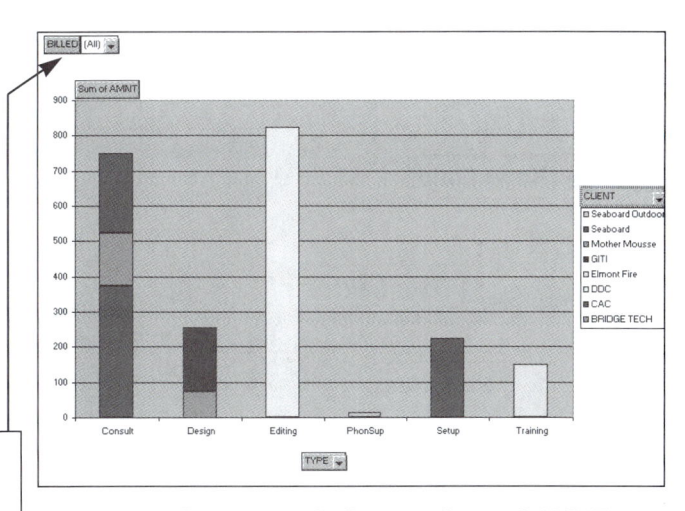

PivotChart Result Graphs Sum of AMNT for Services Provided to Each Client

TIP: You can create a PivotChart based on an existing PivotTable: Select any cell in the PivotTable, then click the Chart Wizard button on the Standard toolbar.

199

Edit PivotChart

Once you create a PivotChart *(see Create PivotChart)*, you can use controls in the PivotChart to reorganize and define the chart. If you make changes to the associated PivotTable, the PivotChart reflects those changes, and vice versa.

Notes:

- Undo actions performed in a PivotTable by pressing **Ctrl+Z** (Undo)
- You can move more than one field onto a PivotChart control.
- You can drag a field onto the **Plot area** to make it a data field.
- **To remove a field**, drag it off the PivotChart.
- **To add a field**, drag it from the Pivot-Table toolbar onto the appropriate area of the PivotChart. (See *Create PivotChart*)

Change PivotChart by Moving or Removing Fields

- Drag field button onto desired area of PivotChart, or off PivotChart to remove it.

  As you drag the field button, the pointer identifies action as follows:

  Drop to place this field on the row axis

  Drop to make this field a data field

  Drop to place this field on the series axis

  Drop to place this field on the category axis

Page (Row) Field

Data field

Plot area

Series Field

Category Field

Field Controls in PivotChart

Notes:

- If the field is a page button, you can select only one option on the list.

- To display all page field items, repeat steps and select (All) from the list. For other field types, click the check box of the field items you wish to show or hide.

Hide or Show Field Items in a PivotChart

1. Click desired field button arrow.
2. Click desired item(s) in list, then click **OK**.

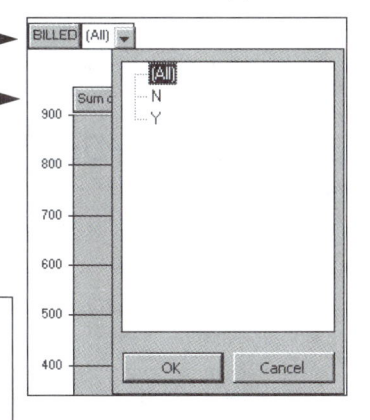

After selecting N, the PivotChart plots only the items that have not been billed.

The Page field lets you filter the chart report for one item.

Other fields let you show or hide specific items.

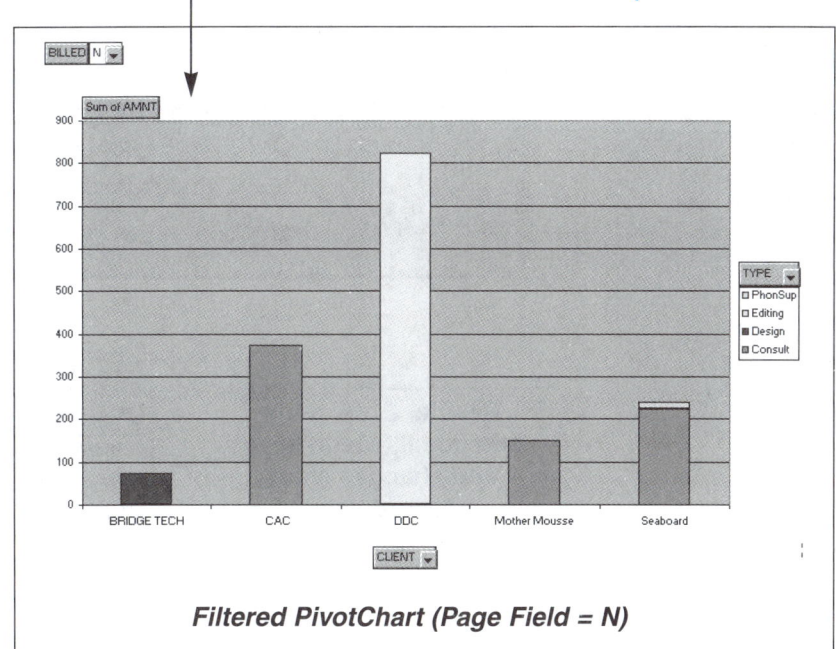

Filtered PivotChart (Page Field = N)

TIP: Excel relates the PivotChart and its associated PivotTable as follows:

PivotTABLE	PivotCHART
Row field	Category field
Column field	Series field

Continued . . .   **201**

Edit PivotChart (continued)

Notes:

- You can achieve the same result by following the procedure to show details in the associated PivotTable. *(See Edit PivotTable — Show or Hide PivotTable Details)*

- The illustration shows the result of adding a field to the series axis. You can also add fields to other field controls:

  Category axis — to plot category combinations, like company and service type.

  Page (row) axis — to filter the chart based on more than one field, such as BILLED = N, and CLIENT = DDC.

  Data area — to plot multiple field values in the same chart.

Add Fields (Details) to PivotChart

- In PivotChart, drag additional field button(s) onto the desired field control.

  As you drag the field button, the pointer identifies the action and placement.

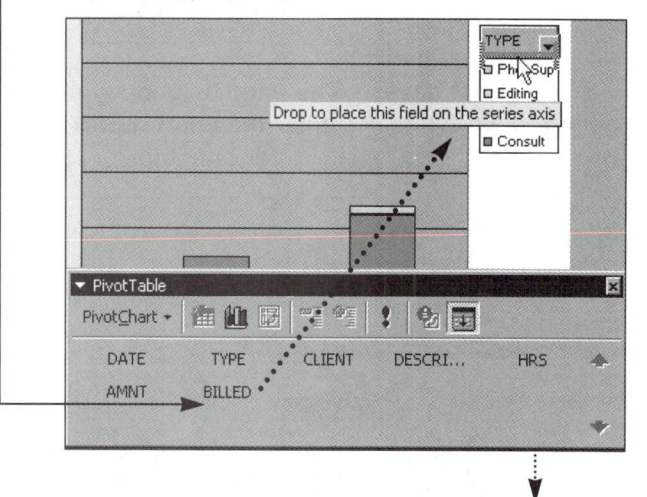

Result: Excel adds additional legend keys and changes chart accordingly.

202

Notes:

- The illustration shows how to reorder fields in a series. You can also reorder fields in other areas of the PivotChart.

Reorder Fields

Use this procedure to change the order of fields in the PivotChart, when more than one field has been added to a field area.

- In PivotTable, select the entire field by pointing to, then clicking the top border of the field button.

  An insertion marker indicates the new location.

Action 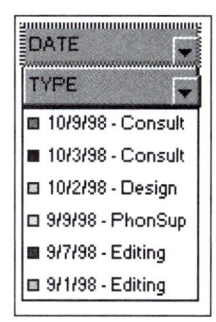   Result

Notes:

- In **step 2**, you can also format data values: Click **Number**, then select desired number style in the Format Cells dialog box that opens.

Change Function of Data Field

Use this procedure when you want use a different function to plot values in the PivotChart.

1 In PivotChart, double-click the data field. Sum of AMNT
2 Select the desired function in the **Summarize by** list, and click **OK**.

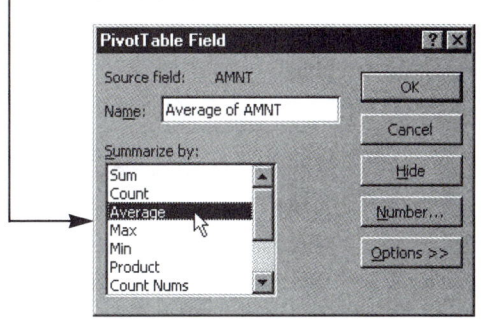

203

Insert Objects in Charts

You can insert objects, such as picture files, AutoShapes, and WordArt, into your chart to add interest and draw attention to information presented.

Insert ➡ Picture

Notes:

- In **step 1**, you should select the chart prior to inserting the object, so the object moves and sizes with chart.

- Once an object is inserted in a chart, you can drag to place it, or drag its sizing handles to change its size.

- After inserting multiple objects, you can change their display order: Right-click an object, point to **Order** on the shortcut menu, then click desired order option, such as **Bring to Front**, or **Send to Back**.

- **From File** option: By default, the **Insert Picture** dialog box previews the selected picture file. From this dialog box, you can navigate folders as you would when opening or saving an Excel workbook.

  Excel accepts many graphic file formats including: JPG, JPEG, BMP, CDR, CGM, EPS, GIF.

Insert Objects in a Chart

1. Click the embedded chart to select it.
   OR
   Select the chart sheet.
2. Click the **Insert** menu, then point to **Picture**.

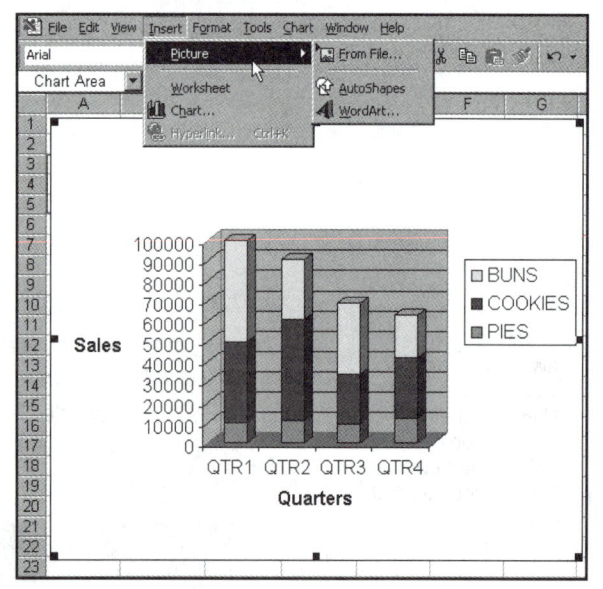

Plain Chart without Chart Title

3. Click one of the following on the submenu:
   From File — to select a picture file stored on disk.
   AutoShapes — to create an AutoShape object.
   WordArt — to create a WordArt object.

To insert From File:

- Select file to insert, then click **Insert** to place the picture in your chart.

continued . . .

Notes:

- **AutoShapes option:**
  You can use tools on the Drawing toolbar to format objects drawn with tools on the AutoShapes toolbar.

- In **step a**, click the button at the bottom of the menu to view additional shape categories.

- **WordArt options:**
  Consider using WordArt for text describing the chart title.

  You can use the tools on the WordArt toolbar to modify the object. For example, you can click the **Edit Text** button to change the text, or click the **Free Rotate** button to rotate the WordArt.

  Point to objects on the WordArt toolbar to identify the buttons.

Insert Objects in Charts (continued)

To insert AutoShapes:

When you select **AutoShapes** from the menu, the AutoShapes toolbar appears.

To display purpose of any button on toolbar:
- Rest pointer on toolbar button.

To create an AutoShape object:

a Click the AutoShapes button on the toolbar, select shape category, then click desired shape.

NOTE: The Drawing toolbar also has tools to create common shapes, such as Line, Arrow, Rectangle and Oval.

b Drag through the chart area to draw the object.

To insert WordArt :

When you select **WordArt** from the menu, Excel opens a WordArt Gallery dialog box.

a Click desired **WordArt** style, then click **OK**.

b Type your text in the box provided, then select the font style for your text in the **Font** list box.

c Select the font size in the **Size** list box.

d Click **OK** to place the WordArt in the chart.

WordArt object

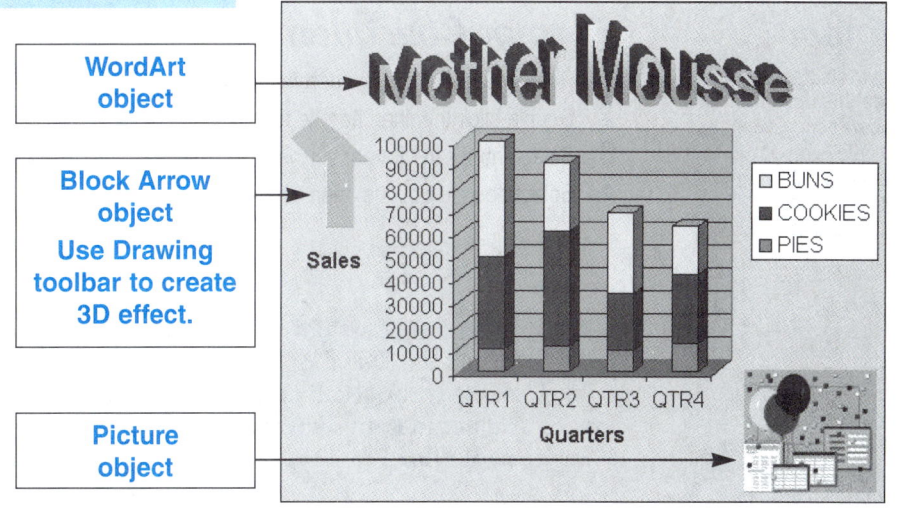

Block Arrow object
Use Drawing toolbar to create 3D effect.

Picture object

Chart with Objects

205

Format Chart Items

Every item in a chart can be changed or formatted. For example, you can change the border or color of the chart area, or fill a series with a blend effect or pictures from a graphic file.

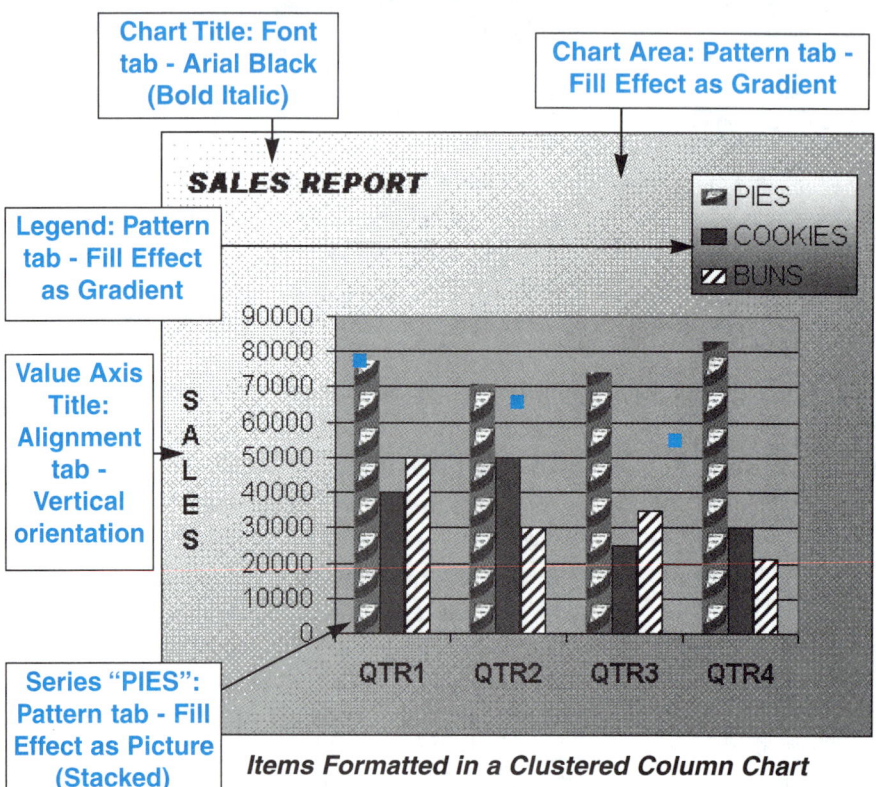

Chart Title: Font tab - Arial Black (Bold Italic)

Chart Area: Pattern tab - Fill Effect as Gradient

Legend: Pattern tab - Fill Effect as Gradient

Value Axis Title: Alignment tab - Vertical orientation

Series "PIES": Pattern tab - Fill Effect as Picture (Stacked)

Items Formatted in a Clustered Column Chart

Notes:

- In **step 1**, when you rest the pointer on a chart item, Excel displays a pop-up label identifying the item.

- In **step 2**, you can also click the **Format** menu and click **Selected** *item name* to format the selected item.

Format Chart Items

1 Rest mouse pointer on chart item to identify it.
2 Double-click the chart item to format.
3 Select tab for the format you want to change.
4 Select desired options, then click **OK**.

TIP: With the chart object or sheet selected, press the Down or Up arrow key to cycle through all chart items. The selected item name will appear in the name box.

> **Notes:**
> - See *About Chart Items* for an illustration of the chart items listed here.
> - Charts will have items or properties unique to their type. For example, pie charts will have properties for a series that describes the angle of the first slice, while line charts will have properties such as drop lines and up-down bars.

Format Options for Chart Items

This is a list of format options for each chart item in the default Clustered Column chart type. Format options may vary for different chart types.

Category Axis (X Axis)
Patterns style of line and tick marks, **Scale** of axis and categories, **Font** style of category labels, **Number** style of category labels, **Alignment** of category labels.

Chart Area
Patterns style of area—shadow, round corners, area color, fill effects (gradient, texture, pattern, picture); **Font** style of text (base font for chart); **Properties** of chart object, such as positioning, printing and locking.

Legend
Patterns style of area—border, shadow, area color, fill effects (gradient, texture, pattern, picture); **Font** style of text; **Placement** of legend in chart.

Legend Key
Patterns style of border— automatic, none, custom (style, color, weight); area—color, invert if negative, fill effects (gradient, texture, pattern, picture).

Plot Area
Patterns style of border, area color, fill effects (gradient, texture, pattern, picture).

Series
Patterns style of border, shadow, and area—color and fill effects (gradient, texture, pattern, picture); **Axis** series on primary or secondary axis; **Y Error Bars** style and criteria, **Data Labels** options; **Series Order**; **Options** specific to chart type, such as overlap and gap width for column charts.

Series Point
Patterns style of border, shadow, and area—color, fill effects (gradient, texture, pattern, picture); **Data Labels** options; **Options** specific to chart type, such as overlap and gap width for column charts.

Value Axis (Y Axis)
Patterns style of axis line; **Scale** of axis and categories; **Font** style category labels; **Number** style of category labels; **Alignment** of category labels.

Value Axis Major Gridlines
Patterns style of gridlines; **Scale** of major and minor gridlines.

Move and Size Chart Items

Charts are composed of items such as the Chart Area and Plot area *(see About Chart Items)*. After you create a chart, you can position and size these items to present the chart data as you like it.

Notes:

- In **step 1**, when you rest the mouse pointer on an item, Excel displays a pop-up label that identifies the item, as shown in the illustration on the right (Plot Area).

Move and Size a Chart Item

1 Rest your pointer on the item to identify it.
2 Click the item to select it.

A border and sizing handles appear around item.

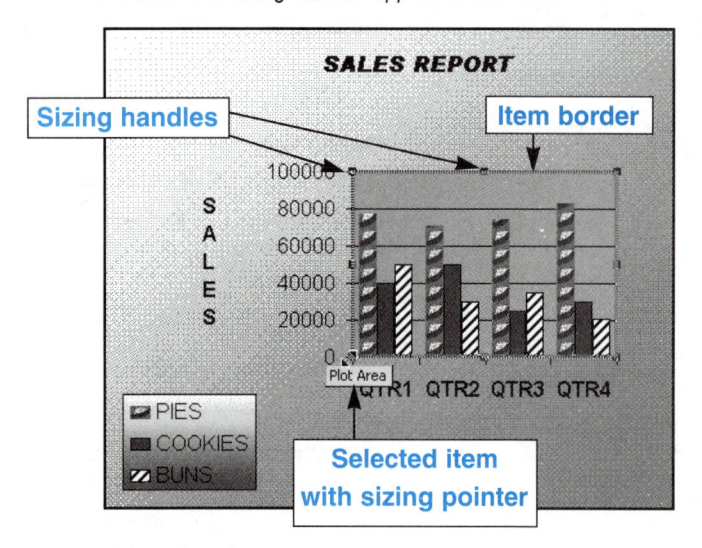

Sizing handles

Item border

Selected item with sizing pointer

To size selected item:

- Drag sizing handles to size the item.

As you drag the sizing handle, a dashed border indicates the new shape of the item.

continued . . .

208

Notes:

- **AutoShapes option:**
  You can use tools on the Drawing toolbar to format objects drawn with tools on the AutoShapes toolbar.

- In **step a**, click the button at the bottom of the menu to view additional shape categories.

- **WordArt options:**
  Consider using WordArt for text describing the chart title.

  You can use the tools on the WordArt toolbar to modify the object. For example, you can click the **Edit Text** button to change the text, or click the **Free Rotate** button to rotate the WordArt.

  Point to objects on the WordArt toolbar to identify the buttons.

Insert Objects in Charts (continued)

To insert AutoShapes:

When you select **AutoShapes** from the menu, the AutoShapes toolbar appears.

To display purpose of any button on toolbar:
- Rest pointer on toolbar button.

To create an AutoShape object:

a Click the AutoShapes button on the toolbar, select shape category, then click desired shape.

NOTE: The Drawing toolbar also has tools to create common shapes, such as Line, Arrow, Rectangle and Oval.

b Drag through the chart area to draw the object.

To insert WordArt :

When you select **WordArt** from the menu, Excel opens a WordArt Gallery dialog box.

a Click desired **WordArt** style, then click **OK**.

b Type your text in the box provided, then select the font style for your text in the **Font** list box.

c Select the font size in the **Size** list box.

d Click **OK** to place the WordArt in the chart.

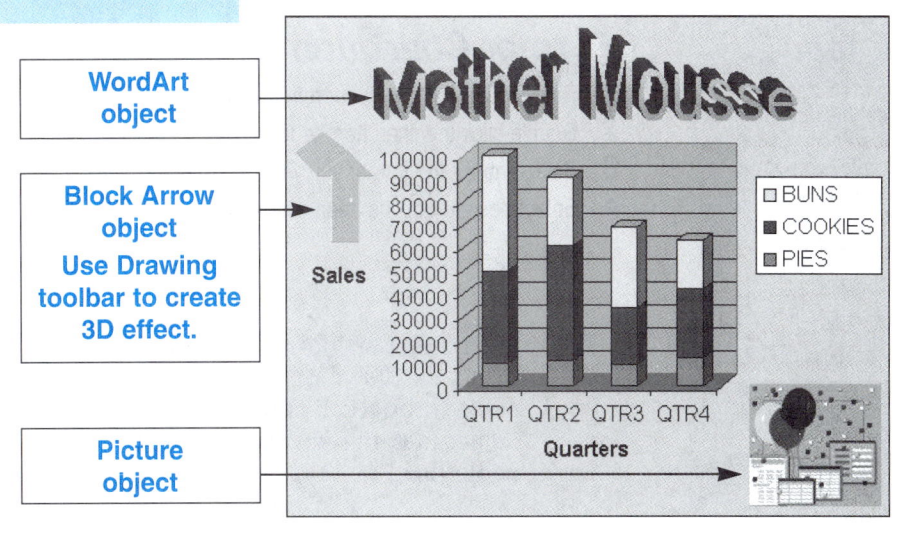

WordArt object

Block Arrow object
Use Drawing toolbar to create 3D effect.

Picture object

Chart with Objects

Format Chart Items

Every item in a chart can be changed or formatted. For example, you can change the border or color of the chart area, or fill a series with a blend effect or pictures from a graphic file.

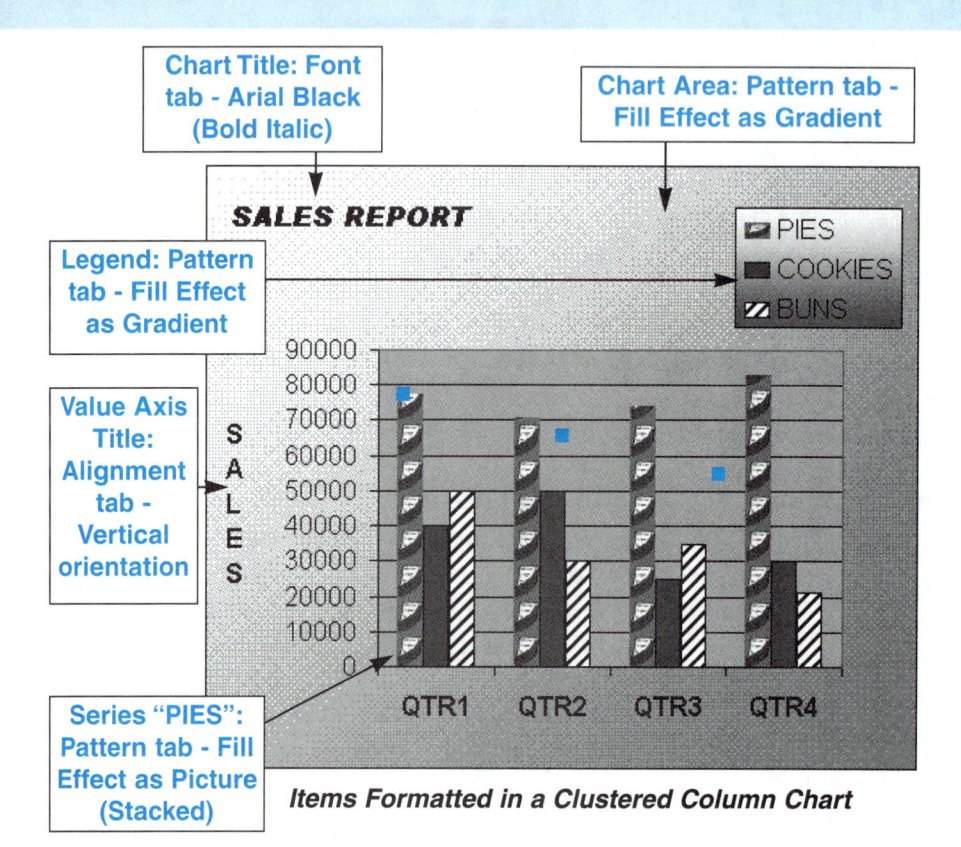

Chart Title: Font tab - Arial Black (Bold Italic)

Chart Area: Pattern tab - Fill Effect as Gradient

Legend: Pattern tab - Fill Effect as Gradient

Value Axis Title: Alignment tab - Vertical orientation

Series "PIES": Pattern tab - Fill Effect as Picture (Stacked)

Items Formatted in a Clustered Column Chart

Notes:

- In **step 1**, when you rest the pointer on a chart item, Excel displays a pop-up label identifying the item.

- In **step 2**, you can also click the **Format** menu and click **Selected** *item name* to format the selected item.

Format Chart Items

1. Rest mouse pointer on chart item to identify it.
2. Double-click the chart item to format.
3. Select tab for the format you want to change.
4. Select desired options, then click **OK**.

TIP: With the chart object or sheet selected, press the Down or Up arrow key to cycle through all chart items. The selected item name will appear in the name box.

Notes:

- Some items, such as axis labels, must be moved by dragging the border. Click inside these items to edit the text.
- Some items, such as Category and Value Axes, cannot be moved and sized directly. These items will change size as you change the size of the **Plot Area**.
- You can size and move the entire chart by dragging the sizing handles when **Chart Area** is selected.

Move and Size a Chart Item (continued)

To move selected item:

- Drag border or empty area of selected item to move the item.

Excel displays the border as you drag it.

Chart Area sizing handles

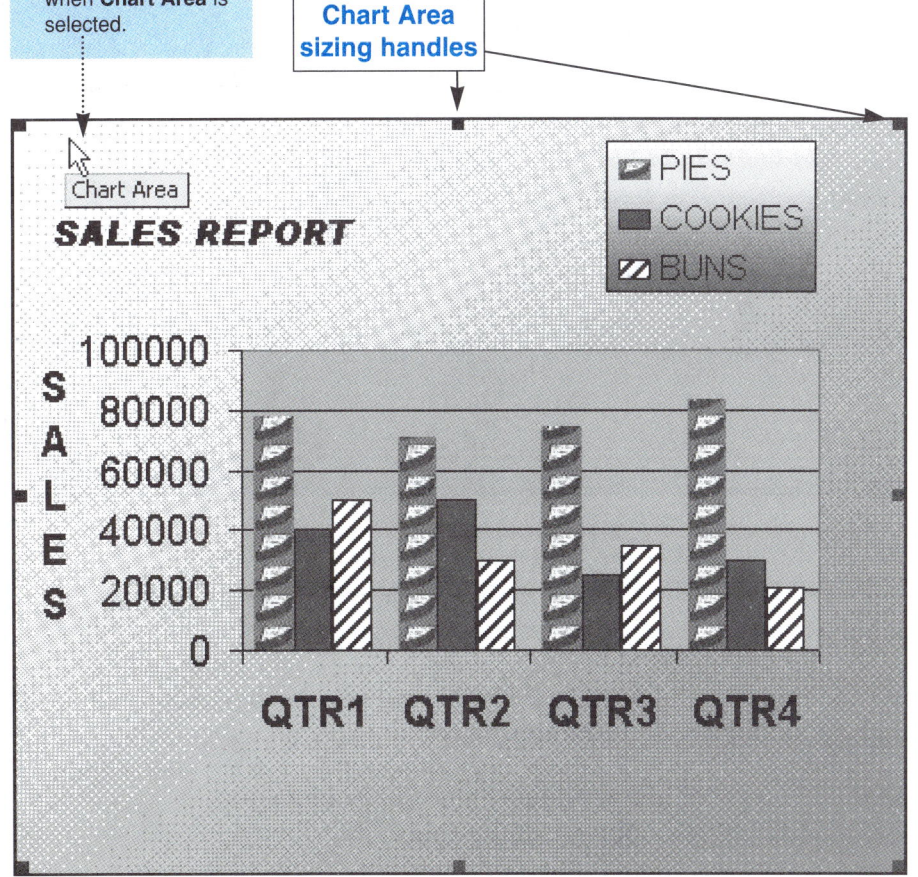

Chart Area (Entire Chart) Selected

209

Print Charts

You can print a chart as part of a worksheet *(see Print Workbook Data)* or print it as a separate item on a page. Prior to printing a chart, you can set options to control the size and position of the chart on the printed page.

File → **Page Setup...**

Notes:
- Chart sheet tabs appear along the bottom of the workbook with the sheet tabs.

Set Page Options for Printing Chart Only

1. Click the chart in worksheet to print.
   OR
   Click chart sheet tab.

2. Click **File** menu, then click **Page Setup**.
   The Page Setup dialog box appears.

3. Click the **Chart** tab.

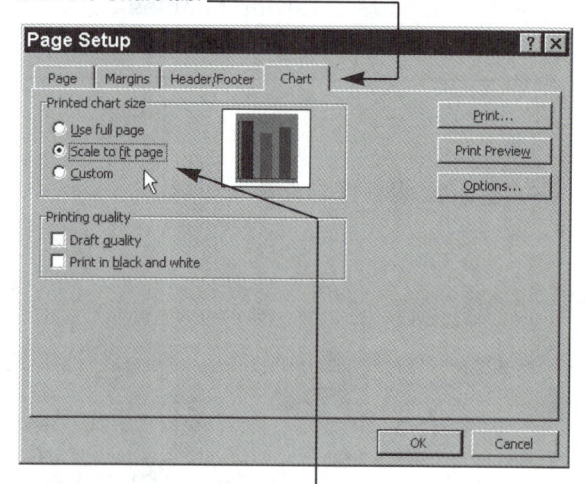

4. Select **Printed chart size**.

5. If you selected **Custom**, select the **Margins** tab to set margins and centering options.

6. By default, charts are printed in landscape orientation. To change the orientation, click the **Page** tab and select the **Portrait** option.

7. If desired, click the **Header/Footer** tab and select or create a header *(see Set Headers and Footers)*.

8. Click **OK** when done.

Notes:

- From Print Preview, you can set margins and access the **Page Setup** dialog box to change page options *(see Print Preview)*.

Preview Chart

1 Click the chart in worksheet to print.

OR

Click desired chart sheet tab.

2 Set page options.

From **Page Setup** dialog box:

- Click `Print Preview`

OR

From worksheet or chart sheet:

- Click **Print Preview button** on Standard toolbar.

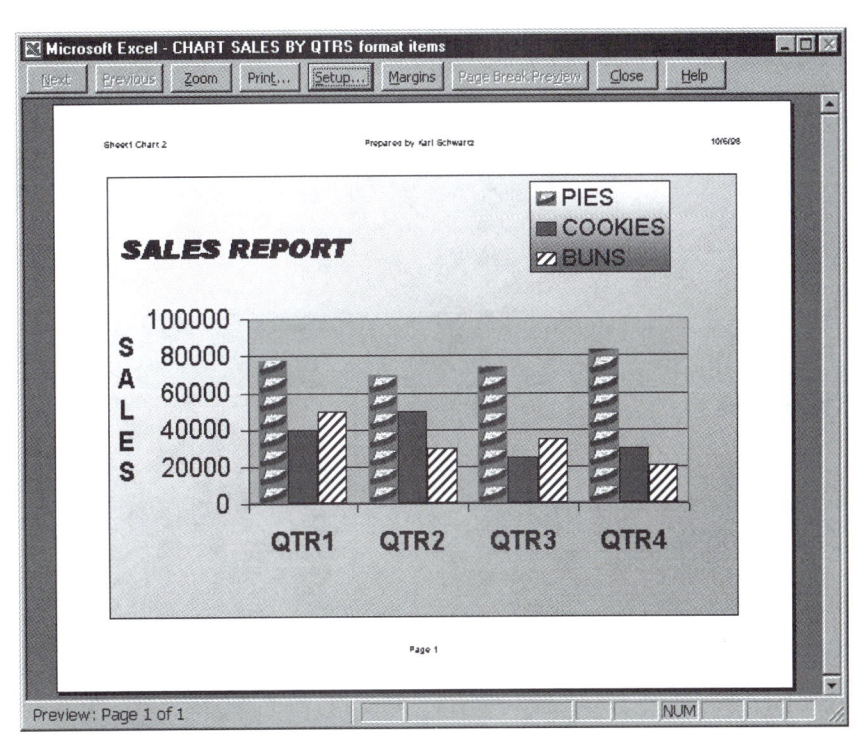

Preview of Chart with Header and Footer

Notes:

- You can also print the chart from Print Preview *(see Print Preview)*.

Print Chart

1 Click the chart in worksheet to print.

OR

Click chart sheet tab.

2 Set page options.

3 Click **Print button** on Standard toolbar.

Select Chart Type

Excel provides 14 standard chart types, such as Area, Column, and Pie charts. Each chart type contains a variety of subtypes, such as Pie with 3-D visual effect. In addition to standard chart types, you can choose from many custom types or define your own.

Chart Wizard button

Chart → Chart Type...

Notes:

- In **step 2**, when you select a chart subtype, a description of the chart also appears in the dialog box.

Select a Chart Type

When charting data, you should keep in mind the kind of data you are plotting and the purpose of the chart. With the Chart Wizard, you can view a sample of your chart without leaving the dialog box, making it easier to choose the appropriate style.

1 Follow steps to create a chart *(see Create a Chart)*.

OR

- Select chart or chart sheet.
- Click the **Chart** menu, then **Chart Type**.

The Chart Type dialog box appears.

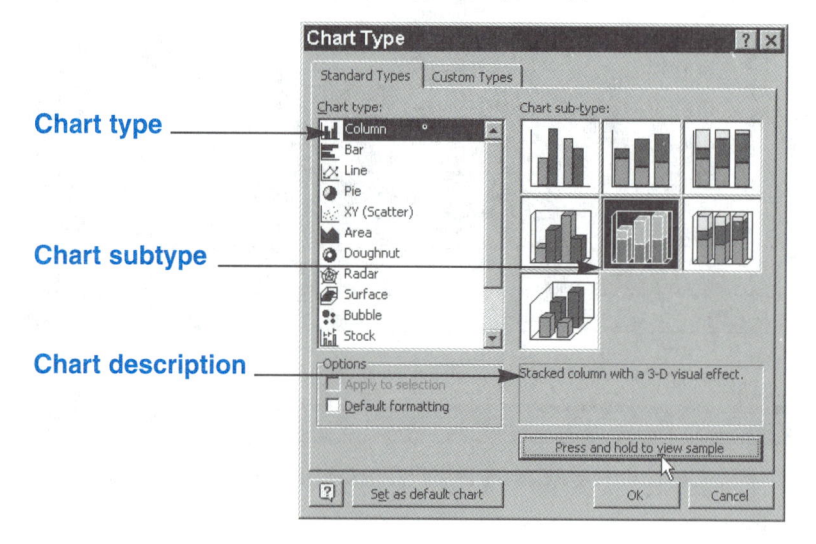

- Chart type
- Chart subtype
- Chart description

2 Click the **Standard** tab and select desired chart type in **Chart type** list.

Excel displays subtypes in Chart sub-type list.

3 Click the desired chart subtype in **Chart sub-type** list.

continued . . .

212

Notes:

- To add a chart to the **User-defined** list: Format the chart, click the **Chart** menu, then **Chart Type**, click the **Custom** tab, select **User-defined**, then click **Add**.

Select a Chart Type (continued)

4 Click and hold mouse on **Press and hold to view sample** button to preview a sample of your chart with selected chart type.

Preview of your chart

Click to set current chart as default chart type

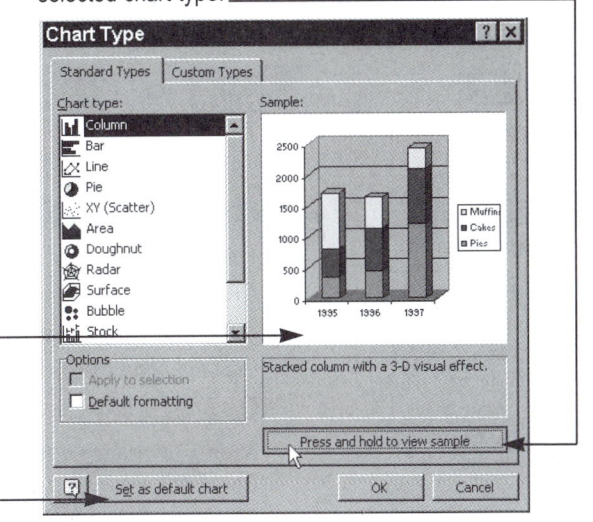

To set current selection as default chart type:

- Click **Set as default chart**.

To select a custom chart type:

- Click the **Custom Types** tab, then select desired chart type in **Chart type** list.

  Excel displays Sample in Sample box.

Click to display custom charts you have defined

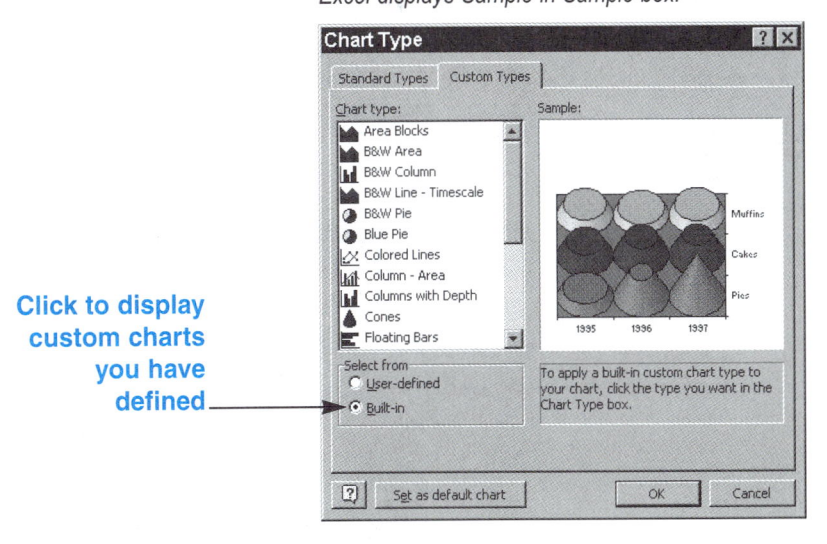

5 Click **OK** or **Finish** when done.

213

Set Chart Options

The Chart Wizard provides the Chart Options dialog box, where you can select from an array of chart options. As you make your selections, the Chart Wizard shows you the results in a sample box. After you create the chart, you can access the dialog box to change options at a later time.

Chart Wizard button

Notes:

- In **step 1**, when you select a chart or chart sheet, the menu bar changes to include the **Chart** menu option.

- When creating a chart, the **Chart Options** dialog box will appear in Chart Wizard - Step 3 of 4.

- [?] To learn the purpose of any setting, click the question mark button, then click the option. A pop-up window will appear to describe it.

- Chart options depend on the chart type. For example, Pie charts will have only three category tabs: **Titles**, **Legend**, and **Data Labels**.

Set Chart Options

1 Follow steps to create a chart *(see Create a Chart)*.
   OR
   Select chart sheet or chart embedded in worksheet.

2 Click the **Chart** menu, then click **Chart Options**.
   The Chart Options dialog box appears.

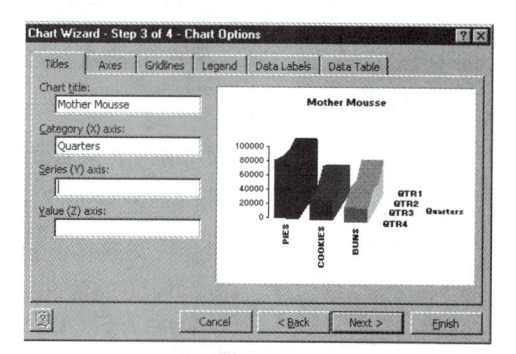

Chart Options: Titles

3 Select the tab containing the option category you want to change, then select options appropriate to your chart type.

4 Click **OK** when done.

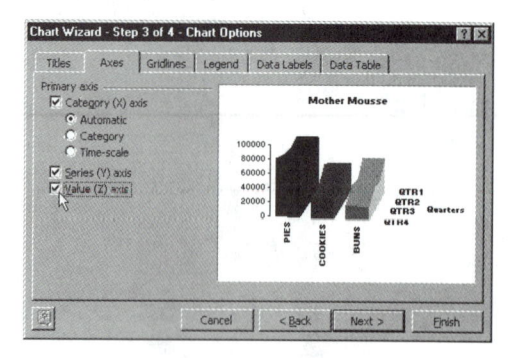

Chart Options: Axes

continued . . .

214

Notes:

- If you add an item (such as a data table) to your chart, but the item does not fit within the chart area, accept the option and size or set the position of the item (or surrounding items) later on *(see Move and Size Chart Items).*

- When you add items to a chart (such as Chart titles and data tables), you do not have to accept the initial format. Double-click the item in the chart to open a Format dialog box specific to the item *(see Format Chart Items).*

Set Chart Options (continued)

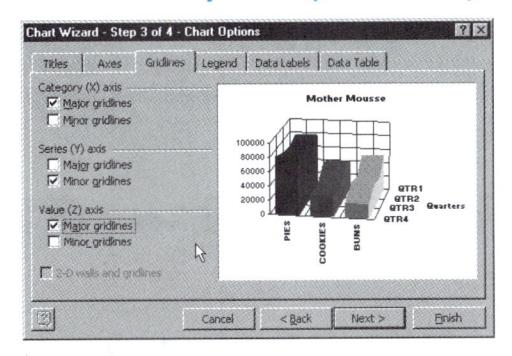

Chart Options: Gridlines

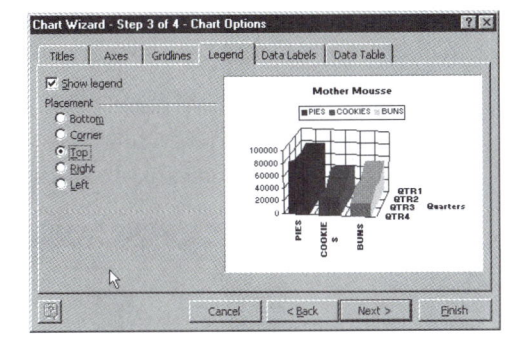

Chart Options: Legend

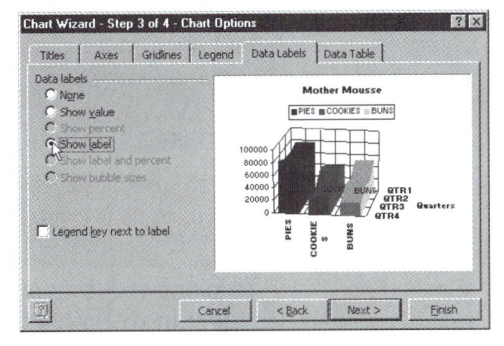

Chart Options: Data Labels

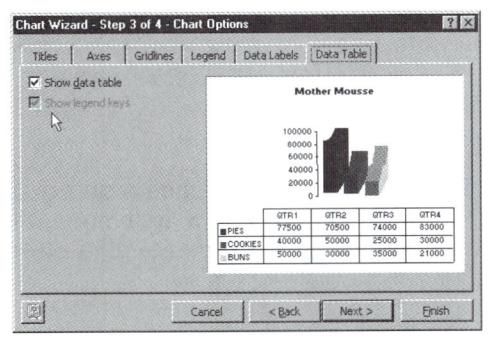

Chart Options: Data Table

215

Set Location of Chart

Use the Chart Location dialog box to set the location of a new chart or change the location of an existing chart. If the destination is a chart sheet, Excel lets you name the sheet. If the destination is a worksheet, you must select the sheet from a list of existing sheet names.

Chart Wizard button

Chart → Location...

Notes:

- In **step 1**, you may have to click the button at the bottom of the menu to view the **Location** command.

- If you want a chart to appear in both locations, copy the sheet containing the chart, then change the location of the chart on the copied sheet *(see Sheet Tabs)*.

Set Location of Chart

1 Follow steps to create a chart *(see Create a Chart)*, and proceed to *Chart Wizard - Step 4 of 4 - Chart Location*.
   OR
   - Select existing chart or chart sheet.
   - Click the **Chart** menu, then **Location**.

   The Chart Location dialog box appears.

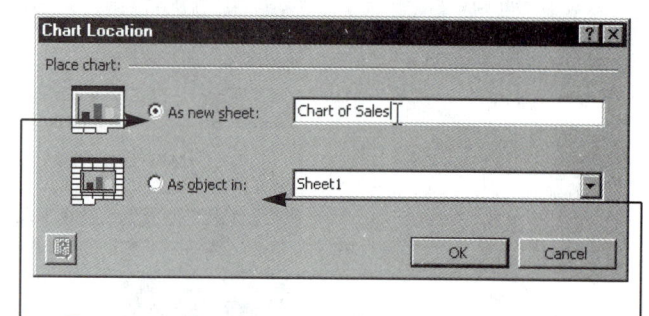

To place chart on a chart sheet:
   a Select **As new sheet**.
   b Type name of chart sheet in text box.

To place chart as an embedded object in worksheet:
   a Select **As object in**.
   b Select sheet name in list box.

2 Click **OK** when done.

continued ...

> **TIP:** Although chart sheets do not automatically show worksheet data, you may include it in the chart by setting the chart option to Show <u>d</u>ata table *(see Set Chart Options)*.

Set Location of Chart (continued)

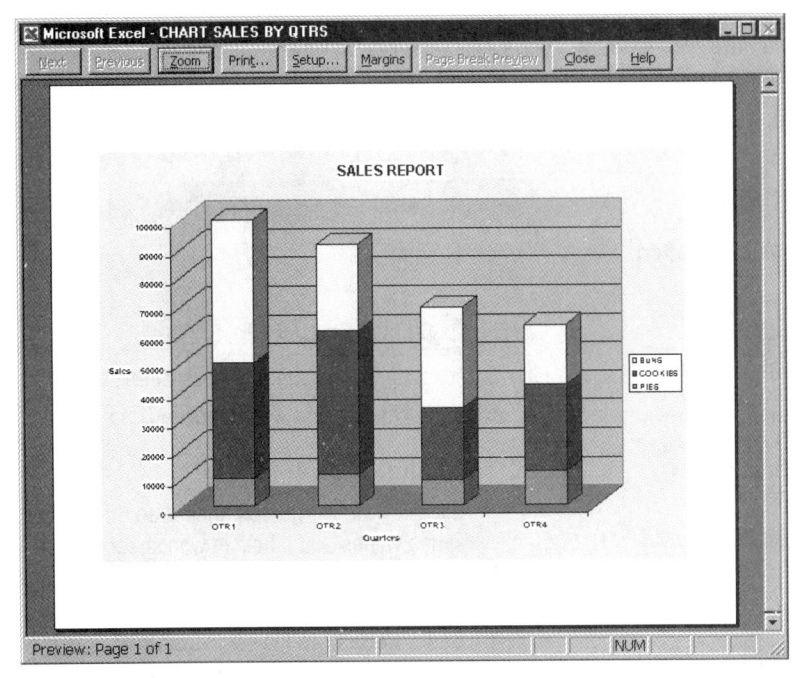

Printed Chart on a Chart Sheet

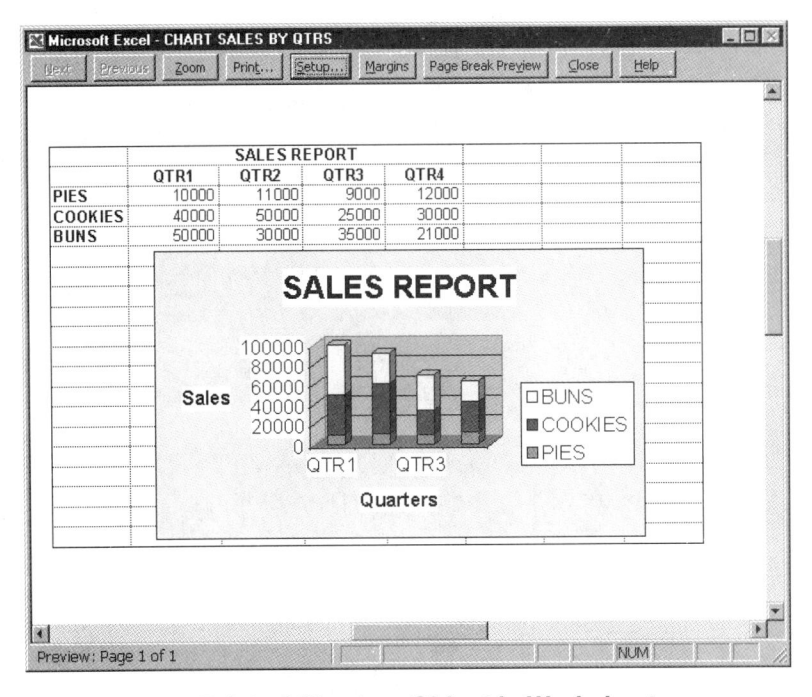

Printed Chart as Object in Worksheet

217

Set Source of Chart Data

Excel provides tools to help you choose the location of worksheet data that you are plotting in a chart. For example, you can add an additional year of data to an existing chart by extending an outline in the worksheet data.

Chart Wizard button

Chart → Source Data...

Notes:

- In **step 2**, you may have to click the button at the bottom of the menu to view the **Source Data** command.

- When changing the plot area, Excel will collapse the dialog box as you drag through the data range in the worksheet. When you complete the selection, Excel returns the dialog box to its normal size.

Set Source Data Using Menu

1 Select chart in worksheet or chart sheet.

2 Click the **Chart** menu, then **Source Data**.

To change the plot area:
- Click in **Data range** box, then drag through series values and labels in worksheet to plot.

To change orientation of series:
- Select **Series in:** **R**ows or Col**u**mns.

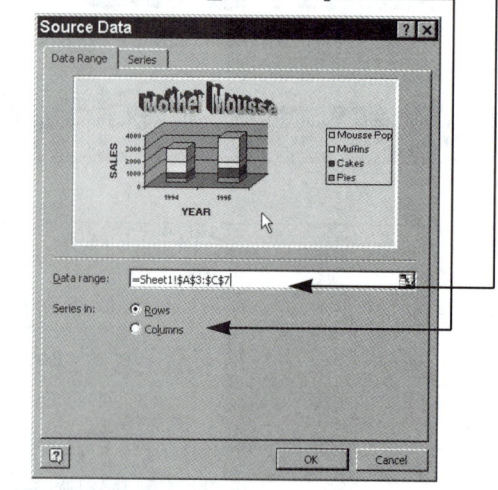

TIP: You can add, remove, and define individual series from the Series tab in the Source Data dialog box.

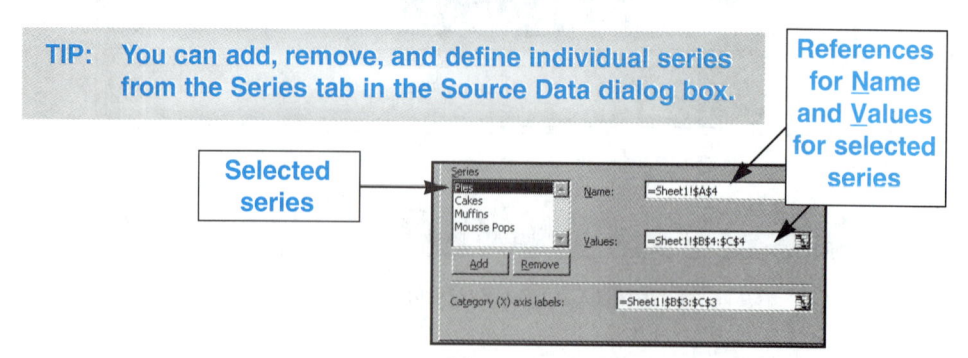

Selected series

References for Name and Values for selected series

Series Tab: Controls

218

Notes:

- You can rest pointer on chart items to identify them.
- When the **Chart Area** is selected, handles appear around the chart.

- You can also add data to a chart using the menu: Select Chart area of chart, click the **Chart** menu, click **Add Data**, from Add Data dialog box. In the **Range** box, insert reference by selecting new cells (include labels and series), then click **OK**.

Set Source Location of Chart Data Using Mouse

Use this procedure only for a chart embedded in a worksheet.

- Select **Chart Area** of chart.

    Excel marks plotted data area in worksheet with borders and extend handles.

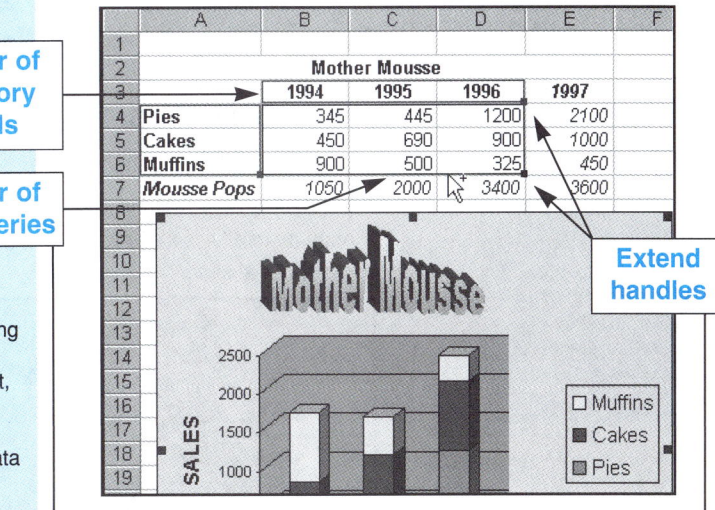

    — Border of category labels
    — Border of chart series
    — Extend handles

To change cells plotted by chart:

- Drag border that surrounds plotted worksheet values to desired location.

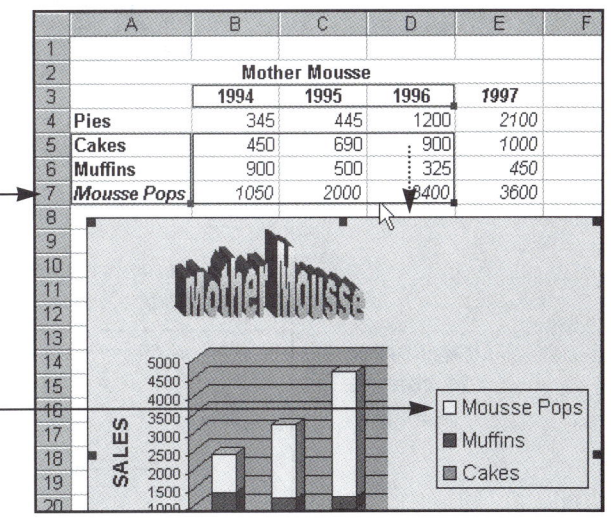

    — New series plotted: Cakes, Muffins, and Mousse Pops.
    — Chart adjusts (note new legend item)

To change range of cells plotted by chart:

- Drag extend handle of border that surrounds values or category to include or exclude data.

Special 3-D Chart Effects

After you create a 3-D chart *(see Select Chart Type)*, you can adjust the view of the chart interactively, or by changing rotation and elevation settings in a dialog box.

Notes:

- In **step 3**, you can rest pointer on any chart item to identify it.
- You can click the **Edit** menu, then **Undo 3-D View** to undo the rotation of the chart.

Rotate 3-D Chart Using Mouse

1 Select the chart in worksheet or chart sheet.

2 Click inside walls of chart.

Corner handles appear around the chart's 3-dimensional space.

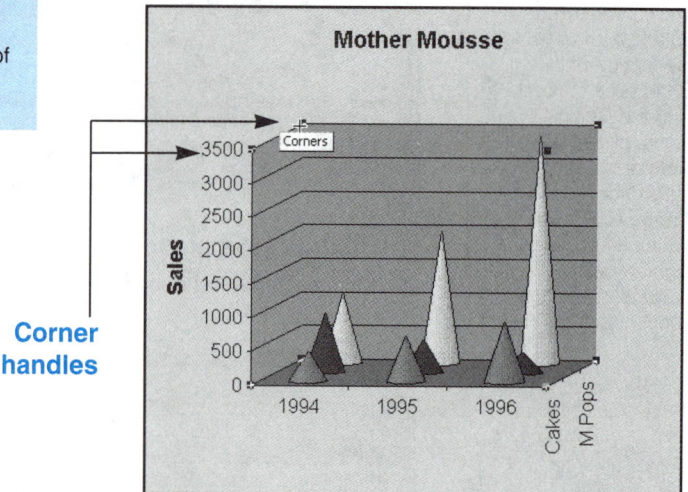

Corner handles

3 Drag any corner handle to rotate and change the elevation of the chart.

The pointer becomes a crosshair and a 3-D box indicates the current rotation and elevation of the chart.

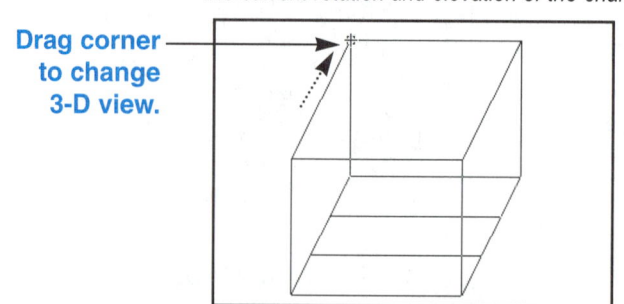

Drag corner to change 3-D view.

4 Release mouse button to accept the rotation and elevation indicated by 3-D outline.

Chart → 3-D View...

Notes:

- Other 3-D View options:

  Auto scaling — scale a 3-D chart to be closer in size to the 2-D version. This setting is available only when **Right angle axes** is selected.

  Right angle axes — deselect to free the chart from the right angle constraint. Excel will enable a Perspective setting, and buttons will appear to let you change the perspective with the mouse.

  Height % of base — type a percentage to control height in relation to length of x axis. This setting is available only when **Right angle axes** is deselected.

  Default — click to return chart to its default 3-D settings.

Rotate 3-D Chart Using Dialog Box Commands

1. Select the chart in worksheet or chart sheet.

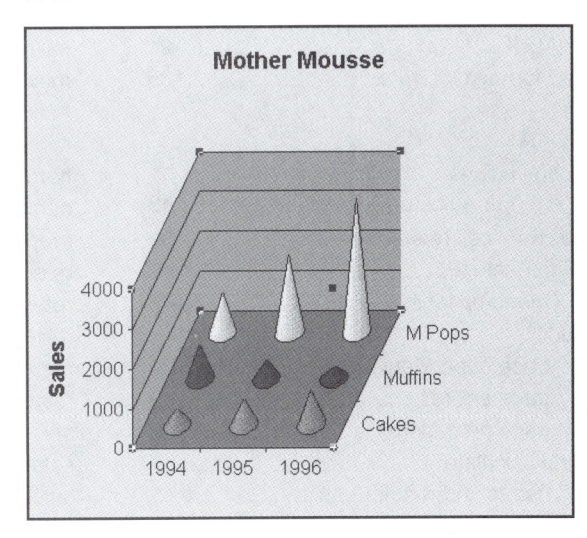

2. Click the **Chart** menu, then **3-D View**.

   The 3-D View dialog box appears.

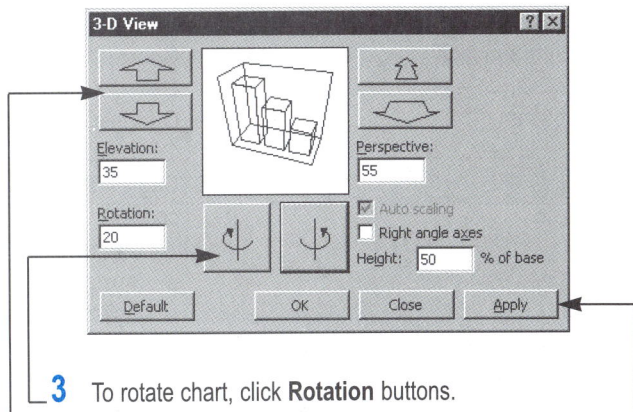

3. To rotate chart, click **Rotation** buttons.
4. To change elevation of chart, click **Elevation** buttons.

   Outline indicates current rotation and elevation settings.

5. To apply changes made, click **Apply**.
6. Click **OK** when done.

221

Index

#DIV/0! 21
#N/A 21
#NAME? 21
#NULL! 21
#NUM! 21
#REF! 21
#VALUE! 21
3-D formula 135

A

abbreviations
    add to AutoCorrect 43
absolute cell reference 131
alignment 42
    menu options 43
audit
    trace dependents 132
    trace errors 133
    trace precedents 133
AutoCalculate 44
    use to find results 45
AutoComplete 67
AutoCorrect 46
    adding to 47
    disable 46
AutoFilter
    AutoFormat 80
    AutoSum function 139
    end 156
    set options 102, 103
    start 156

C

cell
    about 22
    absolute reference 131
    cancel changes 65
    change range definition 97
    clear contents 48
    clear options using menu 49
    copy contents 52
    delete using menu 60
    edit data by double-clicking 64
    enter data 66
    enter special data 67

cell (continued)
    enter whole number 66
    fill by dragging 68
    fill using menu 69
    insert using menu 88
    insert using shortcut menu 89
    locations 22
    lock in a worksheet 100
    mixed reference 131
    move contents by dragging 95
    move contents using menu 94
    move part of contents 95
    name range using name box 96
    name range using titles 96
    properties and controls 23
    reference locations 130
    references in formula 130
    relative reference 131
    replace an entry 65
    restrict entries 124
    select entire column 27
    select entire row 27
    select named range 27
    selecting 26
    validate entries 124
cell range
    select adjacent 26
    select nonadjacent 26
Chart Wizard 196, 212
Chart→3-D View 221
Chart→Chart Options 214
Chart→Chart Type 212
Chart→Location 216
Chart→Source Data 218
chart
    create 196, 197
    format item 206, 207
    insert objects 204, 205
    items 194, 195
    move and size items 208, 209
    Print Preview 211
    print 210, 211
    rotate using dialog box 221
    rotate using mouse 220
    select type 212, 213
    set location 216, 217
    set options 214, 215
    set source of data using menu 218

chart (continued)
    set source of data using mouse 219
    size items 208, 209
    special 3-D effects..................220, 221
circular...21
close
    Excel..35
    workbook 34
close button..............................11, 34, 35
column
    adjust...38
    adjust from Print Preview 177
    adjust using menu 39
    adjust width automatically 38
    change width using mouse...............38
    delete...61
    hide..38
    insert using menu............................89
    insert using shortcut menu..............89
    selecting 27
command 12
    choose from menu 12
    keyboard..13
    shortcut 12
comment
    delete...87
    edit...87
    insert 86
controls for cell 23
copy
    and paste special 50
    cell contents 52
    cell data in special ways..................50
    cell data using Menu 52
    data by dragging cell border............53
    data by dragging fill handle 53
    formats with Format Painter 79
    mutiple items 54, 55
    worksheet using tab 111
copy and paste special 50
customize Excel 56

D

Data→Filter→Advanced Filter 158
Data→Filter→AutoFilter 156
Data→Form..170

Data→Group and Outline→Auto-
    Outline 164
Data→PivotTable Report 142, 143
Data→Sort 166
Data→Subtotals 168
Data→Table 144, 146
Data→Validation 124
data
    align in cells....................................42
    align using toolbar 43
    enter text 66
    find in worksheet 70
    link on different worksheets.............51
    merge and center 43
    replace in worksheet 71
data form
    edit records....................................171
    find records....................................171
    open and navigate.........................170
delete
    cell 60
    column 61
    comment...87
    records from list.............................163
    results in a data table............145, 147
    row...61
    worksheet using tab 110
dependents trace 132
dialog box
    collapse buttons 17
    controls..16
    getting help.....................................19
dragging
    copy data using cell border 53
    copy data using fill handle................53
    fill 68
    hide column 39
    hide row..41
    move cell contents..........................95
    unhide row......................................41
draw 62

E

Edit→Clear..48
Edit→Copy..52
Edit→Cut...94
Edit→Delete..60

Edit→Fill→Series 68
Edit→Find 70
Edit→Paste 52, 94
Edit→Repeat....................................122
Edit→Replace 70
Edit→Undo.......................................122
edit
    cell data by double-clicking 64
    comment..87
    formula 148
    function..139
    options 104, 105
    PivotTable 151
    records in data form 171
    template file....................................115
error message, restricted cell 125
errors
    common causes 21
    trace 133
Excel
    customize 56
    exit Excel 34
    Window..4, 5

F

Favorites, add folder/document...............29
File→Close...34
File→Exit..34
File→Open......................................28, 56
File→Page Setup, Chart tab 210
File→Page Setup, Header/Footer tab ..180
File→Page Setup, Margins tab 182
File→Page Setup, Page tab..................188
File→Page Setup,
    Sheet tab 186, 190, 191
File→Print 178
File→Print Area→Set Print Area 184
File→Print Preview...............................176
File→Properties 116
File→Save..30
File→Save As 30
File→Save As→Save as type 114
file
    create new based on template.......115
    properties for workbook.................116
    view properties 117

fill
    by dragging.......................................68
    using menu.......................................69
filter
    advanced..158
    criteria...159
    items in PivotTable 151
    lists automatically 156
find
    data in worksheet 70
    records in data form 171
    workbook in current folder................72
    workbook using advanced Find........73
folder
    add new..31
    create 31
    folder pane 28, 30
    manage 31
font
    format using menu 83
    format using toolbar 82
    Format Painter..................................78
    headers/footers 180, 181
Format→AutoFormat..............................80
Format→Cells, Alignment tab 42
Format→Cells, Border/Patterns tab.......74
Format→Cells, Font tab 82
Format→Cells, Number tab 84
Format→Cells, Protection tab..............100
Format→Column....................................40
Format→Conditional Formatting............42
Format→Copy 50
Format→Copy→Paste Special 50
Format→Rows 40
format
    add and delete conditions 77
    cell based on cell content.................76
    cell based on formula 77
    cell borders using menu 75
    cell borders using toolbar 74
    cell using Format Painter 78
    chart item 206, 207
    data table automatically 80
    fill using menu 75
    fill using toolbar 74
    font using menu................................83
    font using toolbar..............................82

format (continued)
    numbers using menu........................85
    numbers using toolbar......................84
    PivotTable automatically 81
Formula Bar 65
formula
    add references 134
    audit..132, 133
    cell reference types 131
    cell references 130
    change reference type....................135
    change reference 149
    create complex 136
    create simple 134
    edit...148
    examples 129
    extend cell range in 149
    insert cell reference........................135
    insert external reference 137
    insert reference to cell in another
        sheet 137
    location 128
    order of operation...........................129
    parts 128
    paste named range 135
freeze, pane 121
function
    AutoSum...139
    combine (nest)................................139
    create 138, 139
    edit...139
Function Wizard 138

G

Goal Seek 160, 161

H

headers 180, 181
    custom...181
Help..18
    additional help on Web.....................20
    automatic Help window positions 20
    classic Help 19
    common error messages 21
    dialog box help 20
    identify screen items 20

Help (continued)
    Office Assistant 18
        turn off Office Assistant 18
        use Office Assistant tips 18
hide
    column..38
    toolbar 56
    workbook window 118

I

input message, restricted cell 125
Insert→Cells 88
Insert→Chart.......................................196
Insert→Columns 88
Insert→Comments 86
Insert→Name 96
Insert→Object 90
Insert→Page Break............................174
Insert→Picture 204
Insert→Remove Page Break 174
Insert→Rows...88
insert
    cell reference in formula 135
    cell using menu 88
    cell using shortcut menu 89
    column using menu 89
    column using shortcut menu 89
    comment...86
    function...138
    manual page breaks.......................174
    new OLE object.........................90, 91
    new worksheet 111
    object in chart.........................204, 205
    records in list 163
    reference to cell in another sheet...137
    row using menu 89
    row using shortcut menu 89

K

keyboard
    commands..13
    use to move to a cell 25

225

L

list
- delete records 163
- filtering 157
- insert records 163
- location 163
- parts of 162
- sort using menu 167
- sort using toolbar 166
- subtotal automatically.............168, 169

lists (continued)
- use data forms with................170, 171

lock cell in worksheet............................100
lookup table, create......................140, 141

M

macro
- assign to graphic object 93
- recording 92
- run (play back)...................................93

margins
- set from Page Setup 183
- set from Print Preview 182

maximize button 11
menu command
- choosing 12
- set options..................................58, 59
- shortcut 12

minimize button 11
misspellings
- add to AutoCorrect 47

mixed cell reference 131
move
- cell contents by dragging 95
- cell contents using menu..................94
- chart items 208, 209
- part of cell contents..........................95
- worksheet using tab 111

N

named range
- paste into formula...........................135
- selecting 27

O

numbers
- format using menu 85
- format using toolbar 84

Office Assistant 18
Office Clipboard 54, 55
OLE objects 90, 91
one-variable tables.......................144, 145
open
- add FTP site to Open dialog box 33
- read-only (option) 28
- as copy (option).................................28
- in browser (option) 28
- workbook on disk 28
- workbook using Look in box............29

options
- calculation 102, 103
- edit...104, 105
- general 106, 107
- view 108, 109

orientation (page)..................................188
outline
- collapse and expand levels 165
- list 164

P

page break 174, 175
- change..175
- open preview 175

Page Setup
- chart options....................................210
- Header/Footer tab 180
- Margins tab......................................182
- orientation..188
- Page tab 188
- print options.....................................190
- scale 188
- Sheet tab.......................186, 178, 179

pane
- adjust or remove.............................120
- freeze 121
- split window 120
- unfreeze 121

226

paste
    collect and paste multiple 54
    special to link data 51
picture, insert in chart 204
PivotTable
    create from list 142, 143
    edit 151
    filter items 151
    format automatically 81
    modify summary fields 151
    move or remove fields 150
print
    chart options 210
    settings 178
    titles (repeating) 186, 187
    using menu 179
    using toolbar 178
    workbook data 178
Print Area
    clear using menu 184
    set from Page Break Preview 185
    set using menu 184
Print Preview 176, 177
    chart 211
property
    cell 23
    create custom for workbook 117
    view in Open dialog box (note) 117
protect
    workbook 98
    worksheet 100, 101
publish Excel documents on Web 32

Q

quit Excel 34

R

range
    change using menu 97
    extend in formula 149
    name using name box 96
    name using titles 96
    paste into formula 135
reference
    absolute 131
    change in formula 149

reference (continued)
    mixed 131
    relative 131
relative cell reference 131
remove manual page breaks 174
rename worksheet 111
repeat last action 122, 123
replace data in worksheet 71
restore button 11
row
    adjust height 40
    adjust height automatically 40
    adjust using menu 41
    delete 61
    hide by dragging 41
    insert using menu 89
    insert using shortcut menu 89
    selecting 27
    unhide by dragging 41

S

save
    add FTP site to Save dialog box 33
    as Web page 32
    create folder 31
    protect workbook 99
    using Save in box 30
    workbook as template 114
    workbook on disk 30
scale (page) 188
scroll in worksheet 24
search *(see Find)*
Search Help 19
show toolbar 56
sort 166, 167
    items in folder workspace 29
spell check 112, 113
start Excel 2
using Start Menu 2
Start→Microsoft Excel 12
Start Menu 2
subtotal lists automatically 168, 169
SUM function
    create with range 136

227

T

Taskbar 11
template
    base new file on 115
    edit 115
    save workbook as 114
Title Bar 11
toolbar 14
    Audit 132
    button (using) 14
    create custom 57
    format cell borders 74
    format fill 74
    move 15
    show/hide toolbars 15, 56
    show/hide buttons on 59
    set options 58
    sort list 166
    using to format font 82
    using to format numbers 84
Tools→AutoCorrect 46
Tools→Customize 56
Tools→Goal Seek 160
Tools→Macro 92
Tools→Options, Calculation tab 102
Tools→Options, Edit tab 104
Tools→Options, General tab 106
Tools→Options, View tab 108
Tools→Protection→Protect Sheet 101
Tools→Protection→Protect Workbook ... 98
Tools→Spelling 112
trace
    dependents 132
    errors 133
    precedents 133
transpose, paste special 50
troubleshooting (error messages) 21
two-variable table 146, 147

U

undo 122, 123
unfreeze pane 121
unhide columns 38
unhide rows 40

V

View→Page Break Preview, Normal 175
view
    automatic page breaks 174
    options 109
VLOOKUP 140

W

Web page, save as 32
width
    change for column 38
Window→Arrange, New Window 118
Window→Arrange, New Window,
    Hide 118
Window→Arrange, New Window,
    Unhide, workbook 118
Window→Freeze Panes 120
Window→Split 120
window
    arrange 119
    close button 11
    controls 10
    hide 119
    maximize button 11
    minimize button 11
    open new 118
    restore button 11
    select for workbook 118
    unhide 119
workbook
    about 6
    close 34
    close button 34
    file properties 116
    navigate 24
    open from disk 28
    open new window 118
    open using Look in box 29
    print data 178
    protect 98
    save and protect 99
    save as template 114
    save on disk 30
    select window 118
    unprotect 99

workbook (continued)
- view properties ...117
- window commands ...118
- window ...7

worksheet
- copy using tab ...111
- delete ...110
- group and ungroup ...110
- insert new ...111
- move using tab ...111
- print options ...190
- protect ...100, 101
- rename ...111
- scroll to an area ...24
- selecting ...25
- split window ...120
- tab controls ...8, 9
- tabs ...8
- unprotect ...101

Notes

Notes

Notes

Notes

Notes

The Visual Reference Series

Each book shows you the *100 most important functions* of your software programs

We explain your computer screen's elements—icons, windows, dialog boxes—with pictures, callouts, and simple, quick "Press this – type that" illustrated commands. You go right into software functions. *No time wasted.* The spiral binding keeps the pages open so you can type what you read.

$15 ea.

Did we make one for you?

CAT. NO.	TITLE
G29	**Microsoft® Access 97**
G21	**Microsoft Excel 97**
G33	**The Internet**
G37	**Internet Explorer 4.0**
G19	**Microsoft Office 97**
G23	**Microsoft Outlook 97**
G50	**Microsoft Outlook 98**
G22	**Microsoft PowerPoint 97**
G20	**Microsoft Word 97**
G36	**Microsoft Windows 98**
G43	**Access 2000**
G58	**ACT! 4.0**
G46	**Excel 2000**
G40	**Office 2000**
G54	**Outlook 2000**
G44	**PowerPoint 2000**
G45	**Word 2000**
G70	**Upgrading to Office 2000**

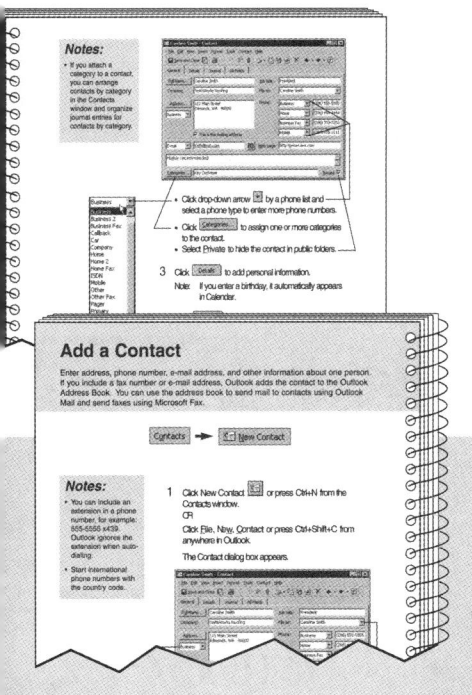

Preview any of our books at our Web site
http://www.ddcpub.com

To order call 800-528-3897
or fax 800-528-3862

DDC Publishing

2/99 V   275 Madison Avenue, New York, NY 10016

Fast-teach Learning Books

How we designed each book

Each self-paced hands-on text gives you the software concept and each exercise's objective in simple language. Next to the exercise we provide the keystrokes and the illustrated layout; step by simple step—graded and cumulative learning.

Did we make one for you?

Titles $27 each   Cat. No.
Creating a Web Page w/ Office 97 ... Z23
Corel Office 7 .... Z12
Corel WordPerfect 7 .... Z16
Corel WordPerfect 8 .... Z31
DOS + Windows Z7
English Skills through
   Word Processing Z34
Excel 97 .... Z21
Excel 5 for Windows E9
Excel 7 for Windows 95 .... Z11
Internet Z30
Internet for Business Z27
Internet for Kids Z25
Keyboarding/Word Processing
   with Word 97 .... Z24
Keyboarding/Word Processing
   for Kids Z33
Lotus 1-2-3 Rel. 2.2–4.0 for DOS L9
Lotus 1-2-3 Rel. 4 & 5 for Windows ... B9
Microsoft Office 97 .... Z19
Microsoft Office for Windows 95 ..... Z6
PowerPoint 97 .... Z22
Windows 3.1 – A Quick Study WQS1
Windows 95 .... Z3
Windows 98 .... Z26
Word 97 .... Z20
Word 6 for Windows 1WDW6
Word 7 for Windows 95 .... Z10
WordPerfect 6 for Windows Z9
WordPerfect 6.1 for Windows H9
Works 4 for Windows 95 .... Z8

Microsoft® OFFICE 2000

Titles $29 each   Cat. No.
Accounting Applications
   with Excel 2000 .... Z41
Access 2000 .... Z38
Create a Web Page
   with Office 2000 .... Z43
Desktop Publishing
   with Publisher 2000 .... Z47
Excel 2000 .... Z39
Office 2000 .... Z35
Office 2000 Deluxe Edition $34 ... Z35D
   • Includes advanced exercises an illustrated
     solutions for each exercise
Office 2000: Advanced Course Z45
PowerPoint 2000 .... Z40
Web Page Design
   with FrontPage 2000 .... Z49
Windows 2000 .... Z44
Word 2000 .... Z37

each with CD-ROM

**Preview any any of our books at:
http://www.ddcpub.com**

DDC Publishing

**to order call:
800-528-3897
fax 800-528-3862**

2/99 L

2/99 OD

Our One-Day Course has you using your software the next day

$18 ea.
Includes diskette

Here's how we do it
We struck out all the unnecessary words that don't teach anything. No introductory nonsense. We get right to the point—in "See spot run" language. No polysyllabic verbiage. We give you the keystrokes and the illustrated layout; step by simple step.

You learn faster because you read less
No fairy tales, novels, or literature. Small words, fewer words, short sentences, and fewer of them. We pen every word as if an idiot had to read it. You understand it faster because it reads easier.

Illustrated exercises show you how
We tell you, show you, and explain what you see. The layout shows you what we just explained. The answers fly off the page and into your brain as if written on invisible glass. No narration or exposition. No time wasted. **Each book comes with a practice disk to eliminate typing the exercises.**

DID WE MAKE ONE FOR YOU?

Cat. No.	Title	Cat. No.	Title
DC2	Access 97, Day 1	DC10	Netscape Navigator w/ Sim. CD
DC29	Access 97, Day 2	DC11	Outlook 97
DC30	Access 97, Day 3	DC52	Outlook 98
DC1	Access 7 for Windows 95	DC12	PageMaker 5
DC50	Basic Computer Skills	DC14	PowerPoint 97, Day 1
DC4	Excel 97, Day 1	DC31	PowerPoint 97, Day 2
DC27	Excel 97, Day 2	DC13	PowerPoint 7 for Windows 95
DC28	Excel 97, Day 3	DC34	Upgrading to Office 97
DC39	Excel 2000	DC47	Upgrading to Windows 98
DC22	FrontPage	DC56	Upgrading to Windows 2000
DC5	Internet E-mail & FTP w/Sim. CD	DC20	Visual Basics 3.0
DC48	Internet for Sales People w/Sim. CD	DC16	Windows 95
DC49	Internet for Managers w/Sim. CD	DC24	Windows NT 4.0
DC6	Intro to Computers and Windows 95	DC18	Word 97, Day 1
		DC25	Word 97, Day 2
DC51	Intro to Office 2000	DC26	Word 97, Day 3
DC21	Local Area Network	DC36	Word 2000
DC35	Lotus Notes 4.5	DC17	Word 7 for Windows 95
DC8	MS Explorer w/ Sim. CD	DC19	WordPerfect 6.1

Preview any of our books at: http://www.ddcpub.com

DDC Publishing To order call **800-528-3897** fax **800-528-3862**
275 Madison Avenue • New York, NY 10016

2/99 HR

Less Surfing, More Answers—FAST

These books bring the specific Internet information you need into focus so that you won't have to spend a lifetime surfing for it. Each book provides you with practical Web sites plus these skills:

- **common e-mail system** (like AOL, Outlook, Messenger)
- **search engines and browsing** (keywords, Yahoo, Lycos, etc.)
- **refining searches** (Boolean searching, etc.), for minimizing search time

FOR BEGINNERS
Cat. No. HR3 • ISBN 1-56243-603-1

FOR MANAGERS
Cat. No. HR2 • ISBN 1-56243-602-3

FOR SALES PEOPLE
Cat. No. HR4 • ISBN 1-56243-604-X

FOR STUDENTS
Cat. No. HR1 • ISBN 1-56243-601-5

BUSINESS COMMUNICATION & E-MAIL
Cat. No. HR6 • ISBN 1-56243-676-7

101 THINGS YOU NEED TO KNOW
Cat. No. HR5 • ISBN 1-56243-675-9

FOR SENIORS
Cat. No. HR7 • ISBN 1-56243-695-3

ENTERTAINMENT & LEISURE
Cat. No. HR8 • ISBN 1-56243-696-1

FOR SHOPPERS & BARGAIN HUNTERS
Cat. No. HR9 • ISBN 1-56243-697-X

HEALTH & MEDICAL RESOURCES
Cat. No. HR10 • ISBN 1-56243-713-5

INVESTING & PERSONAL FINANCE
Cat. No. HR11 • ISBN 1-56243-758-5

ROMANCE & RELATIONSHIPS
Cat. No. HR12 • ISBN 1-56243-772-0

**Preview any of our books at:
http://www.ddcpub.com**

$10 ea.

DDC Publishing
275 Madison Ave.
New York, NY 10016

To order call 800-528-3897 fax 800-528-386

Quick Reference Guides find software answers faster because you read less

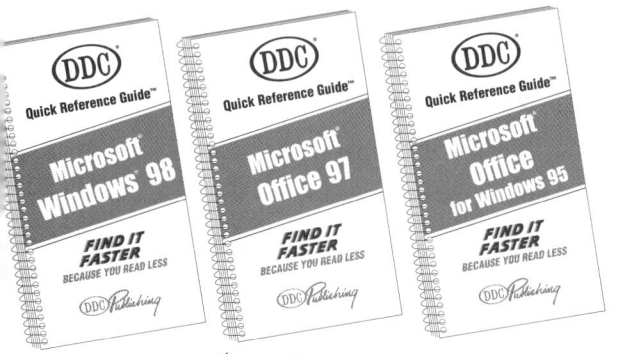

Find it quickly and get back to the keyboard—fast

The index becomes your quick locator. Just follow the step-by-step illustrated instructions. We tell you what to do in five or six words.

Sometimes only two.

No narration or exposition. Just "press this—type that" illustrated commands.

The spiral binding keeps pages open so you can type what you read. You save countless hours of lost time by locating the illustrated answer in seconds.

$12 ea.

Did We Make One for You?

The time you save when this guide goes to work for you will pay for it the very first day

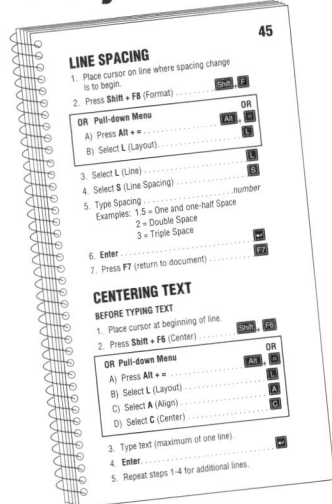

TITLE	CAT.No	TITLE	CAT.No
...ess 2 for Windows	OAX2	Office for Win 95	MO95
...ess 7 for Windows 95	AX95	Office 97	G25
...ess 97	G28	Office 2000	G47
...ess 2000	G55	PageMaker 5 for Win & Mac	PM18
...iness Communication & Style	G41	PowerPoint 4 for Win	OPPW4
...is Works 5 for Macintosh	G39	PowerPoint 7 for Win 95	PPW7
...mputer & Internet Dictionary	G42	PowerPoint 97	G31
...mputer Terms	D18	PowerPoint 2000	G51
...el WordPerfect Suite 8	G32	Quattro Pro 6 for Win	QPW6
...el WordPerfect 7 Win 95	G12	Quicken 4 for Windows	G7
...el WordPerfect Suite7 Win 95	G11	Quicken 7.0 (DOS)	OQK7
...5	J17	Quicken 8.0 (DOS)	QKD8
...6.0 - 6.22	ODS62	Windows NT 4	G16
...el 5 for Windows	F18	Windows 3.1 & 3.11	N317
...el 7 for Windows 95	XL7	Windows 95	G6
...el 97	G27	Windows 98	G35
...el 2000	G49	Word 6 for Windows	OWDW6
...rnet, 2nd Edition	I217	Word 7 for Windows 95	WDW7
...us 1-2-3 Rel. 3.1 DOS	J18	Word 97	G26
...us 1-2-3 Rel. 3.4 DOS	L317	Word 2000	G48
...us 1-2-3 Rel. 4 DOS	G4	WordPerfect 5.1+ for DOS	W-5.1
...us 1-2-3 Rel. 4 Win	03013	WordPerfect 6 for DOS	W18
...us 1-2-3 Rel. 5 Win	L19	WordPerfect 6 for Win	OWPW6
...us 1-2-3 Rel. 6 Win 95	G13	WordPerfect 6.1 for Win	W19
...us Notes 4.5	G15	Works 3 for Win	OWKW3
...us Smart Suite 97	G34	Works 4 for Win 95	WKW4
...ce for Win. 3.1	MO17		

Preview any of our books at our Web site:
http://www.ddcpub.com

To order call 800-528-3897
fax 800-528-3862

DDC Publishing
275 Madison Ave., New York, NY 10016

2/99 Q

MOUS

Microsoft® initiated the **MOUS (Microsoft® Office User Specialist) program** to provide Office users a means of demonstrating their level of proficiency in each application in the Office suite. After the successful completion of the certification test in an application, users receive a certificate that reflects their level of proficiency.

The **MOUS program** establishes the criteria for both proficient and expert levels in Word, Excel, PowerPoint, FrontPage, and Access, and proficient skill levels in Outlook.

Tests are given at Authorized Testing Centers around the country. Each test takes about 45 minutes to complete.

For more information on how you can become MOUS certified, visit our Web site!

www.ddcpub.com